What Others Are Saying about This Book . . .

"In this breathtakingly honest biogranot only lets us in on all the gossip of an ут also into his soul. It is a roller-coaster ysterically funny to the heart-wrenching—all told by a man with a razor sharp observation and a deep compassion for humanity." —**Frank Howsen, Award-winning Director, Writer & Lyricist**

"Danné King is one of the most dashing, dramatic and accomplished gentlemen I have met in my career as a Hollywood Reporter. He could have been a great actor, physician, lawyer, architect—any profession which requires talent, presence, confidence, and of course, knowledge. He is taking his turn as a writer—and with his impeccable taste and eye for detail; the reader is drawn into this exciting tale of love, desire, envy and intrigue. You will become fascinated with this man of a thousand faces, and love them all!"—**Marci Weiner, Entertainment Reporter and Columnist**

"LIGHTS, CAMERA, ACTION: the modeling gigs, the rock bands, the bodyguards, the fast cars, I was there! Who would not feel like a star, we were the beautiful people, and the spotlight never dimmed. Anyone who passed through 212 Brown Drive left a different person. Danné is a dream maker. Anyone who is fortunate enough to meet Danné would never be the same; it is all a life changing experience! He changed Evelyn's life as well, and 'Miss Maybelline' was never happier!"—**Robert Shannon, Artist, San Miguel, Mexico**

"Danné… the king of skin care is now an author. This book (by a man who was and still is a fulfiller of dreams) tells it like it is and pulls no punches. I was taken aback by a lot of it. The twists and turns and the suspense is mind stimulating. I can promise you that this book will not put you to sleep. I give it a thumbs up. Buy it, read it and love it as much as we all do."—**Ron Russell, Television Talk Show Host/Actor**

"This is an exciting, outrageous read—you will like it!" —Grace Robbins, author of *Cinderella and The Carpetbagger*

"This is glorious writing at its best! An exciting book told with tongue-in-cheek humor, and filled with history and details of a most amazing life that spans decades!" —Melissa McCarty, Host of Larry King's ORA TV and author of *News Girls Don't Cry*

"What an amazing book. *The Maybelline Prince* reads like a juicy novel but is in fact a story of a skin-care giant who has lived a most extra-ordinary life! After spending transformative years with the 'real' Ms. Maybelline of the Maybelline Co. Dysnasty, Danné went on to create a world-wide skin care company of his own! And more! From his incredible journey of a May-December relationship that transcends sex yet bound a man and woman together in a lifestyle that influenced and helped so many young people struggling for identity in the 1970s, he has become a worldwide activist in the Harvey Milk Foundation today! His motto *everyone deserves the right to be who and what they are—as long as it is with dignity, style and a passion to enrich the lives of everybody around them,* is alive and well today. An emotional real-life read." —Sheena Metal, Talk LA Radio Host

The Maybelline Prince

. . . Founder of DMK TransGenesis International, and Ambassador for Leadership in Human Rights with the Harvey Milk Foundation

Danné Montague King

BETTIE YOUNGS BOOKS

Cover design: Tatomir Pitariu
Senior Editor: Mary Kay
Content Editor: Mark A. Clements
Text Design: Jazmin Gomez
Photo of Danné Montague King: Drue Assiter

BETTIE YOUNGS BOOK PUBLISHERS
www.BettieYoungsBooks.com
info@BettieYoungsBooks.com

Bettie Youngs Books are distributed to the Trade by Baker-Taylor. If you are unable to order this book from your local bookseller, or online from Amazon or Barnes & Noble.com, or from the Espresso Book Machine (Print), or Read How You Want (Large Print, Braille, Daisy), you may order directly from the publisher: Sales@BettieYoungs.com / www.BettieYoungsBooks.com

Paperback ISBN: 978-1-940784-14-4
Digital ISBN: 978-1-940784-15-1
Hardcover ISBN: 978-1-940784-25-0

Library of Congress Control Number: 2014933195

1. King, Danné Montague. 2. Maybelline Co. 3. Williams, Tom Lyle. 4. Williams, Evelyn. 5. Williams, Sharrie. 6. Sexual Revolution. 7. DNK Skin Revision Network. 8. Gay Relationships. 9. Lesbian Relationships. 10. The Maybelline Story—and the Spirited Family Dynasty Behind It. 11. Transgenders. 12. Transgenesis International. 13. Self-esteem. 14. Newport Beach, CA. 15. Bettie Youngs Books. 16. Danie King. 17. DMK Skin Care Co. 18. Arson. 19. Drugs. 20. 1960s-1990s, History. 21. LGBT.

I dedicate this book to Stuart Milk, who with great giant steps on behalf of us all, "walks the walk."

Contents

Part 1: Burnt Cork

Part 2: First Star to The Left

Acknowledgements

I want to thank Drue Assiter—my other and far better half—for dogging me to finally sit down and write a book, and for his help in restoring the faded photos from the past.

I also would like to thank Mary Kay in Australia, the magazine publisher who made Danné Montague-King the Skin Revisionist a star in her wonderful country so many years ago, and who helped me make sense in the re-telling of an emotional time of my life.

And I'd like to thank Bettie Youngs Books, especially Bettie Youngs, who encouraged me time and again to expand the text beyond my Maybelline years with Evelyn F. Williams, to include the other facets of my life, especially in the creation of my own skincare line over the years. It wasn't until I started doing that that I realized what a long and productive life I've had, and oh what fun (and work!) it has been. I'd also like to thank Bettie's staff, especially novelist Mark A. Clements for his brilliant editing; Adrian Pitariu for the fascinating cover; and, Jazmin Gomez for her good eye and attention to detail! It "takes a village" is never more true than in turning out a book.

Foreword

Since I have met Danné Montague-King and his alter egos, I knew that I had discovered a fellow traveler on the road to helping mankind understand acceptance and love of all God's creation despite race, orientation and identity. Following the very large footsteps of my uncle Harvey Milk who openly gave his life so barriers of ignorance, hatred and prejudice could be broken down. We have had the chance to bring diversity and inclusion to audiences all over the world.

Danné has a way of reaching everyone from all walks of life—from the poorest ghetto child trying to reach the stars from a gutter of poverty, to celebrities and Royalty who seem entranced by his personae and unique brand of elegant courage.

In this book, he transparently opens his life and heart without reservation and takes the reader on a journey that seems almost magical; events happening around him and lives CHANGED BECAUSE HE WAS THERE. And yet with almost child-like aplomb, he takes no credit for many of the things he has created…seizing the day with vigor and curiosity and excited when someone else gets to shine in the many spotlights he turns on for so many.

Read this book about his incredible journey; you'll be better for it. Enjoy!

I personally would like to dedicate this book to those who have lived their lives in the light—being exactly who they are without compromise and facing adversity head-on with grace and passion.

—Stuart Milk, activist and founder, the Harvey Milk Foundation

A Word from the Author

In writing this book, a true story, I have changed the names of some of the people who were involved. Many of us do things in our youth that don't define us for the rest of our lives, and of course it is always important to protect, to the degree possible, the spouses, children and significant others who came along long after the events. In relating the things that happened in the 1970s, I have no wish to embarrass anyone.

My own life, however, is an open book of few regrets. And oh, what a life it has been!

This chapter of that book begins when Evelyn Williams called me and, relying on the many years of friendship we already shared, asked me to come to Arkansas and help her start a business and serve as her business partner and confident. Evelyn, the most glamorous and outspoken member of the Maybelline family, and who was so instrumental in the origin of the Maybelline cosmetic empire, was a true Grande Dame, and newsworthy for sure! Once our lives intersected, an amazing journey was the result!

That journey ended in a most unfortunate manner. Evelyn, who lived life to the hilt, died in a terrible house fire that became the source of much speculation. Some of the speculation involved me, the young man who was with her almost to the end, and who dared to be different.

So this is our story, mine and Evelyn's—and how from those beginnings, the rest of my life unfolded.

—**Danné Montague-King, Southern California, 2014**

PART 1:

Burnt Cork

1

The Last Days of Miss Maybelline

The man opened the lid of the giant freezer that stood in the dank, smoke-damaged basement of Maybelline Manor, and gagged at the eruption of sweet, corrupt fumes from over a hundred rotting chickens. Months before the birds had been frozen solid while awaiting the culinary skills of Chef Bearbra Coleman of The Palace Dinner Theatre in Hot Springs, Arkansas. Now they swarmed with maggots.

One of the chickens had killed Maybelline heiress Evelyn Francis Williams.

Despite the maggots, the man plunged his hands deep into the freezer and groped for money. He had to take *something* back to Danie King.

Danie was broke, having being so overwhelmed with work and getting The Palace Dinner Theatre open on time for the Hot Springs racing season that he had not banked his last three paychecks. The EVDAN corporate account held by Danie King and Evelyn Williams had been frozen pending the investigation into the fire and her death. Wild rumors were circulating around town alleging that her death had been murder or at least manslaughter, the perpetrators being members of the Dixie Mafia hired by jealous club owners, or one of Danie's boyfriends, or even Danie himself.

The last rumor had been squelched by the chief detective investigating the fire, who pointed out that Danie had been mentioned as a minor beneficiary in Evelyn's Last Will and Testament when she had it altered a year previously. Since her legacy to him was worth only as much as the business they had created together, he was hardly likely to have killed the goose that was busy laying the golden egg.

Finding nothing in the freezer, the man followed the beam of his flashlight through the rest of the lower floor of the sprawling house known as Maybelline Manor. He passed Danie's *en suite* quarters where all Danie's earthly possessions and clothing still waited, damaged by smoke. He passed the butler's pantry with the hole burned through the ceiling directly below the kitchen where the fire had started. This possibly accounted for the rumor that there had been two separate fires the day Maybelline Manor burned.

The fire chief later was angry over this idea: "Fires burn *up*, not down, at the point of inception. That hole was from the main fire—nothing downstairs was even touched by flames."

Finally, behind some liquor bottles in the back of the bar the man found a plastic bag containing some old photos and $1,500 in cash. He was elated. Neither he nor Danie possessed clothing or much else; everything was being held by the authorities until the insurance investigator was finished—and the investigator, functioning on Arkansas country time, was doing everything as slowly as possible.

The man glanced at the photos in the beam of his flashlight. One showed a young lady with bobbed, curly hair and dark red cupid-bow lips, wearing a spaghetti-strap "flapper" style dress of the 1930s. The photo was torn in half, as if the woman it portrayed did not want anyone to know who she was, nor the time frame in which the picture had been taken. But the man knew the picture was of Evelyn from back in her Chicago days.

There were other family photos as well—including some of Tom Lyle Williams, the Maybelline King. But most were of Evelyn, her son Bill, and various other family members through time up until the 1960s. Evelyn, forever the gracious lady, always wore the most fashionable attire and flashed her famous megawatt smile with the Texas Guinean naughtiness glimmering underneath.

Danie was ecstatic when he received the cash and photos. His life had taken a major nosedive after the front-page sensationalism of the fire. Suddenly he had nothing in a town where he once seemed to have everything. The main problem was Evelyn's son, Bill Williams, who had come to Arkansas to grandstand and pull strings with his "Palm Springs-Newport Beach Millionaire" image. His goal: to stop Danie from running The Palace Dinner theatre that Evelyn and he had worked so hard to get up and running. To make matters worse, many of Danie's so-called friends were fleeing like rats from a sinking ship—and places to stay were getting scarce.

That was why Danie had asked Steve Wyatt, once their house man (or major domo, as Evelyn liked to say), to go out to the shell of Maybelline Manor and look for anything at all. Danie knew that Evelyn had had a habit of stashing cash in corsets, under mattresses or in other odd places she would later forget about. Once he'd found a dividend check of $19,000 under a mattress in the maid's quarters. When he showed it to Evelyn she had shrieked with delight, as if it were money from home that had been just sent to her.

When Steve handed Danie the cash, Danie looked turned his gaze to the ceiling and said, "Thank you, Evelyn."

It has been written that Danie King left Hot Springs immediately after the fire, never to be heard from again. He didn't. He stayed in town for two more years, surviving the much maligned probate of Evelyn's Will, the ongoing speculations around town, the homophobic and illegal (by today's standards) attempts of Bill Williams to destroy him—and above all the haunting loss of an incredible woman who had set the stage for what Danie would become.

After the fire Danie formed a business with a wonderful Christian family in town that ran a photo shop. Their son, Roger, was a talented photographer who had done advertising work for the EVDAN Corp.—first for the Disco Roller Rink and later for The Palace Dinner Theatre. It was Roger who took a photo of Evelyn from her "Hollywood on Wheels" show and blew it up into a huge poster that was later cut out, glued to a wooden backing and installed on the roof of The Dinner Theatre where her white-gloved hand welcomed all—very old Las Vegas.

Together Roger and Danie launched the *Lewin and King Modeling and Photography Agency*. Working with a young lady who taught modeling at the local Garland County Community College, they also offered glamour portraits of anyone who wanted to look Hollywood-special. Danie would supply the wigs and do the makeup, and Roger would take the photos. As word spread, every wannabe model came to the studio for head shots, and every "society woman" or social climber came to be portrayed as a Hollywood film star or an elegant model.

During this time Danie was introduced to Mary Anderson, an extremely wealthy African-American woman who had semi-retired in Hot Springs Village, an upscale rural gated compound bordering on Lake Katherine. Mary was a colorful character from Chicago with her own Horatio Alger rags-to-riches story built on a chain of "southern sea food delicacies" restaurants called *Queen of The Sea*. The restaurants featured soul food of course, but more New Orleans French than down-home farm style.

Danie and Mary got along like two peas in a pod; for him it was as if Mary were a dark version of Evelyn. Mary liked the fact that Danie could play the grand piano like Liberace (whom Danie had known as a teenager), that he could do her wigs better than anyone else, and that he was the "former Maybelline Prince," as she liked to call him. She rented him and Roger one of the beautiful homes she had bought at Lake Katherine as an investment property, and tried to help them with their modeling and photo business. She was especially interested in Danie's unusual approach to skin care—especially for dark skin—and was giving thought to helping finance the dream he and Evelyn had had of launching a medi-spa in the Hot Springs area.

One evening when Danie came to Hot Springs Village for one of Mary's superb gumbo dinners, she asked him how much money Evelyn was worth. When he said, "Oh, about two million dollars, one million of it in Maybelline stocks," Mary exclaimed, "Why, that ain't no money! I thought y'all was rich!"

By her standards, two million dollars could not possibly fuel the legend that Evelyn and Danie had created of wealth, power, bodyguards, newspaper write-ups and glamour. When Danie explained how both of them knew how to *appear* tremendously rich and possessed of vast connections—the whole story concocted to enhance their business and protect Evelyn from enemies, real or imagined—Mary laughed and said, "Well, honey, she sounds like my type of gal. You just relax now and pay attention to business and we'll see 'bout getting you and Miz Williams' name back up there again!"

That was when Danie sat down and told her the story of how he and Evelyn got their names "up there" in the first place.

2

Before Arkansas...

It was the middle sixties, at the tail end of the Flower Children movement and the beginning of the hippy era. Everyone was "loving the one they were with even if they weren't with the one that they loved." There were no real sexual boundaries as long as you were pretty, hip and open-minded—and we all thought we were just that in those days in Newport Beach, California. In fact all the Southern California beach cities, from artsy and gay Laguna Beach all the way down to the darker and more seedy Long Beach, were "in." We would often hit all the cities along the Pacific Coast Highway in a single weekend.

In those days I owned a shop called The Londoner Wig Boutique on 32nd street in Newport, right across from Town Hall and the police station. It was quite a place. The shop's decor was very British, the UK being the fashion leader of the world at that time, with Vidal Sassoon and Mary Quant as reigning fashionistas. It featured watered moray silk wallpaper, (faux) crystal chandeliers and an oak beamed ceiling (also faux). It was the epitome of style for wealthy Newport residents. I made wigs between running back and forth to Hong Kong where I designed the wigs for a factory owned by a man called Benny Wong. I also hired hairdressers to handle real hairdos and do makeup and makeovers.

I probably helped invent the first "sculptured nails" as well. It happened because of the unusual way I ran my shop. I had a friend named Philip, who was a barber school student and very clever at sculpting. He sold some of his pieces out of my shop, along with an older transsexual woman named Billie who sold shell art. I also showcased another local artist, an older, once-wealthy woman who sold her paintings to get by.

In addition, I let a strange Hungarian manicurist named ZaZa ply her trade in one area of the shop. I was fascinated by her method of nail growth called "The Juliette Nail Wrap," where paper would be wrapped around women's nails for weeks while they grew longer. As ZaZa built her clientele she demanded more and more room. I refused, so she moved out and opened down the street, a place called Nail Cura by Zaza which stayed in business for many years.

After she left, I was sitting around talking to Philip about nails. Surely there was a way that some kind of material could be placed on a nail, allowed to harden, and then sculpted into the perfect shape. During this conversation a dental assistant was getting her wig styled, and she said she could get me some powder called Kadon that the dentist used to make teeth. Maybe it would work. It was like liquid porcelain which, when mixed with activator, became hard as a rock.

A few days later she brought some. We mixed it and applied it to one of our lady friend's fingers, but it would not extend beyond the fingertip—just flopped over once dried. I suddenly realized it needed a *form* on which to brush the solution so it would hold the mixture in place while it dried, which only took minutes. I grabbed some aluminum foil we used for color highlights for hair and fashioned little "hooves" that wrapped around the finger then ledged out from the tip of the nail.

Philip gently stroked the solution on the nail and out over the "hoof" and we waited breathlessly while it dried. When we removed the foil, *voila*, there was a long but crude "nail," solid as granite. Phil took a diamond nail file and a half hour later he had sculpted the crude and lumpy hooves into long, elegant, thin nails as strong as false teeth. We called them porcelain nails, and within two weeks Philip was booked up until 10 o'clock at night.

Later, as other salons picked up the technique, the FDA cracked down on the use of dental Kadon. Fortunately I was too naive in those days to try to patent a chemical whose sole legal purpose was for dentistry. Later, other companies used acrylics instead and a multibillion dollar industry was born.

This was an easy, breezy time; celebrities taking LSD went on television with their psychiatrists to talk about their "trips." Pot was selling for $25 a "lid" (a small plastic bag full, which in today's market would cost about $300). Everyone was slightly stoned. It was the era of Glam

Rock, with David Bowie and other androgynous rock stars leading the way, but there were none of the hard, home lab, street drugs of today. LSD was common, as well as "magic mushrooms" (peyote). As an hallucinogenic, mushrooms affected mainly the optic nerves of the eyes, in addition to "slowing down time" the way marijuana did.

On peyote, when one got tired of "seeing things that were not really there" one just blinked one's eyes and it all went away. Not so with LSD, which went directly to the brain cells and could not be controlled once "dropped" (taken). I tried it one time only at a friend's house in the hills above Laguna Beach. It did bring on all kinds of illusions, especially in mirrors and lit fireplaces. Friends became other people, some unbelievably beautiful and some almost demonic looking.

All I really remember was standing on the peak of a roof, stark naked, watching the sun go down over the Pacific. The flora and fauna of the neighborhood looked like a painting by Van Gogh and early stars were swirling and moving in circles like his *Starry Night* painting—life imitating art.

A girl who lived there, a plain little redhead inelegantly nicknamed "Fast Fuck Fran" because of her dozens of male admirers, poked her head out of an upper story window and yelled, "Danie, what in the hell are you doing up there?"

I called back, "I'm Giselle, greeting the morn," as I executed a clumsy arabesque.

"You look more like indecent exposure greeting the police. Get down!" Somehow this got through to me and I did get down, even as I realized with shock that I could have gotten killed.

I never dropped acid again. I did try the popular cocaine once at a party—there were tons of celebrity-ridden parties in those pre-AIDS days, each complete with its compulsory "orgy room." All that happened was that I ran around yelling like an evangelist about how tacky orgy rooms were, talking a mile a minute for about an hour—then nothing.

I couldn't see spending all that money for cocaine; in fact, I became unpopular at these soirees for breaking up orgies. I would wander into the rooms as if I were encircled by some kind of light. People entwined in all kinds of configurations would reach out to me to join in but I shrugged them off, just staring at the spectacle with incredulous eyes. I thought it terribly clinical and not romantic at all! What was worse was the fact that some of the people I had seen come to the party and really liked, were there on the floor or the couches. *How could they?* I thought.

Many times, influenced by my "angelic" attitude, people would get up and leave, and later complain to the host!

Most Newport Beach socialites living on Lido Isle and Balboa Island were either heavy drinkers, dopers, or both. It was acceptable as long as you were young and looked good and kept it all private. The older citizens, who did not indulge, turned a blind eye to it all—it was "the norm" at the time.

Harland Sanders, who created Kentucky Fried Chicken, lived on Lido Isle. We would see him with his little white-headed wife, leaving their condo—every bit Mr. and Mrs. Santa Claus; they probably had no idea that there had been a massive orgy party right in their condo complex the night before!

I knew a lot of celebrities in Newport Beach at the time. Jane Russell used to push a shopping cart next to me at Hugh's market in Newport. At the time, I was a skinny kid with huge sun-streaked Afro. June Allison, with her thinning hair, came to me for "demi wigs"—a sort of half-wig-fall. And, the still-glamorous at age 75 Mexican film star, Delores Del Rio, was a regular when she and her husband came up to Newport to service their boat.

I was also hired by film star photographer Harry Langdon Jr. to come up to Hollywood to style wigs on Diana Ross and other stars for album covers or fashion layouts. *Wigs and Hair Today* magazine, one of the more popular publications of the time, featured me constantly as if I were a wealthy stylist of great renown. I wasn't. Yes, I worked hard and I do believe I had talent and an eye for style and how women should look "naturally," but I also played hard and picked up everyone's tabs—a bad habit that somewhat exists to this day. I certainly had no clue how to "manage" money.

I was living in a beautiful condo on the water at Huntington Beach with LaVerne Lanyon-Spence, a sexy redhead of 43 who had inherited a fortune from her deceased husband, lost a great deal of it to a second scoundrel husband, and decided to go into an up-market dress business called "Aunty Mame's" in my catch-all location. Ours was an odd relationship. During the week we were lovers and on weekends my boyfriend would come and stay at the condo.

LaVerne was a very open-minded woman who always lived for the moment. She was also best friends with blonde bombshell Mamie Van Doran, who became a client. Mamie would come into the shop with LaVerne to look at my human hair falls. In those days Mamie still looked unbelievably young, with long straight blonde hair, a tiny waist and her famous "boobage"!

At about this time two other women—women who would change my life—entered the shop. One was a fading, so-called socialite named Delyle Compton, and the other was the famed Maybelline heiress, Evelyn F. Williams.

I was standing behind the counter when the door opened and the most remarkable little woman walked in with a huge smile that lit up the entire place. She was tiny but big-busted, and had a strong, theatrical face that reminded one of a cross between the Barrymores and Joan Crawford in her best days. With her silver-blonde hair, designer blouse and pearl earrings, she looked like she had just left a garden party.

The first words out of her mouth were, "My darling, aren't you so handsome, I can't stand it!" Her huge blue eyes, fringed with long fake eyelashes, looked coyly up at me and I turned three shades of red, thinking of every movie star I had ever heard of all at the same time. I was used to glamorous women, but this was something different.

I stammered that she was also a beauty. Very coy, she said, "How old do you think I am?"

I replied with a line that over the next decades became one of my standards with women of age: "Somewhere between forty and death?"

She laughed uproariously and replied, "I'm 71-years-old." And with that, her pants fell down.

There she stood in her underpants, little white legs with the toes of her gold boots peeking from under her pants. Without batting an eye, she pulled the pants up and requested "a safety pin, darling; I've lost a bit of weight lately." I called Billie, the transsexual, to get a pin and help Evelyn out. Once she was settled, we got down to the business of why she was in the shop.

In a private booth she took off her wig and wanted to try on some others. She had hair, but it was thinning—a result, she claimed, of being given ether when she had her one and only son decades ago. I had heard of this before, so we spent the afternoon trying on wigs of various colors and styles and telling each other our life stories. She told me her money came from Maybelline Cosmetics, and mentioned over and over again how "like Tom Lyle Williams, the inventor of Maybelline mascara" I was.

I was to hear this comparison many times over the next few years, and later on her love of Tom Lyle (T. L.) would start to make sense to me, along with her unfailing belief in me and my so-called abilities. She loved my makeup techniques, but was more interested in my skin care and a protein "skin tightening masque" I was experimenting with. She became, in fact, an early Guinea pig for the very enzyme masque that is now the flagship treatment of the DMK Skin Revision network.

On one occasion I applied the masque on her in a darkened private room I kept in the back of the shop. After covering her entire face with the luminous greenish mixture, I pulled a satin quilt up over her and she went to sleep for the forty-five minutes it took for the masque to activate. During that time Bobby Shannon, a close friend of mine who was always pulling pranks on me, came into the shop for a visit. I scrunched my face up into an expression of extreme worry and said, "Bobby, I think you should go across the street and get the police. Miss Williams came in this morning and I think she has had a heart attack. I laid her down in the back room."

He was all concerned and asked if she were breathing. I told him to come and take a look. When he gazed into the room at her motionless form, face stiff and glowing in the dark, he screamed and ran out of the building! I chased him down and told him it was a joke. At that moment Evelyn woke up and wanted to know what was going on. When we told her we were passing her off as a corpse, she said, "Well, I hope you're selling tickets and will give me my cut."

Evelyn had a marvelous sense of humor. We became very good friends right away. She came in for a "touch up" nearly every day and eventually invited me to party at her small but elegant home on the water on Lido Island. It was at that party that I met her sisters, Verona and Bunny—Verona being a quiet, regal woman as opposed to Bunny's more down-to-earth personality. I also at that time met her son Bill Williams, a person she almost talked about constantly—one time very positive and another time angry at his attempts to "control her life."

Bill was intimidating. Tall and husky, he had a face that reminded me of a cross between Rex Harrison and one of the Barrymores, a look that seemed to be inherent in the entire family. He seemed pleasant enough, but I sensed a self-important air of entitlement. I also sensed that he was homophobic (although he never admitted to this in a day of openness and free love) and thought of me as just another one of "mama's pet projects"—a common "queer" hairdresser; never mind the fact that Jon Peters, heterosexual, was a hairdresser in Newport Beach at the time and would later marry Barbara Streisand and become an important film producer. I saw Bill Williams as someone who thought that hairdressers were all "fags," and tolerated because they kept women pretty, but of no real importance aside from that.

3

The Maybelline Heiress

I'm afraid I'm responsible for creating that title—or at least for the publicity and acclaim that eventually made it seem real for Evelyn F. Williams, and which would define her as a person in Arkansas. She never described herself as such in the Newport Beach days. Of course she talked about Maybelline and her close relationship with its creator, Tom Lyle Williams. She also admitted that her wealth came from Maybelline stock—but so did other members of the Williams family. However, over the months and years we were together in Hot Springs, the stories of her involvement with the two Williams brothers—Tom Lyle: gentle, elegant, brilliant and gay; and Preston Williams: muscular, handsome and a lady-killer-around-town—and the huge part Evelyn played in Maybelline company, caused me to think that she really was *the* Maybelline heiress. Never mind how much stock she actually held in the Shearing Plough company that owned Maybelline at that time.

Since then I have read and heard other versions of these stories, though Evelyn's versions were told to me in her own words, over cocktails or dinner, in the car or when I did or said something that reminded her of Tom Lyle. As time went by, somehow the persona of Tom Lyle's brother Preston Williams, whom she married, would appear in the mix, especially when we were faced with some daunting task for the business, or she was fearful of reprisals from a small-time gangster called Sam Saleem. It was then that she pushed me to go beyond myself, go out of the box—to be a man and take things head on, regardless of outcome. In other words, to have no fear.

Looking back, I see the things she made me do that I could have never done on my own. She had a way of making a man feel like he *could* pull anything off—that she was behind him 100% but needed his protection and help. This was the Preston half of how she saw me, and it was an entirely different Evelyn than the one on whom I did skin treatment experiments or applied makeup while planning what we would wear to appearances.

It has been said that Evelyn, Preston and Tom Lyle were in a strange love triangle. Physically, this was not true. Tom Lyle Williams was gay in a time when it was not talked about except in Hollywood, the theatre and in beauty salons. His lover, Emory Shaver, a partner in the business, was promoted as his "spokesperson." The fact that Tom Lyle never married was lightly explained away by "He's married to Maybelline." As a youth in Kentucky he *did* father a son, Cecil, followed by a very strange shotgun marriage to legitimize the child and then an annulment. The fact that a gay boy could have sex with a girl is not remarkable, especially in those days when youths often did not *know* they were gay until much later. Being a romantic at heart, Tom Lyle fancied himself to be in love with the girl, and nature did the rest. Regardless, even as a child, Tom Lyle took care of Cecil extremely well, and in time he would bring Cecil into the company. And, it would be Cecil who inherited the bulk of Tom Lyle's estate upon Tom Lyle's death.

His brother Preston Williams was a well-built, good-looking, pugilistic man who appealed to Evelyn's healthy physical side, and in her own way she loved him as a husband and the father of her sole child, Bill. But her romantic and spiritual side always loved Tom Lyle, who embodied the grace and regal style she admired in certain movie actors of the day, as well as members of royalty.

One night while talking about the early days of Maybelline, she told me about the time she was in a car in downtown Chicago, stopped at a light, when she looked over at the corner "and there was the most beautiful man I ever saw." She described his elegant dark, sleek hair, aquiline profile, long gray Chesterfield coat with a velvet collar, the white scarf at her throat held with a diamond stick pin, and his black, silver-headed cane. He looked up at her, raised his cane in a salute and smiled, and she was shocked to see it was Tom Lyle Williams, her brother-in-law!

So yes, part of her was very much in love with T. L., but there were no lurid love triangles or behind the scenes hanky-panky. At some level she knew he was a homosexual. Much later, I came right out and asked her if she knew. After looking down for a moment, she raised her eyes and replied, "Well, yes, we sort of always thought so, but that was not talked about in those days in polite society. In fact those kind of people were referred to as 'ice cream cones,' and Tom Lyle was a popular and important man—he could never be thought of that way—he was married to Maybelline and that was that." If, in fact, there *was* gossip about her and both brothers, that would only enhance the myth that Tom Lyle was a normal guy—after all, didn't he have a son?

When Tom Lyle was a young lad in Morganfield, Kentucky, he was always doing something for extra money. An entrepreneur at heart, he sold postcards and other notions to people on the trains that came through town, bought a flashy motorcycle and put on "Actor-bat" shows, complete with posters all over town announcing himself (he later advertised the cycle and sold it at a considerable profit). He also ran the early movie projector at the local nickelodeon and passionately watched every detail of every film, scrutinizing the beautiful movie stars of the day—a habit that helped him later in building the Maybelline empire.

The story of the mascara, as Evelyn told it to me, was this, Tom Lyle's sister, Maybel, had singed off her eyelashes and eyebrows while cooking. This gave her a very eerie and un-feminine appearance. Desperate to look presentable (this was in the early 1900s when decent women did not wear "make up"), she concocted a mixture of burnt cork, lamp black and Vaseline petrolatum jelly and applied it to the scanty hairs still present on her lashes and brows. The effect was so stunning to Tom Lyle that it gave him an idea. According to Evelyn, he approached what she called "a raw chemist" in town to make up a little black base in a small box for women to apply to their brows and lashes, and named it "Maybelline" after his sister. Apparently he advertised this in the local gazette and other publications for 10 cents a box, and the dimes started rolling in. The cake base was actually soap base and sometimes irritated the eyes, but nonetheless it sold.

Eventually, feeling he had a real winner, Tom Lyle decided that he and Maybel had to leave Morganfield and go to Chicago to "really manufacture Maybelline big time," but he did not have sufficient capital. He begged his brother Noel, who was working in Chicago, to take a chance on him and invest in a small lab and manufacturing facility for which he would give him 50% of Maybelline profits (needless to say Noel became a very rich man for this sibling leap of faith).

Although often touted as "the creator of mascara," Tom Lyle did not actually invent either the word or the product. Ancient Egypt did—producing a mixture of galena, malachite, charcoal, honey, crocodile poop and water known as *kohl*. The Egyptians used this throughout history to line their eyes and darken their lashes, and the product segued into the Middle East where a version of kohl (minus the croc feces) is still used today. The word "mascara" itself is believed to have come from the Spanish word *máscara* meaning "mask or stain," and the Italian word *machera*, meaning "masque."

Despite the story told to me by Evelyn—and that is all I have to go on—the product that people would recognize as mascara today was developed in the late 19th century when a chemist, Eugene Rimmel, developed a cosmetic using the newly-invented petroleum jelly from which the popular Vaseline would be made. The name *Rimmel* became synonymous with the substance and still translates to "mascara" in several languages, including Italian and Spanish, to this day. Rimmel never became mainstream really—I occasionally see an old Rimmel makeup or powder box—all fine quality, but without American marketing and The Movies. There does seem to be a resurgence of Rimmel Cosmetics in some US store chains today!

But here is the strange part: Rimmel was in Europe, and Tom Lyle was across the Atlantic, yet history tells us that T. L. Williams created a remarkably similar product for his sister Maybel at the same time, and a few years later started a mail-order business that would eventually become the giant icon Maybelline! There was no internet in those days, no television and not much transatlantic radio. There were wireless messages and ships, but no airplanes crossing the ocean regularly. Did these two men just happen to think of the same thing at the same time?

Still other reports keep to the story that Maybel herself made up the petrolatum-burnt cork and lamp black ratio—after seeing the "recipe" in *Photoplay* magazine!

Ahh, the media. Controlling everything as usual.

Yet it *was* Tom Lyle's strong sense of "self" and purpose and vision that put mascara on the map to the masses; that, and his creative talents—along with his muse, his sister-in-law Evelyn F. Williams.

Evelyn Francis Williams was born Evelyn Francis Boecher on February 1, 1901. Her father, known to everyone as Papa Boecher, was a first-generation German-American who had become wealthy in the plumbing and early air conditioning business in Chicago, and used his three beautiful daughters, Bunny, Evelyn and Verona to display his success. They were the quintessential society girls with every privilege, including music lessons at The Chicago Institute of Music. Bunny played the trumpet, Verona nearly became a concert pianist and Evelyn played the violin—but her real passion was dance, followed by fashion and being the first to try any new trend that came along. She was also the apple of her father's eye and was, according to her, spoiled rotten. Small and petite with a provocative bosom, she had endless queues of admirers, but being a romantic at heart and with the energy and gusto of a Jack Russell terrier, she flirted with them all but stuck with none.

As adventuresome as a boy, she briefly ran away to join the circus, being billed as a "bareback horse dancer."

"I couldn't *really* bare back dance," she once admitted to me. "They rigged this special cinch around the horse with a funny little stand at the top and a belt went around my waist. My costume was all-flowing chiffon and tulle with a short front to show my legs and a long train that covered the rig. I wore a long, shiny auburn wig with a sparkling rhinestone tiara and long plumes. They would lead me out to a huge fanfare and music. There were *real* bareback dancers behind me and I would smile, pose and execute sort of ballet steps, up on my toes, leg extended, arms gracefully over my head and pretend to do arabesques while smiling and bowing and turning from side to side. Most of the time I was scared I would fall off, but the audience seemed to love it!"

She also met the great circus Impresario, P. T. Barnum—in a less-than-tasteful way.

"He would make advances to me," she fumed, indignant still after decades. "He appeared one time in my dressing room and exposed himself." She described a lurid scene of a nasty little boy trying to play doctor with a female schoolmate—very much the same story Tippy Hedren would tell me about Alfred Hitchcock years later.

I asked Evelyn what she did to get out of the situation—a man like that with such an ego, used to easy conquests, would not be easily put off! She lowered her eyelashes for a moment and then looked up at me, eyes sparkling, with that naughty twinkle that only women with great confidence seemed to have: "Well, Danie," she said, "there *are* ways to calm an overheated man down without hurting his feelings."

Having survived a P. T. Barnum attack, she left the circus and used that experience to convince her parents to send her to the much more socially acceptable ballet school. Papa Boecher was a man who wanted his daughters to be refined with Old World traditions and manners.

The amazing thing about these "fireside chats" I had with Evelyn (some of them actually conducted around the massive fireplace at Maybelline Manor, sitting on her huge green velvet tuxedo-style couches, drinks in hand) was that she never attached any time period to the stories. She hated it when, upon meeting her for the first time, people would say, "You look wonderful for your age!"

"Why can't they just say I look wonderful?" she would hiss. "What's this habit of chopping life up into 10 year increments and then everyone has to age ten years each time and act and dress accordingly?" She went on to point out that we are born and then we die—everything in between is up to us. She was a big believer in healthy eating. She met Gaylord Hauser, the great American health food guru of the 1940s, and tried to follow his advice. She also believed in a woman's obligation to maintain illusion.

Evelyn knew she was older—she had no illusions or even regrets about that. At night, when she took off her elaborate foundation garments and saw that still-splendid cleavage drop toward her waist, removed her wigs and exposed the scanty gray hair beneath, and watched her large, magnetic eyes shrink down without makeup and false lashes, she did not bemoan her age and cry like Bette Davis in *Whatever happened to Baby Jane*. She simply accepted it as part of life. She knew she had the skills, aided by me and my treatments, to burst forth on the public scene still beautiful and glamorous, and she dressed with great flair, innovation and dignity.

She did, however, have one small, secret vanity that she tried to hide, even from me: the famous "Verona teeth."

She had told me that her sister Verona had lost all her teeth and had a Beverly Hills "dentist to the stars" create a set of special chompers that had flanges built in the sides that filled out her cheeks, giving her a more youthful appearance. Fascinated, I intended to scope the design out if Verona ever visited us in Hot Springs. As it turned out, I didn't have to wait for Verona. One night Stephan, our major domo and my personal companion and assistant, brought me something he'd found in the laundry room whilst going around the estate checking locks and the security system. He handed me the largest and oddest set of false teeth I had ever seen—large enough for a horse, with high, thin gums that flanged up on either side. I said, "Omigod Stephan, those must be the famous 'Verona Teeth'—but they're not Verona's!"

He told me that he had noticed that Miss Williams' voice often sounded muffled and funny when she was issuing household instructions to him from behind her closed door in the morning. Embarrassed for Evelyn that her little secret was discovered, I told him to quietly sneak into her bathroom which was across the hall from her bedroom, mix the Verona Teeth up in a towel and stick it into a drawer. My hope was that she would think she had gotten absent minded, as she often did, and left it there.

About two days later, while we were at dinner, the subject of Verona's Teeth surfaced again. "Remember when I was telling you about Verona's special teeth, Danie?" Evelyn trilled casually.

I pretended to not remember at first, then said, "Oh, yes, I do believe you mentioned it, and what extraordinary invention."

"Well, she laughed, "I guess she left a spare set in my guest room in Newport Beach because I was going through some old boxes looking for bras and scarves I loved, and there they were." With a flourish she banged the offending teeth on the table. I almost expected them to start chattering across the tablecloth like those trick teeth.

I looked up at her million dollar smile. Her eyes glittered with challenge, and all I could think of to say was, "Good God, Evelyn, how in heck did she get those into her mouth? Does she nail them to the wall and then run at them?"

She thought this was very funny and we laughed and laughed, coming up with even more crazy scenarios of how Verona Got Her Teeth Into Her Mouth.

She was satisfied that her little ruse had worked—the teeth were never brought up again, or appeared outside her mouth again—but I could not help but wonder what the spare teeth had cost her. I learned to adapt her concept of time to my own life, foregoing dates as they related to life's journey. She never lied about her actual age because she never looked or acted her chronological age—not in front of other people, at least.

Neither have I. Even now, when I'm lecturing to a crowd of people at various venues around the world and at some point announce my age, I wait to hear the gasps and see bosoms being clutched in disbelief. And then I always say, "When I don't hear the gasps anymore, I'll retire."

Evelyn had no intention of retiring from life—despite the demands of her son, Bill Williams. Every time she called him to say hi, he would harangue her to "quit all that Hot Springs nonsense," sell everything she could and come back to the peace and comfort of Newport Beach. She did not want to return to Newport Beach to live as a little old lady clipping coupons on Lido Isle, or in a senior living center like her sister Verona—no matter how luxurious. She also did not want to face the gossip about her disastrous marriage. She wanted to "visit" in the future, appearing as a successful businesswoman and a "somebody"; not just another wealthy widow/divorcee in a town already filled with older widow/divorcees.

This was, after all, a woman who had dazzled Chicago society and, later, Hollywood society during their respective "golden eras." She had been loved as a muse by one of the century's most creative men, inspiring him to try new ways of advertising, emphasizing the "power of women's eyes"—a power that she herself knew how to use to great advantage. She had the German practical side that knew what women wanted and the best way to use cosmetic tools at home, such as the Maybelline eyebrow and eyeliner pencils that came out later in black, brown, auburn and, even later, the soft gray. It was Evelyn who backed up the plan for the Maybelline Company to leave Chicago and go to the movie capital of the world, Hollywood. There were times, she told me, that she would get all dressed up in furs and jewels like a movie star with full makeup, and pass out Maybelline fliers on Chicago's windy streets!

She kept hounding everyone that Hollywood was the place to be. To be sure, tentative plans were already being made in this direction. Tom Lyle and his life partner had discovered on a visit out there that they could live their private lives more openly in "fantasy land" than in the more rigid Chicago, and Evelyn, with her unbridled enthusiasm and commitment to the Maybelline family, made the move seem not only doable but necessary. This was, after all, a woman who had bested Barnum, met and flirted with Al Capone (a vulgar, greasy-looking man with mean, cold eyes, according to her; she claimed that she had "felt dirty" when he took her arm, and later felt that she had escaped from the cage of an animal). She met and flirted with the top politicians of the day, and later with celebrities and movie stars. Much of what is now American history was graced by her sparkling presence. She was even sitting in a front row seat when the immortal race horse, Seabiscuit, won the Derby.

Later, ensconced in Hollywood in a house formerly owned by Rudolf Valentino, Tom Lyle became the first cosmetics creator to use the services of up and coming starlets, most of whom later became major stars, in advertising campaigns. Soon the general public could see their favorite stars, with lustrous eyes, gracing the pages of magazines. Ordinary women everywhere could now share in the glamour and be like Jean Harlow or Betty Grable for a few hours a day or night. In other words, it was Tom Lyle Williams who started the celebrity endorsement trend that exists to this day.

Although shy by nature, Tom Lyle held "star crossed" parties up at his mansion in the Hollywood Hills, making sure that reporters and other publicists were present. According to Evelyn, he was a teetotaler, and hard liquor was never served at these soirees—something I can hardly imagine, knowing the Hollywood crowd as I do.

This was the woman who seduced me into moving from coastal Southern California to Hot Springs, Arkansas, a place in which I would never have imagined ending up. Her constant comparison of me to Tom Lyle baffled me. I would stare at photos of him, trying to see myself in this dark haired, refined and shy looking man. From all she had told me, we were nothing alike. I was outgoing, bombastic and let it all hang out. He lived much of his life "in the closet" and depended upon others to front for him. He seemed effete, although not effeminate. I was masculine and at times, according to others, intimidating.

Tom Lyle stayed in one serious relationship, from what I was told, for most of his life. Although I myself had many lovers of both sexes, I was always the romantic and was never one for the "quickies" that ran amuck in gay society during the '60s, '70s and '80s before HIV took a lot of that away. I had to be "in love" even for a one night stand.

Another big difference between us was that Tom Lyle depended upon his spokesperson Emory Shaver, while I was ever the public orator and could have gone into politics or organized religion.

But recently, whilst writing this book at age 69, I began to see the similarities between me and Tom Lyle that Evelyn had noticed so many years ago. It had nothing to do with looks or mannerisms. Both Tom Lyle and I knew pretty much who we were at an early age. Both of us were curious as to how things worked, and the possibilities of new things that no one had done before. His fortune came from a mixture of burnt cork, Vaseline and lamp soot. Mine came from a cryotherapy gel that froze away body aches and pains for extended periods of time, which I called BIOFREEZE™.

To be sure, my real work would be in skin revision and paramedical adjunctive treatments for acne, age management and other serious anomalies; a methodology of natural pharmacology for skin disorders that made me famous in the field of aesthetics and in the scientific community—but did not make me rich. In fact, years ago a venture capital expert in Century City, California was trying to raise money from other companies to take my methods and creations to a commercially viable level—to become the "Gucci" of the skin care industry. He performed a due-diligence search of me all over the world, based upon my many published articles in trade magazines and my travels and lectures all over the planet—even as far away as Tibet, where a painting of me 30 feet high and 25 feet wide, in a white suit, is fastened to the side of a building in Lhasa.

He came back wondering, "How come your reputation far exceeds your income, Danie?" Apparently my reputation also included the fact that from a corporate standpoint I was hard to work with, a control freak and "not a team player"—the venture capitalist could not raise big cash for such a time bomb eccentric maverick. I told him to forget it—if I were owned and forced to do things as they had always been done, the magic would vanish. Time proved me right, and I know now that Tom Lyle felt the same way—which is why Maybelline stayed pretty much family-controlled until Tom Lyle retired and sold the company to Shearing Plough for millions of dollars.

Tom played the piano, and so do I. When I was a kid I performed stories for the kids at church, acting out all the characters and dramatizing it with music. I put on puppet shows; Tom put on his "Actor-Bat" shows and other promotions in his home town. We both worshiped the movies—he absorbed the original films of the "golden era" as they were released; I saw them decades later and viewed every one over and over again, and still do. We both had insight into what it took to make and keep women beautiful, and pioneered many things that later became standard in the beauty and health industries.

We both were gay but had an offspring from a heterosexual affair. He acknowledged his son; I could not acknowledge my daughter—her British mother's family, hating me, married her mother off to a very wealthy man upon discovering she was pregnant. The girl never knew that I was her real father, and if her husband knew he did not acknowledge it. Her mother, however, sent me a baby photo after our daughter's birth with a note that said, "Who does our daughter look like? If you really loved me, please keep this to yourself and don't contact me, ever."

The baby looked like me—my eyes and face shape and hair. I never did contact them, of course, but often wonder if the girl, now a mature woman, knows who I am, maybe even follows my work and career. Has she passed me on the street in London? Does she use DMK products or treatments? If she knows me is she proud of her father?

Both Tom Lyle and I had long-time lovers who were a huge part of our success. He had Emory and I had a Son of Chicago, Randy Allen Larsen. When Randy met me, he was 25 and I was 43. He thought I was in my early 30s at first, and was furious when the white lie was later revealed, although not because of the age difference—he is a moral and good man who hates lies.

For 22 years this pillar of integrity, salt of the earth, direct and honest businessman who has always given his all 24/7 has put up with "The Danné Show." I was always "famous" in my field no matter where I went—I always made money, but had no concept of how to manage it. Brought up as a gentleman who does not talk about one's finances, I ignored the finances. I was a bright and fantastic ship of hope to the world under full sail.

And leaking in a thousand places.

I knew this, but did not know what do to. Randy finally quit his high-paying job at a large market research company, and invested the liquidation of his stock sharing in that company into mine. Fearful that my ego and reluctance to relinquish control of the administrative and basic running of my company would cause trouble, he took over. He didn't realize how much I needed and wanted this; I totally gave up control and did not look back.

In a short period of time he had my mess cleared up to the point of doing normal business, and for the next 22 years he helped me build the company to what DMK is today—and we are still building. Although we are sadly not together anymore as lovers—we are each with other people, my "other half" being an incredible, caring and beautiful human being—Randy is still my business partner.

The last thing I had in common with T. L. Williams was that the great city of Chicago was our mutual starting point. But this story is not so much about who Evelyn Williams was during the formative years of

Maybelline. It is about who she became after an age when most people are set in their ways, tottering down the road to forgotten antiquity and waiting for the parade to pass on by. Not only was Evelyn still part of the parade in the years I was with her, she led it!

A short while after Evelyn became my client and friend, into my shop walked Delyle Compton—a vague sort of woman who seemed "all beige." She exuded an aura of old money "class" and quiet refinement. She always had her nails done by Philip, but kept looking over at me and smiling. She had a face that was once beautiful, rather doll like, with full, pouty lips and large Bette Davis eyes that she used to express everything.

She came back for nails several times before she began to seriously talk to me. Thinking she *was* a real lady fallen upon hard times and living with her nerdy and reclusive, acne-ridden son Stuart in a modest house in Costa Mesa, I began confiding in her. I didn't realize that she was actually pumping me for information, trying to figure out how she could cash in on my unusual shop. Despite my insight into people, I was still the product of a strong, moral upbringing by highly intelligent parents. My mother was a woman of strong emotions and drama—and very precise as to how her first born son should behave in public. My father was a dignified man of science and culture, very British and old school. I had been sent to private schools, taught to be a gentleman and to believe that poverty was a state of mind, not pocketbook. I'd also been taught to respect women at all costs and to accept them at face value. In this manner I was fooled many times by women who had agendas.

Delyle had a way of moving very slowly and speaking exactly. I thought this represented old-money upbringing, an impression enhanced by photos she showed me of her younger years in which she wore smart suits and hats at garden parties and dinners, sometimes with film star Jeanette McDonald.

Delyle was more vague about her recent past and her son Stuart's father—she told me a legitimate-sounding story about how she had been left with a fixed income and was "OK," but it turned out to be all lies. Nor was Delyle ever my business partner, as later rumored, although she did insist that I redecorate my shop to be more "tasteful and subdued" to attract the "really wealthy" people. She called my friend La-Verne a "painted whore" and said I should "purge" any suggestion of her from the area of her dress display (LaVerne's son-in-law had painted it hot pink with mirrored walls). Eventually Delyle had her son, Stuart, paint it dull brown.

I was actually buying into this woman's gentle and tasteful approach and listened to her ideas of how I could "build an empire" with her guidance (I was to hear this same thing from many other women over the years). I did not actually introduce her to Evelyn; the two women introduced themselves one day when they both came into the shop for various services. They were yakking up a storm by the time the first meeting was over—and suddenly they announced they were going to lunch together at the Blue Dolphin, and swept out into Evelyn's yellow Cadillac.

Later Delyle told me that Evelyn was a marvelous woman but lonely and saddled with a controlling family. For her part, Evelyn told me that Delyle was a marvelous and elegant woman of good taste, but lonely and saddled with a fatherless son.

And with that the goose with the golden eggs became a sitting duck. Delyle introduced us to Hobby Derrick, a good ol' boy from Arkansas who was allegedly her stepfather. Hobby seemed harmless and down to earth and did not talk much—although he could come off as another Will Rogers. Delyle talked about his military record being the cause of his limp (fake) and what a wonderful, down to earth, *salt* of the earth man he was, a real champion of truth, justice and the American way.

He also wore horrible toupees that looked like Davy Crockett raccoon hats on his head—and of course I had to restyle them to make him presentable because, lo and behold, he and Evelyn were falling in love.

This was not actually shocking—he seemed very nice and conservative, and he treated Evelyn like a lady. They dated for some weeks— quiet dinners out, road trips and serene evenings at home with Delyle serving tasteful meals. Evelyn seemed to feel sorry for Delyle and her shy son, and actually appeared to be taking over their lives, although secretly the situation was reversed.

Later Evelyn confided to me that Hobby had asked her to marry him, although they had not "been intimate" because he was old-fashioned in that respect. Actually she had another reason not to be intimate: she was suffering from prolapse of the uterus, a condition that was not conducive to the "missionary style" of senior sex. Fearful of surgery, Evelyn was keeping herself in place with cotton pads. She also alluded to a variety of special skills that a woman could employ to keep her husband happy until she could bring herself to endure surgery. She feared that if she vacillated too long he would "get away"—a prime bachelor like him being much in demand.

She was also afraid of what her son Bill would think of Hobby. My advice was simple: If two older persons fall in love, why not get married? And Bill be damned. She was a grown woman; Bill had his own courtship going with the Rosan Yacht family's daughter Gloria, so why should Evelyn not do what she wanted to do?

The wedding was held at the Balboa Bay Club. Delyle had handled all the arrangements—a fact that was brought up later at the divorce trial—and it was a fun time. Evelyn was resplendent in a silver-sequined jacket with a silver-gray Carmeuse silk skirt; Delyle was a vision of elegant restraint in tones of beige, including her wig. The men were in black tie, with Bobby sporting a new toupee I had made especially for the occasion.

I was in charge of entertainment, so I organized a comedy skit from an old Jeanette McDonald movie where she sang her famous "Indian Love Call" song. A local woman with an opera-trained voice played Jeanette and I, with my wobbly baritone, played Nelson Eddy. I had huge balloons put into the singer's bodice, and as we rushed into each other's arms during the grand finale "...you belong to *meeeeee*..." she hit a high note, I crushed her to my breast and the balloons exploded with a BANG! It brought the house down. Evelyn, having a very Germanic sense of humor, loved it. Later I played the grand piano and she sang.

Afterward Hobby swept her off to his native Arkansas for a honeymoon and to find a home. Meanwhile Delyle and Stuart moved into Evelyn's Lido Isle home to "look after it." Later they would join Evelyn and Hobby in Arkansas, where Stuart could attend a decent school and have a wholesome country life away from the glitz of Southern California and all the beautiful bronzed teenagers who made fun of his virulent acne and pasty-white skin. I felt sorry for the kid and tried to clear up his skin problem inasmuch as I too had suffered from terrible acne as a teen.

While they were living at Evelyn's house, Delyle went through all Evelyn's belongings "to get them ready for shipping to Arkansas," clucking over all Evelyn's "terrible excesses and buying ten of everything, including household cleaners."

I privately thought this was rather bitchy, and that Evelyn could do what she wanted with her money. But again I said nothing to this slow and pedantic-sounding woman. It was not until later, during the divorce proceedings, that I discovered that her slow, careful, understated way of talking and acting were classic hallmarks of a long-time alcoholic.

In the following months I wrote Evelyn a few times and talked on the phone with her. She seemed very happy, going on about how beautiful and peaceful Hot Springs was and the wonderful home on which she and Hobby had finally bid—a real show place on Lake Hamilton.

All at once Delyle and Stuart were leaving for Arkansas, and Evelyn's furniture was put into storage in L.A. I thought Evelyn's life was set and I would probably never see her again.

I was wrong.

One day, out of the blue, Evelyn and a Los Angeles attorney named Joe E. Lewis pulled up in front of my shop in Joe's black Cadillac. Evelyn rushed in, crying, "Danie, you have to help us—they're trying to contest the divorce and take everything!"

I told her to calm down and tell me what was wrong. She introduced me to Joe, who suggested we close the door to the shop, lock it and talk. Although Evelyn was still as sparkly and vibrant as ever, her face had aged ten years from fear and stress. Joe was a kind of mousy older man with stooped shoulders, thinning hair, a basset hound face and a whispery voice. He looked more like a Charles Dickens clerk than the high-powered attorney he turned out to be.

Together they told me a lurid tale of con artists, collusion and possible intended murder—Evelyn's. From what I gathered, the moment Delyle Compton arrived in Hot Springs she changed from Betty Beige to Hanna Horrendous. She took over the large home Evelyn had bought, dictating how it should be decorated—no more of Evelyn's crass Hollywood style. She controlled Hobby and all his daily activities, and catered to Evelyn just enough to keep her off balance. She had also kept Evelyn drugged with larger and larger doses of prescription mood enhancers and "just one more little cocktail for the evening, darling."

Hobby had to have a business, Delyle claimed; he could not be perceived in his native state as a gigolo to a rich woman. So they conned Evelyn into buying a large property called Gulpha Gorge, right at the entrance to Hot Springs. A roller rink was built there called "Hobby's," of course, and plans for a go-cart track were laid out with preliminary work being done.

At first Evelyn saw some sense in all this. Her husband had pride, and the fact that he wanted to do things for the kids and families in town made it seem all right. She even pictured herself as a benevolent patron of youth…plus she'd have a place to dress up and go to in the evenings where people were having fun.

But Delyle had other plans—she perceived *herself* as the true Mistress of the Manor, the person who ran everything—and of course her miserable son Stuart would be a rich kid at last. And popular, too, because his Mom and stepdad ran the hottest spot for teens in town. He might even finally get laid!

Evelyn kept herself more and more in the background and became increasingly disenchanted with the marriage. Her attempts to keep Hobby happy as a husband were failing, and Delyle was emerging as a garish, showy and pretentious woman—the little beige wren a thing of the past.

But Evelyn was reluctant to tell anyone, most of all her son, about the circumstances of her marriage. Having spent a great deal of money on properties and new Cadillacs for everyone, plus a roller rink, she did not want to admit that she had been bilked and defrauded.

Then one night she overheard Hobby and Delyle bickering. The argument got louder and louder until she heard Delyle say, "Hobby, you *have* to do something with Evelyn, and do it soon."

Fearing for her life, Evelyn screwed up the courage to get out of bed, dress herself and march into the room where the other two were arguing. She even had the presence of mind to call the police first. Standing in the doorway, she yelled, "I heard every word between you two! This is collusion—get out of my house!"

Then she locked herself in her room until the police arrived.

Either the law goes where the money is, or Delyle was not quite as popular in Hot Springs as she imagined herself to be—or perhaps information about Hobby's time in prison had finally leaked out; whatever the reason, the police did indeed remove Hobby and Delyle from the house.

The next day Evelyn filed for divorce.

Delyle and Hobby then made a big mistake: they counter-sued. They thought they had the little old rich lady sequestered in Arkansas where they could run herd over her. They hired a great lawyer, but there were three things they failed to factor into their plans: Evelyn's spirit of survival, her sense of life's dramas—and me.

4

The Divorce Trial

Joe E. Lewis was one of those lawyers who researched everything before making a court appearance. His Los Angeles firm was old, venerable and had vast resources. Despite his humble, shabby, almost "sad sack" appearance, there was an aura of class about him. He was even dating a European countess at the time.

He presented me with a deal. If I were to go to Arkansas, stay for the length of the trial and testify on behalf of Evelyn in the double-suit divorce, I would be compensated $5,000. I can't pretend that didn't sound like a lot of money. The shop was getting by, but I lived up to my reputation of being an artist who far exceeded his income. So I told my assistant I'd be gone for a few weeks, put $3,000 into the business bank account to cover expenses, and left for Hot Springs, Arkansas.

Evelyn and Joe met me at the airport in a huge new baby-blue Cadillac, accompanied by a "bodyguard" named Greig. He was a stocky young man, seemed sensible and down to earth, and definitely knew about the security business. He was also somewhat in awe of "Mizz Williams," as he called her.

Evelyn had hired another "security man" right after Delyle and Hobby vacated the house. Through an Arkansas lawyer—she was required to have *local* legal representation as well as her out-of-state attorney—she had acquired a Cajun thug named Sam Saleem. He apparently frightened the hell out of her. Later I confronted him personally and saw why, but in the beginning her descriptions of him and his attempts to imprison and extort more money from her seemed exaggerated. He sounded like a cartoon gangster character from the 1930s—like Al Capone, in fact. Apparently Joe got rid of Saleem and hired Greig from an agency.

From the airport we drove into the city that would change both our lives.

It was hot and sultry in Arkansas. At first I thought I could never stay there for long; I was used to the cool, dry air of Newport Beach. But within three days I got used to it; in fact it felt rather sensual, as was the town itself. Evelyn's huge house on Brown Drive was not a mansion per se, but the driveway was private and ended at a pillared brick entrance with a huge circular area in front and an island in the middle bearing tall pine trees and shrubs. There was no lawn and few flowers; I had both put in later. "Rustic" was the word that described the place. The center of the house held the main door entrance, with the kitchen as a focal point. Wings extended out on either side, the left wing housing the maid's quarters, and the right wing Mrs. Williams' quarters, which consisted of her office, two guest rooms and her large en suite master bedroom. She actually hated the master bedroom and its built-in spa bath—memories of Hobby and being imprisoned there were sharp in her mind. Instead she took one of the smaller guest rooms, saying "It's so much cozier and homey."

My quarters were on the ground level, which consisted of a long line of odd rooms that started with a laundry at the bottom of the stairs, wound through a living room with a stone fireplace, then a bedroom, card room, butler's pantry with a hallway, store rooms, and finally a large, formal bar with an old upright piano. My living room opened onto a natural rock patio that overlooked a sweeping lawn dotted with majestic pines and Lake Hamilton beyond. The edges of the property down to the lake were draped with sweet-smelling wild honeysuckle vines and a tangle of nearly tropical Arkansas bushes and shrubs. It was all very peaceful and sequestered. Above my patio was the upper deck, which opened into a narrow upstairs living room with an A-frame ceiling and really massive stone fireplace, an extension of my own. It was the only ceiling in the house high enough to be described as "grand." Next to it was a narrow dining room.

The foyer at the front door was also grand—marble floored and wainscoted. The huge front door had a large, embossed, solid brass knob in the middle of the door that came off in one's hand if a certain amount of pressure was not applied when turning it. I told Evelyn this had to be fixed, but for some reason she seemed to feel it was a "security measure" against anyone trying to come in the front door—she often took the knob off at night and put it on the floor. Still, I intended to go ahead and get it fixed, as it annoyed me when people would visit. I never got around to doing that chore…which might, in the end, have contributed to Evelyn's demise.

All in all it the house was basically a big vacation home for people who liked the woodsy look and feel, and hardly the Hollywood glamour spot we would try to make it into later. There was very little furniture in the place—a few beds, a couch and some tables, all picked out by Delyle who was "in the process of decorating." There was nothing downstairs but a very old couch of the tuxedo design that was also a hide-bed. I rather liked it.

That night we sat around the table laughing and joking about old times. Evelyn seemed almost hysterically happy to have me there. Greig kept looking back and forth between us with a perplexed look on his face as if we were from another planet. Evelyn talked about her fear of Sam Saleem and how he had vowed revenge upon her when she fired him. Greig assured her that he was armed (he showed us his guns) and would be on the alert 24 hours a day; when he needed to sleep he'd bring in relief from friends of his moonlighting from the local sheriff's department.

Joe and I sat and discussed the trial and what my part would be. The next day, Jim Gooch, Evelyn's Arkansas attorney, would arrive to meet with Joe and me to further strategize. Evelyn described Gooch as a "wonderful Southern gentleman."

It appeared that Hobby and Delyle were contesting Evelyn's accusations of collusion and having them removed forcibly from the house. Hobby asserted that he had married Evelyn in good faith, she having been the one to pursue him in the first place. They contended that he did not even know she was wealthy when they met, owing to the fact the fact that her car was "not new." They claimed that she was the one who had insisted they make a fresh start in Arkansas, she being weary of Newport Beach and her controlling family. Furthermore Evelyn had promised to make provisions for his stepdaughter, Delyle, and her son Stuart, insisting they tear up their roots and move to Arkansas as well.

This may have sounded reasonable to anyone else, but not to me. I had witnessed the courtship from its inception, knew all the parties well (except that I didn't really know Delyle and Hobby at all, as Joe's research later proved). This was to be the basis of my testimony: a description of Evelyn's obvious wealth, how everyone had actually met… and one trump card that I held that was given to Joe before the trial started.

On the evening before the trial, James Gooch, from Arkadelphia, Arkansas appeared. I will admit he did look like Central Casting's version of the Southern Gentleman: tall, well dressed, with a string tie and a big, white hat. His face was sun- and bourbon-reddened, with small piercing blue eyes that looked coldly over rimless glasses; even with his big white-toothed "perma-grin" and hearty, rich, southern, booming voice. He flooded the house with cornball oratory, full of assurances that we were "gonna *git* those four-flushin' sidewinders." He looked and talked like a human version of the pompous cartoon rooster Foghorn Leghorn. I could hardly keep from laughing in disbelief. Later , when he took me aside for some private pre-trial prepping, I discovered that he was not quite so funny.

"Son," he said in a fatherly manner, eyes piercing mine, "we have to establish ya'll as a solid citizen and a truthful man." I agreed that this was necessary, and stated that I had no criminal record of any kind and could supply many high-profile character witnesses.

"Thass fine, thass fine," he said, "but they're going to say y'all *are* some kind of faggot. Now if y'all are, why, just go on and admit to it, son. They'll respect y'all more for it."

I looked up at him sharply, and suddenly saw someone in there besides the "real Southern Gentleman." I also knew he was in cahoots with everyone else. I didn't have the heart to tell Evelyn this; instead, I got up, shook Gooch's hand and said, "I think I'll know how to handle myself, Mr. Gooch—and by the way, whose lawyer did you say you are?"

His face turned even more red as I walked out of the room.

Later, when I confided this experience to Joe, he was not surprised. He already planned to minimize Jim Gooch at the trial, and I already intended to pour cold water all over the hated faggot image they were expecting. That night I cut off my wavy, shoulder length hair, and when morning dawned over the Manor, Evelyn was shocked to see standing in her hallway, a strange man with Republican-parted short hair, a dull tweed blazer, blue chambray shirt and an old-school striped tie, faded jeans and scuffed cowboy boots.

"But I wanted you to look elegant!" she cried. "You look like a Baptist youth counselor, a young redneck!"

Chuckling, Joe Lewis informed her that I looked exactly right, and we set off for the Garland County Courthouse.

It was a venerable old building like in a movie set. I could almost see Gregory Peck going up the steps in *To Kill a Mocking Bird*. The Judge had a stern, no-nonsense face, and considering the fact that I later discovered he and *all* the local attorneys were "old buddies" in real life, I felt that he was fair and just, and well aware of the media and the high profile case this had become.

The courtroom was packed. It was agreed that Evelyn would not take the witness stand, but remain visible in court as the "victimized old lady." This was a role she had a hard time dealing with, never mind looking like, despite Joe's pleas to play down her appearance and wardrobe. He felt that sitting in the courtroom looking sad and haggard was best, and she did try to appear that way.

While I was waiting in the foyer with Greig while Evelyn visited the lady's room, Delyle suddenly stood before me. I was shocked by her appearance. Gone was the Beige Lady. In her place was what looked like an ageing hooker trying to hang onto her youth for a few more years. She had on a shiny green dress with a full skirt, tightly belted with a gold belt that emphasized her thick waist rather than disguised it. Her feet were encased in gold plastic spring-a-lator pumps covered with rhinestones. But it was her face that was the shocker. She had on more make-up than Tammy Faye ever thought of wearing; false eyelashes rimming puffy eyes, bright orange lipstick over-painted like a fish, and her hair dyed bright red, combed over a long fall that cascaded down her back. She was grotesque, and I actually felt sorry for her.

I was braced for some kind of threat or sarcasm over my being there, but all she did was ask me the time in a mumbling voice and then drift away. I realized she was either drunk or high.

Her testimony was curiously sad. She played the single parent card, claiming to care only about her son's welfare. The real drama came when Joe Lewis took the stand and revealed that Delyle's son was not her son at all; he had been adopted as part of a marriage agreement between her and his real father. Stuart, sitting in the back of the courtroom, obviously did not know this. The look of shock and disbelief on the Mama's boy's face will never leave my mind—that and the look of betrayal. I've often wondered what happened to the poor kid after he walked out of the courtroom.

Joe shattered Delyle Compton on the stand. He brought up her alcoholism, asking her if she "needed a little drink right now." Despite objections from her attorney, she collapsed into a whimper, fumbling in her large bag for tissues. One could almost hear "Ding, dong, the witch is dead!" wafting through the air.

But it was Hobby Derrick who was the real show. When confronted with the fact that he had served time in the Arkansas State Penitentiary for armed robbery and trafficking in stolen goods, he just sat there with a fixed smile on his face and his toupee slightly askew, muttering something about "That was a long time ago, and ah paid mah debt."

Joe E. Lewis had also discovered that Hobby had been married a total of seven times, Delyle being both Wife Number Six *and* his stepdaughter, due to the fact that her mother was wife number five. Delyle's mother had shot Hobby in the shoulder and then disappeared, never to be heard from again, and was presumed dead.

Hobby married Delyle in 1970. Although they divorced a year later he continued to live with her and Stuart up until he married Evelyn. During that time Hobby had no visible source of income. Delyle claimed to be a nurse, an accountant, a public relations expert and a journalist. She was in fact none of these; Evelyn appeared to be their "ship that had come in at last."

Hobby's rebuttal was that Evelyn was not the woman she made out to be and was reneging on her promises to take care of him and his little family. When Joe Lewis asked him to elaborate on how Evelyn was not the wife she claimed to be, Hobby blurted that she would never make love the "regular way," and only offered oral sex.

"I just got damn tired of it," Hobby said, and the courtroom burst into laughter. Evelyn sat there stricken, cheeks flaming. Greig clapped his hands over his mouth, cheeks bursting, to avoid embarrassing her further. I was livid with rage.

The rest of the afternoon was taken up with the presentation of documents proving that Delyle and Hobby's conspiracy had been planned and launched long before the wedding and included financial misappropriations after the wedding. A large sum of cash was still unaccounted for. When pressed on this issue, Hobby said that the money was stashed in his car. Asked to go out and get it by Joe Lewis and his own attorney, Hobby smugly said, "I don't believe I want to do that."

Judge Chestnut turned to him. "Mr. Derrick, you *will* go get that money right now, or my deputy will be escorting you to another room in this building."

Red-faced, Hobby stumbled out of the courtroom accompanied by a Bailiff, leaving the audience sitting there shaking its collective head in disbelief over his blatant stupidity. It was obvious that Delyle and not Hobby was the so-called mastermind of this debacle.

On the ride home I tried to defuse Evelyn's embarrassment by insisting she take the stand in her defense. Slowly her shame turned to the rage I wanted to see, and she told us that Hobby had an impotence problem that he'd promised to have medically repaired at some future date. In the meantime she had tried to please him as best she could.

I privately viewed the marriage as a sad comedy of errors and vanity, because I knew Evelyn had her own secret issues that would require surgery as well. But Joe and I did convince her to appear on the stand the next day.

We'd won that battle, but Evelyn chose to go against her lawyer's advice to appear as an "old, misused woman," and be herself instead. Clad in a chic charcoal gray silk Chanel suit, pearl earrings and necklace and Ferragamo pumps, she swept into the courtroom, leaving a cloud of Balenciaga perfume behind her. Hobby looked stunned and shrank down in his seat as far as he could go. Delyle and Stuart were nowhere to be seen.

When questioned by Joe E. Lewis regarding her courtship with Hobby Derrick, Evelyn maintained that she knew he had little money, but thought he was supporting his stepdaughter and grandson. She elaborated upon his old-fashioned southern courtesy and how she'd thought him to be a simple but caring Will Rogers sort of man with a great sense of humor. When asked about Delyle, Evelyn maintained that she felt sorry for her and was happy to include her in their plans as a lady's companion, and also because the boy needed a good background and education.

In short, Evelyn came off as a cross between Mother Theresa and the Queen of England.

Then Joe brought up the sexual allegations, and I will never forget this. First, the lighting in the courtroom was perfect. There was a key spotlight, for some reason, right above the witness stand. It enhanced all of Evelyn's best features, giving her an elegant and gracious look. Her eyes appeared huge and as expressive as Bette Davis'.

But her testimony was pure Loretta Young. In carefully modulated tones she said, "When I married my husband, I was aware of certain physical difficulties, but at that time it did not seem to matter. We both were older people, and at certain ages companionship and good fun are more important than sex. However, I did my best, as his wife, to make him feel as manly and complete as possible until he received medical help."

There was dead silence in the courtroom. Hobby looked like the worst heel in the world to everyone present, and put his head down. I resisted the urge to burst into applause.

There was no cross examination from Hobby's attorney. He knew it *was* over—and it was over. The Judge stated that although there had been much exaggeration from both sides, the case was clearly in favor of Evelyn F. Williams, and all monies and properties were to be returned to her in full. Off the record, he suggested that "Hobby and company" leave town.

Later that evening we were in a celebratory mood. I forget whether we dined out or went back to the estate, but Evelyn, especially, was energized. She recapped the day over and over, using a lot of body language. She was especially happy with Joe E. Lewis and his seemingly fumbling courtroom manner, which had lulled the witness into a false sense of security before Lewis came out swinging with hard facts. Evelyn recreated this with clenched fists swinging dramatically in the air. "Pow, Joe, you *got* her—the bitch didn't know what hit her!"

I was under the impression that despite all the cost and stress, Evelyn quite enjoyed the show. Then she turned to me and, with shining eyes, laid her small slim hand on my arm and told me I was her hero and no one had ever been more powerful on the stand—fending off all attempts by the attorney to discredit me. In reality, the highly intelligent attorney for the plaintiffs had tried to discredit me at the outset, but one look at me and he knew it was hopeless to play the "queer card." My answers to his first tentative questions were straight to the point and made the courtroom chuckle. He clearly decided "not to go there" with me, a fact he confirmed much later when we met again socially.

Apparently Evelyn and Joe had already discussed the possibility of me staying on in Hot Springs. Evelyn downplayed my clinic in Newport Beach as a "mom and pop" operation that was not good enough for all I had to offer the world. She went on to propose that if I stayed to help her turn the Roller Rink around as its manager, I could continue my skin revision experiments at the estate. Later, she said, we could venture into a really big treatment spa that I had always envisioned, combining dermatology with adjunctive skin treatments—not realizing at the time that this would be a forerunner to the now internationally popular medi-spa.

That night I lay downstairs in my little roll-away bed and mulled over all the pros and cons of such a move. I didn't really have much to hold me in Newport Beach—a lot of friends but no real relationship, and a shop that was popular but financially barely keeping my head above water.

It was when I got up early in the morning and found myself walking around, looking at all the empty rooms downstairs and planning where I would conduct my homespun research and treatments, that I knew I had already made the decision. At the same time I decided to keep the shop in Newport, letting the young lady run it, just in case things didn't work out in Hot Springs.

When I told Evelyn what I had decided, she was ecstatic. "You won't regret this, Dan!" she exclaimed (I would be "Dan" to her from then on). "We'll build an empire together." (I'd heard this before and have again since, but when she said it, it sounded real.)

The next two days were spent with Evelyn, Joe and me planning how we would establish Evelyn in Hot Springs. She wanted to change the name of the roller rink from Hobby's to something else. I suggested Spa City Roller Rink with a red, white and blue striped background. I pointed out that this would be a grand gesture to Arkansas civic pride, and patriotic at the same time. Joe agreed. I also pointed out that since Evelyn really *was* "an heiress" in the Maybelline family and that there was a Maybelline plant near Little Rock, why not capitalize on the glamour and legend of a household name?

At first she seemed a little shy about this scheme, wondering what Tom Lyle would think. As he was still alive at the time, I suggested we get a little publicity underway and then send it to him in a letter and see what he thought. Since the publicity I had in mind was of the highest caliber and dignity, I felt sure he would approve.

I had no intention of presenting Ms. Evelyn F. Williams as just a colorful, wealthy old lady from California. Her marriage was over. Everyone knew what she had gone through and were sympathetic. Now we had to make public the fact that rather than run away from Hot Springs she was going to stay and continue providing the youth of the city with good clean fun, and entertainment for the church groups.

She was already thrilled with the beauty and tranquility of the area, and the warm and hospitable people of Arkansas. She was keen to use her wealth, glamour and style to assist in Civic and political endeavors, yet remain a "show woman" at heart. This was not so hard to do in this most unusual of all American cities. Hot Springs was a place where religious and moral standards co-existed nicely with gambling, horse racing, strippers, bars, nightclubs and sex—for sale or rent. Everybody knew everybody else, and also knew where their place was and where the boundaries were. As long as you had a label that was out in the open, and lived within the parameters of that label, you were OK. After all, Hot Springs had been a mafia playground in the roaring '20s and '30s, with a lot of under-the-table money changing hands to make town leaders look the other way.

Once a year there was the horse racing season, at which point Hot Springs filled to overflowing and all the restaurants and night clubs made a fortune. Big name entertainers would come to town, and top local talent was often "discovered" by talent scouts. The Race Meet was on everyone's lips for the rest of the year as the city went about the ordinary business of a small resort city. Plans were underway to create an outdoor amphitheater in which a huge production would be staged portraying how the Spanish conquistador De Desoto came to the natural healing springs area in the Quachita Valley, made friends with the local Indians who revered the mystical place, established what would end up as Hot Springs. When the amphitheater was complete, actors, singers and actresses from all over the USA auditioned. Later, after Evelyn and I were made official members of the Showman's Association which headquartered in Hot Springs, we entertained many of these actors. Through our friendship with banker Mort Cox (who became a mentor to me, often advising me on how to deal with various aspects of the city and its movers and shakers), we were often VIP guests at this wonderful pageant—sitting in the audience with our security man Grieg while he got out his cell phone—an expensive and rare tool at that time—to call Mort high up above the arena to see if he "had a little vodka" to ease Mizz Williams' back pains. Evelyn suffered from various neck and back osteo problems and used hot, hydrocallator packs at night to take away the pain. These kinds of problems in older people usually result in a dowager's hump or bent spine. Evelyn refused to cave into this, always standing and sitting erect, but many times a "little nip" of vodka was needed to help her through public appearances. Mort was flabbergasted the first time he got a call in his office from us, knowing we were down in the audience.

After three days of planning our moves while getting phone calls about what Delyle and Hobby were doing and having their personal belongings removed from the Roller Rink under the watchful eye of hired security, we thought it best we go down and take a look at what we had to work with. I was officially named General Manager with a huge salary of $250 a week, a sum which Evelyn would point out "was the salary of a Senator." I guess in the early 1970s that may have been a good wage, but now my housekeeper would turn her nose up at it. Inflation changes everything.

When we got to the rink there were kids all over the place, with roller rink music—the old-fashioned kind—pumping away. A nice sort of school-teacherish lady greeted us, her hands twisting nervously. She had been the cashier under Hobby's management, a decent and honest woman, a Christian woman who was either a widow or a spinster. Odd, I can see her as I write this—slender, with wavy light brown hair, a narrow face and glasses—but I cannot remember her name even though she was to become Evelyn's Personal Assistant and run the entire office and administration of the rink very well for years. But at the moment of meeting her for the first time I could see that she had been underpaid and under-used, yet needed the job and feared the worst from us.

She showed us the place and told us how the roller business worked: skate rentals, hours and times of operation, church group bookings, books, ticket sales office and cash boxes.

But there were no books, and the cash was gone. Hobby and Delyle had cleaned everything out and taken a great many other things as well. Evelyn was furious at the security man, who pleaded ignorance over what was theirs and not theirs, and wanted me to call the police. But the cashier lady (I'll call her Gracie) said that the cash hadn't been that much because she'd gone to the bank the day the trial ended and deposited the week's take, and she knew the books by heart. She also admitted to not really liking Delyle or trusting her, and had been suspicious of her from the "get go"—so when the trial began, Gracie decided to keep her eye on the money, just in case.

Feeling that Gracie was going to be a gem, I told Evelyn I wanted her to work under me as assistant manager. Until further notice we'd also keep the employees who issued the skate shoes, worked the concession and taught skating. Gracie had tears in her eyes over her new title and slight raise, so I told her to assemble all the employees into what would become Evelyn's office—a large room with a private bathroom and a two-way mirror Hobby had used. After everyone shuffled in, eyes lowered with apprehension about the fact that Delyle had told them the rink was being taken over by a crazy old drunk lady and a raving California queer, I presented Mrs. Evelyn Williams to them. She was wonderful. She graciously acknowledged each employee, asking their names, inquiring about their families and complimenting the women on any little thing she could see to mention ("You have the most amazing eyes, my dear, but perhaps a little more Maybelline?").

The boys she called "handsome," and as she greeted each one you could see them visibly straighten and puff their chests out. This was the effect she had on all men, young and old.

As for me, I suddenly became very "southern," my speech laced with "y'all" and "ah tell you what." I could not seem to help this, it just came—the old "holding a mirror up to people" trick I had used all my life. After a while it became my normal manner of speech and people back in California got a huge kick out of it.

I informed the employees they all still had a job if they wanted it. I said we knew nothing about the roller skating business but would learn fast—from them.

Then I told them of the name change and the fact that I was planning to update the image of roller skating into Disco Roller Skating, and change the music to the more modern and with-it songs that teens enjoyed. We'd keep the organ music for the church groups. I also informed them we were open to any and all suggestions for a better rink, and reminded them that we were the very first business people saw as they drove into Hot Springs through the Gulpha Gorge area. We had to shine and catch the tourists!

They were excited and started talking at once. Some started to tell Delyle and Hobby horror stories, along with a few Stuart tidbits, but I waved it all aside. That was history, I told them. Ms. Williams had been through enough with these crooks, and did not want to hear it. (This was not entirely true; later Evelyn would cackle, "Did you hear what they said? Oh, those crooks; they should have been put in jail!")

But that day as we walked to the entrance of the rink to leave, I noticed a large group of sullen, teenage boys standing to one side, legs spread, arms folded, glaring at us. Wondering what this was all about, I slowed down, gave them the once over, then opened the front doors and ushered Evelyn out into the evening twilight.

When I saw her Cadillac, I knew what the tough boys were all about.

5

The Spa City Roller Disco Roller Rink

*S*pray painted along the entire side of the Caddy in black was the word FAGGOT.

Evelyn gasped, clutched her throat and moaned, "Oh, no!" I stood there stunned for about a minute, then a quiet rage rose up inside me. This rage would recur again and again for the rest of my life. Evelyn saw it for the first time that day and would use it many times over the next two years.

I whirled and glared at the gang of boys that had followed us outside, followed by a group of girls who were posing and whispering with many under-the-eyelash looks at me.

One boy stood out immediately: a slight, cocky kid with short jet black hair like a prison cut, flawless skin, a skinny moustache outlining smirking lips, and snapping defiant black eyes. His features reminded me of old 1940 movie stars. I instinctively knew he was the ringleader; later I would learn that his name was Doug Berry.

"Who in the hell is responsible for this?" I barked, staring directly into Doug's eyes.

The rest of the boys shuffled and muttered, but Doug drew himself up and yelled, "Ms. Compton warned us about you, man. She said you were a queer and would try to hit on us."

I knew at that moment that I had to either fish or cut bait; I'd have no second chance with these kids, and any show of fear on my part would undo everything before it began.

Although I was from a level of society in relaxed California that these boys could not even dream of, I had confronted bullies before. I walked up to Doug, grabbed the front of his tank top in both hands and pushed him against the side of the roller rink wall. Glaring down into his angry eyes, I growled, "What in the fuck did you just call me?"

His eyes flickered back and forth like a computer screen, then grew uncertain. I repeated my question, louder.

"Ahhh, man, Ms. Compton and Hobby said you were a fag and would try to make this place into a fag club."

Releasing him, I stood up and spoke to everyone present: "Do those little gals over there think I look like some kinda fag?" The young ladies tittered and blushed; one in particular gave me a bold smile and struck a teen version of a calendar girl pose. Doug put his head down for a moment, and then looked up at me with a totally different expression on his face. I could see that he was very intelligent, crafty and a born leader, even if he didn't know it himself.

The rest of the boys started all talking at once, telling me all the horrible things Delyle and Hobby had said about Mrs. Williams and me—I was a fag, Evelyn was a crazy old lady on drugs, and together we were going to wreck the roller rink.

I yelled "Shut the f—up!" and they all fell silent. I pointed to Evelyn who was by this time standing next to the car, looking at the spray paint and shaking her head. "Does she look crazy?" I demanded. "Do I look like a fag?"

Embarrassed by now, the kids stood silent, shuffling their feet.

"OK guys, listen up. I'm taking Mrs. Williams home. She's very tired after this ordeal, but she wants the best for everyone and we are not closing this rink. I want you, you, you and you (pointing at Doug and four of his friends) in the office at 10 sharp tomorrow morning. You all have jobs and we're going to upgrade this rink into the 20th Century. No more boring organ music; we're going for roller disco dancing with the occasional live band; we'll put Hot Springs on the map!"

They cheered and hollered. Doug's face lit up like a lamp and he put out his hand and said, "Sorry, man."

At the Caddy I turned around. "And I want this crap removed from this car tomorrow morning—understand?"

They understood—and it was removed.

On the way home in the evening twilight Evelyn breathed, "You were wonderful back there, so masterful!"

"I couldn't let that bitch get away with that, Evelyn," I said, grimly staring at the road to Brown Drive unfolding before us. I had no idea how many times would that same road would take me back and forth in a life that was to become a roller coaster, never mind a roller rink.

"You made this a lot of promises, darling, do you think we can do all that? A roller disco dance?"

Glancing at her eyes sparkling in the dim light of the dashboard, I knew she was up for the challenge. She could not resist any form of show business.

"Sure we can. Tomorrow I'll look over everything and see how we can install a disc jockey booth, get some new music and start promoting disco dancing weekends. Every kid in town will come, it will be the new, cool place to hang out and we'll have live bands. There are always little local garage bands that want exposure."

"Oh, yes," she enthused, "and we can still have special bookings for the church groups and local children's shelters and civic groups, and we can put on roller shows like Ice Capades!"

The more we talked the better it sounded, and we talked long into the night. Hobby had started a Go-Kart track on the adjoining Gulpha Gorge property, basically just brush cleared and a little dirt moved around, but he had also purchased a fleet of Go-Karts that were sitting in the garage at the house.

We decided to call Tommy Peterson, the contractor who had built the rink, to budget the cost of finishing the Go-Kart track and build a small clubhouse that would feature pinball machines, Foosball and a food canteen for soft drinks—everything to keep the youth of Hot Springs out of trouble and off the streets; with security hired to watch everything.

The next day I met with Doug and the boys, as promised. They turned out to be the best skaters in town and the most popular guys with the other kids. I gave them all jobs, with Doug as sort of a "chief" to keep them in line, and told them Gracie was to work the box office and be Evelyn's assistant. We kept the food concession as it was, no one was fired as rumored, and I completely re-decorated Evelyn's private office with its huge, two-way mirror window. I installed a bar for grownup clients and business associates, hung western-motif paintings on the wall along with Maybelline advertisement photos, and installed a comfortable lounge chair where Evelyn could take a load off and watch everything, unseen, behind the two-way glass mirror.

We immediately had the sign "Hobby's Roller Rink" taken down and erected a new sign with a new name: "The Spa City Roller Rink" against a red, white and blue striped background. It was as All-American as apple pie, and as civic and patriotic as you could get.

The kids were caught up in getting the place ready for a new grand opening. A disco booth was designed with a professional turntable and microphone setup. I made friends with a young man who owned the only "hip" record store in town, Apple Records; he supplied us with all the latest hits and people who could professionally disc jock. Later he would be the head man in my rock band KIDZ.

I had met many rock stars back in California at The Golden Bear in Huntington Beach and The Troubadour in Hollywood—Jim Morrison of The Doors and Roy Orbison, among others, so this part of my promise to the kids was easy. In fact, to offset the "faggot" image yet be able to live my life openly, I knew I had to become a sort of rock star figure myself.

Even in right-wing Baptist Hot Springs, Arkansas, "Glam Rock" was popular as David Bowie and Lou Reed strutted their androgynous selves across concert stages. Members of the heavy metal band KISS were demigods to these kids, thus making men wearing makeup OK and "cool."

I already had a hip wardrobe a la Newport Beach, and I became a frequent shopper at the one store in town that had trendy clothes to fit the image. I let my hair grow long again, wore tight jeans and tighter Levi jumpsuits. I had Edwardian suits and pointed toe boots and platform shoes.

In those days I also had muscles, was very strong and had a penchant for the heavy silver and turquoise rings, necklaces and bracelets that were popular at the time. It was all a little Aerosmith and Mick Jagger with a touch of Britain and a little cowboy thrown in!

Needless to say, I stood out—and although I never announced I was gay, it became an accepted fact with the kids.

Doug Berry became my best and most trusted friend. His mother, Nessie Berry, was a hard working single mom who had a big old house in the middle of a small plot of trees where she sewed, kept house and did odd jobs to keep food on the table and care for her family. She was salt of the earth.

Although no stranger to trouble and the usual delinquent shenanigans, Doug nonetheless had a mature sense of honor and obligation once he gave his word. He was a natural born salesman who could sometimes be a con artist as well—he could talk anyone into anything. Especially the girls. I did sit down with Doug several times and explain my life style. He could not understand at first how a "dude that all the girls wanted" could not be straight. "You have everything man, you could get any girl in town, why would you want a guy?"

I explained that being gay was not a choice. Why would someone like me choose to face prejudice and be socially ostracized? I also explained that being gay was no different than being heterosexual. Not all gay men hit on every guy they see or even try to, any more than a straight man chases after every female who comes along—even if he secretly wants to. And there were relationships of love between members of the same sex, some lasting for many years, just like a marriage.

He then tried to categorize me as being "bi" after I told him of the women I had been with, including the mother of my only child.

"There's no such thing as being bisexual, really," was my reply. "Certainly there are people who have sexual experiences with the same sex at some points in their lives for various reasons, but in the end, there's always a decided preference." I went on to conclude that mental cretins and sexual addicts who would take on anything were the only exceptions, as well as men in prison.

Doug seemed to accept all this because I was me, always up front with him, always trying to keep my word. The other boys went along with Doug. Many of them were curious about a man who looked like me, had money, lived in an estate and seemed to have the world by the tail.

Then the closet door opened and out came the kids who were secretly gay, along with the hustlers! It was bound to happen. Those young men, all eighteen and over, who had been living a lie or in denial all their lives, saw a chance to come out. Some were poignantly beautiful and actually poetic, writing me strange and sad little notes about themselves, often unsigned. They managed to hang out, undetected, with the other kids. One of them was actually forbidden by his drunken father to come to the rink on the weekends where that "fag" ran the joint. He came anyway and much later, when he moved out of town and I ran into him at a gay bar in Little Rock; confided to me that when he would come home from a night at the rink he would be beaten with a belt, the buckle end flaying the skin off his back.

He told me he'd tried to emulate me in every way, copying my clothes the best he could, even to imitating my mannerisms. He also told me he had been in love with me from the first day I showed up and had tried to get my attention but did not know how. This confession broke my heart and I was glad that he had escaped from a terrible home and found himself.

But others were hustlers, and they became a thorn in my side.

When I say "hustlers" I don't mean it in the negative sense. There are young men who want a better life style, have looks and charm and don't mind doing whatever it takes to elevate their position. The word "bisexual" probably applies here—and I was a sitting duck, having left my former life behind, along with any relationships that could have been.

The first was Gabriel.

Gabriel was from a Greek-American family; poor, of course. He would stand out in front of the roller rink under the lights with his shirt open as I was leaving for the evening. He didn't hang out with the other kids and no one seemed to know much about him.

He was cute as opposed to handsome, had a muscular body that was somewhat thick (Mrs. Williams said he had a "peasant's build"), and soulful brown eyes. I didn't speak to him at first, but noticed the posing and the secret looks. He was 20 years old and appeared lonely. I felt sorry for him.

Evelyn and I were getting weary of the various security guard schemes that we were prey to. After Grieg was let go, we endured a young gentleman who looked exactly like Ricky Nelson and came to us offering professional services complete with a deputy from the Sheriff's Department, who was his "partner in the business." His name actually was Rick!

Swayed by his looks and suave demeanor, Evelyn thought he was ideal. I also was fooled at first. He was the opposite of "redneck," and had a load of security devices that he installed all over the lake property, including trip wires that could be activated at night and stop anyone from coming up to the house from the lake.

There was a boat dock, and an old, huge party barge came with the purchase of the property. Hobby had used it for fishing but Evelyn had other ideas. We had it all cleaned up and painted red, gold and black with curtains and a little bar. The seats were re-upholstered in red and "The Maybelline Queen" was painted in gold on the bow and the aft deck. We made quite a sight cruising around Lake Hamilton, me in my captain's hat and Evelyn dressed to the teeth.

Looking back now, it was all very garish and corny but the locals seemed to love it and it added to the legend we would create. Rick had the boat wired as well, and he set up his "security office" in the large maid's quarters at the north end of the house. The maid's quarters was actually a well-designed mother-in-law apartment created by the previous owners. It had a separate bedroom, bath and kitchen and a very large living area with a balcony that overlooked the lake.

Fear of Sam Saleem overruled Evelyn's need for a live-in maid. We would have girls from the roller rink come in twice a week to clean and sometime cook—always southern fried everything. Once ensconced in the house, Rick soon waylaid her fears of the dreaded Mr. Saleem. Well, that and the fact that the Sheriff's deputy official car was often parked in front at night, which reassured us both.

Then one night it all changed.

My quarters led onto the formal bar area, several rooms down from my bedroom. I was awakened about midnight by the sounds of clinking glass and a low voice cursing. I got out of my waterbed carefully and crept through the card room, the butler's pantry and the rooms where I carried on my experiments in skin revision and also styled all Evelyn's wigs and finally making my way to the door of the bar. I pushed it open carefully and peered inside. The bar refrigerator was open and from its light I could see that several glasses had fallen off the shelf and broken. Also, the sliding door to the outside patio was open, the cold lake breeze blowing the curtains like in a horror movie! Tiptoeing through the slider and onto the path that ran around the back of the house and past my patio, I heard footsteps ahead of me and saw a figure in the dark moving towards the maid's quarters.

"Rick?" I hissed, fearing to wake Evelyn, who would have heard the glass crashing already.

"No, it ain't Rick," a muffled voice came back, "it's Duane from the Sheriff's office." Recognizing the voice, I ran up beside him and noticed he had about four half-gallons of vodka and whiskey clutched in each hand.

"What do you think you are doing with our liquor?" I demanded, outraged.

"Ahhh, we just having a little party upstairs," he whined. "Rick said y'all wouldn't mind, that you're a cool dude."

"What party? At this hour? Mrs. Williams will have a heart attack!" I was livid at the downright cheek. The very thought that he assumed I was so "cool" that they could just do what they wanted in our home, enraged me.

I also thought that Rick knew better than to pull off something like this. So, assuming a jovial tone, I said, "Well hell, invite me to the party."

He brightened up. "Shit yes, Rick said you were a party animal. C'mon up."

Grabbing two of the liquor bottles from him, I followed him through the maid's kitchen into a scene right out of Boogie Nights, the porno theme movie with Burt Reynolds that came out years later. They had set up the entire living quarters as a studio, complete with lights, reflectors and cameras. There was a naked girl being taken "doggy style" by a young man with long blond hippy hair. I had seen him around town panhandling, basically a street-person. The girl was a stripper from one of the many strip joints that lined Central Avenue in those days. I had made friends with the owners of many of those establishments after Evelyn and I were inducted into the Arkansas Showman's Association—fully aware that Hot Springs was a "two-world" city, each world co-existing with the other—and clearly with blind eyes all around. The club owners would send their kids to my roller disco dance and promote it with their clients, and in return I would drop in occasionally, tip the girls like a "good ol' boy" and donate to their various charities. Evelyn was aware of this and did not like it really, although one night insisted on going with me.

They were all shocked when Evelyn walked in the door decked out in her designer hat and jewels. Everyone acted nervous, ushered us to a private booth and offered drinks on the house. I took the owner aside and cautioned him to downplay my patronage.

One of the bar managers, a French woman actually named Frenchy, took a liking to Evelyn and I could see that it was mutual. Frenchy eventually became kind of an assistant to Evelyn at civic social events and was very kind to her.

The show that night was much less raunchy than usual, and one of the girls came down to say "Hi" to Evelyn, very shy and awed by The Miss Maybelline presence.

"I always wear your makeup, Ms. Williams," she exclaimed, "and I think you are just beautiful."

"Well, thank you, my dear" Evelyn purred, "but let me give you a little tip for your act, honey: Don't wear those clunky K-Mart shoes with the straps, wear high heel pumps the color of your stockings. It makes the legs look much longer and more seductive.

"W-w-why thanks," the girl stuttered, and Evelyn told me behind her hand, "See she gets a new pair of pumps, those look terrible."

The K-Mart girl was the one in the porno scene I'd witnessed in the maid's quarters that night. Setting the bottles down, I marched over to the wall and switched on all the lights. Blinking foolishly, the actors stopped their somewhat clinical-looking routine.

"What in the hell is going on in here?" I bellowed. "Rick!"

Clutching her blouse, the young lady started crying. "Don't tell Ms. Williams about this, Danie, or my boss, I just needed the extra money for my kid!"

I told her and the young hippy-looking man to get dressed and leave very quietly or Ms. Williams would find out.

Thanking me profusely, she got dressed and jerked the young man's arm. "C'mon, let's get out of here." They left.

I then turned to the guilty-faced deputy and demanded to know where Rick was.

"I'm here, Danie, what's going on?" said a muffled voice, and Rick walked out of the bedroom in his underwear scratching his head. Through the doorway behind him I could see a naked female in the bed, trying to pull the sheets up over her head.

"What's going on, Rick?" I demanded. "You have a little porno business going on here? How long has this been going on?"

"Ohhh, don't get upset, Danie." He was amazingly calm, as if I had interrupted a séance rather than an orgy. "This is just a little something to make extra money—we sell the films out of State to dealers in Georgia, the kids get well paid and no one gets hurt, and we're very careful to be quiet."

"Are you out of your mind? If Mrs. Williams got onto this it would kill her, not to mention the scandal—and you'd end up in jail."

"So would you, Danie," he smirked. "It's your home, and we could say you paid us to put this little show together."

I lit into him, determined to wipe the confident smile off his face. I informed him that both Mrs. Williams and I enjoyed a personal friendship with the Sheriff and the police department because of the events we staged on behalf of their charity funding. This was something he was unaware of. I also pointed out that his partner, the deputy, would lose his job. Then I let him know that the strip club owner was a friend of ours along with everyone who was a member of the Showman's Association, and a lot of them were carnival people, well known for taking care of their own.

Finally I told him that he didn't really know me that well, or what I was capable of, or how much I would spend to see him run out of town on a rail.

"Mrs. Williams may be scared to death of Sam Saleem," I said, "but I'm not, Rick. Pack up your gear, send us a final bill for your security services, and get out."

He looked at me for a moment, his face red and angry. I could see that he was trying to think of some kind of threat, but I was too "out there" for any kind of blackmail attempt. Being a smart young man after all, he knew when the show was over. He shook his head and said, "Well, I would have cut you in, you know."

I told him I had my own money and to leave and not a word of this would be spoken to anyone, including the sheriff.

To his credit, Rick smiled and told Duane to pack everything up. When I watched the tail lights of their cars disappear beyond our property and into the night, I sat down with my head in my hands trembling at how close we had come to disaster.

I saw the sheriff's deputy many times after that, and even hired him off duty as security for the roller rink. I always believed in keeping enemies as close to me as friends. But I never saw Rick again.

Following him came a series of the boys from the Roller Rink, their older cousins and sometimes even a father or two. They were all very respectful to Evelyn, although I sometimes wondered what they really thought of us with our emotional outbursts, arguments (which she always won) and sudden bursts of laughter.

I often thought that Evelyn fancied herself The Lady of the Manor with myself as Squire. Perhaps this went back to her youthful days in

Chicago when servants and bodyguards were a way of life for many people.

For a long time she would accompany me to the office and go over everything with a fine tooth comb, making suggestions on how to cut expenses, and improve the menu in the concession. "People love a good sandwich Dan, not all this deep-fat-fried junk."

We hired an exuberant nutcase of a man to run the concession. Fat and jolly, he persuaded Mrs. Williams that he could prepare such fast-food triumphs that the entire town would rush to eat dinner at The Spa City Roller Rink. He impressed her with a ham-free ham salad sandwich and boiled broccoli stalks that when sliced and fried, were indistinguishable from scallops. He actually did come up with some tasty things, but he was inconsistent, emotional with the rest of the staff, and eventually absconded with the evening's take on his last night of employment.

We would often walk over to the property next door and plan the "Hot Springs Disneyland" that Hobby had started. The contractor had built the recreational building, but it was empty, awaiting games, pinball machines and another concession. The Go-Karts were stored somewhere, but to keep interest up for the Theme Park (as Evelyn called it) I had the cars brought out and gassed up, and held "Go-Kart Races" out on Brown Drive. Maybelline Manor's driveway was circular, so the carts would careen around the drive like a miniature Indy Race, with kids screaming and hollering at their favorites to win.

Evelyn actually took one spin—which surprised me, not to mention that the watching neighbors were stunned to see the tiny little lady with one hand holding down her silver hair as she spun madly down the road laughing like a hyena.

Evelyn was a curious blend of stand-offish Society Lady and the Unsinkable Molly Brown. The kids loved her as their very own cartoon, a bigger-than-life celebrity.

6

The Skillful Art of Illusion

Many people back then, and even now, want to know about the so-called magic I performed on Evelyn that always made her appear young and vibrant in public.

In the beginning, when I first came to Hot Springs, the stress of the divorce and fear of Sam Saleem had taken its toll on her, so for a while I employed some of the "tricks" that makeup artists have used on aging film stars since the 1930s.

First of all, Evelyn had created herself a long time ago. In the 1930s the flapper look was in: boyish chests, cupid-bow lips and frizzy bobbed hair. Evelyn's full bust and strong facial features did not suit this look, which is why I have long suspected that the torn-in-half photo of her from that era that Steve found in the basement after the fire was not the way she really perceived herself to be. I think she modelled herself more after Greta Garbo and, later, Joan Crawford—who she actually resembled.

Most women fear illusion, usually because they lack a strong sense of identity that can survive the erosion of the years. They tend to pull back from skillful makeup, wigs and foundation garments, fearing that they will look "over-the-top" or delusional…and indeed there *are* some women I know who do look like delusional clowns—the "Baby Jane in the Mirror" syndrome.

But Evelyn was all about the art of illusion. She did not hang onto the trappings of her youth in any way, such as keeping her hair dyed an improbable auburn or flashy blonde. She was age-appropriate with her silver-blonde wigs and wonderfully tailored gowns, suits and dresses—but her face always had to shine and her makeup had to be flawless.

I used face-lift tapes at first. These are transparent, one-inch square tapes attached to long elastic bands with loops at the end. Using surgical adhesive, I would glue one tape to each side of her face, just in front of each ear, and pull them up and back to the crown of her head, securing them with a pin curl. I would also attach one on each side of her neck in back. This pulled the neck tissue up and back, banishing any turkey neck or loose flesh that might get in the way of necklaces and chokers.

Although the tapes are self-adhesive, she never trusted this. "Put some glue on them, Dan, I don't want one to snap in public and look like I had a stroke," she would laugh.

Makeup and her wig covered everything, and no one ever knew.

Eventually the weekly enzyme treatments firmed up her face and neck enough to where the tapes were not needed as much—and then, of course, her final facelift surgery made everything easier.

I would apply a makeup foundation to her face and neck, selecting a tone darker than her normal skin, then I would apply a lighter foundation to her forehead, cheeks and chin. This "low light/highlight" trick would naturally sculpt her face with a model's cheekbones and camouflage areas that tended to sag a little or be puffy.

Next I would outline her eyes with black liquid liner, similar to that which a ballet dancer would wear for a stage performance. The black outline would tilt up at the ends, "lifting" her eyes and giving them an exotic frame; and I would blend, blend, blend a lighter shadow to soften the lines and highlight under her brow. I would then stroke a color directly on her upper lids that would pick up what she was wearing, without being obvious.

Mascara (Maybelline, of course) would then be brushed onto her natural lashes and finally, her false eyelashes would be applied. I taught her to *never* put eyelashes on first and then apply mascara to both her own lashes and the false ones. This destroys false lashes, especially if one tries to clean them with acetone—and in those days, they were not as inexpensive as they are now.

Evelyn would dampen her false eyelashes with a little water at night, and roll them around a ballpoint pen in a small square of tissue, keeping them in place with a rubber band until they dried, nicely curled.

Because of the medications she was on she had extremely dry lips, flaking and peeling to the point where she would almost not want to go out. So, after exfoliating her lips with the enzyme masque treatment, I would use a soft brush to apply raw pomegranate oil mixed with a little beeswax. Pomegranate oil is one of the few oils that is self-humectant: whenever it is hit with water or saliva it becomes oily again, but not greasy.

After waiting a moment, I would seal it with a small amount of corn starch and then outline her lips with a wax pencil so that her lipstick would not overrun the lip line created. Thus treated, her lipstick would stay on and the peeling disappeared for hours at a time.

"You should create a lipstick with that oil, Dan," she said time and time again—and now, decades later, I'm working on that very thing.

Her wigs were all the same color: silver-blonde. In Newport I'd sold her a couple of human-hair, hand-tied wigs that looked totally natural and could be brushed back off her face or even done up in a French twist. Working there with me was an older woman who knew the art of double-knot hand-tying human hair, and between us we could turn out a new wig in one week.

But in Hot Springs this was not practical. I didn't have time to devote to such tedious work, nor anyone to help me do it. Besides, I was an "executive" and Evelyn didn't want anyone else in town to know about her wig secrets.

Instead, we ordered synthetic wigs from an out of state source I knew, and I would hand-tie synthetic fibers to lace fronts which I would then sew onto the wig. Her hairlines always looked completely natural. She also had me sew in little "intrusions," as she called them, of platinum synthetic fibers to add a subtle sparkle and depth to her hair. Most people thought it was natural. Since she never went to any local hair salon, people assumed she had her hair done in Little Rock. I said nothing to change this opinion.

Once the makeup and hair were in place and Evelyn had given it her "mirror test" (she would turn on all the lights in the room and sit in front of the mirror, turning her head all different ways, using hand mirrors to view the sides and back), the final touch was a quick dusting of pale pink powder under her eyes. This brought a sparkle and "youth" to her eyes like nothing else.

Evelyn disliked contouring with blush or "contour powders." "Looks like they got racing stripes on their face," she would scoff. My application of a darker foundation *first* and then highlighting the high points of her face made more sense to her, and gave a totally natural look.

"I don't know where you think of these things, Dan," she would say, "but they work and seem logical."

I actually assumed it *was* logical and everyone did makeup that way. It was only when I kept hearing about "his magic touch" even from Evelyn's granddaughter Sharrie Williams that I felt maybe I was doing something different after all.

In reality, makeup is art. It is highly individual, and the so-called "magic touch" cannot be taught to anyone. Certainly the principles of makeup can be taught—techniques for special effects, color work, prosthetics and so on. But these are tools. The real skill is in the hands of the artists and the way the models carry themselves and show the work off.

Evelyn was a genius at showing it off, making it look natural and glamorous.

She was very aware of lighting—always positioning herself in a room where the lights were most advantageous. When we visited the roller rink for the first time and she stepped into the glare of the hanging fluorescent lights in the concession area, she barked, "These lights are not kind, Dan, get them changed immediately!"

I finally found some warmer toned bulbs actually called "people lighting"; even the teens liked the effect better. People came and sat in the concession area much more frequently and food sales went up.

If we visited someone who had glaring lights in their living room, Evelyn would raise her hand to her forehead as if she were looking out to see in the sun, bat her eyes furiously and say, "My dear, *could* you turn that light down a little? I have *such* a problem with my eyes in strong light."

The hostess would rush to dim or turn off the light, and Evelyn would give me a little smug smile.

Now, in my early seventies, I understand her light manipulation. It was not a case of excess vanity, it was simply the choice of someone who loved life and lived it full stop, wishing to appear as youthful as possible in order to interact with the much younger people around her. Young people shut the door to persons who look old and tired, simply not seeing them except perhaps as a grandma or elderly aunt.

But Evelyn was a role model, even to the teenage girls around us. Far from overlooking her as a geriatric, they crowded around her whenever we could appear at the rink; asking questions about makeup and style and how to deal with their boyfriends. To them Evelyn really was a celebrity and a Hollywood star.

I recently saw a Facebook page of one of the teenage girls back then. Now a grandmother herself, she had a photo album of key people from her past.

There were two photos of Evelyn.

7

A New Identity: "My Nephew Danie King, Son of..."

The rink soon became *the* place in town to go on weekends. During the week, church groups and other organizations booked events. There was another roller rink in town, a small affair with an unfortunate pillar in the middle of the skating floor. The young lady who owned the place had had some kind of private run-in with the owner of a local free-press paper called *The Garland County Register*. Because of this the owner approached me with free advertising schemes for the Spa City Roller Rink—basically he wanted to starve her out. Although I had nothing personal against the young lady, I also knew that there was not enough room in town for both of us, so I went along with his ideas and we became front-page news for months. I even ended up writing a regular column for the paper entitled "Inside Out"—my first stab at becoming a journalist on human affairs and activities in a small town.

Cole, the owner of the Register, was an open-minded man who let me pontificate on just about any subject, but the main reason I wrote my column was to promote the roller rink indirectly by allowing the people of Hot Springs to see me in a trustworthy and favorable light.

Both Evelyn and I knew we were not like other people in Hot Springs, so we had to build a reputation. The press came first in the form of a reporter from the *Sentinel Record*. I will call him Steve. He was a fifty -year-old gay bachelor who lived with his sister in a very New York-style apartment. He was sophisticated, intuitive and lonely. Because I was out there without making announcements about my private life, he was almost desperately glad to meet me. He loved Evelyn from the beginning and enjoyed many candlelit dinners at Maybelline Manor.

Finally committed to using the Maybelline name to identify herself, Evelyn had me commission a sign that said Maybelline Manor in red, black and gold and place it on one of the brick pillars at the entrance of the estate. Steve went along with this plan and came out to interview her "at home" with the paper's photographer Les Beale, who later did not become my friend with subsequent photos he shot for the *Sentinel Record*.

The interview, titled IN SPA FOR A REASON, was front-page news the following weekend. I had told him the details of Evelyn's divorce and the gossip it had started about Evelyn being crazy and old and drugged-out on prescription medications. The article reversed every-one's opinions. It detailed Evelyn's love of the beauty and tranquility of Hot Springs, the warmth and hospitality of the people, and her vision of helping the youth of the city forgo activities that promoted delinquency and problems with the law. It was a very "pay it forward" article...but the accompanying photo did not please Evelyn at all.

It was a clever photograph, showing a double image of her looking pensively out the window, her finger delicately touching her chin. But it also showed her age. I pointed out to her that it was already published and not to complain (she wanted to call the paper immediately) and that "Front page is front page, after all."

The article had an immediate effect I call "the domino phenomenon." Soon people were calling us up, one after the other, inviting her to var-ious civic events. I will never forget the first call because it established Evelyn as a show business "star" and also endeared her to everyone. I forget the actual event—suffice to say all the city fathers and everyone who was anybody would be attending. Evelyn was excited because in addition to actually meeting the movers and shakers of Hot Springs, she would be arriving in a new car such as no one had seen in decades.

The car situation came about because of Gabriel. Gabriel, the strange young man who had posed under the roller rink lights off and on again when I left the office, had come to work for us. Evelyn, noting my friendship with the young people of Hot Springs and growing tired of hiring so-called security people like Rick, asked me if perhaps some of the kids could be hired at small wages to help with the household chores. She would train a housekeeper, while I suggested that she should also get a young man to help patrol the grounds and do the heavier work such as gardening and keeping the lawns mowed.

Evelyn agreed, so I put the word out at the Roller Rink. Soon some of the girls applied for the housekeeping job. Gabriel was the first young man to come into my office and, with warm and suggestive eyes, apply for the guarding and heavy work. I was vulnerable as he told about his karate skills, being able to shoot a rifle like a marksman and not being opposed to gardening, patrolling the grounds at night and being a major domo for me and Mrs. Williams.

The young lady Evelyn hired was a sweet, down to earth little blonde and as country as Dolly Parton. She cooked old-fashioned style food and listened to Evelyn's instructions on how to be a "Lady's maid" with full attention (after being coached almost daily by me).

Gabriel was another matter.

Evelyn admired his strength and respectful manner, but railed against his "ignorance" when it came to details such as trimming bushes and replacing things after he used them. He made her feel safe after he displayed his shooting skills, knocking over bottles that I'd set up on the boat dock all the way from the house, using a rifle we had purchased. Evelyn impressed upon him that Sam Saleem was still "at large" and could appear at any time, perhaps in disguise. Of course all the kids knew about this potential threat and were excited to be assigned to "protect Ms. Williams," taking turns filling in for Gabriel at night when we went out to dinner or to an event.

I will say now, looking back, that Gabriel and I did not have to become close. He knew what he was doing when he told stories about previous sexual encounters with distant family members and how he always felt he had to "hide" his true nature from his Dad. Later he would rescind these tales as just lies he told to get the job, but at the time I believed him. Within a month he moved from his little cot in a side room into my room. I did caution him to keep our relationship to himself because while Mrs. Williams was aware of my lifestyle, we never talked about it.

And we never did.

One afternoon, after we sent Gabriel out on an errand in Evelyn's blue Cadillac Coup De Ville, we got a call from the Sheriff saying they had a hysterical young man at their office and I had to get down there right away. Having a good relationship with the law enforcement in Palm Springs, I thanked the officer and rushed down to find a swollen-eyed Gabriel shaking in a chair in the reception.

"I wrecked Miss William's car," he wailed. "I couldn't help it, but she'll kill me and fire me!"

After informing him that "killing" would come *after* "firing," I asked what had happened.

It was an accident. Having a hard time finding one of the things Evelyn had sent him shopping for and running late, he had tried to take a short cut on a hairpin-turn road in the foothills outside Hot Springs. Going too fast, he'd come around a turn to be confronted by a large dog in the middle of the road, and in an attempt to avoid hitting it he had swerved onto a sandy portion of the road that led down into a rocky canyon. The car plunged over the drop-off, crumpling the entire front and breaking the windshield. Gabriel managed to open the door as the car skidded down the embankment, and rolled free just before it crashed. His flip flop sandals were still on the floor of the car when I went with a tow truck to examine it.

He could have been killed—a fact that smoothed Evelyn over—and to my surprise, she showed more concern for his well-being than the loss of a Cadillac. She even insisted he go to the doctor immediately to be examined.

On the way to the doctor, I told him, grimly, that he was damn lucky, and to be even more attentive and precise in his duties; our personal relationship would not allow him to be careless and to slack off. I somehow did not quite believe his story of taking a shortcut over a winding road far from the city, but he kept to his story with big pleading brown eyes and I caved in.

"Insurance will cover the car," Evelyn trilled later, sounding oddly pleased that it had been wrecked. "I never liked it anyway—Hobby picked it out—so let's go down to the Cadillac agency tomorrow and order a new one."

As we swept into the agency the next morning, the owner personally came out, bowing and scraping and offering us cocktails in his office; which Evelyn graciously declined. So much for the rumors spread by Delyle and Hobby about the abuse of drugs and booze!

Evelyn tried to explain that she did not want a big, boxy Coup De Ville again; she wanted something a woman would look good in, with sleek styling. His eyes gleaming with anticipation, the owner flipped open an elegant faux leather booklet and informed us that Cadillac had just released its new Eldorado Biarritz, and no one in Arkansas had one yet. I looked down at the glossy photos and gasped—it was the most beautiful cars I had ever seen outside of the legendary Biarritz of the 1960s.

The model shown was white with deep red detail lines, a long sleek hood, a wonderful leather-covered cabin and a Rolls Royce sculpturing of the trunk. The result was an automobile that had both grace and power, instead of the massive chunkiness of the Cadillacs of that period. Evelyn and I looked at each other, and she said, "Order it!"

When the car arrived at last, it was even more spectacular than in the photos. We were thrilled. I insisted she drive it off the lot, but she was afraid of all the new electronic gadgets, the incredible smooth power and the long, long front. She was also embarrassed that the agency people, all of whom were waving us off, would realize she could not operate her own new car. It would be several weeks before she finally drove herself into town, head up, elegant profile framed by one of her signature hats, a small smile on her face. Evelyn loved that car, and insisted Gabriel wash and wax it every other day.

It was in this showy conveyance that we attended our first black tie civic event. Two days before the event she was in a dither of what we should wear.

"Well, the Cadillac *is* white, and it *is* Spring, so why not show up in all white?"

And so we did. I wore my white linen suit, a Valentino design, and Evelyn was resplendent in a white lace suit with a long skirt and pearls. When we drove up to the building it was about an hour past the time the even began and there was no parking. "What will we do, Dan? We're late!"

Noting a ramp that led to the front of the building, which was all glass windows through which I could see everyone inside sitting at tables and standing around with cocktails in hand, I decided to pull up and park in full view right outside the window.

"You can't!" Evelyn gasped with a giggle.

"Oh no? Watch me!"

And I roared up the ramp, stopped the Cadillac in front of the windows and with a flourish, opened her door and gave her my hand. She gracefully swung onto her feet, but I could feel her trembling. Putting my arm around her, I whispered, "You look fabulous, darling. Now chin up and let's go in."

Everyone in the place was gawping at us. Evelyn gave them a cheery wave, an apologetic shrug and her million-watt smile as I ushered her toward the door. Most of the attendees smiled back. Once inside Evelyn was surrounded by people. I kept apologizing for our unorthodox entrance, claiming we had nowhere else to park, but one of the town's main bankers, Mort Cox, kept saying, "Not at all, not at all—would have done the same thing myself."

Later, eyes twinkling, Mort took me aside and said, "That was quite an entrance, young man. Haven't seen anything like that since Sinatra came to town."

Later, Mort would become my best mentor in Hot Springs. It was he who told me how to talk to people in power if I needed something done; who to be careful with, and who I could trust. Mort knew where all the skeletons were (having a few of his own) and truly thought Evelyn was the most elegant woman he had ever met.

That night Evelyn and I did meet everyone. We were both at the top of our games—in fact, I was aghast at the way Evelyn so adroitly handled even the toughest and crustiest man and gained the confidence of all the ladies with her compliments of their wardrobes and accessories.

Meanwhile, I found within myself a different Danie King. Despite our age difference, Evelyn and I were the couple of the hour. Flushed with excitement on the way home, she cattily told me what she thought of some of the women and their fashion sense, and the men she wanted me to befriend.

"That banker seems to like you," she mused. "Hobby never did get licensing to open the Go-Kart track." She was referring to the fact that there were laws against totally demolishing the natural, rural beauty of the Gulpha Gorge area at the entrance of Hot Springs with anything commercial. We also talked about how our friendship was perceived by people and exchanged the very first hint that I might someday run for office, an idea that Joe E. Lewis had brought up several times during the trial.

That was the night I ceased to be a "friend" to Evelyn F. Williams and became a relative. "You can be my nephew, son of my sister Bunny," she exclaimed. "Bunny loves me and will go along with it once she understands how necessary it is in this town where all the Baptists will say you're a gigolo with a wealthy divorcee."

I reminded her that her son Bill would definitely not approve of me becoming a blood relative, but she waved this off. "I can handle him—he owes me." Soon it seemed logical to me that the entire Williams family would approve of this little "joke" contrived to protect Evelyn's reputation in a small and gossipy town.

After a while, being introduced as "My nephew, Danie King" became almost real to me, and no one ever really challenged it.

We became members of the Sertoma Club, an exclusive businessman's association, which we added to our Showman's Club membership. The Maybelline Heiress legend took flight.

Our accountant and lawyer insisted that we incorporate the Roller Rink and any other business interest that we may develop. Jim, the accountant, informed us that a corporation would allow us to avoid suffering excess taxes and be a protection against law suit or garnishment—in other words, protect Mrs. Williams' money. Which is why I always found it rather odd that years later, after she was gone, her son implied that the corporation was a scam of mine to "slush fund" money and rob Evelyn blind the way Bobby and Delyle had tried to do.

Jim was not the kind of accountant that millionaires would hire to keep their books. He was a churchgoing man who would not take risky tax cuts or write-offs that were not totally legitimate. "Offshore accounts" was not in his vocabulary, nor speculation on the stock market. He told Evelyn to put away her Maybelline stock documents and pretend they were not there. He did everything he could to teach me about cash flow liquidity and keeping careful paper trails. I'm afraid I was a less than an avid student, but I retained Jim because in the back of my mind I feared anyone questioning my motives with Mrs. Williams, particularly her son Bill, who still bombarded her with letters and calls to give up "all this nonsense trying to run a business at your age and come home."

Our attorney, Eudox Patterson, was the same. A slim and intellectual young man, he was not a member of the old guard of scheming Arkansas attorneys Evelyn had suffered from during the divorce. He seemed to like me and I would come to his office for advice on nearly everything. I actually felt that there was something more in my future in Hot Springs, perhaps even public office—as unlikely as that would have seemed in my Newport Beach days. I had to surround myself with the most legitimate and well respected people possible, yet still be myself.

I had one of these "running for office" discussions with Senator Bud Canada, a distinguished and handsome man, and was bemoaning the fact that my colorful nature might give opposing candidates plenty of gossip and speculation to fire at me in order to weaken my reputation.

"Danie, I know one thing after years in office," Bud said, pointing down at the leather desk cover on his desk. "You have to learn to have the hide of an elephant if you're going to put yourself in the public eye."

I never forgot that advice and used it many times when confronted by a heckler or a competitor. Years later, a Swedish doctor called me a "madman" in the press due to my published articles attacking the worldwide overuse of the then-popular Alpha Hydroxy Acid Peels. I'd simply told the scientific truth about these so-called "natural acid peels" and how they were not harmless at all and should be respected by practitioners and the public alike. Time and research repudiated the plethora of nasty emails I received, mostly from companies who were basing their entire product ranges on these AHAs. I was hurt, of course, to see such downright meanness directed at me in print—but, remembering Bud's advice, I continued my consumer and professional advocacy.

I also had a father whose dignity and morals meant a lot to me. I was the number one son, the renegade with the weird life style. I wanted him to be proud. Trying to think of a name for our corporation, Evelyn and I agreed to blend our names together, forming EVDAN—which probably gave root to the rumors that I was taking over everything. Evelyn was hard-headed, emotive and often did not err on the side of caution—this was a lifelong habit—but she was nobody's fool. She trusted me one hundred percent and I felt that I had to earn that trust. She saw everything all the time, even if she chose not to mention it or talk about it. Out of nowhere, she would often say, "Dan, let's go into my office and go over the books."

Then she would examine every expenditure, every receipt, often screaming how this cost too much and what was that spent for? Despite her glamour and look of extravagance, she was very frugal at heart. Her wardrobe was re-worked many times over, easy to do when you purchase expensive classics. She would take her old stockings and cleverly braid them as hat bands around her many hats; her shoes were sent for repair often and I reworked her wig collection many, many times.

She would scan the papers for food sales, often buying a dozen hams, roasts and several chickens that were ensconced in the massive old freezer downstairs. The only thing she never scrimped on was anything to do with promoting the roller rink (a write-off), and my skin revision experiments—which she was convinced would someday make us a fortune that would rival Maybelline's.

We allocated two rooms on the ground floor for her wig collection and my home lab. There I kept shelves filled with bottles of tinctures that I had hand-made from herbs and other botanicals that I had ordered from all over the USA. There was a metal sink and heavy rubber pans where I would macerate the herbs (cold-soaked for two weeks, then the liquid drained through a fine mesh screen and bottled). The room reeked of ingredients being cooked in a double boiler on a hot plate, often resulting in a *beep-beep-beep* on one of the many intercoms Evelyn had installed throughout the house and her voice, tinny and shrill, "Dan, what on earth is that horrible smell?"

She forgot about the smell when I flourished a new crème or a treatment for which she would be the Guinea pig. How she trusted me with her skin through all this I will never know. My brain functioned on a logical basis, never going along with what was normally done in skincare in the late 1960s early 1970s. My original mentor, a part-American Indian botanist and medical chemist in California, was a guide to me as I developed my hypothesis regarding how our skin systems really work and what was a buzzword or old wives' tale.

For example, I discovered that the very word "moisturizer" is a misnomer, a word contrived by an advertising firm in New York City in 1962 to sell beauty creams. It had nothing to do with trans epidermal water loss at all. My very first attempt to revise skin back to the way nature intended it to be was to mock the two secretions in the skin that we are all born with: the sudoriferous secretion (water or sweat) and the sebaceous gland secretion (a highly fractionated and protective oil).

Creating a fine oil blend where the oil molecule was rendered small enough to piggy-back on the water molecule, thus re-creating nature's natural acid mantle that we have from birth, was not an easy task. I blended all sort of oils together, principally those containing high amounts of vitamin E, a natural antioxidant, and after spraying my skin (and everyone else's who happened to be around) with polarized water, I attempted to mock these two secretions which gave us our natural fresh, moist and supple skins we had in our pre-teen years.

Evelyn became a willing test subject. She loved my enzymatic lifting and tightening masques (in themselves difficult to blend using amino acids and other proteins in an albumin base) which I obtained in those days from the Eggo Food Company. But after filling her bathroom with oil blends and water spray bottles, she would exclaim that she could not use them, they were "too greasy and shiny"; she suggested that my theory, though logical, was impossible. I stubbornly persisted, often getting up late at night and poring over textbooks on anatomy and histology, mainly my old standby Gray's Anatomy, 35th British Edition. How to create a replica of human sebum with botanical oils?

The answer finally came from a friend of mine who taught biology at the University of British Columbia in Canada. He told me of a small lab up there that could render any oil into fractionated molecules though a process known as fractional distillation, but warned me that it was expensive and never used for topical skin care products or cosmetics. As it turned out, my California mentor, medical chemist Dr. Johnson, also knew of these people and had them manufacture some wound-healing extracts and volatile oils as well.

Excited, I called them and told them what I wanted. To my surprise, they said my theory made sense. Two weeks later my expensive gallon of fractionated oils arrived, and with anticipation I sprayed my face and neck with my water, put a couple of drops of the precious oils in my hand, rubbed my palms together and patted the oils over my damp skin. Instantly my skin bloomed with color, felt released from that tight feeling you often get after you've washed your face—yet it did not feel greasy at all. In fact my skin felt "normal" as I vaguely remembered it had when I was a kid. I rushed upstairs and told Evelyn to wash her face right away, but not to put on any of my crèmes.

"What on earth, Dan?" she exclaimed as I hustled her into her bathroom. She washed her face, patted it dry and presented it to me with trepidation. She protested when I started to spray it. "Not another grease job!" she yelled as I gently patted the oil over her skin.

Then she looked into the mirror and said, "My word, I look ten years younger!"

Evelyn spread the word amongst the ladies she met in town, and soon there were people calling up Maybelline Manor wanting to know if I could "take a look at their skin." Because of my bouts of terrible teenage acne and my self-experiments at home using Gilbert Chemistry sets, local plants and household food items, I also used a lot of the kids at the roller rink as test subjects. Fortunately almost everything worked; many results were stunning, so people trusted me. This brought me to the attention of a dermatologist in town who was extremely wealthy, being the owner of several cattle farms and other interests.

Because his money came from sources outside his practice, he was a forward-thinking man not dependent on the standard dermatology of that time to make a living. Originally I took Evelyn to him to remove some skin tags on her neck. When he complimented her on her porcelain skin she impulsively told him all about my experiments. Later he called me and asked me what I had done and how many face-lifts had Evelyn had.

When I told him "None," he was taken back and asked if he could come over and see what I was doing. I invited him to a big barbecue we were having that weekend for some of the leading townspeople.

The barbecue was a huge success, people wandering all over the grounds with plates filled with what I look back at now as the best barbecue we ever put on.

I had concocted a sauce made from tomato puree, molasses, brown sugar, cinnamon, maple syrup and lemons and oranges—sort of an early El Pollo Loco. But it was the skill of the parents of one of the young teens at the rink—poor backwoods people who you would expect to be running moonshine for a living—that made the meat tender, juicy and memorable.

The father had never rubbed shoulders with "the rich people" of Hot Springs, outside of doing odd jobs, so he bent over backwards to dig the fire pits just right and get the coals to a perfect temperature while he looked with heavy suspicion at the gallons of "strange sauce" I had made. But after barbecuing everything with the skill of a French Chef and taking a bite out of a rack of ribs, he grinned toothlessly and said, "Well I be damned, this here is somethin' I got to git the recipe to."

Everyone got very tipsy from cocktails and beer, people were diving off the Maybelline Queen and dancing in the bar, the Dermatologist was having a great time, so the reason for him being there became less and less important. But eventually we made our way into my little home lab and I explained the concept of skin revision that I had been working on. After looking at everything and nodding, he asked me what I intended doing with all my research.

I told him about my shop in Newport and that Mrs. Williams and I sort of had plans to find a little lab in Little Rock that could make my products for sale to salons and stores. His take was that everything I was doing was too medical in concept for that, and had I ever thought about opening a spa? Hot Springs was famous for spa treatments due to the many natural healing springs in the area. In fact, ancient Indian tribes used to gather together in the Quichita valley for the healing waters, even if they were at war with each other, putting all fighting on hold in the mystical and magical place.

Intrigued by this idea, I asked what was wrong with mixing dermatology and special skin treatments along with spa programs. His face brightened at this idea, but the concept had never really been done before outside certain spas in Europe. The more we talked, the more real the idea became, but the party was winding down and Mrs. Williams appeared, demanding that I get back to the guests and see them out. Evelyn had been talking about having a facelift for weeks. Her headline photo in the *Sentinel Record* had bothered her a great deal. Every few days she told me she had not liked her appearance ever since the divorce.

Taking advantage of the fact that the good doctor was standing right there, I said, "Evelyn, let's ask Doctor D——who the best surgeon in the area is." Then I challenged, "You *do* know the best?"

Admitting that he indeed did have a great referral in Kansas City, he told us to make an appointment the following week. Then, thanking us profusely for inviting him, he left. Quietly he told me, "We'll talk more about this when everyone is sober."

Evelyn and I sat up for two hours talking about his idea of a medical spa. By the time we were through speculating on this controversial idea, we were convinced that half of Hollywood would fly in for the treatments, not to mention Europe and the rest of the world. We would house the top clients at Maybelline Manor; Evelyn could be the gracious hostess and a fabulous advertisement for the treatments. We'd make package deals with the hotels, and during the Race Meet when the entire town was booked up, we would offer top name entertainment packages for clients. They could go to the track, have a great time experiencing Hot Springs, then convalesce from their treatments in beautiful surroundings. Why, the entire town would love us and our fantasy plans for my having a public office would become reality. I might even end up in the State Senate; after all, I was already getting a Senator's salary! (This was said tongue-in-cheek, Evelyn's little way of being funny.)

If everything had worked out the way we were fantasizing, our spa would have been the forerunner of the hugely popular Medi Spa that we know of today.

We did go to see Dr. D——, who, after examining Evelyn's skin, recommended the Kansas City surgeon. He added that he would perform a phenolic peel around her mouth to banish the fine lines that were beginning to creep upwards from her lip line. We treated him to lunch and laid out the plans on which I had elaborated the previous week. I actually had constructed a treatment schedule that encompassed all age groups and skin conditions with a provision for dermatology (drugs and skin anomaly removals) when needed. I kept to myself my feeling that drugs and surgery might not even be needed.

The doctor liked everything in the proposal, and told us he had several country locations he owned that would be perfect for a private spa. He suggested we go into it as a joint venture, 50/50, and said he was prepared to invest a million dollars—would that be OK?

I inwardly blanched, knowing that to fork over a million dollars on such a scheme would eat heavily into Evelyn's Maybelline stocks. To her credit Evelyn did not bat an eye and said we would go home and work out more details with our attorney and accountant and get back to him.

Again on that familiar winding road to Brown Drive I tried not to show my disappointment. In fact I was almost relieved. "Honey," I said, "you cannot go into your Maybelline stocks for this idea."

"I know, Dan," she sighed. "But it is *such* a good idea, better than babysitting these kids every weekend and having your rock band KIDZ rehearsing in the maid's quarters all the time, which is driving me crazy."

I had sponsored KIDZ, a group that was becoming as well known locally as rock stars, and taught them how to stage their appearances by creating a mystique around themselves, not fraternizing with the audience after each concert; and how to dress and make up and present their dynamic music. They were a hit at the roller rink, where we had installed special effects and a stage. Mrs. Williams would often come on stage and announce them—but the rehearsals were loud and annoying to her.

I tried to soften our disappointment by saying we'd work harder to make more profit with the rink, stop work on the Go-Kart track to save money, and come back to the doctor at a later date.

"But he thinks we're super-rich," she moaned. "Oh, why did I let Hobby and Delyle rip me off so much?"

As we pulled up to the house, suddenly she sat up straight and exclaimed, "Tom Lyle would love this idea."

I knew Tom Lyle Williams was still living in his home in the hills above Hollywood. Evelyn often spoke of us taking a trip out there and me finally meeting him. As we went into the house she kept saying, "A million dollars is nothing to him—he would like this idea, we must write him."

Her enthusiasm and conviction that such an appeal would work started to convince even me. After all, who knew him better than Evelyn? She marched me into her little home study, and pulling out sheets of her personally monogrammed paper, insisted I dictate the details of this enterprise as carefully and as professionally as I could.

Carried away by her excitement, I tried to sound professional and businesslike. She of course added personal family sentiments and an over-glowing description of me, comparing me to a younger version of Tom Lyle.

After re-reading the letter five times and re-writing it twice, she finally signed her name with a flourish, slipped it into an envelope and stated firmly that not only would Tom Lyle go for the plan, he would probably make the trip to Hot Springs despite the fact he had not travelled for years.

Then we got caught up in her person dilemma again. She wanted all the furniture she had stored in Los Angeles brought to her, and she wanted the facelift. Medi Spas could wait; besides, if she had the surgery first, she would be able to surprise Tom Lyle. "I would not want him to see me this way," she said with a sigh.

When no reply came in the mail from Tom Lyle, Evelyn decided to call him and ask if he had received our letter. An African-American woman answered the phone, a housekeeper he had with him for years. Knowing this lady well, Evelyn asked her how Tom Lyle was—burbled on about what we were doing in Hot Springs, and did Tom get her letter?

There was a moment of silence. Then, "Mrs. Williams, Mr. Tom Lyle passed away a few days ago."

Putting down the phone, Evelyn started to cry—her shoulders heaving and tears pouring down her face. Finally she wiped her eyes, she looked up at and exclaimed, "Why did no one tell us?"

She was sad all the next day, going through old photos of her and Tom Lyle, telling me a little story with each one. I looked down at the images of this sensitive-faced man, trying to see why she compared us—and not seeing it at all, I assured her that he would have no doubt come to our rescue on our project and that we would work towards it anyway, in his honor.

Somewhat mollified by this, she said, "Yes, Dan. We'll have a dedication plaque on the door of the Spa—it was Tom Lyle who gave me what I have now, anyway."

Gabriel and I flew out to LA to collect her furniture. To save money she'd decided to rent a moving van and have us drive it to Arkansas. Me and my big mouth told her I had driven an 18 wheeler, loaded with furniture, from Houston Texas to Los Angeles for a friend a few years before. "But darling, you and Gabriel can have *such* an adventure," she burbled. "Why, you'll be like road warriors bringing the Queen's possessions safely to her."

Although again she was talking tongue-in-cheek, she really meant "It will be much cheaper and safer than using those crooks at the moving companies who just throw things on the truck any old way."

I did have some loose ends to take care of in Newport Beach. The young lady I'd left to operate my shop had quit and disappeared, and the landlord had kindly put my things in one of his storage units pending my shipping them to Arkansas. Evelyn said that this made the trip even more important: I could put my few belongings in the truck with her furniture and it would cost nothing.

So I made arrangements to stay with friends in Laguna Beach and Gabriel and I flew west. We arrived in Laguna via rental car. My friends were glad to see me and wanted to hear all about my new life. They kept looking at Gabriel, who was tongue-tied in the presence of the more sophisticated beach people. "They all talk too fast for me," he complained, and they of course gave me knowing looks as they took in his muscles, long hair and cute Greek face. He was not used to me being as openly gay as I was in California, and spent most of the time looking at his feet.

I rang Evelyn's oldest granddaughter, Sharrie Williams, and invited her and her husband to dinner at Delaney's Sea Shanty, a popular watering hole and restaurant down on the piers in Newport.

Sharrie looked very much like her grandmother—but in a more modern and edgy way. She was always on the go, bristling with energy, like a Jack Russell Terrier. She also had that air of privilege and entitlement that her father Bill had, but seemed much more down to earth and liberal. In fact, she exuded trendiness and appeared to be in command of herself and everyone connected to her.

No stranger to gay people and indeed all the *in crowd* of Newport, she was very supportive of what she called my many talents. I do not recall her criticizing Evelyn's marriage to Hobby Derrick, and when I told her of the offer from Evelyn and Joe Lewis for me to go to Hot Springs as a witness for Evelyn and her divorce suit, she was supportive of the fact that I could expose the con artists for what they were. She urged me to keep her posted on everything, but before I left she wanted me to help her with an unusual, Maybelline–sponsored fashion show for a charity she was involved with.

This was to be a fashion show like none other, with music and teen models, some dressing like film stars of yesteryear and others in updated fashions showing the influence of the movies on the current trends. I had just done a layout for movie photographer Harry Langdon where I engaged models that I could make up to look like Bette Davis, Joan Crawford, Sonja Henie, Greta Garbo and others. I actually met Bette Davis's "other daughter," Monica Henreid, the progeny of one of Hollywood's best-kept secrets at the time, Bette and Paul Henreid, not long after they made the movie *Now Voyager*. Monica was a dead ringer for her mother and told me many interesting stories about her, all positive—unlike the book Bette's other daughter, B.D., had written—that broke Bette's heart.

I also had a young friend, a very dynamic and popular Newport Beach kid named Bobby Shannon. Bobby was tall and surfer tan, with a huge mane of curly red hair, His Irish eyes sparkled with mischief and intelligence, he was outlandish and outspoken and we had this secret sense of humor about everyone and everything that created a friendship that lasts until this day. He resembled Sharrie's brother Preston, a fact that was not lost on Evelyn later, but where Preston was shy and retiring at the time, Bobby was out there, often on the edge. He actually ended up with his own Harry Langdon portfolio, even though he never became a professional model. It was his personae that glowed from the pictures.

Sharrie's plan for the fashion show followed this format, so I asked Bobby to help me get other models and after days of casting and talking to be people in addition to many script writing meetings with Sharrie, the show was on.

In actual fact the show was probably sponsored by her father Bill, but there were Maybelline gifts on every table in the large local ballroom where it was held. I knew that Bill still did not like me; I knew that he was basically homophobic and not happy with his mother and her marital dilemma. I conveyed this to Sharrie, reminding her that there were a lot of gay kids in the cast.

She waved this all aside, even agreeing to a young female impersonator, who swore he could do a flawless Barbra Streisand with his own voice. Sharrie maintained that this was the 70s and she wanted to portray all walks of life with fashion.

The day of the show brought backstage nerves and kids developing stage fright. Sharrie calmed them all down somehow, her brisk and commanding presence giving them assurance that they would all be wonderful. Bill appeared, treating me with distant civility, and the show went off without a hitch…until the kid who was to do Streisand came on. He had assured me during rehearsals that he could make himself up exactly like Barbara. His voice *was* similar, although with a weak falsetto, and he looked enough like her son that I believed everything he said.

But when they played the *Funny Girl* overture and the spotlight shown on the empty picture frame that was part of the set, he walked out wearing a black, male leotard, no makeup at all, with his curly dark hair parted hippy fashion in the middle. There wasn't any sound track as he had assured me there would be. Instead, he sang "People" in a Baritone Acappella voice with passion and his eyes closed.

I was furious at the deception. Years later I realized that this young man was using that stage to "come out" and say "This is me—take it or leave it," but that evening I was livid with rage—the audience was stunned and embarrassed for him, the applause tentative and polite. Bill Williams' face was red with an "I told you so" look on it.

Sharrie seemed unconcerned. "Well, he made the effort. Don't say anything, Danie."

Based on this, I felt she was an understanding person who, beneath her shiny and brittle and always on-the-go demeanor, was someone and something else.

When Gabriel and I entered Delaney's, he kept looking around with frightened eyes. "Is this all rich people in here?"

"Well, yes," I replied, "but a lot of other people come in here also. I've had transsexual people come in here with me and just regular beach bums; it's a very open minded place."

Sharrie and her husband, a husky dark haired man, were waiting for us at the table. Sharrie's eyes danced with anticipation to hear all the news from Arkansas. I realized how much her expressions were like her grandmother's, but she had a direct way of looking at you instead of all the coy and flirtatious looks that Evelyn made use of. There did not seem to be a lot of husband and wife connection going on. He was pleasant enough, the kind of a man who wanted you to think he was cool, hip and informed and liberal, but I had the feeling there was a much darker person lurking inside him, and Sharrie was afraid of this other person. She seemed to be putting on a performance of her own—asking me all kinds of questions about the activities in Hot Springs, almost as if it were an ongoing television series she was hooked on.

Gabriel was uncomfortable with them, feeling out of his depth. Sharrie tried to draw him into the conversation, telling him how handsome he was, and then stating, "He looks good on you, Danie."

This made him even more uncomfortable. I could tell he wanted to get back to Arkansas as soon as possible.

The next day we rented the truck and drove into Hollywood to the storage warehouse where he and the warehouse workers loaded Evelyn's furniture on board. Then we drove to Newport Beach to collect my belongings. As I looked around my empty shop that had been host to so many unusual things and people, I wistfully thought, *Am I doing the right thing, leaving here?*

With one of his sudden deep understandings of things, Gabriel gently hugged me, took my hand and said, "Let's go home."

We left as the California sun sank below the Pacific.

I don't remember much about the trip to back to Arkansas. I remember driving miles and miles across vast spaces, with Gabriel telling me his life story. He was very kind to me on that journey—almost as if we had been in a relationship forever. He was protective of me, insisted on doing much of the driving and wanted me to teach him everything about life. He especially wanted to know how to look and act around people so he would not feel like a redneck bumbling fool. He knew I saw him as beautiful in his own way—but he did not perceive himself as anything much at all.

This fact came out in a dramatic and sad way later.

8

Rock & Roll, Wolfman Jack—and "The Silver Ghost"

*K*IDZ was developing into a major rock band, despite Evelyn's complaints of "that damn racket in the maid's quarters" where they had set up their rehearsal hall.

I can still see the three of the band members in my mind's eye, especially the oldest man with his long auburn hair and white highlights, and the young, handsome bass guitar player, a dark haired youth who looked like he came straight from a prep school.

Then there was Clint, the drummer. He had it all as a potential star—a face that was androgynous and beautiful, a lean sculpted body with smooth, almost statue-like skin which he did not mind flaunting on stage and off. Clint was an aggressive and forceful drummer, almost as if he was embarrassed by his pretty face and flowing dark-blond curls. He was always barking and fighting with the others and often with me—shoving his face right up to mine, eyes angry and snapping. He also made subtle gay jibes in my direction, like he was *defying* me to make a pass at him. The fact I never did made him spit out one evening after a rehearsal, "Well, I *could* be with a dude if I wanted to!"

I laughed, said, "Go ahead," and walked away.

Clint was the face of KIDZ. The heavy metal band KISS was at its height of popularity at the time; my take was that KIDZ would be the opposite. Angelic, where KISS was demonic looking; beautiful, where KISS was hardcore. But nonetheless full-on rock and roll.

The older man was the lead singer and songwriter. He owned APPLE RECORDS, the only place in town where wannabe musicians and a few professionals hung out; he was very talented and serious. I became the band's manager after I asked them to perform at the roller rink and told them that they had far more potential than just doing college gigs. I was actually grooming them to appear as a warm-up band at Barton's Coliseum in Little Rock, where top groups like Boston, Foghat and Aerosmith played. I was convinced that their fresh look and talent would propel them into the big time, so I re-designed their style, bought them some new sound equipment including a synthesizer, and made them rehearse, rehearse, rehearse.

Whenever they had a new set of songs ready and a new act, I would feature them at the Spa City Roller rink and plaster posters all over town, emblazoned with their logo, which I had hand-drawn.

Evelyn had to be in on this to make up for the rehearsal noise, so she would appear dressed in a costume—once as a Russian Czarina in a huge fur hat—and announce them from the stage. The kids in the audience had to feel that the Maybelline Heiress not only understood them, but supported their form of entertainment.

The technology for lighting effects was not as sophisticated as it is today. Although laser was just coming in, it was way too expensive for a roller rink, so we relied on a huge mirror ball in the center of the rink and a multi-colored spotlight panel. To achieve really spectacular effects I had to use fog machines that often blew up, and two huge cast iron kettles placed on either side of the stage. They were filled with kerosene, and at key points in their concert, the KIDZ roadies would sneak up and light the fuel. The effect was pillars of flame suddenly erupting; the band looked like Las Vegas royalty.

Rick Warren, a brilliant young pianist who was very popular in the clubs around town, drove an old but pristine Cadillac Limo in which we would have KIDZ arrive. I insisted that they be flanked by their "roadies" like real stars and not talk to, or even look at, any of the audience as they entered the rink. This was hard for them, as in real life they knew everyone in town, but it paid off. The young people of Hot Springs went along with these theatrics and screamed hysterically when the band appeared. Later, Clint told me he felt like Mick Jagger.

But even the best of bands fall apart without strong management, and I could not babysit them 24/7. When my own life took another turn a year after KIDZ got going strong, they fell apart after a few false starts on their own.

Once rock and roll mixed with disco took off, I decided to create an on-air personality to keep the interest of the young people fresh and going.

I had a friend who was the manager of a local radio station where we advertised the rink. He was heavy set, with John Lennon glasses—everyone's favorite college nerd. He also had an incredible wit. When we invited him out to Maybelline Manor to discuss the live ads, he'd have Evelyn rolling on the floor and snapping right back with her own one-liners and stories.

One evening when I went down to the radio station to listen to our ads being run, I was informed that he was up to his neck in recording some announcements for college football teams. He asked me if I could put the headphones on and record our ad from the script we'd written. I sat at the console, and for some reason, as I began to speak, I affected a Wolfman Jack imitation. Wolfman was probably the most popular radio jock in the Nation at that time, with his gravelly voice and "Heeeeeyyyyy, Baaabbbbby!" byline. Many people thought Wolfman was black, when in fact he was a chubby, middle-aged white man.

After I finished the bit, my friend rushed into the room and said, "That was *great*! Why don't you do all your ads?"

Flushed with success, I began to envision a short talk show featuring popular music—kind of like my newspaper column, except for the kids. We thought of creating a mystical character that no one ever saw—sort of a "ghost on the air," using the same fake Wolfman voice.

Thus, the air personality, "The Silver Ghost," was born. Few people knew it was me. I solicited the services of a young pastor's son, Danny, to be my "field spy." Danny was a tall, serious kid whom everyone liked but most girls did not pay attention to because of his Jimmy Stewart-style quiet manner. I told him that the job I was proposing would put him into the thick of things on the weekend, and that girls would eventually see all his sterling qualities and looks (he was actually an attractive, sort of Nordic blond type). Giving him several rolls of dimes, I had him hang around all the popular meeting spots for the kids—certain parking lots, fast food joints and school grounds. He also attended all the sports events.

He would hang around with the other kids, watching and listening, until my little show came on the air; then he would rush to a phone booth, call me up and tell me what was going on (this was, of course, before cell phones). Imagine you were a pretty girl about to climb into a car with someone who had a bad reputation. Suddenly the Silver Ghost's voice comes out of the car radio: "Uh–uh, Debbie Baaaby, you don't *want* to get into this car—you *know* your mama would not like it—and by the way, you look soooo pretty in that little orange tank top."

At first the kids freaked—who in the hell was this Silver Ghost and how could he be everywhere? Well, he explained at the end of the show that he had eyes everywhere a ghost could go, so everyone had to listen up.

And they did. The next week, a packed roller rink was buzzing about the Silver Ghost and who he really was. True to his word, Danny said nothing—until the Silver Ghost finally appeared at the roller rink in person as the DJ, and everyone saw that it was Zeke. Zeke, who later become an obsession of Evelyn's and mine—and upset an entire town.

I still needed a car, the Austin Healy having been towed to the only foreign car "specialist" in Hot Springs, who informed me, while chewing on a tobacco plug, that the parts needed were rare and he might have to order them from England.

Two weeks went by and not a part for the car in sight, so I purchased a marine blue Corvette on a time payment plan in Little Rock. Evelyn did not like "the blue job," as she called it, either. The one time she took a ride in it she was frightened of the raw power and fiberglass body. She did, however, see the value in a "man's glamour car," as far as the kids were concerned.

The 'Vette did become legendary around town. There were a few other Corvettes, of course, driven by middle aged men, but the "Blue Flash" would be seen from Little Rock to Hot Springs, often violating speed rules. Like most adults in the early 1970s, both Evelyn and I had our cocktails and wines with dinner. I, however, had an enormous capacity for alcohol that today I cannot even relate to. I thought nothing of having three or four dry martinis before dinner, champagne and wine during, and several Drambuie's afterward. In fact, a bottle of Drambuie was always in my car and became my signature high. Today, although I keep a wine cellar in my home and a full bar, I'm lucky to have one or two glasses of very top drawer champagne without getting sick. The thought of that sweet and burning Scotch-based liquor makes me gag!

How I survived those days, eating so much gourmet and Southern food and drinking so much alcohol yet still looking trim and fresh, is beyond me. Having the metabolism of a Jack Russell terrier may have something to do with it. But many times, in the wee hours of the morning after leaving a party or one of the bars, I would be merrily speeding down the roads to Brown Drive and police cars would switch on their lights and pull me over. When they approached the 'Vette and saw it was me, they would always politely ask if I was all right, then offer to escort me to Maybelline Manor, always thanking me for the work we were doing at the rink and for the funds we helped raise for Police Charities. Evelyn, at times hearing cars out front, would ask me in the morning why the police were there.

I would reply, "Oh, they offered to escort me home and check the grounds for any intruders."

The fear of Sam Saleem seemed to have disappeared from Evelyn's mind; at least she never talked about him anymore. So we got by with just a new housekeeper, a beautiful, tall, dark haired woman called Mary. I had one or more of the guys from the rink, usually Doug Berry, come out and stay on the grounds if Evelyn and I were going to an event late in the evening, and we started to relax.

Then one night, after an evening at The Saw Mill Depot—a high-end restaurant and bar that catered to the town's elite and also the more colorful people—we got home to find the young man who had been watching the estate for us standing outside with a rifle in his hands.

"Ms. Williams," he shouted breathlessly, "a weird guy drove up an hour or so ago asking to see you."

I asked why he was so weird. The kid said he was a black man wearing an Afro and driving a big Cadillac. He was also smoking a cigar.

Evelyn screamed, "That was Sam Saleem, Dan—he's going to get me!"

I reminded her that Sam Saleem was not an African-American, to which she insisted, "He always told me he disguises himself as a Black person, and he does drive Cadillacs and smoke cigars!" She was trembling with fright.

I told the kid to call Doug and a few of the other boys to sit around the house that night and not let anyone in. We had a long, heavy chain that could be used as a barrier between the brick posts at the front of the drive to stop a car from coming in, and I had them lock it in place.

Fortified for the night, I promised her we would inform the sheriff's department and police the next day. Coming onto the property in disguise was, in my opinion, against the law. However, the next day we were informed that person's dressing a certain way was not against the law until it was proven that a crime was being committed.

"Oh, yes, they'll do something after I'm dead," Evelyn moaned.

To calm her down, I said we'd get professional security again—put Saleem's description out and finally trap him on the premises. I vowed to get him for her and erase him from our lives.

I got a chance to do exactly that a few days later.

We'd gone into town to do some shopping and to stop at a little dressmaker's Evelyn liked. I took her to a nice luncheon and we had a few Bloody Marys to get her mind off Sam Saleem. He still didn't seem to be a real person to me, at least not as formidable as she made him seem. And the thought that he would drive up to the house disguised as an African-American made him seem like an almost harmless nutcase.

We had parked the Eldorado behind some buildings in a parking lot. When we came back to it, our arms laden with purchases, I saw another large Cadillac parked next to us with a bulky figure sitting in the driver's seat.

"Oh, Dan," Evelyn hissed, "that's Sam!"

"Get in the car, honey," I said in a low tone. "Let me handle this."

After putting her into the car and locking it with the automatic clicker—a new innovation in those days—I approached Sam's car.

He immediately pulled himself out of the driver's side with a big, toothy smile on his face. Broad, with nearly no neck, swarthy skin and short black hair, he had the olive black Cajun eyes people from down in New Orleans have—and they were as cold as ice, despite his wide smile.

I was taller than he was, so I drew myself up, puffed out my chest and walked right up to him. "What the hell do you want, Saleem?"

"Ohhh boy," he crooned in an accent so thick it sounded like he was tongue-tied, "so you know who I am? Well, I believe Ms. Williams wants to talk to me 'bout a little bidness she and I have."

"No, she doesn't, Sam," I hissed. "She has nothing to say to you."

Looking at me with narrowed eyes, he said he knew who I was, with my little boys with rifles hanging around the property. Again he insisted he and Evelyn had "bidness" to discuss.

Using a ploy I had learned as a misfit child, I held an invisible mirror up to him. I *became* him and my own accent took on a Deep South patina.

"Sam, you don't know a damn thing about me, who I am or what I'm capable of. Those boys are just part of an army to protect my territory and interests."

I informed him I had the law in my pocket and my army included sheriff's deputies. His eyes widened with sudden comprehension. This was a field he understood playing on.

"So, you have interests too, huh? Well, I understand that, but Ms. Williams made me some promises that I want kept."

I stepped closer to him and, in as deadly a tone as I could muster, said: "You know she was under stress and sedation after those two were done with her. Old people, especially women, will say anything when they're afraid. Anything she promised you is null and void. I control everything now, and if you need proof of that, why, let's go on down to the sheriff's office, call my attorney to meet us and you'll see how much those promises are worth."

After putting his head down and looking at his feet while he digested all this, he suddenly looked up with a conspiratorial smile and gave me a wink. "Well, well, looks like you got all this wrapped up nice and cozy—OK, OK, I get it now—looks like I am a bit late. Sure you don't need some 'hep?"

Firmly refusing any help, I asked him to leave us alone. There was nothing to gain by hassling Mrs. Williams.

"Well boy, watch out for her—she's a crazy bitch."

Without another word he waved his hand in resignation and opened his car door. As he bent down to get in, his suit coat stretched over a muscular, bull back and revealed a tell-tale bulge under his arm: a holstered pistol.

I stood there shaking like a leaf.

Evelyn's head popped up over the roof of the Eldorado, face white as a sheet. "Dan. Dan, what happened, what did he say?"

"Never mind, my dear, get back in the car and let's get outta here. I'll tell you on the way home."

As we approached that familiar drive again, I knew I could hardly tell her that I had diffused this crook by pretending to be like him. So I simply said, "Well, darling, I just told him that if he didn't leave you alone I'd have him shot and buried in a shallow grave by Lake Hamilton."

"You didn't!" she gasped, and then, giggling, informed me that murder threats were against the law.

"I know, Evelyn, I know, but he's hardly in league with the law, and this was the only language he would understand."

Grabbing my arm so hard that I nearly drove off the road, she exclaimed, "Oh, you are my *savior*! You gave it to him, Dan—socko!" She smacked a fist into her other palm. "Rode him out of town on a rail!"

She settled back in her seat with a big smile on her face and kept repeating that she knew his type, he was a coward at heart, and with the fear put into him he would never try to see her again. He never did, but the story of how I routed the dreaded Sam Saleem got bigger each time she told it to someone. By the end I had thrashed him soundly, dragged him into his car and kicked him in the butt. The boys at the roller rink looked at me with new respect, and I heard the rumor of how "Danie can really kick ass" floating around.

Later this would save me from physical attack several times.

9

Gabriel

$\mathcal{I}$ needed a car. Evelyn did not like her wonderful machine being driven so much or parked down at the roller rink at night. Placing calls to friends of mine in California, I found an Austin Healy Le Mans sports racer in pristine condition for $2,000. It was a distress sale that would normally never have happened, so I phoned him and said I would come out to Los Angeles immediately.

Since I had a meeting with Joe Lewis on some legal matters anyway, Gabriel and I flew out once again with the idea that he would drive the car back for me. I had only two days to be away from the roller rink as we were planning rehearsals for "Hollywood on Wheels," an Ice Capades-style spectacular in which Evelyn had a prominent role.

The car was indeed beautiful. The owner had tears in his eyes as he took my check. "Please treat her nice," he begged.

I assuring him that I understood British motor works from my private school days in England and that his baby would showcase at a beautiful estate. Then I flew back home, leaving Gabriel with enough cash to stay at a motel or two and buy food and gas. I gave him three days to get the car to Hot Springs.

A week later he still had not shown up, and there was no way to contact him. Evelyn was furious, expecting the worst and admonishing me daily for trusting "that ignorant foreigner!" (Gabriel constantly talked about his Greek heritage.)

Finally, just before we were ready to call the State Patrol, a call came through from a gas station owner in New Mexico: "I got a very tired young man here, who is out of gas and out of money and said to call you."

I told him to put Gabriel on the phone and was confronted by tears and gulps again as Gabriel said he'd lost most of the cash by leaving it in the car in an envelope and forgetting to lock the door while he went into a cafe to eat.

As cold as ice, I asked him to inquire where the nearest Western Union was, then go there and wait until we wired $200 through. Then he was to drive non-stop until he was home.

I asked the gas station owner if we could use his address for Western Union, and he complied after I told him that Gabriel would fill the car up there. Evelyn, of course, was dancing around, eyes bright with suspicion: "What happened, Dan?"

I lied and said the car had broken down and Gabriel did not have enough money to fix it—the gas station owner said it would cost another $200.

"Well, that serves you right for buying a fancy foreign car that's old," she snapped, "you should have just got a decent used Cadillac or something."

Evelyn was prepared to hate my new car, and sure enough, when Gabriel finally drove up a day and a half later, she was all over him like a mother hen. "Ohh you poor *baby*, having to drive this old thing so far—you must be frantic."

She didn't get much of a chance to hate the car or like it—neither did I. I drove it proudly for two days, and on day three it vanished. So did Gabriel, along with a bag of petty cash we kept on hand for incidentals at the estate, about $600.

After we discovered the car gone early one morning, we assumed he had decided to go somewhere for his own purposes—he had been very moody since returning from Los Angeles. But we were furious at the cheek of just helping one's self. "He mistakes kindness for weakness, Dan, you have to get rid of him," Evelyn snapped.

At first I decided to give him the benefit of the doubt, but by the third day I knew something was wrong and with a heavy heart I phoned the police. After getting all the details, they put out an all-state bulletin on him and the car. A day later Gabriel called me up from some little town downstate and confessed that he had "borrowed" the car so he could get away with his "girlfriend-soon-to-be-wife" and get married. Apparently she was pregnant.

I was aghast and asked him how long this had been going on. He turned nasty and said they'd been having an affair for months so he could prove to her that I had not "turned him gay." Apparently the only way they could be happy was to run off and somehow return the car to me after they got married and settled.

When I asked about the cash he said he still had most of it and to tell Ms. Williams he was sorry and would pay it back. The girl was someone I knew from the roller rink. Her name was Cherie; she came from a nice, middle class family. She also wanted to be a musician—a guitar player—and whenever KIDZ appeared, she would be in the front row, intently listening to everything rather than jumping up and down like the other girls.

How she could be enamored with an uneducated, slow-thinking boy like Gabriel was beyond me, until I remembered my own fondness for him and how "spiritual and romantic" he could seem at times. Also, at times he was a very giving person as well. I knew his little fantasy was not going to work the way he imagined—not to Cherie's family and not to Mrs. Williams, who would not allow me to just let my car go, nor cash from the house, on speculation that it would all be returned someday.

I talked to Gabriel about this for nearly an hour, using all my persuasive powers to make him realize that if this were indeed true love and they were future parents, they needed to come back and let their families in on it. I maintained that Evelyn and I would actually help them through this, but if Gabriel did not comply with this plan, the All-State's Bulletin would stand and he would face jail time—and perhaps Cherie as well.

He finally broke down (again), sobbing that he'd hoped I would say all this and he was sorry he could not be gay for me.

Evelyn was amazed at the events that had happened. She seemed almost curious about the pregnancy and agreed that under the circumstances the girl needed an abortion. Gabriel would of course have to find job elsewhere. "We cannot have the two of them here," she warned. "Abortions could be a scandal." No doubt she was thinking of her own experiences decades ago.

Gabriel finally limped my poor English car up the drive again. It had thrown a rod and smoke was pouring out from under the hood (bonnet). He practically crawled on his hands and knees to Evelyn who was sitting regally in a chair in the living room. I will never forget the sight of him burying his head in her lap and sobbing, "Please forgive me, I love her, I love her," and Evelyn placing on him a slim hand with that huge, emerald cut diamond ring flashing in the shaft of light from the high widow near the ceiling. She looked like an Empress offering a benediction to a Knight who had fallen from grace and favor.

Observing this scene from an MGM movie, I realized how corny it all was—Gabriel's constant emotional outbursts and self-centered thinking, and how he really believed that my affection for him allowed him to do anything. He looked up at my frozen face, realized he'd made an enemy, and left the estate on foot.

I informed the roller rink he was off payroll and then went to visit Cherie's parents. She was there when I arrived, her swollen red eyes defiant, daring me to challenge her. Her parents were nice people who obviously didn't know all the details except that their daughter had run off with her boyfriend in our car, and thanked me profusely for not pressing charges (Gabriel is such a *nice boy* we just don't know what got into them!). I asked to speak to Cherie alone and we walked outside into the garden.

"He's not like you, you know—you can't change him," she muttered.

"I have no intention of changing him. People cannot be made to be what they are not."

"But he isn't gay!" she protested, "I know that for sure." And she launched into all the cute and romantic things he would say and how he treated her. "There's one thing he says to me that just makes me love him more—it's so sweet…"

"'Anything that pleases you just tickles me plum to death?'" I said.

Her eyes widened. "*Omigod!* Did he say that to you?"

"Nearly every day, honey." And I told her all about Gabriel.

When she realized I knew as much about him as she did, in every possible way, I took her to the car and showed her the cartoon portrait he had had sketched of himself at Laguna Beach by a street artist. On it he had written: "Think of me forever, love Gabriel."

She broke down and cried.

I asked about the baby, and she admitted this was just a ruse to get Gabriel to commit to a relationship. She'd believed him when he told her I had loaned him the car and money to get married out of town, and that Mrs. Williams and I would help them later. Wondering how young women could be so gullible (wasn't I?), I pointed out that a relationship with a man who was confused as to his own identity never worked. Drying her eyes with the bottom of her blouse, she sighed and vowed not to see him again.

Gabriel disappeared from Hot Springs for a long time, so I knew Cherie had kept her word to me and to herself.

A long time later, after my life had changed in Hot Springs, I was walking out of the photo shop where Roger Lewin and I had our Lewin and King Modeling Agency. It was twilight, with that beautiful and strange purple light that fell over the city in the fall. Street lamps were glowing amber in the light fog that sometimes gets trapped in the valleys between the ancient mountains surrounding the city, and down at the bottom of the street I saw a lone figure standing under a street lamp. He was wearing a long overcoat and had a hat jammed down over his forehead, obscuring his face. As I sauntered by a soft voice whispered, "Hello Danie," and I looked up into a more mature and oddly thin Gabriel face.

He had cut his hair short, but he still had that warm smile and merry brown eyes, somehow sadder looking than before,

I asked him where he had been. "Oh—away," he replied vaguely. He then wanted to know about what had happened to Mrs. Williams. I told him, and described some of the details about the roller rink, the Hollywood on Wheels show and The Palace Dinner Theatre. He did not reply to anything, and I felt oddly uncomfortable, ending the conversation ending with, "Well, Gab, come on out to Hot Springs Village and visit Mary Anderson and myself."

He lifted his hat, smiled and said, "Whatever pleases you tickles me jest plum to death."

I never saw him again.

10

Blue Flash, Sam Saleem ~and a Little More Respect

$\mathcal{I}$ still needed a car, the Austin Healy having been towed to the only foreign car "specialist" in Hot Springs, who informed me, while chewing on a tobacco plug, that the parts needed were rare and he might have to order them from England.

Two weeks went by and not a part for the car in sight, so I purchased a marine blue Corvette on a time payment plan in Little Rock. Evelyn did not like "the blue job," as she called it, either. The one time she took a ride in it she was frightened of the raw power and fiberglass body. She did, however, see the value in a "man's glamour car," as far as the kids were concerned.

The 'Vette did become legendary around town. There were a few other Corvettes, of course, driven by middle aged men, but the "Blue Flash" would be seen from Little Rock to Hot Springs, often violating speed rules. Like most adults in the early 1970s, both Evelyn and I had our cocktails and wines with dinner. I, however, had an enormous capacity for alcohol that today I cannot even relate to. I thought nothing of having three or four dry martinis before dinner, champagne and wine during, and several Drambuie's afterward. In fact a bottle of Drambuie was always in my car and became my signature high. Today, although I keep a wine cellar in my home and a full bar, I'm lucky to have one or two glasses of very top drawer champagne without getting sick. The thought of that sweet and burning Scotch-based liquor makes me gag!

How I survived those days, eating so much gourmet and Southern food and drinking so much alcohol yet still looking trim and fresh, is beyond me. Having the metabolism of a Jack Russell terrier may have something to do with it. But many times, in the wee hours of the morning after leaving a party or one of the bars, I would be merrily speeding down the roads to Brown Drive and police cars would switch on their lights and pull me over. When they approached the 'Vette and saw it was me, they would always politely ask if I was all right, then offer to escort me to Maybelline Manor, always thanking me for the work we were doing at the rink and for the funds we helped raise for Police Charities. Evelyn, at times hearing cars out front, would ask me in the morning why the police were there.

I would reply, "Oh, they offered to escort me home and check the grounds for any intruders."

The fear of Sam Saleem seemed to have disappeared from Evelyn's mind; at least she never talked about him anymore. So we got by with just a new housekeeper, a beautiful, tall, dark haired woman called Mary. I had one or more of the guys from the rink, usually Doug Berry, come out and stay on the grounds if Evelyn and I were going to an event late in the evening, and we started to relax.

Then one night, after an evening at The Saw Mill Depot—a high-end restaurant and bar that catered to the town's elite and also the more colorful people—we got home to find the young man who had been watching the estate for us standing outside with a rifle in his hands.

"Ms. Williams," he shouted breathlessly, "a weird guy drove up an hour or so ago asking to see you."

I asked why he was so weird. The kid said he was a black man wearing an Afro and driving a big Cadillac. He was also smoking a cigar.

Evelyn screamed, "That was Sam Saleem, Dan—he's going to get me!"

I reminded her that Sam Saleem was not an African-American, to which she insisted, "He always told me he disguises himself as a black person, and he does drive Cadillacs and smoke cigars!" She was trembling with fright.

I told the kid to call Doug and a few of the other boys to sit around the house that night and not let anyone in. We had a long, heavy chain that could be used as a barrier between the brick posts at the front of the drive to stop a car from coming in, and I had them lock it in place.

Fortified for the night, I promised her we would inform the sheriff's department and police the next day. Coming onto the property in disguise was, in my opinion, against the law. However, the next day we were informed that person's dressing a certain way was not against the law until it was proven that a crime was being committed.

"Oh, yes, they'll do something after I'm dead," Evelyn moaned.

To calm her down, I said we'd get professional security again—put Saleem's description out and finally trap him on the premises. I vowed to get him for her and erase him from our lives.

I got a chance to do exactly that a few days later.

We'd gone into town to do some shopping and to stop at a little dressmaker's Evelyn liked. I took her to a nice luncheon and we had a few Bloody Marys to get her mind off Sam Saleem. He still didn't seem to be a real person to me, at least not as formidable as she made him seem. And the thought that he would drive up to the house disguised as an African-American made him seem like an almost harmless nutcase.

We had parked the Eldorado behind some buildings in a parking lot. When we came back to it, our arms laden with purchases, I saw another large Cadillac parked next to us with a bulky figure sitting in the driver's seat.

"Oh, Dan," Evelyn hissed, "that's Sam!"

"Get in the car, honey," I said in a low tone. "Let me handle this."

After putting her into the car and locking it with the automatic clicker—a new innovation in those days—I approached Sam's car.

He immediately pulled himself out of the driver's side with a big, toothy smile on his face. Broad, with nearly no neck, swarthy skin and short black hair, he had the olive black Cajun eyes people from down in New Orleans have—and they were as cold as ice, despite his wide smile.

I was taller than he was, so I drew myself up, puffed out my chest and walked right up to him. "What the hell do you want, Saleem?"

"Ohhh boy," he crooned in an accent so thick it sounded like he was tongue-tied, "so you know who I am? Well, I believe Ms. Williams wants to talk to me 'bout a little bidness she and I have."

"No, she doesn't, Sam," I hissed. "She has nothing to say to you."

Looking at me with narrowed eyes, he said he knew who I was, with my little boys with rifles hanging around the property. Again he insisted he and Evelyn had "bidness" to discuss.

Using a ploy I had learned as a misfit child, I held an invisible mirror up to him. I *became* him and my own accent took on a Deep South patina.

"Sam, you don't know a damn thing about me, who I am or what I'm capable of. Those boys are just part of an army to protect my territory and interests."

I informed him I had the law in my pocket and my army included sheriff's deputies. His eyes widened with sudden comprehension. This was a field he understood playing on.

"So, you have interests too, huh? Well, I understand that, but Ms. Williams made me some promises that I want kept."

I stepped closer to him and, in as deadly a tone as I could muster, said: "You know she was under stress and sedation after those two were done with her. Old people, especially women, will say anything when they're afraid. Anything she promised you is null and void. I control everything now, and if you need proof of that, why, let's go on down to the sheriff's office, call my attorney to meet us and you'll see how much those promises are worth."

After putting his head down and looking at his feet while he digested all this, he suddenly looked up with a conspiratorial smile and gave me a wink. "Well, well, looks like you got all this wrapped up nice and cozy. Okay, I get it now—looks like I am a bit late. Sure you don't need some 'hep?'"

Firmly refusing any help, I asked him to leave us alone. There was nothing to gain by hassling Mrs. Williams.

"Well boy, watch out for her; she's a crazy bitch."

Without another word he waved his hand in resignation and opened his car door. As he bent down to get in, his suit coat stretched over a muscular, bull back and revealed a tell-tale bulge under his arm: a holstered pistol.

I stood there shaking like a leaf.

Evelyn's head popped up over the roof of the Eldorado, face white as a sheet. "Dan. Dan, what happened, what did he say?"

"Never mind, my dear, get back in the car and let's get outta here. I'll tell you on the way home."

As we approached that familiar drive again, I knew I could hardly tell her that I had diffused this crook by pretending to be like him. So I simply said, "Well, darling, I just told him that if he didn't leave you alone I'd have him shot and buried in a shallow grave by Lake Hamilton."

"You didn't!" she gasped, and then, giggling, informed me that murder threats were against the law.

"I know, Evelyn, I know, but he's hardly in league with the law, and this was the only language he would understand."

Grabbing my arm so hard that I nearly drove off the road, she exclaimed, "Oh, you are my *savior*! You gave it to him, Dan—socko!" She smacked a fist into her other palm. "Rode him out of town on a rail!"

The divine Miss Maybelline settled back in her seat with a big smile on her face and kept repeating that she knew his type: he was a coward at heart, and with the fear put into him he would never try to see her again. He never did, but the story of how I routed the dreaded Sam Saleem got bigger each time she told it to someone. By the end I had thrashed him soundly, dragged him into his car and kicked him in the butt. The boys at the roller rink looked at me with new respect, and I heard the rumor of how "Danie can really kick ass" floating around.

Later this would save me from physical attack several times.

11

Sexual Escapades: Mary, and Zeke

Handling KIDZ was looking like a full-time job, and they couldn't play the Spa City Roller Rink forever. They were fighting amongst themselves but also getting a few paying gigs around Garland County; so, promising to still represent them when I could, I had them vacate the maid's quarters, mainly because Mary came to work for us.

Mary was tall, with a figure like Raquel Welch in her early movies. She had rich black hair, large liquid dark eyes and a very quiet, almost regal way of acting and moving. She was exceptionally beautiful, which was why I almost turned her down when she appeared in my office inquiring about a housekeeping position. She said she could cook well, sew, was a hard worker and just loved all the things she had heard about Mrs. Williams. She also pointed out that she was 30 years-old, not one of the teenagers we hired part time and who were driving Evelyn crazy with their lack of decorum. For example, when the phone rang, the maid of the week would shout out, "Evelyn, I mean Miss Williams, someone wants to talk at ya!"

Mary seemed so sweet and genteel and refined that I was hooked. But I feared her extraordinary beauty would put Evelyn off, so I told her to show up at Maybelline Manor dressed in a plain sack dress, her hair slicked back and no make-up.

That evening I described her to Evelyn as the "perfect find." Quiet and lady-like, she was an accomplished housekeeper who had worked for a family in Georgia (a fiction I warned Mary about in advance, knowing Evelyn would never check it out).

"Well, dear, if you think so, have her come out for an interview with me and we will see. I am rather tired of all these farm girls."

Mary did appear and Evelyn and I were both impressed with her description of the food she could prepare, including a few of Evelyn's favorite German dishes. She dressed as I had asked, but not even the ugly brown skirt and beige top, lack of makeup and hair pulled back in a bun could disguise her Ava Gardener beauty.

However Evelyn did not seem to notice this, or the quiet fire burning in the girl's eyes when she looked at me; and told her she could have a week's trial. Smiling shyly, Mary thanked us and said she would report for duty the following Monday.

As Mary left in an older car with a driver I couldn't see, Evelyn said, "Well Dan, she appears to be what we need, but I really have to help her with her appearance, the poor thing."

Mary proved to be everything Evelyn needed in a housekeeper. She answered the phone like a professional receptionist, could cook like Martha Stewart and could even do all the garment alterations that Evelyn normally had to take into town. The only flaw was that she seemed very preoccupied with my quarters and laundry. Evelyn, often wondering where she was, once caught her going through my closets garment by garment, a smile on her face.

"She is my housekeeper, not yours, Dan," she complained. "She spends far too much time down there."

When I told this to Mary she cast her eyes down, smiled and said softly, "You have such nice things; I want to keep them nice for you."

She made me feel uncomfortable.

A long time later I found out how Mary really came to us. I had met this strange, almost mystical young man whom I can only describe as a gypsy. I do not mean that in a negative sense. I have met many of the "Romany Folk" all over the world in subsequent years, some who were mysteriously provocative and helpful, others downright con artists. He was a little of both. He lived in a small wooded area close to town, in a cabin filled with objects d'art, fake antiques and wonderful fake jewelry with a few real creations thrown in.

He came around to my office one day, a dark slender figure in a long leather coat—sort of a Vampire look that is popular in films today. He showed me several silver rings and huge turquoise bracelets and necklaces. I bought one ring with the head of Medusa, which I still have to this day, and a squash necklace for Evelyn. Preferring diamonds and pearls, she wore the necklace a few times as a nod to what she called "high-end hippy fashion," but told me not to bring "that odd man" into the house again.

He did enter again in the guise of his cousin Mary. She had been watching me around town for a long time. When the gypsy found out from comments I had made, that we were looking for a good housekeeper. He set it up so that she would be interviewed. I do not know to this day what made her feel she could "get me." It was common knowledge that I was gay—she knew this for sure. Sometimes women who think they're in love feel that this overrides anything and that they can "change" a man. They cannot, as she found out the night I came home from a social event and there she was, laying in my king size waterbed, completely nude.

As I entered the room where a single candle was glowing, she threw back the duvet and, smiling, opened her arms to me. I remember thinking that at that moment, most heterosexual men would have gone weak in the knees and fallen over. Mary was magnificent in ways that most women only dream of. Vargas could never have captured her body on canvas with all its subtle, creamy rich tones. Her breasts, with dark rose areolas, were a triumph of nature; thrusting naturally upward without the fake stiffness of implants. Her eyes glittered like black coals set with jewels and her midnight hair cascaded down one satin shoulder. Even Hugh Hefner would have been struck dumb.

"Mary, what are you doing in my bed?" I whispered.

"Waiting for y'all to get home, now get in bed," she whispered back in a husky voice.

Terrified that Evelyn could hear this exchange, I tried to explain to her that as beautiful as she was, I was not of "that persuasion" and Mrs. Williams would fire her on the spot if she knew she was in my bed.

"But y'all had that guy in your bed," she said.

This irritated me, and I informed her that those situations were different. Because I never discussed my personal life with Mrs. Williams, she, being an "old fashioned woman of high moral standards," thought it perfectly normal that men could bunk together—but a woman in my bed was not to be tolerated.

In actual fact, Evelyn was no stranger to gay life, even back in the 1930s, and knew what was going on. The real truth was that she was jealous of any female influence on me—particularly that of a raving beauty.

Mary got up, a sheet wrapped around her, and sat on a chair, her head down. "I feel so embarrassed," she muttered, "such a fool. I thought y'all liked me."

Putting my arms around her, I told her that I did like her—just not in that way. I went on to say that if I were a regular guy, I would have fallen in love with her by now.

Looking up with tear-hurt eyes, she brushed her hair from her forehead and said: "Really? Someone like you would fall in love with someone like me?"

I then knew that our lifestyle was far beyond her imagination or dreams, and once having her foot in the door, she had fantasized that she could make a dream come true and marry into great wealth and happiness. If I were straight, this might very well have come true for her.

Mary never approached me again and became a model housekeeper, although every once in a while she would give me a quick look with a question mark in her eyes. Evelyn took her under her wing, gave her many dresses and casual outfits and bought her smart shoes. She always referred to her as "that poor, plain Mary."

But soon this domestic tranquility was shattered by a young man called Zeke.

Zeke was the son of Hot Springs' best electrician. He had been part of the original gang of so-called hoodlums Evelyn and I inherited when we took over the roller rink.

I didn't pay much attention to him at first; he was one of those rangy people, all sinew and no fat, prominent veins and very long hands and feet. He had to buy his own roller skates to get anything to fit and he was an extremely fast and aggressive skater, often careering through the rink recklessly, causing the slower kids to shriek in terror and rush to the rails.

Zeke had one of those British-type faces: a high–bridged, aquiline nose; triangular piercing blue eyes; and fine long hair, the kind that had to be washed every day or it would look lank and greasy. Which it often did, sticking out in all directions.

He seemed popular with everyone—sort of a buffoon and jokester. He hung around the girls the same way Doug Berry and the other boys did, but I never saw him in any relationship. He would come out to Maybelline Manor to do minor electrical work for his dad from time to time, and Evelyn liked him. "He is so respectful" she would say, "and so efficient—and has a wonderful voice."

She invited him, on occasion, to one of our weekly home-cooked meals where she and I would be gourmet cooks and plan elaborate re-pasts, complete with wines and after dinner drinks. These meals would be served in the kitchen dining room, the formal dining room being for important occasions only. But still Evelyn would light a candelabra, set the table beautifully with old silver and napery, and insist that we treat the meal like a ritual. "Dinner should be eaten slowly and with good conversation, not gulped down in a hurry like you do, Dan,"

I did eat fast, and still do—and pay for it now, at my age, with various gastric problems and dyspepsia.

It was strange to see Zeke calmly sitting there in this elegant setting wearing cut-off jeans and a tank top. I was highly amused and a bit snobby, thinking that Evelyn had lost her mind to invite this "redneck" 20-year-old for dinner.

Later it was revealed that he had a well-off Aunt from out of town who was liberal-minded and sophisticated; he had picked up manners from her.

Usually he would leave right after dinner, mumbling to me, "See you at the rink" and profusely thanking Mrs. Williams for her hospitality while she tittered and batted her eyes.

One evening he asked me if he could come downstairs and see some of my record albums, which he had noticed while installing our inter-com system.

Taking him to my quarters I showed him my huge collection of clas-sics, jazz, soul, R and B and rock. He loved the rock and enthused over my collection. As we stood by the fireplace he suddenly announced that this room had been the office of his mother when she was the accoun-tant for the previous owners of the estate. She currently worked for a hotel chain.

All at once I did notice the voice Evelyn was talking about: deep and rumbling and sort of muffled-sounding—and somehow sensual.

As we stood close during the stilted conversation about his Mom, I felt strangely too hot; almost faint. It was the most extraordinary situation I had ever encountered in my life, and I wanted him out of there.

He felt something odd, as well. His face turned red and he suddenly wheeled around and yelled, "Well, got to get on home; my Dad will whip my butt!"

I could not define the burning feeling at all—I was not the least bit attracted to Zeke's raggedy and rambunctious style. In a few days I forgot about it and he faded back into the roller rink gang.

Then one weekend he turned up at what we called The Lake Hamilton Yacht Club. This was a well-decorated bar and lounge on the water where people could tie their boats and spend an evening. Once in a while I would take the big, cumbersome Maybelline Queen over, returning home over a tranquil, moonlit lake before midnight. On this particular occasion I was restless and lonely. The club was full as I escorted Evelyn back to the boat, so I decided to get her to bed, wait awhile and then come back. With Sam Saleem out of the picture, Mary in the house and the club only about twenty minutes away, I felt that she would be safe for a couple of hours. We also had some of the security apparatus still active from Rick's days.

When I arrived at the club Zeke was in the bar. He loudly laughed his way to where I sat, accompanied by some of his buddies. They sat down, happy to see me in a relaxed mood and expansive with drinks. We got plastered. Zeke wanted to know all about my California life, what it was like to meet celebrities, and what was the story behind my rock band KIDZ.

As the evening wore on, his buddies got bored with the chitchat and wanted to leave. Zeke, by then three sheets to the wind, claimed he didn't want to leave yet and asked me if he could crash at Maybelline Manor and have someone pick him up the next day?

I said, "Sure, there's a roll-away in the card room."

We stayed at the Yacht Club for another hour while he told me about his immediate dream: to be a professional disc jockey. Noting his unusual voice, I said that I might let him do a commercial for the roller rink on The Silver Ghost show.

"You know The Silver Ghost?" he exclaimed.

I put on my faux Wolfman Jack voice. "Sure I know him, Zeke—I *am* The Silver Ghost."

Zeke thought this was incredible, and laughed insanely all the way down to the pier. We boarded the *Maybelline Queen* on unsteady legs and zigzagged across the lake, shrieking with laughter as I continued with my Silver Ghost routine, doing spoofs on everyone in town. I said "Shhhhhhshh!" as we approached the Manor in the feeble grounds lights. "We can't wake up Mrs. Williams."

As I opened my patio doors with Zeke close behind me, I felt that strange burning sensation again. We tiptoed to my bedroom and he grabbed my arm gently. "Hey, man, can I sleep in the waterbed?" His voice had gotten very deep and both kind and intimate. I looked at him for a moment, uncertain of what to think or do—and suddenly, we were nude in bed.

I won't go into graphic detail; the experience would be impossible to describe in a manner that did not sound like a cross between a Victoria Holt corset-buster novel and pornography. Suffice to say that Zeke and I shared a chemistry that neither of us understood. It was if we'd known each other for many years, down to the last toenail and hair.

You hear talk about "chemistry between people" all the time—but this was a physical reaction that transcended gender or sexual preference. I don't think he cared if I was a man or woman that night. I did not care either. There were no roles played, no special interests, no romance.

Over the next few months I discovered that Zeke was one of those intensely sexual people who liked most everything and everyone. But on that night, during and for several hours after, as I left the bedroom to lie on the couch and catch my breath while he snored away—I burned. I have never had this experience since. And I have known great love. This was not love; it was obsession—an obsession that almost ruined us all.

Zeke became The Silver Ghost turned real. His DJ dreams came true. The next morning he woke up, looking sheepish. "Man, were we drunk last night?" (How many times has that been said over the decades?)

Not knowing what else to do, I made light of the situation even though I was sure this could not be the only time we would be together.

When we went upstairs, Evelyn was in the kitchen with Mary, and said in a bright voice, "Why, hello, Zeke. Did Dan ask you over this morning?"

I told her that his friends had gotten very drunk in the neighborhood and Zeke, frightened of getting into trouble or a car wreck, insisted that they drop him off here.

"Well, that was wise, Zeke, drunks can kill people—and you're welcome any time, isn't that right, Dan?"

Could she not see how flushed I was? "Anytime," I said. Evelyn offered Zeke breakfast. Mary, on the other hand, gave me a long side look that said she knew.

That weekend, after re-creating the disco booth and adding even better mike and sound systems, I introduced The Silver Ghost. Zeke had practiced my fake voice, doing an even better job with it, and his deeper pitch was explained away by the reverb on the mike and the booming speakers as opposed to the more tinny radio speakers. I taught him to make up his face in a version of KISS, using silver with black outlines, and then punked out his hair with silver hair spray.

He was a hit.

Most of the kids knew who he was, of course—but theatre does funny things to people. A good act and a great costume, like a department store Santa, make everyone believe for a little while.

Our affair grew more intense and ended up accompanied by Zeke's favorite rock music. Hour after hour after Evelyn was asleep—and sometimes, dangerously, in the middle of the day, "What are you doing right now, Dan?" would come her voice over the intercom.

"Nothing!" I would holler as Zeke and I struggled into our clothes, giggling like teenagers. "Zeke is here to fix my sound system!"

To this day I cannot listen to *Boston* or *Frampton Comes Alive* without thinking of Zeke.

I didn't put any definition on our relationship then, or boundaries. He'd already detailed all his sexual conquests with girls. I was the first man. He claimed he saw no difference and that sex was sex; he said he couldn't understand "gay life" at all.

This changed one weekend when I took him to a gay party at a well-to-do friend's house in Little Rock. He sat on the floor of the beautifully decorated home filled with equally beautifully dressed men and women, looking mostly amazed and shy. He seemed painfully conscious of his worn Levis, beat up Nikes, Fog Hat tee shirt and plaid jacket. Evelyn suggested many times that I dress him up in my clothes if we went out (by then she was treating us like a couple, David and Jonathan), but they did not fit him well. I thought he was beautiful anyway. Funny how someone you barely noticed for a long time or thought was quite ordinary can become unbelievably beautiful in every way.

My friends took little notice of him, and I explained him away as "a Mrs. Williams makeover project," and straight—suggesting that she was grooming him for our plain and lonely housekeeper. I wanted their lack of attention to stay that way.

At that party I met a male model from Atlanta—a very nice, sweet natured blond with a weight lifter's build and a very open manner. When he indicated he liked me, I invited him home to Maybelline Manor, and told him I would return him to Little Rock the next day.

Zeke was quiet when I dropped him off at his place. The model was stunned when we turned into the entrance of the manor.

"I didn't know y'all were rich!"

He was a nice guy and very sweet-natured. Too much so. All night I kept thinking of Zeke and his dark wild ways and intensity. The next day I drove the model home—I think he knew there was no fire there—even though he expressed a desire to get to know me better. That night, as I sat reading on my couch, there was a knock at the sliding patio door. I looked up and there was Zeke, a haunted look on his face. I could tell he was a little stoned on home-grown pot.

I invited him in and sat back down on the sofa. He stood before me, arms crossed and legs spread—taking deep breaths, his face red.

"I…I don't know how to say this to ya, Danie…" He faltered. "Well, hell, I'll just say it: I really like ya—I mean—more than like—well, okay, when you're tired of the pretty people, let me know!"

And he sped out the door, slamming the slider closed with a bang that almost broke the glass.

Evelyn came rushing down the stairs, "What on earth, Dan?"

I told her Zeke had had another fight with his mother, a woman Evelyn had met and did not like.

Later I hugged myself with glee, crossed the mental boundary—and fell in love.

A huge mistake.

My experiences in Hot Spring may sound like I think I am an incredibly handsome and irresistible creature. I don't view myself that way at all. I have always, and still do, maintain myself: it's part of my career to do so; one must look like what one does or where is the credibility. But I view myself as somewhat average, with the ability to dress and act like

I might be "somebody." I think my early sexual adventures as a boy with straight men, and later on with so-called straight or "bi-sexual" men, were based on something I inherited from my mother: a way of making anyone I was with feel good about themselves. Also, being somewhat of a giver rather than a taker, make them feel good—period. I could, however, be domineering and possessive once I loved someone—again a trait of my mother. But as far as being beautiful is concerned, I have been with enough really beautiful people to know that I was ordinary.

My falling in lust with this young man was doomed from the start.

12

Evelyn's Grandchildren "Take Hot Springs"

Evelyn wanted her grandchildren to visit Hot Springs. Apparently they had come out for the original opening of Hobby's Roller Rink and she wanted them to see how much better everything was now. I suspected that she really wanted to report favorably back to their father, Bill Williams, who continued to pressure her to give it all up and come back to California.

Bill's son Preston was a tall, quiet boy with normal shy teenager interests. One of them was playing the drums. "He could play with your KIDZ band," Evelyn enthused, and I mentally made a note to persuade the group to let him sit in on *one* set.

Billee Rae, Preston's sister, was another matter. Extremely pretty, she had a lithe, marvelous dancer's body and in fact possessed all the dancing grace that Evelyn had had as a girl. She also had her grandmother's come-hither eyes.

At first the both treated me with mild suspicion, as if I were a zoo exhibit. But after a few days, seeing how the kids regarded me, they warmed up.

"You're nothing like Dad said," Billee Rae commented with her Paris Hilton rich-girl aplomb.

She was a great deal like Paris—whom I briefly met at a fundraiser, decades later. Far from the manufactured blond bimbo wild child she portrayed—100% contrived for publicity, Paris was a cool, calm, ladylike creature, lovely and with that special hauteur and restraint that only old-dynasty money can breed.

Billee Rae was also accustomed to the hot discos of California, mostly made popular by the young gay crowd, and could do all the latest dances with flash and style. So Evelyn and I billed her as Billee Rae the Disco Queen straight from Hollywood and devised several outfits, dance routines and lighting effects to show her off. I appeared as her male counterpart in some of the numbers, but she sizzled on her own.

The kids in Hot Springs had never seen anyone like Billee Rae. Doug Berry fell madly in love with her. Unbeknown to Evelyn, indeed to anyone but me, they carried on a wild affair during that visit. Despite the fact that Doug could charm the birds out of the trees, he was out of his depth with Billee Rae, a sad fact I had to tell him after she left town and he came to me, face forlorn, aching with love.

I knew that Billee Rae was equally turned-on by Doug, but I had to explain to him about her father and her family—that they would never allow a serious relationship to develop between their daughter and a young man with no money to speak of, and little background.

"Rich sons-of-bitches and snobs!" he growled. "I know she feels the same way as me, man."

Billee Rae did indeed bring in the boys, who brought in the girls, most of whom came because they were curious to see what this Beauty from Hollywood had that was so "darn special."

What she had was star quality, like her grandmother—no matter how reserved and aloof she looked ordinarily, when she went onstage she lit up the entire room. All the girls wanted to be her friend. All wanted to be *her*!

Evelyn, of course, was proud and regaled her son Bill on frequent phone calls to Palm Springs how wonderful Billee Rae was, how much money was being made, and how popular Preston was as well.

Actually Preston was just there, basking in his sister's shadow. The boys treated him well enough, although I warned them not to include him in any of their parties where home-grown weed was smoked and a lot of beer consumed. Not to mention the sex. Most of the boys were now 18 and over, but Preston was a younger teen with a father who was suspicious of me. I was not about to give Bill Williams any excuse to react to wild party stories.

Classed as "the quiet rich boy," Preston was pretty much left alone, accepted as part of our glamour show but not a player. He did get to sit in one time with KIDZ on the drums—for one number. He wasn't at all bad, got a round of applause, and seemed happy. I liked Preston, and back at The Manor I would spend time with him, talking about his future, what we were planning to do to elevate the business, and share with some insights into my own life—knowing that his Father had presented only negative things about me. I had a feeling that Evelyn was concerned about Preston and instinctively trusted his quiet, thoughtful manners beyond those of her granddaughter. But then Evelyn never was a woman's woman, except when it came to herself.

With the disco show going well, the occasional appearance of Evelyn in exotic costumes and hats to introduce performers (the crowd loved this) and Zeke playing The Silver Ghost for the roller skating sets, the Spa City Roller Rink was getting a huge reputation all over Arkansas. Everywhere Evelyn and I went in town, people treated us like celebrities. She couldn't pick up a tab at the high-end eateries like the Saw Mill Depot, our favorite hangout, although I seldom received the same courtesy on my own.

Still, there were those who did not think we were wonderful. They viewed us as over-the-top Hollywood types: gaudy, with loose morals, catering to the wildness of the teenagers with our rock 'n' roll and half nude girls shimmying onstage.

"Heaven knows *what* goes on down there!"

"Why, I've heard all kinds of things go on in that old house behind the rink…and it's *her* property!"

Actually, there *were* things going on in the old house beside the unfinished Go-Kart track. Once, when I was showing banker Mort Cox our plans for development, we walked into the stale, rat-infested dump, the floor was littered with condoms and roaches (the marijuana kind, not the insects, which I was sure were also present).

With knowing eyes, Mort said, "You need to tear this eyesore down, Danie…someone could get hurt in more ways than one."

Although I realized he was right, I told him Evelyn would scream over the expense for demolition unless she was *forced* to tear it down.

Two days later she was served with a paper stating that the building at Gulpha Gorge was to be razed immediately due to being deemed as an unsafe structure located too close to public businesses frequented by children.

This got me off the hook with the older boys who now had reason to growl that their "pad" was gone—damn the City! But Zeke had somehow acquired a large trailer house in a wooded lot not far from the rink, and this became their new clubhouse. I was to visit there many times—another line I crossed, another mistake.

Tearing down the old shack did score us some points with what I call "the Church People"; there were a few more tentative smiles and "hellos" when Evelyn and I appeared downtown. Gushing matrons urged us to visit their churches. We always said we would, and we never did. Being a free thinker, Evelyn did not like organized religion. She especially shuddered at thought of potluck suppers, quilting bees, rummage sales ("I keep my designer garments forever," she would say). The fact that everyone was so nosy at Church events irritated her no end.

Perhaps she was trying to protect me and my private life despite the fact I'd been brought up Church of England as a boy, and later my parents became decent Baptists. I knew very well how to "work" the church scene and fit right in—I had played piano in church, sung in the choir and had sex with cute Danny Johnson up in the dark classrooms while revivals were going on downstairs. We'd told ourselves we were just practicing "how to make out with our girlfriends if they ever decide to go all the way."

But Evelyn was firm about not joining a church. "Tell 'em I follow the Buddha philosophy," she would say.

My final story to the Church People was that as a new resident in Hot Springs, Mrs. Williams felt she had to be impartial and not favor one church over another. I added that she and I observed Sundays at home in prayer and meditation, and I played sacred music for Mrs. Williams while our cook prepared Sunday dinner. Actually I played Broadway hits and we sang along, Evelyn hitting the high notes in her warbling coloratura, arms flung out, chest expanded, head back. Mary, walking past the archway between the kitchen and living room, would roll her eyes and put her head down. Once I asked if she thought we were a little crazy, and she replied, "Noooo, rich people have their ways."

A long time later, after our Major Domo Steve Wyatt appeared, Evelyn and I were asked by Henderson College in Arkadelphia to judge The Miss Henderson Beauty Pageant.

"I don't know anything about judging," complained Evelyn. I assured her I would help her out, and we prepared for the event. They had also requested that I play the grand piano on the stage as part of the entertainment. This made Evelyn more enthusiastic to appear. "You can be like Liberace, Dan—knock their socks off!"

When the day arrived for the pageant, Mrs. Williams and I—and even Steve—all came down with the flu; we had temperatures of 102. "We can't let them down!" croaked Evelyn. "It's been all over the radio that I'm judging the pageant—we have to go."

We did go, and I, dressed in a powder blue tuxedo with a ruffled shirt, ascended the stage with weak knees to play a religious medley I had arranged, a mix of "In the Garden" and "How Great Thou Art" with a lot of arpeggios and Liberace runs. There were even candelabra on the piano to complete the image. As I thundered down the keyboard to the grand finale of "How Great Thou Art," I looked down at a white-faced but beaming Evelyn in the front row, and knew the Church people accepted us at last.

The applause was prolonged, and on the way out of the auditorium people grabbed our hands and clapped me on the back, thanking me profusely for such an inspirational rendition. "God has his hands on yours," enthused one woman. "And bless you, Mrs. Williams, for helping us out."

Nodding wanly, her face dotted with perspiration, she whispered, "Let's get out of here, Dan; I don't think I can make it home."

Along the way both Steve and I stopped to throw up in the bushes by the road. Evelyn sat stoically in the car. We all were laid up for three days, living on juice and Evelyn's famous chicken soup—but we had, I was sure, secured our reputation with the Church People for good.

Or not.

13

Catering to the "Sinners" in Town

One morning over a breakfast of scrambled eggs, country ham, biscuits and red eye gravy, I approached Evelyn. "My dear, remember your bareback riding days with the circus?" Giggling coyly, her blue eyes turned up and sparkled under the chandelier light overhead—always on a soft focus dimmer, even in the morning—she replied, "Well, yes, Dan, I do think about that now and then, especially when I see how the crowd reacted when Billee Ray danced." (Billee Rae and Preston had left for home the week before, much to the agony of Douglas Berry).

"Darling, how would you like to be up there again?"

"But I couldn't get up on a *horse*!" she gasped. Then, giggling, "Besides, it was mostly fake."

"Yes, but the point is—they loved *you*, fake bareback or not, and you still have that pizzazz."

Her eyes sharpened with curiosity. "What scheme are you hatching now, Dan? Remember my time of life."

She never use the word "age" for herself, it was always "my time of life."

I told her I was concerned about the rising gossip from certain factors in Hot Springs that we were too showy, less than moral, and catering only to the "sinners" in town.

Indignant over the possibility that her respectability was in question, Evelyn huffed and puffed for the next half-hour about what two-faced hypocrites they all were, how her Father was a monument of class and respectability, and practically supported their grand church in Chicago. He was always insisting his girls be dressed flawlessly, complete with white gloves every Sunday, as opposed to the local Hot Springs bumpkins who wore K-Mart dresses and thought a gaudy brooch or fake pearls were fashionable.

As Evelyn went on her tirade she literally puffed air out of the side of her mouth, her shoulder jerking in tandem. Suddenly she stopped and, resigned, asked me what we should do.

With the enthusiasm born of many nights putting together my plan for a roller skating show modelled after ice shows like Ice Capades, I proposed that we postpone the Disco Dance, Rock Shows, and The Silver Ghost acts for a few weeks and instead, present family entertainment for all. We could revive the weekday kiddy and senior citizen sessions by offering discounted package deals and special theme music for civic and senior groups. There was a large retired community in and around Hot Springs. At Lake Katherine these people had their own club, and young piano virtuoso Rick Warren made good money playing there. I figured he'd be an excellent source of PR for our 40s and 50s weeknight swing parties, which even the dourest church person would find fun and wholesome. The fact that we had good food—gourmet hamburgers and southern-fried everything—was a plus.

To my surprise this plan seemed to work almost immediately, as if all the church people had been waiting for us to come to our senses.

Evelyn, meanwhile, seemed to always know which deacon or Sunday school teacher would not be opposed to sharing a "little snort" in her private bar behind the two-way mirror. Several times I'd open the door to gales of laughter as Evelyn regaled one of the church people with one of her more sanitized risqué stories.

"Y'all really *did* watch Seabiscuit win the Preakness?" bellowed one thin, gray-skinned teacher as he brandished a wine glass, his eyes glassy and bright. "Why, Ms. Williams, y'all don't look old enough to have been there."

Again with her famous twitter and coy under–the–lashes look, Evelyn murmured "A woman is born, eventually she passes on; what she does in between is up to her. Age is only a number."

Looking up to see me standing there with amusement on my face, Evelyn would add, "Oh, Dan, Deacon So-and-So here was feeling a lot of back pain from the skating. I thought a little wine would ease him... just for medicinal purposes, you know, dear."

The Deacon found an excuse to leave at that point, mumbling in my ear, "Don't tell my wife" on his way out the door.

I didn't. The success of *Hollywood on Wheels,* as we called it, would depend on the goodwill and attendance of all the co-existing townspeople—the goodie-two-shoes and everyone else, including tourists.

To be fair to all the young people I held auditions for the show. I knew in advance who my principals would be; I even wrote the script around their appearances and skills. Fortunately a few of the church people's children proved to be very good, and some were beautiful—but at first the rehearsals were a nightmare, with the church kids standing arrogantly off to the side looking at my group as if they were covered in dog turds.

Kids, however, are pretty much all the same under the patina of circumstance and upbringing. After a lot if diplomatic grandstanding on my part they finally settled down. Everyone was given equally important roles, and the show itself levelled the social field. I put together *Hollywood on Wheels* as opposed to writing it. Evelyn was delighted—we were at last giving a real show after all that Rock 'N' Roll. She was a vital source of information on old Hollywood and the Golden Age. Not only had she actually been there for some of it, she had met a lot of the stars such as Sonja Henie, whom I was to portray in the show—beard, moustache and all.

I collected sound tracks from the top musicals of the Golden Era. Steve, my friend from *The Sentinel Record*, had a huge collection and my buddy over at the radio station recorded them onto tape.

We had Fred Astaire and Ginger Rogers dancing "The Continental"; wacky music from Spike Jones that we used for a Laurel and Hardy skit; tracks from *Guys and Dolls*; music from Sonja Henie's skating films; "Indian Fire Dance" for the Jeanette McDonald and Nelson Eddie skit; and, the *Hiawatha* theme.

Nadia's Theme became the balletic background for a skit I wrote where the ugly duckling becomes the White Swan by stepping through the same mirror in which she bemoaned her ugliness every night. Sort of *Cinderella Becomes Princess via Ugly Duckling and Black Swan*. Walt Disney would have been proud to have been so cleverly plagiarized.

Knowing you could un-freeze even the toughest audience if you got them to laugh, I decided to go "butch drag" and play the Norwegian star, Sonja Henie, myself. This involved having a special snow sleigh built and painted—in the Maybelline colors, of course. Instead of sleigh runners, it moved onto the rink floor on wheels, the whole rig pulled by some of the younger, less talented kids dressed as snow elves. (Well, it *was* a tribute to Hollywood, where anything is possible, and deer costumes were not in the budget.)

When Opening Night arrived, nobody knew what they were about to see. Including me.

I entered the lights backward so the audience saw only the back of the glamorous Miss Henie wearing a long, flowing, red velvet cape trimmed in ermine; her long, shining blonde hair cascading down her back and one white gloved hand regally waving.

Once in position at the back of the rink, she turned, smiled, and regally stepped down onto the floor, shedding her cape as she commenced her famous solo number on roller skates. Her sparkling silver dress sent shimmers of light across the darkened rink; her tanned legs were delicately poised to skim out over the wooden floor like a feather.

Except…wait! Ms. Henie has a beard and moustache, eyes with sword-length lashes, and round spots of rouge on her cheeks. And she can't skate! She *thinks* she can skate because there she goes, staggering all around the rink, but her arms flail wildly as she struggles to keep balance. Then she pirouettes and skates backward with all the grace of a grizzly bear on a frozen pond—all the while turning her delusional red joker-lipped smile on the stunned audience.

Finally they get it—it's a *clown*! And everyone starts to laugh.

I had two, huge over-inflated balloons as boobs, and after a couple of staggering passes around the rink, nearly but never quite falling down (which takes some skill and a lot of rehearsals). I came to a stop at the back of the rink, again with one arm raised as if I had just executed the most brilliant skate-waltz in the world and expected huge applause.

The announcer boomed, "Miss Henie will now attempt to do a 'never been done before' leap over five people lying on the floor. Are there any volunteers, please?" A portion of the overhead rafters was draped in black so as to hide the little wood platform where Doug Berry was sitting to handle the rope-and-bar rig we'd installed the week before. We'd had only rehearsed this trick twice.

The volunteers laid side-by-side on the floor, five people deep. After a drum roll, I pawed my skates back like a bullfight bull, then put on a burst of speed and skated as fast as possible towards the prone bodies, the idea being that I leap as gracefully as a gazelle over them and land on my feet daintily on the other side: *Ta Daaaaa!*

I could have no more pulled that off than I could have flown to moon, but at the last moment the rope and bar rig, securely fastened like a trapeze, would be dropped down by Doug. I would grab it and swing out over the bodies, landing on the other side with flair.

When I look back on it now, I wonder how I did it without breaking my arms or legs. During the two rehearsals I'd landed fairly well on my feet long enough to strike the dramatic *Ta Daaaaaa!* pose. In reality there should have been twenty rehearsals and coaching by a trapeze artist. But when you're young and committed you think everything will go great.

Ironically, had things actually gone that way on opening night, the act would have bombed. It was not a funny finale, and I was the show's clown. I got a few laughs during the first portion of my act as I mugged and stumbled around the floor, but after the drumroll the room fell deadly silent as the audience waited to see this fool kill himself. I started my approach. The bar did drop on time (please be there Doug I prayed) and I did grab it with sweating hands and I did barely skim up and over the prone volunteers, one of whom who actually clamped his hands over his head in fear. I landed on the other side with a thump, on both feet, and struggled to get into the Sonja *Ta Daaaa!* pose. Instead I pinwheeled madly towards the audience, fighting for balance, and fell forward onto the floor with my hands jutting out at the last minute to save my face.

And with a loud BANG, my rubber boobs exploded.

The audience roared with laughter as I sat up, a woebegone look on my face as my hands scrambled all over my drooping gown looking for the lost knockers. I had the presence of mind to go with it, crying "*Ooohhh noooo!*" and throwing the skirt over my head as I skated offstage to thunderous applause. Sonja was a hit.

We kept that finale in the show.

Everyone in town, it seemed, was in on the production. I had independent carpenters build the flat sets, the sleigh and Mrs. Williams' skating platform. A sweet and shy and adorable girl named Angela (Sugar as a nickname) helped Evelyn decorate and sew the costumes that I had designed. Angela was in Evelyn's eye, the perfect girl for her equally shy grandson, Preston. I think the kids actually dated a time or two, and they looked natural together. But of course, Preston went back home and that was that. Had something actually developed as Evelyn hoped, perhaps Angela would today be a millionaire's wife here in Southern California. But she married Hot Spring's top plumber's son and had a lovely family instead.

We foraged as many attics and thrift stores in Little Rock as we could find for evening gowns and old tuxedos for the principle acts, and The Showman's association actually came up with a Laurel and Hardy costume set that included padding for Hardy. The chorus costumes were red, black and white—Maybelline colors again—but it was Evelyn's ensemble that was spared no expense.

She only learned during rehearsals what her starring role would be. The finale number was a rousing chorus of the upbeat rendition of the song "Hollywood." At the beginning of the number the skaters and principals would all be on the floor executing figure 8 patterns, with Mrs. Williams waiting in the wings in her Mae West costume. As the music progressed, the skaters would wind around to Evelyn and two of the male skaters would grasp her firmly by the waist and pull her out onto the rink floor, her long, billowing skirt hiding the little platform with its swiveling skate wheels that made her appear to glide. I taught her to move her hips and legs slightly to give the impression she was really roller skating, and she remembered how to gracefully wave her arms around and smile, from her circus bareback-riding days.

Her costume was made of 45 yards of Italian silk taffeta, deep red with ruching and flounces billowing down over a full skirt hooped underneath. The bodice began with a sharp "V" at the waist, widening up to a heart shaped bust-line—her corset padded to enhance the Mae West image we were trying for. The entire ensemble was trimmed in sparkling silver sequins and lace and her up-swept platinum wig was topped by a huge portrait hat with white feathers cascading down. Mae had never looked so good!

The rest of the chorus had an initial in silver rhinestones on the front of their costume that spelled out the word "Hollywood"; Evelyn was the

"Y" in the center. After gliding her around the rink once, the chorus assembled itself with Evelyn in the center of the floor facing the audience. They did a series of high kicks and knee pumps in synchronized rhythm, all very Busby Berkley, while Evelyn swayed back and forth to the music, which changed to "There's No Business like Show Business." They sang along to the sound track, Evelyn's warbling soprano rising over everyone else. Just as they approached the finale of the song where is goes "So let's go on with the SHOOOOWWWW!" the line began a "wheel." A wheel on skates takes precision as the entire line turns a full circle, half the skaters going forward and the other half skating backward. Evelyn, being in the middle, simply turned, waved, smiled and sang.

It was very strenuous for anyone, let alone a woman in her 70s, but she did it with great aplomb and energy night after night and never complained. Indeed it seemed to energize her more each time—and each time the applause was thunderous.

But Doug Berry's "Indian Fire Dance" nearly stole the show. We placed two of the old iron cauldrons filled with kerosene from the KIDZ act on the rink floor and dimmed the lights. Doug appeared in only a leather loin cloth and a head band with a feather. His hairless, chiseled body gleamed with bronze body paint and his natural dark good looks were enhanced by makeup sculpting—he was a true Hiawatha, Longfellow's Indian Prince.

Skating fast in a series of complicated patterns all over the rink, he approach one cauldron with flames leaping up and trailing black smoke, pre-lit by stage hands dressed in black. Without stopping he would leap over the cauldron, his body in full extension, land on the other side and continue skating to the next cauldron, where he would repeat the stunt.

Since Doug wore only a jock strap under his loincloth, I feared each night for his ability to procreate later on in life. My script for this number was much more sedate, but he wanted to do it this way, so I let him. People gasped and *ooo'd* and *awwww'd* each time he flew over the flames.

I had tears in my eyes ever night as I stood in the dark at the side of the rink and watched Ginger Rogers float on wings of white chiffon and feathers with Fred Astaire under a follow spot, Laurel and Hardy doing hilarious pratfalls and an ugly duckling step regally forth from a magic mirror as a beautiful white swan. These were the misfit kids of

Hot Springs. The poor and disenfranchised, many of them considered by the more fortunate to be "scummy lowlifes."

But in *Hollywood on Wheels* they were *somebody*. They were stars. And they did shine.

14

A Different Kind of Drama

This discovery of how youth can be galvanized into wanting to be better people, how they can be assured that it is OK to dare to have a dream or two with the knowledge that at least one dream could come true—how their lives could change no matter if they were poor, ethnic, gay, lesbian or transgender—stayed with me all through the decades that followed. But in Hot Springs all I knew was that these young people had talents that they did not know they had, while I had a stage and a big mouth and simply put them on it. The fact that they did star and shine and their self-worth elevated, equalized their position in the community. Though I had it all, I was their friend.

I think this was in part the reason so many of them tried to get up close and personal with me, often appearing unexpectedly in the manor when I came home after an evening out. One very cute young man, obsessed with getting a high-class girlfriend who would help him out of a life of drunken and abusive parents living on welfare, appeared in the famed water bed one evening.

Amused, because I knew he had no gay tendencies whatsoever and was too shy and naive to be a horn-dog hustler, I said "Eric, why would you want to try to sleep with me?"

He looked down and blushed. "Well, you've done a lot for me, giving me a job at the rink and helping me read better and all—"

"So that's a reason to try to sleep with someone when you don't want to? Those are things I do all the time for a lot of people who are trying."

"I know," he replied, "but that's all I have to give you."

I was deeply touched by this innocence—I hugged him for a second and told him to go on home, assuring him that he would find a great girl someday and would know how to bring up his kids right.

But at the same time I was having problems with Zeke. *Hollywood on Wheels* took almost all my time and Zeke had been acting a bit distant—spending most of his spare time at his new "party pad," the trailer house on the hill above the rink. Because it was in a wooded and secluded area, he could crank up the rock music with no complaints and the trailer was always crowded with guys and gals getting drunk or stoned on homegrown weed.

Now and then I sneaked in through the back door which opened to his private master bedroom. Without talking much we would fly at each other, the strange chemistry that bound us sizzling like bacon in a frying pan, and often burning up! Every once in a while I'd see his triangular eyes boring into mine as if he were searching to see where and what I was. But most of the time it was like a wrestling exercise straight out of the *Kama Sutra*—no position too difficult, no action too wild.

Hours later, exhausted, I would leave him snoring and sneak out the back door in the cold light of pre-dawn to be home before Evelyn woke up.

Despite the intense sex, Zeke became more and more uncommunicative and I sensed something else was going on in his life beyond my influence.

One weekend night I wasn't worried about leaving early because it was a weekend and I'd told Evelyn I would be working late and would just stay overnight at the nearby trailer ("But Dan, I hope you don't become white trash!" she'd cautioned). As Zeke and I were falling into a Drambuie-induced sleep, I heard two girls talking loudly and drunkenly through the thin wall between Zeke's bedroom and the next.

"I could do Zeke," proclaimed one girl. I recognized her voice as belonging to one of our employees, a young lady whose reputation was that she would sleep with anyone and everyone. She was the least attractive of our group, possessing a pudgy face, kinky black hair, a thick waist and huge thighs. In fact the boys nicknamed her "Thunder-thighs," at which she would just laugh, toss back her frizzy hair and retort, "All the more to grab ya with!"

I was fully awake now, outraged at her bold bragging. Zeke had known her since grammar school and had never given her the time of day. She had never given him the come-on either, but that was before his professionally hi-lighted and cut hair, trendy clothes, party pad and fame as The Silver Ghost.

"But you can't hit on Zeke," protested the other girl, "you'd have to deal with Danie King."

"Shit, I can handle *that* old fag," scorned thunder-thighs, and she continued on with a list of all the things she would like to do with my lover.

I rose, went into Zeke's small bathroom, cleaned up, dressed and walked out the door to the front of the trailer. As I passed by the bedroom with its door open framing the two girls gossiping on the bed, I stopped, leaned in and with a smile said, "Good evening ladies; have a good time," and left the trailer as they sat there with their mouths open.

15

The Post Hollywood on Wheels Party

Evelyn decided to throw a post-*Hollywood on Wheels* cast party, and invited everyone in town along with the cast members and their parents. Stories of how lavish this party would be sent a lot of parents to the attic or thrift stores to find something formal to wear—Evelyn insisted on black tie.

It was a perfect late spring night. The front of the estate was glowing with lights, both from the house itself and candles in hurricane lamps placed all around the circular drive. These same candles continued at the back of the Manor, lining the pathways to the lake, the pier and even the *Maybelline Queen*, which was also decked out with twinkling white Christmas lights. Evelyn had wanted arc lights at the entrance to the property "Academy Award style" she said, but the closest rental place was Little Rock, too far away to bother.

The buffet table was a triumph of crystal, antique silverware, and damask napery in Evelyn's gold and white pattern. Glimmering tapers, illuminating the cascading freesia, white roses, lilies and ivy that decorated the massive table. It groaned with succulent sea food gumbo, smoked turkeys sliced and then reassembled back to their original shapes, poached salmon, ratatouille and other vegetable dishes swimming in butter sauce. A complicated Melrose salad served in red cabbage bowls created a sensation, and the kitchen table groaned under the weight of deserts which included a huge English trifle, *crème brûlée*, shoo-fly and pecan pies with crusts made of bacon grease instead of shortening. This was a recipe I had learned from an old black lady years before and once tasted, makes any other crust taste like cardboard. Mary and I worked hard on the food, which everyone assumed had been catered somehow from Hollywood.

Evelyn was a vision in a gold lace theatre suit, her ears twinkling with diamonds and pearls and her famous huge emerald cut diamond ring trailing fire from her small and perfectly manicured hand.

She was everywhere at once—throwing out jazzy one-liner *bon mots*, laughing uproariously at some cornball southern joke as if Johnny Carson himself had told it. Senator Bud Canada, a widower or divorcee, was a next-door neighbor and appeared with his daughter. Evelyn immediately took possession of this handsome and distinguished man, laying her hand lightly on his arm as she steered him around the Manor, eyes looking coyly up at him, sparking with humor and suggestion. Evelyn fancied Bud and had told me earlier that she had been "thinking of having that little surgery down there" so she could start dating him.

Knowing the much younger women in Bud's social circle and how sought after he was, I did not have the heart to tell her that he would never marry or have an affair with a woman 20 years older, no matter how glamorous or rich. I let her have this one delusion, figuring it would take its own course and Bud would get married to someone soon.

We had hired two hunky bartenders, one of them being Bruce, a half-breed American Indian who was almost impossibly handsome (Bruce did a lot of "show pony" appearances for us as a chauffeur, bartender, escort, and so on. He was always trying to get me to sleep with him and his girlfriend, but I was far too proud to—he was just too impossibly good looking and knew it); and the other one who was also Hollywood handsome in the manner of Alan Ladd—his fiancée being a half-breed Indian girl related to Bruce. He actually went home with me after a big night at the yacht club, telling me he was curious about gay sex. So I showed him—and was surprised to find him gentle, reciprocal and easygoing about it all. We became friends after that one time and later I was saddened to find out he OD'd from heroin in Little Rock.

Evelyn had also hired a pianist whose playing kept the downstairs bar packed, and Zeke finally arrived. Dressed only in a black shirt and jeans, he walked into the kitchen and peered into the living room where Evelyn and I were surrounded with people. He gave me a small, wry smile and a heads-up sign and slouched down to the bar were most of the young crowd were.

After a while I grew tired and hot and decided to go to my quarters and change out of my tuxedo into more casual attire. After taking off my clothes, I wandered naked out onto my flagstone patio. Above me I could hear the crowd in the living room, but they could not see me unless they knew where to look. A full moon had risen over Lake Hamilton and added its radiant light to the hundreds of candles we had placed everywhere. Curtains of wild honeysuckle vines cascaded down over the trees and bushes on either side of the property, their white blossoms glowing like stars in the ambient light from the moon, the hot and humid air redolent with their sweet scent.

Looking at even more light patterns wavering on the waves lapping the shoreline, I suddenly did not care who saw me and ran towards the water, feet springing on the lawn grass. I dove in, scattering diamonds of light. Coming to the surface and flinging mossy lake water out of my hair, I stared up at the glowing and pulsing house, party in full swing—and felt suddenly very alone. What was I doing here, anyway?

Feeling depressed and isolated, I slowly made my barefoot way back to my quarters, slightly annoyed that no one had even seen me running nude in the moonlight, a tragic and beautiful Greek statue come to life.

My pity-party ended moments later. I entered my rooms, dripping wet, and crossed to the little hall leading to the laundry room for a bath towel. The door was locked, but through it I heard a man's muffled voice and a female's giggle followed by moans. Thinking that some of the kids had gone in there for a quickie, I was filled with rage over the rudeness of such a scene at Evelyn's wonderful, upscale party given for them.

I pounded on the door. "Open up!"

The door opened a crack and Zeke stuck his head out, eyes bleary with booze. "Hey man, cool it; I'm just having a little weed in here so Ms. Williams wouldn't find out."

Not smelling the distinctive herb on his breath and knowing he could have taken a sneak-a-toke outside anywhere on the spacious grounds without discovery, I pushed the door wide open.

Zeke stood there stark naked, his erect, considerable endowment slowly descending. Backed up against the dryer, her mouth open in surprise, was thunder-thighs, her large, floppy breasts swaying over her pudgy stomach, her kinky hair sticking out in all directions. She had kept her threat; she had "done" Zeke, or was in the process.

She started to wail that she was sorry, words stuttering out between hiccups, begging me not to let Ms. William's know.

"She isn't going to know," I said in a quiet voice, "because you're fired."

By this time Zeke had his pants on and thunder-thighs was struggling into her own underwear, hair flopping all over as she struggled to cram her gelatinous breasts into her cheap bra.

She burst into tears at my statement, and I told a confused-looking Zeke to get her the hell out of the house by the back door.

They left in a cloud of sobs and hiccups, and with an even heavier heart I went upstairs to thank everyone and tell Evelyn I was going to bed. No one seemed to notice I was leaving.

16

Zeke Goes AWOL

The next week was slow, and I felt like I was walking underwater. Evelyn noticed something was wrong and told me to take a few days off and stay at home relaxing with her and watching old classics. I did just that, and she started to lift my spirits. Several times she would say "Dan, I have been thinking..." and then stop. I would inquire what she had been thinking and she would murmur, "Oh, nothing," and change the subject.

The Silver Ghost show was to resume the next weekend, but Zeke did not show up for it. A few days later he called and begged that I reinstate thunder-thighs as an employee. Resigned and just plain weary of drama, I said, "Your girlfriend can come back if you come back and do your Silver Ghost routine again."

"She's not my girlfriend!" he yelled. "Can't you understand, Danie? She or any other girl I f— has nothing to do with you and me and what we have; can't you lighten up?"

With hope blooming in my heart I did lighten up and told him I was a fool and sorry—that basically I was just mad that he was having sex where Mrs. Williams could have walked in. "Well," he snickered, sounding like the old Zeke, "she could walk in on *us* anytime."

The conversation ended with funny possibilities of what Evelyn would do if she walked in on us, and Zeke promised to show up Friday as usual.

Friday night came and Zeke sauntered into my office carrying his costume and makeup kit. With a curt nod to me at my desk, he went into the bathroom and started applying the Silver Ghost face. As he had not said a word, I walked to the door and watched him stare at himself in the mirror. His expression seemed grim and haunted somehow, his eyes staring wide open with the whites showing all around the irises.

"Zeke, what's the matter?" I whispered. "Are you okay?" I moved into the bathroom to put my arms around him.

He recoiled like a rattlesnake, whipping around to face me—and suddenly his long, strong fingers were around my throat as he screamed, "*The matter is leave me alone, leave me alone Danie, I don't want nothing from you anymore, I don't want this face, leave me alone!*" And with each tortured word he banged my head against the tile wall—his fingers getting tighter and tighter.

All of my life, whenever I'm confronted by violence I am suddenly unafraid. Something like rage rises up and I kind of black out and meet the violence head on—perhaps a throwback to some ancient British Noble who said, "How dare thou lay a finger upon my person?"

Jamming my knee into Zeke's crotch broke his stranglehold, but I must have followed it with a right hook to his head, for when I came to my senses he was on the floor weeping like a child, looking up at me with tear–filled, frightened eyes, his hand covered with blood from a cut on his cheek made by my big Medusa ring.

Filled with instant remorse, I leaned over, exclaiming, "Oh, Zeke, Babe I am so sorry!"

He leaped to his feet, looked wildly around, and fled out of the rink.

Just at that time Evelyn had arrived with Mary. Rushing into the office Evelyn exclaimed, "Dan, that was Zeke running out of here like the devil was chasing him and all bloody; what on earth—?"

Lamely I told her that Zeke's mom didn't want him to hang out at the Roller Rink anymore—we had had words over this, he had run into the bathroom to slam the door on me and crashed his cheek against the hard metal edge of the mirror, which happened to be standing open.

"Why, that bitch," growled Evelyn. "I'll handle *her*, you just go after Zeke and calm him down. Take my car, maybe he'll think I'm in it and let you at least talk to him."

Seeing the logic in this illogical suggestion, and knowing she hated being driven in my "blue job," I tore out of the rink parking lot in her Cadillac. I knew Zeke had not taken off with the friends who had brought him because they were all standing around the parking lot gossiping about what happened between Zeke and King.

As I drove up the dark, winding woodland road to his trailer I vowed to get to the bottom of everything. The problem could not be because I was too possessive; we'd already resolved our "space case," and I was determined to keep my end of the bargain.

Suddenly I saw him in the headlights, trudging slowly along with his head down. He limping, having lost one of his rubber thongs. Overcome with guilt and feeling like a monster, I pulled over, rolled down the passenger window and softly called, "Hey Zeke, please get in and let's talk quietly. I am so, so sorry, man."

Turning a white face to me, black streaks of blood still running down from his cut, he bellowed, "*I told you—just leave me alone!*" and plunged into the bushes. Knowing that it would be hard to find him in the dark in this frame of mind, I slowly drove back to the rink and parked in the shadows to think for a moment. I noticed that my Corvette was gone, Mary having taken Evelyn back to the Manor, where she was probably waiting for me to bring a contrite Zeke back and have a wonderful "making up" party. I decided to drive on up to his trailer and give one more chance to any kind of reconciliation—our relationship could not end on this bad of a note.

As I drove the big Caddy into Zeke's parking area all I heard was the crunch of gravel. The night was silent, not a cricket or a bird to be heard. I could see the outline of the trailer against the night sky, but no lights were on. He wasn't there yet, probably wandering around the woods, sobbing and bleeding.

Sighing and laden with even more guilt, I rolled down the window and lit a cigarette, my hand illuminated only by the car's spaceship dashboard lights. All at once there was an explosion of brilliant light accompanied by a flash of intense pain as a fist came out of nowhere and crashed into my forehead. Dazed, I looked up into a face filled with malevolence and hatred. At first I thought it was Zeke—it looked like Zeke, except that Zeke did not have jutting breasts or wear a dress.

It was Zeke's mother, Rhonda, standing there with balled fists. She shrieked "You are *not* going to butt f— my son again, you—" and here she let loose a string of sexual expletives that would make a hardened criminal serving life in prison blush.

Somewhere in the back of my mind another Danie was amused at her accusations of predator and butt f—ing amongst other scummy titles; she obviously did not know her seductive and predatory son at all, and was jealous that anything or anyone could take him away from her control. The control factor I knew about from many long conversations with Zeke.

Her tirade, which flecked my face with spittle, ran on another three minutes, then she drew her arm back for another punch. But her husband loomed up out of the dark behind her and pinned her arms to her side.

"There, there, that's enough, honey," he admonished. "Son, y'all just better leave now and don't come back here no more."

He was no doubt fearing assault and battery suits from our attorney and maybe remembering all the money he'd made doing electrical work at the Spa City Roller Rink and at Maybelline Manor, often with Evelyn's pretty maid bringing him hot lunch and cold beer. He also *knew* me, and I think on some level he knew about Zeke and me—perhaps he'd even have had a little *mano y mano* himself as a youth.

As I drove slowly away, head throbbing, Rhonda screamed, "And get yourself another Silver Fox!"

I stopped the car with a screech and yelled back: "*Not 'Fox'— 'GHOST!' It's 'The Silver GHOST'!*", and tore down the driveway, shaking like a leaf.

Looking back now, and having met and even counseled hundreds of women of all ages, I know that under extreme duress, mothers can have a complete personality change when they feel that they have to protect their young. Mrs. Williams and I had met Rhonda when we came into the hotel restaurant as customer, and while not very friendly, she was civil enough. I remember her looking at me with a guarded expression on her face, as if trying to figure me out or place me in some zone where she was comfortable. She may have been, for personal reasons, homophobic; I'll never know. And heaven knows what Zeke may have told her when she questioned him about why he spent so much time with me and at Maybelline Manor.

My assessment is that when Zeke started to feel trapped by my assuming we were a "couple," however secret we thought we were being, his mother's mental images of "enslavement" may have gotten worse and more graphic—with her son as some kind of victim led along by the evil Pied Piper King. The strange thing about this is: why would a seemingly intelligent woman not know that it takes two to tango, and that our relationship had gone on far too long for Zeke to claim a gun had been metaphorically pointed at his head while I demanded he drop his trousers?

The guilt I felt during the next few weeks was not based upon Rhonda's venomous accusations; I never seduced or took advantage of her precious boy. It was that strange chemistry that burned us and pulled us together, not who did what to whom. Always the romantic and never clinical about sex (I hate people who always ask, "What are you into?" or worse yet, "Are you a top or bottom?" These things are so limiting in life's experiences and rather cretinous.) Zeke and I played all roles when it came down to it—but if anything, he was the more aggressive and domineering, at least sexually.

Evelyn was uncharacteristically calm about the Zeke incident, even after he suddenly disappeared from Hot Springs and no one knew where he had gone. I panicked when this happened. It seemed so extreme; what would the witch do next?

Rumors went flying around town: supposedly Zeke was in an institution with a nervous breakdown; he'd been sent to Jackson, Mississippi to live with kinfolk; he was in Kentucky, same deal (Rhonda apparently had kinfolk all over the south). I actually paid some of the boys to search for him everywhere except in an institution. That was a stretch, even for Rhonda.

Knowing Zeke loved pool, the boys partied and played pool in Jackson. No Zeke. They took off for Bowling Green, Kentucky—beer busts and pool houses. He wasn't there. Of course all the guys loved this spy vs. spy stuff—there were more Zeke sightings than sightings of Elvis, who would pass away a few months later. In their minds the boys were The King's Knights, sallying forth to rescue a poor soldier imprisoned by an evil witch.

Rhonda was hit hard for her son's vanishing act. No one blamed me—they all knew how close Zeke and I were...in fact, a few closet-case kids would write me little sympathy notes slipped under my door.

One of the boys was only 13 years-old and looked like a little Mick Jagger. Acted like Mick too, swaggering around slightly effeminately, with tight jeans and wild hair. The little girls loved him, and he was always with a gaggle of girls. Few guys bothered with him due to his outspoken cheekiness. He knew who he was, which impressed me, but the letters and poems and gifts (once a crystal snack set—perhaps re-gifted from his mother) became annoying. Evelyn seemed afraid of him and tried to steer him away from me when she was at the rink. All we need-ed was a trumped-up pedophilia charge adding to Rhonda's arsenal!

The boys were terrible to Rhonda, giving her the "finger" each time she appeared in public, roaring by the hotel where she worked and shouting out "Super bitch, where is your son?"

Finally Evelyn called them all into her office and admonished them all to calm down and leave Rhonda alone. She wisely pointed out that Rhonda could train her sights on them and cause trouble.

"Yeah?" barked Doug Berry at this meeting. "Let her try!"

She did try, the very next day.

Doug called me at my office. "That bitch has gone and done it!"

"Done what?"

"She's had Bobby G. arrested for selling drugs and it ain't true. You gotta help!"

I asked him to calm down. I wanted the whole story before I com-mitted to anything.

Apparently Bobby, one of our top weekend floor workers, had been arrested in the hotel parking lot while getting into his car. A security guard had seen him give another boy a full paper sack, and the kid then ran into the woods on top of a small rise behind the building. Police were called and Bobby was taken, handcuffed, into the town jail pend-ing a hearing the next morning. Rhonda issued the formal complaint, backed up by the security guard's story.

The whole thing sounded fishy to me. Bobby was a nice, laid back kid who had never been in any trouble. He was a reliable worker with a steady girlfriend whom he intended to marry once he'd saved up a little security. He was one of the politer boys and Evelyn liked him very much, always commenting on his manners. I called Eudox Patterson and asked the lawyer to meet me at the courthouse the next day.

That afternoon I went to the sheriff's office, where I was known pret-ty well, and asked to see Bobby. He sat in his cell, frightened and ner-vous. He told me he had parked his car in the hotel lot because it was the only place available from which he could run errands. He'd had to go to a clothing store to pay on a lay-away plan, and a gas station to see if he could get a battery. The battery he needed had to be ordered, as they were out of the cheaper brand he needed.

When he went back to the car to drive home, two officers drove up, searched the car, found a small marijuana joint under his seat and ar-rested him, hounding him as to where was "The other boy with the bag." Bobby denied everything all the way to jail. His father, an only parent, was out of town on a highway crew, so he called Nessie Berry to get some help. Doug, answering the phone, had called me.

"I know it was her!" Bobby said over and over. "She swore she would get me one time when I was driving some of the guys around and they were yelling at her and giving her the finger—you were right, Danie, we shoulda kept our mouths shut!"

Feeling like this was somehow my fault, I was determined that this kid was not going to be part of the Zeke and Danie vengeance campaign.

The next day, dressed in my best conservative banker suit, I met Eudox on the courthouse steps. An entire platoon of kids climbed out of cars and off motorcycles and followed us into the courtroom. Bobby, sitting in front with a deputy standing next to him, turned around with a surprised smile on his face—the kids were all hollering, "Be cool, man; don't worry, Bobby," until the Judge, who had entered the courtroom and was speaking quietly with Eudox, the hotel security guard and the arresting officers, banged his gavel down and roared, "Silence in the court!" I kind of felt sorry for him; he had a look on his face that said, "Oh, no, I hope this won't escalate into a sideshow like the Evelyn Williams divorce trial," which was where he had seen me last.

Rhonda stood at the back wall, arms folded, one foot tapping. She looked defiant and somehow smug, as if she had last gotten to me through one of my boys, whom she no doubt imagined was a regular at perverted orgies at Maybelline Manor.

After the little conference at the bench was over, the charges were read and Eudox got up to address the judge and the court openly. He pointed out that there was no evidence of drug selling or money exchanging hands prior to the arrest, and only about five dollars found on the defendant. There was a receipt in Bobby's wallet indicating that he had paid a time payment at a store on that day, and a call to the gas station proved that he did indeed place an order in person in the same time frame.

The small joint found in his car was a misdemeanor for personal usage, usually punishable by an overnight sentence at the jailhouse, which he had already served. Somehow the security guard, who technically worked under Rhonda, became confused over actually seeing a fleeing boy with Bobby, claiming he saw a boy with a paper bag running along the top of the wooded bank when he went outside the back of the hotel to have a smoke. The security guard, who by this time was hunched down in his seat, clearly not expecting a high-end lawyer and a crowd of people to show up at the court room; looked over with a red face at the now-furious Rhonda, and shrugged.

The judge released Bobby with a stern admonition to not have any pot in his car ever again, and ruled the session over.

The kids burst into cheers and applause, some shaking the bemused Eudox's hand (he later sent me a substantial bill) and some clapping me on the back. I was their champion, and ding dong to the witch! Rhonda, her face set in cement-like hatred, stomped out of the courtroom without looking back. I would never see her in person again, although years later I would see her as a smiling grandma with her gorgeous great-grandkids on Facebook, hardly the Harpy I remembered in the 1970s.

When that happened I sighed and thought that time does change everyone. To be fair, in the earlier era of censure, gay people in Hot Springs typically stayed in their place, having drinks at Norma Cristy's bar on Central or at home in the closet quietly having dinner parties and then going to Little Rock on weekends. They did not drive around in flashy Cadillacs directing the youth traffic of town. In Rhonda's mind I was an openly gay man living with a flamboyant old lady in the house where she used to work as a bookkeeper, and where her 21 year-old son spent most his time.

Weary of youth, drama and the empty hole left by Zeke's total change towards me followed by his disappearance, I drove down to the Sawmill Depot for an early happy hour Bloody Mary.

I was far from happy, wondering again what I was doing in this city and where my life was going, other than living with Evelyn. She was wonderful, challenging, and supportive of my work with my formulas and all my other ideas for our business. Occasionally she would freshen up the dream of an exclusive treatment spa with a world-class line of products that would rival Erno Lazlo, the current reigning skin Guru, but she was in her twilight years and anything could happen. She could suddenly become ill and have to have intensive care or worse, and then Bill Williams would enter the picture and move me out of it with very little to my name except my small savings.

Despite the fact that he claimed he respected me and all that we were doing, based on Bill's one and only visit with his new wife, Rosan Yacht Heiress Gloria, I did not believe him. Although we had bent over backwards to impress him with our Hot Springs popularity, and introduce him to all the important people we were friends with, as well as to entertain him royally at Maybelline Manor—with Mary serving all his favorite foods and drinks—he still acted in a guarded way around me, as if I were suddenly going to burst forth dressed like Liberace and grope him. Gloria, on the other hand, was lovely, gracious and very supportive of all our plans.

We went to a great deal of trouble to have all the accounts prepared and our bookkeeper laid it all out for Bill to go over. He barely glanced at everything, seeming more concerned about the safety of Evelyn's Maybelline Stock than anything else. Perhaps our roller rink earnings were just chicken feed to keep Mama thinking she was making money and occupied. Bill did, however, really admire the Eldorado, and drove it around every day.

17

Hot Springs' Favorite Gay Bar

Arriving at the Sawmill Depot, I spotted my favorite waitress, Mary Mo, sitting at a table close to the entrance with my friend and town advisor, "Tourism Queen" Cheeta Connell. They both looked at me with sharp eyes that had a gleeful glint in them and waved me over.

"Sit down, Danie, I have something to tell you," said Cheets. I sat.

"Are you ready for this? He's back," she said in hushed tones.

"Who's back?" I asked, my heart in my mouth.

"Zeke. Zeke has been back a week, and he's working here."

"That's right, Danie," Mary chimed in, "he's working here; he's here in the bar now."

Standing up on shaky legs, I slowly walked to the huge bar, the two ladies trailing behind me. A slender young man was standing by a long table at the back, stacking glasses. I almost passed out; I didn't know what to do or say. It was Zeke!

"Go on, talk to him—he's cool now," whispered Mary Mo.

As I approached, he turned that oh-so-familiar profile towards me, the sunlight filtering through his lashes. "Hey, Zeke," I said.

"I beg your pardon?" The young man turned to me full face; it was not Zeke. An uncanny doppelganger, and from the neck down, Zeke in the flesh. But where Zeke's eyes were penetrating and triangular, these eyes were round and childlike. Where Zeke's mouth was thinly sculptured, this mouth was red, full-lipped, framing very white but very jagged teeth.

The nose, the hair, the long hands and feet were identical—but it was not him.

"Danie," boomed Cheeta, "meet Steve Wyatt; he's new in town." But behind her jocular introduction I could see she was worried that their little ploy had maybe backfired. I was white as a sheet, she told me later, and at that moment she knew how much I cared for Zeke.

Stuttering that I was glad to meet him, too, I made some excuse about going to get a drink and fled back to the table, the girls swooping after me.

"I'm sorry, Danie, we thought it was Zeke too when he first walked in to work, but then we thought you might like him and get your mind off that ingrate rug rat and his crazy mother," consoled Cheeta, her Irish eyes suddenly worried and serious.

They went on to say that he was gay, had been there a week, was 30 years-old and had heard all about me. After the shock wore off I forgave the girls, realizing they were just trying to help, and soon we were all watching Steve move back and forth in the bar, occasionally giving us a side glance.

"I think he's *much* better looking than Zeke," giggled Mary Mo, "but you'll have to get his teeth sorted out."

They were already assuming we were an item. "But what if he doesn't like me?" I asked Cheeta.

She snorted. "Like you? He'll *love* you, honey, don't they all?"

Ignoring her friendly sarcasm, I kept watching Steve, fascinated by the unbelievable resemblance—so close that later when we walked down the street, people who knew Zeke would say, "Well, why not say hello, Zeke? Where ya been?" and then pass on with a confused look. Finally, emboldened by two Bloody Marys, I sucked in my gut and swaggered over to the bar, re-introduced myself, apologized for acting so weird and asked him if we could meet for drink later, when he got off. I offered to show him Norma Cristy's, Hot Springs' favorite gay bar.

Amused, he informed me he had already been there several times, having moved into a small flat across the street from it, and agreed to meet there at 7:00. I rushed home and showered and changed, and telling Evelyn I had a meeting with Eudox and attorney Q. Byron Hurst for a political campaign (knowing these things bored her to tears), then I drove back into town, my spirits lifting. Q. Byron actually *did* run for office later, and I did campaign. It seemed that every story I concocted to placate Evelyn came true somehow.

Norma Cristy's was a dimly lit, comfortable neighborhood bar that also catered to the occasional Arkansas traveler looking for a little action, and tourists. Norma (Norman) was an astute entrepreneur with fingers in many pies, and ran a tight ship.

In addition to strong drinks the bar featured male dancers, many of whom were from out of town and straight, but enjoyed the easy money. There was also a surprisingly good drag show. It starred Tuna Star (who later became a good friend); the Lady Baronessa; and at times, Norma herself.

Occasionally a drunken redneck would wander in, not realizing what kind of place it was, and then try to get into a fight. They never won and were ejected by Norma's muscled bar boys. It was always amazing to me to hear some fat, ugly drunk yell, "If any of you goddamn queers try to touch me, I'll kill ya!" Didn't they realize that only the most desperate and ugly Queens would even consider looking at them, never mind touching them?

Gay bar pickup life is based mostly on good looks and a hunky body, or young hustlers looking for the older man who will hire them or keep them.

There is a group of gay men who are big, burly and hairy—they are called "Bears" and even have clubs. But they usually lean towards butch young men with swimmers' bodies who like to fish, camp and mountain climb—manly sports, including sex. Others are Daddy figures to a few disenfranchised youths who are attracted to fatherly types. But these blubbery rednecks with baseball caps pulled down over their greasy hair, pig-like eyes red with cheap booze, guts hanging low over belts that cut into their crotches—they make fools of themselves when they wander into a gay bar and then start announcing what terror they will create in any queer who comes near them.

As Tuna Star would say to these threats, "Puh-*leeeeeze*, Mary!"

I've known a lot of drag queens over the years, including many of the great ones all the way back to The Jewel Box Review, Lynne Carter, T.C. Jones and the immortal Charles Pierce, who was a friend. Charley had a full-page obituary about his life and career in *Life* Magazine after he was gone. He would have liked that. The only oil painting ever done of Charles and all his characters once hung in my house. I knew Divine as well, and later Jackie Beat (think Divine only prettier and thinner and with a much better voice) and the incredible Jimmy James who stunned the world for 17 years with his almost otherworldly portrayals of Marilyn Monroe—almost more Marilyn than Marilyn was. Jimmy is still writing hit songs like *Fashionista* and appearing in top clubs with one of the best voices in the industry—all 30 of them! Then there's young Peter Mac, whose portrayals of Judy Garland are different than any other Garland impersonator's. They all have one thing in common: more balls than the so-carefully-masculine butch type of gay man who sometimes scorns feminine guys unless they're on a stage as a major Diva. The drunks who acted up at the odd time at Norma's never messed with Tuna Star or any of the other drag queens—they were too afraid to.

The show was just starting as I walked in, and seeing Steve sitting near the back, I sat down with him, suddenly nervous about what to say. Sliding a long "Zeke like" hand over mine, he said, "I know I look like your ex-boyfriend, everyone in the bar has told me this for days. That is why I wanted to meet you."

I sat there taken back by this candid admission, and felt even more nervous when Steve went on to tell me that it was okay, that he was himself and would like to prove it to me. All at once the air seemed to clear and we both relaxed over drinks. We tried to tell each other our life stories in a few minutes.

Steve was from a mountain town in Northern California and had come to Hot Springs to visit an eccentric old friend named Dallas, who had purchased a small village of pyramids in the low hills outside the city. Dallas had an entourage of ageing hippies, new agers and whack-job ladies all living in his compound to extend their lives and health through the energies of the pyramids. He also, at an advanced age, would hit on any young man who came along and often succeeded in bedding them. I actually admired the old fraud for his tenacity of life.

Steve fell in love with the Spa City, got a job at the Sawmill Depot and moved into a tiny flat. After a couple of drinks and almost non-stop life-story chatter, we left Norma's and ended up in that Spartan flat, both knowing this was going to happen all along. Funny how sometimes conversation becomes foreplay when you already know it's a done deal!

It was in bed where the major differences between Steve and Zeke became apparent. Zeke was wild and intense, Steve was gentle and giving. Zeke was always in a hurry to do everything at once while listening to rock 'n' roll at the same time. Steve liked classical music in the background, and took his time. Zeke would tell me whenever I dressed up for an event that I looked "cool" or "hot" if it were one of my glam rock costumes, but never said a word about how I appeared when we were making love. Steve would look down at me every so often, and with shining eyes tell me I was beautiful.

Although Zeke had been well-endowed to be sure, Steve could have substituted for Johnny Holmes in porno flicks! I would tease him by asking him how he kept from passing out when he had an erection. The two men did not smell the same or feel the same, and the dark and burning chemistry that Zeke put out was not there. Still, I fantasized and was not feeling lonely anymore.

The first time I drove Steve up to the Manor, he fell in love with the place immediately. He cooked a gourmet, German-style dinner for us, and Evelyn was all over him like a cheap suit. She laughed and joked, running through her repertoire of one-liners and corny risqué but never vulgar stories, especially the one about the two spinster sisters who ran a drugstore in the middle of the desert and the cowboy who had fallen off his horse, then got bitten in the crotch by a rattlesnake. Crawling through the sand with his member swelling bigger and bigger, the cowboy finally spotted the store's lights in the darkness. Collapsing on the front porch in front of the two maiden ladies who were staring at him in disbelief and shock, he gasped: "Help me; you gotta give me something for this! Anything! Help me—what can you give me for this?"

The old gals looked at each other, whispered in each other's ears, and then turning to the cowboy said, "Well all we have is about $500 and the deed to the store, will that be ok?"

Of course Steve roared at this subtle not-so-dirty joke and countered with a few of his own, the two of them cackling like crazed chickens for hours while we gorged on delicious Sauerbraten and butter-fried potatoes. Steve insisted on cleaning up the kitchen, since our housekeeper was gone, and did so with astonishing speed and skill. Looking at him speculatively, Evelyn asked if he knew anything about keeping up a big house and dealing with helping a lady with her domestic necessities.

He informed her that as the only male child in a family of five sisters and a domineering mother who was more of a clean freak then Joan Crawford, he was indeed familiar with running a big house, indoors and out, and we already knew he could cook. Before the evening was over, Evelyn had persuaded him to quit the Sawmill Depot. They agreed upon a salary nearly equal to mine (which had gone up to $400 a week—a President's salary, she would claim) and that the maid's quarters were his as soon as he wanted to move in.

"In fact, Steve, dear," she gushed, "why don't you stay the night and try out the bedroom? It's getting late and Dan has to be up early tomorrow morning—isn't that right, Dan?" And she gave me a sweet and somewhat conspiratorial smile.

Steve gave me a look of his own: "Is this for real?" I replied with a small affirmative nod, and Steve informed Her Graceness that he would be delighted to work for us in any capacity she felt he was needed.

Sneaking downstairs to my room for the first time after she went to bed, Steve was all excited. We talked for hours about plans for The Manor, weekend trips with Evelyn in tow—he seemed to love her already. Zeke had been polite to her, and afraid of her, but had acted like she was an old lady not worth hanging out with.

The electric orthopedic bed in the maid's quarters was a monster that Evelyn had purchased for her back and hip pains that sometimes came on like a fury at night. But she could not control the many buttons and positions it offered, each movement accompanied by an annoying grind and buzzing sound. She banished the bed to the maid's bedroom where everyone else, including Mary, hated it. Mary had purchased a foam rubber pad to soften the Ortho Bed's hard surface. Claiming leg and hip problems also, Steve convinced Evelyn that my water bed, which was also heated, would help him a couple of nights a week (this led to Evelyn wanting to lie on it during the day when I was at the office, but she soon hated the water movement, claiming it made her seasick). Evelyn agreed that this would indeed be therapeutic for Steve, "As long as Dan doesn't mind." (Yeah, right.) Soon it became accepted that the maid's quarters was once again an empty guest room and art gallery. We had hung all of our leftover paintings and framed photos all over the walls in the large lounge area of the suite.

Steve was amazing on many levels. Sometimes on cold nights we'd get home-grown pot stoned sitting in front of my fireplace, and of course the munchies always followed. Steve would dash up to the kitchen and reappear moments later with incredible snacks, such as Albacore Tuna Salad Nicoise with perfectly sliced avocados and grapefruit arranged around the rim of the bowl. This would be handed to me with a head waiter's flourish followed by anything else he could do to make me happy.

Like Mary had at first, Steve spent far too much time on keeping my quarters clean and my wardrobe categorized. But Evelyn did not seem to notice, perhaps because he was a man. Each morning a long list, written in her distinctive flowing script, would appear outside her door, many of the items starting with, "Have Dan do..."

Every evening the list would be shoved back under her door with all items checked off or memo'd as to why they could not be done that day and when they would be finished. Evelyn was utterly in heaven—there was nothing Steve could not do or find out about. Even Evelyn's private closets, which Mary had never gotten to view, were open to him for suggestions on how to arrange things. He told me of seeing incredible gowns and furs from the 1940s and 1950s carefully wrapped in cheesecloth or soft canvas bags reeking of the cedar chips used as a moth preventative.

"I will not smell like an old lady with moth balls," Evelyn would say in indignation, and then, grinning slyly, she would ask whoever was listening, "Why do moths have such small balls?"

Thinking this was a joke with an unknown dirty punch line, the listener would say they did not know. Hooting with glee, she would reply, *Because they don't dance very well!*" You'd be surprised how long it took intelligent people to get that one—which is why she seized every opportunity to talk about closets and moth balls.

I think the secret to Steve's success at Maybelline Manor was that he really enjoyed what he did for Evelyn *and* he was clearly falling in love with me—a fact that made me feel uncomfortable yet secure and mellow at the same time. Steve never demanded labels or boundaries on what we had together.

Not even when Zeke really did come back.

18

The Return of the Lone Disc Jockey

It seems as if it was always Doug Berry who first gave me any news. My phone rang at the office one afternoon and there was his familiar voice, hushed and vibrating with excitement. "Dude, he's back—Zeke is back, man!"

Somehow this did not draw my heart up into my throat as it would have a month or so earlier. In fact my heart sank; I did not need this complication. Asking for more details, I discovered that Zeke had come back and that Rhonda, his mother, had set him up at her hotel bar as a disc jockey with all new equipment. And, an ad campaign ready to roll out that would attract all the 18 and over crowd from the Spa City Roller Rink. "They have a laser light machine ordered," he warned, and hinted that I order two or three right away. In addition to that, Zeke was now dating Bethany Anderson—that admission *did* shock me, and my heartbeat started ascending again.

How in the world did a low-life like Zeke get an angel like Bethany Anderson to date him? Bethany was one of those beautiful girls who went beyond being just "good." Coming from a very devout Christian family, she was angelic, sweet and big-hearted. She was also as shy as a Unicorn in a forest, always dressed impeccably, and her big-hearted ways kept the other girls with far less charms from being jealous.

Bethany had never had a boyfriend that we knew of—preferring to just hang out with the girls in general. The boys were a little intimidated by her—almost as if she walked in a circle of light. If you looked up the word "virgin" in the dictionary, you would see her photo!

I sensed that Bethany liked me, but not in a carnal way; she seemed to look up to me as a strong man who really did want to help the kids through their growing pains. I'm sure she knew I was gay; I'm also sure that if I were not, she would be the type of girl I'd marry—and I think that at some level she knew this. I was outraged that Zeke would even dare to throw his dark and horny charms on this girl! It was an odd feeling to be jealous of someone I had lost and someone I would never have, at the same time.

I railed about all this to Steve when I returned home that night and was surprised when he told me I should go down to the hotel and see Zeke for myself.

"I couldn't," I gasped. "Rhonda would be there and probably have her security goons try to escort me off the property!"

"But if you took Evelyn with you, she wouldn't dare pull anything. It *is* a public place and you'd be there as customers."

Evelyn was busy refurbishing her wardrobe and planning a visit from her son Bill, and I did not want to drag her into any more Zeke drama anyway. She'd already heard about Steve's resemblance to Zeke and thought it nonsense: "Why, Steve is so much handsomer than that boy, and a real gentleman. They look nothing alike, Dan."

I had a sudden thought, and turned to Steve. "Why don't *you* go down there tonight, meet him under the guise of a new person in town, and find out what's going on?" I secretly wanted Zeke to see Steve and notice the resemblance between them, yet see how Steve, so much more sophisticated, was like one of the "pretty people" Zeke had been so jealous of long ago.

Steve looked at me with an impassive face, then grinned and said, "Oh, all right, it'll be fun. I'll find out everything!" I think he was curious to see why I'd been so obsessed with this Zeke person.

We spent an hour carefully dressing Steve. When it was over I had him all in black with a long, leather coat that flared at the bottom and a huge Stetson hat I'd given him as a present. Rayban sunglasses completed the picture and he'd grown a trim goatee and moustache. He looked the very essence of a hip, wealthy player out on the town looking for action. I told him to park my 'Vette at the back of the hotel lot so Zeke wouldn't recognize it (although I'd make sure he'd recognize it later when I chose to reveal who Steve really was, after Zeke spilled his guts and they became friends).

Since Rhonda had never seen Steve either, our spy game was perfect and about to begin. I told Evelyn all about it the next day, fearing she would try to stop our ploy if she knew about it beforehand, but she actually seemed intrigued, although irritated that Zeke's mother was attempting to try and sabotage our business with an effort of her own. "That woman knows *nothing* about show business or how to attract an audience, Dan—she is an idiot. Don't worry; no one will go to hear her untalented son."

After waiting for three hours, nerves revved to a high pitch and wondering if I had sent Steve into a lion's den where he might even be beat up or badly hurt, he appeared at the patio door. His calm story was anticlimactic to the point that I almost felt sorry for the delusional Rhonda and her small-time attempt to raise her son's career in show business to heights I could never have attained.

As Steve rambled on about his boring experience, I envisioned Rhonda, her son and long-suffering husband all sitting around their kitchen table, laying out plans to use the hotel's resources to topple EVDAN and all of its business. Zeke, of course, was swearing he could "kick ass when it came to spinning music and attracting a crowd—the money crowd that's old enough to drink a lot of liquor. Good, *straight* people's entertainment, that's what this town wants!"

Steve said he'd felt very conspicuous as he entered the bar, mainly because of the way he was dressed and the fact that hardly anyone was there. Zeke was hunched over in a corner behind a makeshift disc jockey booth that resembled one of those cheap home bars available at Wal-Mart or a discount furniture store, the kind with faux wood paneling and a plastic, marble-finished top. Apparently he was engrossed in thumbing through albums and occasionally sticking his head up to a mike where he would mumble "and now we're going to hear a little something from Queen"—hardly the growling and dynamic Silver Ghost of a few months ago. His hair was cut short, his highlights gone. Steve admitted that there was some basic resemblance between them but gently said, "Danie, this is not the man you used to know, not from the way you described him; I think this is the real Zeke."

He said there was a beautiful girl who fit Bethany's description hanging over the edge of the bar, but mostly she sat laughing and talking to a hatchet-faced woman who kept staring over at Steve with a haughty and suspicious look. Rhonda, of course. Steve sat at the main bar and ordered a drink. Eventually Rhonda walked over and welcomed him to the club. She asked him to invite all his friends; big plans and big names were being booked for the immediate future, along with a big new light show for dancing.

Apparently satisfied with his claim to be a newcomer to Hot Springs, with a tight smile she informed him that "This is *the* place to come for a great time; a lot of pretty girls love the disc jockey we brought in from California."

It turned out Zeke had been shuffled off to California to stay with the liberal Aunt who had moved there shortly after I spoke to her on the phone. I felt betrayed that Miss "When You're Hooked, You're Hooked" could be so shallow with me. Blood really is thicker than water. After being assaulted by this blatant PR, Steve walked over to the disco bar and asked if Zeke could play any *America*.

"Sure, Dude, coming right up." As Zeke fumbled through the albums, he dropped several on the floor. After "Ventura Highway" was played and over, Zeke took a break at the bar and Steve casually drew him into conversation.

Zeke admired Steve's coat and the large turquoise ring I had just purchased. Now I was glad I hadn't given in to my urge to let Steve wear my Medusa ring as a secret signal to Zeke. Steve mentioned there was faint, bluish scar on Zeke's cheek—a lifetime reminder of that ring.

Playing down any interest in Zeke outside of the most inane and general questions, Steve learned that this was the third night of the Disco Dance operation at the hotel, and if they proved they could attract a crowd, the hotel would finance a laser light show. Zeke's manager (Rhonda) was also trying to contact talent agents in the South to get some well-known live bands and singers in. Zeke admitted, with sheepish laugh, that he wasn't really from California but had just recently come back from there after a long visit with his aunt, who knew all the top people in San Jose and was going to help promote the club. He also claimed that all the friends he had grown up with in Hot Springs were excited about the club and would be packing in the following weekend. "You should drop by, Dude," said Zeke with a wink. "I know all the hot chicks in town."

Steve's take on the whole rather sad scene was that apart from his deep voice, Zeke had no talent at all for disc jockeying. "Danie," told me, "Zeke was only good because you created a character for him, one based on your own radio personality. You coached him, dressed him, taught him makeup and advertised all this everywhere. Without all that he's just a redneck kid basically living in a dream world that started to come true because it was handed to him."

They say love is blind, and this is true—I never thought of Zeke in that way. I felt that yes, I handed him a stage and a few costumes, but it was his intense chemistry that made The Silver Ghost a hit. But Steve was right. I was the *real* Silver Ghost and Zeke's chemistry had never extended beyond a bed.

Finishing his drink, Steve then made his way out the door while Zeke, his mom and Bethany all waved goodbye and yelled, "Y'all come back, ya hear?"

It was sad and pathetic and after this mundane report I suddenly saw all of them, Zeke included, shrink down and down some more, revealing what and who they really were. I felt sorry for Bethany, knowing she must have felt the strange, burning chemistry also. Long after I left Hot Springs I heard they got married, and then later, divorced. Well, Rhonda did accomplish one thing: she got her baby boy married to the most beautiful girl in town. Didn't that prove to everyone he was not a queer?

Recently, while browsing through the many photos online depicting the Maybelline dynasty and references to the "mysterious, unsolved murder of Evelyn Williams," I came across a post from Bethany. Surprised at the sweet and somewhat naive comments about her knowing Evelyn, I went onto her Facebook page and pulled up her photos. I froze in shock. They were all family photos showing beautiful babies being cuddled while relatives sat around gazing fondly. I saw a more benevolent Rhonda, older and heavier—very Grandmother-ish, beaming at all her offspring's offspring.

Then I saw Zeke, holding a beautiful child and looking into its eyes with love.

Bethany's photo showed the same Bethany I remembered except for a change of hair color. As I stared at Zeke, memory lane beckoned and once again I saw those same lips, those long, tactile hands that now held the child, and that strong profile. At first I wondered how they all looked so young. Zeke looked a little older than I recalled and more mature, but still! I began to think that these must be old photos. But why just these on her Facebook page, not something more current?

Peering closer, I noticed that Zeke's nose seemed more refined than I remembered, and the clothes everyone was wearing were current fashions (although Levis will always be Levis). And his eyes were not so triangular anymore—they were rounder and a dark, rich brown. But Zeke's eyes were blue!

My gaze wandered up to Bethany's profile photo, and looking closely I noted that time had taken some toll on her face. Although still lovely, I was looking at a woman in her late forties or early fifties.

Finally I noted the dates the photos were posted. It was this year, and I was looking not at Zeke but at his son holding *his* children! Bethany was a grandmother! Their son was now slightly older than Zeke had been when we were together. Funny how people in our pasts remained frozen in time—always young and always there. Seeing the physical characteristics I knew so well handed down to another person was eerie and made me feel terribly old.

The rink business was slowing down, but not because of competition. I was spending more time out with Evelyn and Michael, letting the long-suffering Gracie run the rink with my gaggle of boys working the floor and the skate rental booth. One night Evelyn, Steve and I all dressed up and went to a new jazz club that had just opened, featuring a young African-American organ/pianist who played like a cross between Billy Preston and Oscar Peterson. I had the privilege, later, of taking a few lessons from him at Mary Anderson's house—he was a genius.

As Steve and I waited in the living room cooling our heels while Evelyn got ready, she suddenly appeared in the archway, so lovely we both involuntarily exclaimed "Wow!" She loved wows, and pirouetted and posed while we both applauded. She had on a dark but brilliant green velvet pantsuit with one of her signature Beaumartin collars. Diamond and pearl earrings sparkled in her ears and the huge, emerald cut diamond on her small, perfectly manicured hand traced fire as she waved it about.

Beaumartin collars were originally worn by the Virgin Queen of England. Evelyn's was made of stiff lace, rising up high behind her head, covered with jewels and sweeping around on either side of her neck. In the 1930s a modified version of this style was seen on fur coats and art modern jackets. Evelyn adapted it to her own style, softer but no less dramatic; it framed her white bosom, neck and face like the frame on a portrait. Handing me her new, white mink sports-length fur coat that she'd had designed by a furrier in Little Rock ("All my furs are too dated," she would complain), she chortled, "My, what a lucky girl I am to be escorted by two such handsome men!" She always had a way of making men, straight or gay, feel seven feet tall and able to accomplish anything.

A few months earlier Evelyn had finally had her face and eyes done, flying to Kansas City and going to the surgeon our Dermatologist friend had recommended. I was to drive out to get her in four days; she was afraid she may still be bruised and puffy and did not want the public to see her.

I talked to a groggy sounding Evelyn several times during those four days, wringing my hands at night and fearing the worst—and the subsequent wrath of Bill. The surgeon also spoke to me on the phone, assuring me Evelyn was robust and healthy aside from her osteo problems and that she had everyone at the convalescent facility treating her like a film star. She wanted to go this alone, such was the level of her vanity. Then, on the way to Kansas City I was delayed by a violent storm that rocked the big Caddy like a small rowboat at sea. At one point the wind blew the rain so hard it came at me horizontally and I could hardly see the road. I pulled off onto a gravel side road that rose up to a small hill under a huge oak tree, parked in the pitch blackness and fell asleep listening to the thunder clap and boom around me, wind and rain lashing the window.

When I awoke with a start, hours later, dawn was just breaking. The air was crystal clear as the rays of sun shot through the remaining clouds, tinting the valley below me with pale gold. I was up much higher than I had imagined, and the huge, black-limbed tree formed a canopy over the car, green leaves dripping on the roof with a soft, almost musical sound. I gazed down the steep side of the hill to my left and saw a little white church gleaming in the early light, almost magical, with birds swooping and diving over and around it. I felt like I was in the middle of a Disney movie.

A middle-aged, slender man came out of the parsonage at the side of the church, wearing a black blazer, hand up above his eyes against the rising sun. He called something up to me and, lowering the window, I called out, "What did you say?"

"I said, are you OK and would you like some coffee?" he hollered back.

Assenting that I would indeed love a cup of coffee, I slipped and staggered down the wet grass to where the Parson was waiting, a friendly smile on his weathered face, to shake my hand and usher me into the tiny, warm and cheerful parsonage kitchen.

His wife, a bubbly plump little woman, talky as a jaybird, said that they had seen the lights come up the hill around one AM and figured it was someone stranded by the storm. "Robert here was going to try to go up and get you, but the wind was blowing so darn hard I wouldn't let him," she laughed. "When I saw that huge white Cadillac parked up there, I figured you would be as safe there as here—you know the rubber tires don't conduct lightning."

Acknowledging that I had also heard this story, but uncertain if it were true, I suddenly realized what time it was.

"Can I use your phone?" I exclaimed. "It's an emergency; I have to pick my aunt up at the hospital in Kansas City."

"Son," the preacher said, "that's about an hour's drive away." He handed me the phone.

Frantically I rang the convalescent center and asked the desk nurse if Evelyn Williams was released to go home yet.

"Not only is she released, honey," said the nurse dryly, "but she's here waiting in the lobby and hopping mad—I'd get here as soon as I could if I were you."

I asked her to put Evelyn on the phone. There was a silence and then I could hear Evelyn complaining all the way to the desk.

"Dan," her voice cracked in my ear, "why are you not here? I've been waiting for over two hours! I am *not* happy about this, Dan!"

I explained about the storm, exaggerating a bit with stories about flooded roads and preachers coming to my rescue, knowing full well that Evelyn lived for high drama. Her tone changed immediately from bitchy to concerned. "Are you OK, dear? Is the car in one piece?" And then told me not to *rush*, but to get there fast. I thanked the Parson and his wife, who handed me a cup of coffee to go, and tore down the hill to the highway.

I did make it in less than an hour, facing speed traps and country cops who love to hide behind bushes or bridges and stop huge speeding Cadillacs. The storm must have had them occupied with other, more serious issues because I glided down an almost empty highway.

As I rushed into the lobby of the facility, which was charming, modern and spacious, almost like a five star hotel, I saw Evelyn sitting in the middle of a couch, surrounded with her garment bags and suitcases. I had forgotten how much stuff she'd taken with her on the plane.

She had a somber look on her face and would have looked disgruntled if she hadn't looked so young. I was amazed, and I think she saw this by my expression, because she brightened, smiled shyly and whispered, "Do I look all right?"

"*All right*?" I nearly yelled, glancing over at the desk nurse who was pretending not to listen, "you look bloody marvelous! I can't believe it! You look about 45 or less!"

After hugging each other and laughing hysterically, which did result in open stares from the nurse, we picked up all her gear and went to the car (which she gave a once-over to ensure no damage was done). On the way home we sang and laughed and commented on the scenery as if we were on a holiday. She kept wondering what "Bill and the rest will think" or, "What the people in town will think."

I advised her to say nothing. I had already let the word out that Mrs. Williams was visiting her family in California for a few days and the facelift was no one's business, not even Bill's. Amazingly, she had no hematoma or bruising except a little around the eyes that she cleverly camouflaged with makeup. The surgeon had said he'd never worked on anyone her age with such healthy, resilient skin. I knew why, of course, and even now plastic surgeons around the world recommend my preoperative skin revision treatments to ensure better and faster healing and less scarring and down time.

Two things frighten plastic surgeons: Hematoma (blood blisters forming under the skin, at times due to Aspirin taking) and sloughs (Alopecia, where lack of circulation along the incision lines and tissue undermining kills off the hair follicle, resulting in permanent hair loss and necrosis of tissue). Nowadays, my DMK pre- and postoperative products, which generate a tremendous *plasmatic effect* of increased circulation and oxygen to the skin at the site of the surgery, the support of the mitochondria (the cells' "battery pack") and the Langerhans cells (our skin immune system), negate both of these contraindications. Especially the sloughs.

Evelyn never did confide to anyone about her facelift, at least not that I heard. To be honest, I forgot about it myself until the night we went to the jazz club and she looked so dazzling I found myself thinking how haggard she had been when I first arrived in Hot Springs. Look at her tonight! Senator Canada was starting to not sound so farfetched after all.

As we entered the dimly lit, well-appointed Jazz Club, there was that wonderful smoky, pre cigarette-ban atmosphere that made one think of the great New York and Chicago Jazz clubs of the '40s and '50s we see in the movies.

Framed by her two handsome escorts, Evelyn called out "Hello, everybody," and proceeded to table hop, talking to total open-mouthed strangers. She would complement one woman on a brooch or a necklace, another on her hairdo, and several gentlemen on their suits or ties. She did not know any of them, just assumed they knew who *she* was: the Maybelline Heiress. Fortunately there were a few folk there who knew us and waved from their tables, calling out, "Hi, Ms. Williams, you look great!"

Energized by this, she waved a waiter over and requested a front row seat. With much moving of the already packed little tables, we were ensconced right beneath the small stage, where the brilliant keyboard artist looked right down at us, smiling at Evelyn's open enthusiasm, and made it sound like every song was for us. After one particularly riveting Errol Garner rendition of "Misty," Evelyn leaned back, sighed with contentment, sipped her flute of Champagne—and then suddenly turned to me, eyes flashing with inspiration.

"We're in the wrong business, Dan," she said as she clutched my arm with surprising strength. "This is where the money is—a good show and booze!"

I looked at her with dawning hope and new respect. I too, was weary of babysitting the town's teens and kids with all of the associated drama. Yes, there was satisfaction in being a mentor and seeing young lives change for the better; yes, I felt I was helping young closeted gay kids find identity—but that had more to do with my open lifestyle and lack of fear in the face of homophobia than any business could provide.

We looked at each other, beaming, yet said not another word. Later, Steve told me it was like watching two aliens communicate with their minds.

That was the moment The Palace Dinner Theatre was born.

19

The Palace Dinner Theatre

If someone were to tell me now that I'd transform a roller rink into a plush dinner theatre with an all-star lineup of performers, in-house orchestra and world-class cuisine, and do it in the four months before the tourist season hit town while going up against the competition of long-established supper clubs, I would suggest that they seek psychiatric help.

But in the 1970s, in Hot Springs Arkansas, I did just that—and for under $300,000. Of course that figure would be a million dollars or more today—but it wasn't money that built The Palace, it was the little people led by a visionary who only saw the end result of a dream, paying little attention to what it took to get there and being driven by a remarkable woman who had pushed many dreams into realities before.

Forty years later it's hard to remember all of the administrative details I became embroiled in and exactly how I handled each one. With a lot of help from friends like Mort Cox at the Bank, who had the ear of the City Council, and other less upscale friends who owned the bars and strip clubs on Central Avenue, and the Showmen's Association, I managed to get a liquor license and permits to build a restaurant/bar. I remember promising a lot of free passes for front row tables on opening night, a promise that backfired on me and caused some ill feelings later on. Evelyn, Steve and I sat up night after night drawing a basic floor plan for the theatre, but nothing really happened until we recruited the help of a pianist, the young Rick Warren.

Rick was thrilled at the project, having been overlooked as a major talent for the up and coming Race Meets. He and his band (which we referred to as The Rick Warren Orchestra in later publicity) had played the very established Vapors and other clubs in the region, but all he had at this time was his gig at The Hot Springs Village, playing sappy standards for retirees. In his mind, we were his door to the big time, and he believed in me.

It was Rick who obtained Chef Bearbra Coleman, a big, affable African-American gentleman who had been The Vapors' chef for years. Apparently the owner, wanting to "upgrade" the popular club in time for the Race Meet, was downgrading his old staff in an effort to modernize and be trendier. Evelyn and I invited Bearbra out to the Manor and, with California liberalism, made him feel he was Cordon Bleu from Paris and promised a better salary. Rick, who had the respect of every musician in town, put together a real supper club orchestra, again with higher salaries than the performers normally made. The real find was another ex-Vapors' employee, a tough little lady named Barbara Wallace who was to be the general manager of The Palace. Barbara came into the Manor like a whirlwind, vowing to do everything in her power to ensure that the dinner club would be a massive success and claiming to have the "inside on every vendor and wholesale liquor dealer" to not only save us money, but get us good credit ratings from the start.

"They all know and trust me," she insisted. "Don't worry, Mrs. Williams; nothing gets by me, and I'll run a tight ship."

Evelyn and I were impressed and relieved; we worried about our lack of knowledge on how to actually *run* a supper club. Sadly, after the fire Barbara, confronted by The Millionaire from Palm Springs—Bill Williams—would turn on me like a dog. Apparently she forgot about approaching me for a loan to help her out of a financial crisis only days after we hired her—a loan that was never paid back. There appeared to be a reason, after all, why she had been let go from the Vapors, but I was naive and in a hurry.

The Race Meet was Hot Springs' biggest money maker each year. Thousands of people would crowd into town from all over the USA, taking every hotel and motel room within fifty miles around. The locals would drive or bus in every day, many walking to the track to bet on the horses and make their fortune. The established clubs depended on this trade and engaged top talent and stars, from country singers to Vegas personalities such as Engelbert Humperdinck and Phyllis Diller. I'm sure they all laughed up their sleeves when they heard that 'crazy' King and that rich old lady thought they were going to open up competition in time for the Race Meet—impossible!

They stopped laughing the first month after we closed the rink and began construction on the club. I felt bad about taking away the kids' one place to go on weekends, so I went to visit the young lady who owned the other rink in town, which had somehow stayed open, and assured her that not only would I help redecorate her place to a more attractive venue, but would give her our disco skate booth and lights setup and all the music that went with it. I'd also help her advertise the All New Disco Skate and plug it to the tourists who would come to The Dinner Theatre as the place to drop their kids off at while eating dinner and seeing a show.

She was grateful and thrilled, actually a very sweet and attractive girl, so I apologized for any part we'd played in the *Garland County Reporter's* campaign to ban her place. Feeling better, I announced all this publicly after our last big promotion at The Spa City Roller Rink, a three-day dance marathon that offered a thousand dollars to the couple that was still on its feet at the end of the marathon.

Dance marathons, which were popular during the war years, are not what most people expect unless they ever participated in one. All the employees, including myself, had to work in shifts as this was a 24 hour event with no rest for the winners except five ten-minute breaks and bathroom visits. I napped on the couch in Evelyn's office, getting up every three or four hours to check that everything was going as planned. It was great publicity because many food vendors and soft drink companies sent in snacks, full meals, water and free sodas for the contestants. Some businesses "sponsored" their favorites with massage therapists doing "on the floor" rubdowns as the dancers sluggishly moved around to the music like zombies. Many times a dancer, mostly women, would fall asleep on her partner's shoulder, which was allowed as long as the partner kept them moving. If both fell asleep they were disqualified, and sometimes near fights broke out as my floor supervisors blew the whistle on the dancers and yelled, "Yer out!"

"We were just dancing really slow" some would complain as they staggered off the floor and collapsed against a wall.

An out-of-town grifter named Johnny Angel (who claimed that the singer Shelly Fabre, who made a song of the same title famous, named him after it) instigated this event. He assured me it would put the Spa City Roller Rink on the map and pave the way for more interest in

The Palace. Johnny, a slight man with long hair and 1960s-style clothes, had a face and manner that seemed slightly British. He was clever and the kind of a friend you could never quite trust, but remained a friend nonetheless—never holding grudges.

At first Mrs. Williams loved this marathon, and appeared in the evening to encourage the dancers to stay on their feet. She told the ladies she had been in a few "back in the day" and had won several.

"Just dance slow, dear; let the man carry you around the floor for a while and then you carry him," she would advise. Eventually she tired of it, complaining, "Isn't that damn marathon over yet, Dan? We have a dinner theatre to open!"

The day after the marathon finally finished and the winners wearily took off with their check for $1,000 waving on their hand amongst a cheering crowd, we took all the employees inside for a meeting.

The much-harassed Gracie had quit her position weeks before, claiming she could no longer handle all those "rude and impossible boys who work here." Evelyn and I begged her to hang on and take over the box office for The Palace, but she did not like Barbara, she claimed, and wanted to retire anyway. She said that due to our generosity she had managed to put quite a bit of money by and would be OK. I should have had my ears tuned better when she mentioned not liking Barbara, but at the time I put it down to Barbara's aggressive personality up against Gracie's old fashioned, conservative nature.

We informed the staff that they would all still have a job in some capacity after The Palace was open. We needed waiters, bartender assistants, waitresses, kitchen help, maintenance people, dishwashers and general "gofers" to help out with the various celebrities we intended to book. Most of the younger people clamored for this position, but I put Doug Berry in charge. I also asked for volunteers to help with demolition and remodeling—every one of the boys wanted in on that—and one of them offered the services of his uncle who was a contractor and had built clubs before in Little Rock and elsewhere in the South. This uncle saved our life. He was a quick-thinking man who appreciated the job, most construction work being tied up by two or three major contractures in town—including the foot-dragging builder who was supposed to be working on our teen theme park, but always had some other project he had to complete first.

Evelyn and I had decided to put the Go-Kart track and clubhouse on hold anyway, until after The Palace made money and I had the property graded for a car park area. When we showed the builder the plans we'd had made up for the look and flow of The Palace, he nodded and made a few suggestions here and there, said it was a great design and asked who we'd hired to create it.

Evelyn and I looked at each other for a moment, and then cried out, "We did, is it really good?"

He told us it was unique, then started going over bare bones costs, permits that needed to be gotten, plumbing that had to be done, a bigger and better stage than the one we had, dressing rooms at the side of the stage, lighting hook-ups and a huge bar at the back of the club. He knew that we had a limited budget, and when we mentioned what we were prepared to spend, he nodded and to our surprise, said it could be done but we'd have to get all the furniture and decor items ourselves, plus outfit the kitchen once the plumbing was put in.

After this the little people took over. It became a neighborhood project, getting The Palace open by Race Meet. I'm sure there were several poker games going on around town in back rooms and home recreation areas where, amidst cigar smoke, bets were being taken as to whether or not Williams and King would manage to pull it off.

My design had to overcome the fact that all we had to work with was one huge wooden floor, a few rooms for skates and skate rentals, two public restrooms with two toilets each, a crude stage at one end and two offices, with mine including a box office at the end of the short hallway at the entrance. Only two doors led out of the back of the building, which was a plain, rectangular cinderblock affair. Somehow we had to transform this into a Palace that would be seen by everyone as they drove into Hot Springs on the main highway.

It was actually the first business to be seen at the City's entrance anyway, but as a roller rink it didn't have to look impressive on the outside. We decided to paint it a soft red and plant conifers along the front, sort of a Las Vegas modern appearance. Colored lights would further soften any harsh lines, and the coup de grace was a photo of Evelyn in her Mae West Costume, one arm up to welcome customers into her dinner theatre. I had Roger Lewin take the photo and enlarge it as much as possible. To get it the size I wanted, Roger suggested blowing it up in sections on the largest paper his dad's photo business could find, and then we fit these together like a puzzle, re-creating the photo into a giant figure that could be seen from the highway. This took an entire night putting everything together over a strong, wooden background

Roger had made, using the rink floor as our work table. It looked like a patchwork doll when it was finished, but, prepared for this, I hand painted the entire photo, covering the seams where the pieces were joined. Roger and I enhanced her eyes, smiling red lips and anything else that needed to be touched up and brought out more dramatically. When it was finished we looked down at it, astounded that it had turned out so well.

"That's the *biggest* airbrush job I ever had to do," Roger chuckled as he started applying several coats of marine varnish over the figure to weather proof and fade proof it. Evelyn did not see it until the night of the opening, when it was erected and tied into place, illuminated by two spotlights.

"Oh my," she whispered, her hand to her mouth as we drove up, "I look like Las Vegas!"

The inside of the building was harder. I had to figure a way to accommodate a dining crowd that could eat while the show was going on yet not be crowded together on one floor. Even though we were featuring full course buffet dinners to minimize waiters taking orders for food while the show was on, people walking back and forth with plates would still get in the way of people trying to see the stage.

Watching a boxing match on TV one night gave me an idea. Calling my builder the next day, I rolled out the floor plan I had found of the original roller rink drawings and then hand drew on them a series of boxes, like small boxing rings, all placed on the floor at catty-corner angles, from the back bar all the way to the stage. They would be about five feet high with steps going up one side and down the other, painted black and equipped with inexpensive black and white tiled floors. Strong chains covered in heavy, faux gold velvet would be suspended from four strong posts at each corner, the twin sets of chains preventing anyone from falling off the mini boxing ring floor by mistake. Four or five tables with red tablecloths and red covered chairs could fit on each raised "box." Between the boxing ring platforms, floor level tables would be placed at random all the way to the edge of the dance floor area in front of the stage, which could be built up another three to give everyone an excellent view of the show from every place in the room. Of course, booking those platform seats would cost the patrons a little extra. Both Evelyn and the builder thought this was a brilliant idea; he mentally calculated what it would take to build them.

"They have to be strong," I cautioned. "We have to prove to the City

Building Department that they're safe."

"They look a lot safer than those bleachers they put up at that theme show they got going on outdoors for the tourists," he exclaimed, and assured me that the platforms would outlast an earthquake and seat the fattest of people without a tremble.

The back bar could also seat diners, I thought, if it were constructed right up against the back wall on a series of elevated platforms running all along the front of it, the first being for bar stools and the other two for smaller cocktail tables and chairs—the cheaper seats, but also a "conversation and drinking area" for people who were not 100% into the show, or for a happy hour crowd.

And then we had a turn of luck—just before a wave of really bad luck hit us.

All kinds of people were bringing things to me for The Palace, to make a little extra money. One elderly lady, her makeup carefully applied and her faded red hair piled on her head (reminiscent of another era), brought me a beautiful lithograph depicting a lovely young girl wearing a blue gown and holding a blue fan, her hair and makeup from the turn of the century. The picture was ornately framed in rich dark wood and had a sweet, haunting quality about it. It was called, appropriately, "The Blue Lady." She said she thought it would go well with our "palace theme" and that it had hung for many years in an upscale brothel in New Orleans. She wanted only $150 dollars for it, so I grabbed the deal. As she turned to leave, clutching her check in trembling, arthritic hands, I stared at the painting and then called out, "Wait a minute; this girl somehow looks familiar. Is this you?" She just gave me a tiny, enigmatic smile and left the building.

Others brought bolts of material from closed-down warehouses. One offering was enough for Nessie Barry, an accomplished seamstress among her many other talents, to make our stage curtains in an opulent, Moray watered silk pattern. Three crystal chandeliers appeared one day at a paltry $200 each, given the amount of crystal and their size, so I also grabbed those, no questions asked. The lighting catalogues I was poring over were charging $1,300 and up for chandeliers not as large or impressive. These had come from a private home that was being foreclosed on.

The parade appeared every day, people down on their luck with a bauble or two to sell, one man bringing 10 boxes of really beautiful bar glasses in various sizes from a failed restaurant he lost his shirt (and his wife) over. They were a third of the cost of new glasses. Evelyn loved to be in the office on these days, although the sawdust in the air, the noise of hammers and saws and men yelling four letter words eventually drove her back to the estate and concentrating on getting her wardrobe ready for her club appearances. Before that she often embarrassed me by haggling with some of these poor creatures, getting them down on prices already ridiculously lower than the items were worth. When they accepted her final offer she would cackle with satisfaction and exclaim, "There, Dan, that's how you do it—you're too soft hearted for all these hard luck stories."

I did put my foot down when one middle aged couple came in offering an enormous amount of silverware, intricately patterned with the letter P stamped into the handles. It was enough flatware for three restaurants—they had been in the restaurant supply business and retired. These had been in their garage for years.

"We thought P for Palace would be perfect," smiled the woman, "and we only want $1,000 for the lot."

"A thousand dollars?" shrieked Evelyn. "Why, those are only silver plate! I can't have my customers eating with those!"

Red-faced, they turned away and I quickly reminded Evelyn that we were not a 5-star restaurant and could not afford real silver for big crowds. She grumbled. Telling her I'd get them to come down a lot, I rushed out the door and caught the couple as the man was loading the sample boxes back into their car. I told them to come back later and I'd give them a check. I said that Mrs. Williams wasn't trying to be rude; it was just that she was used to only the best and wanted the same thing for her clients. They brightened and said they understood and brought the silverware back that evening. I told Evelyn I'd gotten them down to $600, at which point she exclaimed, "See, you're learning, Dan!"

On the night of the opening I was amused to hear her tell several people that she had ordered the flatware especially with The Palace "P" inscribed.

But Steve was the person who found us our biggest break. He'd run into a handsome man of about 40 who was from California and a seasoned bartender with references. This man had come to Hot Springs hoping to get a bartender's gig at one of the big clubs and clean up on tips during the Race Meet. He was also an avid race fan himself and claimed to have made a ton of money in the past.

I had Steve bring him out to the Manor for an interview that went on into dinner—Evelyn liking the fact he was from California, and therefore to be trusted to be in charge of all the liquor (she thought a lot of the locals were boozers and feared loss of stock). They got along like a house on fire, even when he requested a salary bigger than I was getting. In Evelyn's mind a good head bartender was everything to the success of a club, and she was right. But even more amazing was the fact that this man had met someone who had a huge bar, already fully fitted out, left from an old dance club in one of the towns in Southern Arkansas. We called his man up and arranged for the bartender and Steve to drive over the next day and take a look at the bar. I had a Polaroid land camera and asked Steve to take photos of everything and bring them back as fast as he could.

The next evening, Steve appeared with a fist full of photos and a big grin on his face. "You're going to love this, Evelyn and Danie." He laid the photos out on the table. It was a huge, deep rich, dark mahogany bar with excessive and ornate scrollwork all around the top, sides and back and around the doors. The front portion, where drinks would be served, was all green Carrera marble, as well as the shelves on the towering back bar portion. The handles and knobs were solid brass, the doors to the cupboards set with stained glass, and it had a full set of copper and brass draft beer dispensers, like an English pub. It also was fitted with refrigerators, copper lined wash-up sinks and faucets; and even a long brass kick rail along the bottom. It looked as if it were made for us: a bar for a Queen and a King in a Palace. It would be the focal point of our club, and no one else in town had anything like it.

Our new bartender, Rod, said it had been all custom-made and everything was in good working order apart from a few electrical fittings that would have to be replaced, and the seller only wanted $10,000 for it. As this was $7,000 less than our builder was going to charge to build a much less stunning bar from scratch, Evelyn didn't say a word except "Let's grab it, Dan—this will knock 'em over!" Of course the bar had to be somewhat taken apart and brought in with a big moving truck, and much of the $7,000 savings was taken up by having the building crew re-fit it into its new space and rewire it to safety code; but it looked like it was *made* for The Palace! It fit perfectly across the entire back, and a sudden richness took over the place. I found a set of bar stools that matched the rich mahogany. I had the seats covered in tufted, red faux leather and I felt we were actually going to pull it off after all, and now we were actually ahead of schedule.

The word got out about the hiring of Chef Bearbra Coleman, Barbara Wallace and the best musicians in town. Soon a bevy of professional cocktail waitresses were showing up hoping for jobs.

Although I had promised the staff of The Spa City Roller Rink they could also have jobs, I knew I needed a few professionals to train them and keep an eye on things. So I hired four—two men and two women. The head waitress was a lovely, sexy and competent woman named Connie who ended up training everyone for a month before opening without asking for a dime extra!

Nessie Berry, in addition to making the massive stage curtains, also made the cocktail waitress costumes to my specific design and in the three Maybelline Colors. They were short, Grecian style gowns, in wearable nylon tricot but looked like chiffon. They were pleated at the waist and up over one shoulder with a single drapery fluttering down the back; the hemlines were "handkerchief" points that floated when the waitresses walked. I began to review hair and makeup with each of the female staff members, letting them know that they were part of the show as much as anyone onstage, every night, and as such they would get better tips. Wigs and hairpieces were purchased and everyone was given skin treatments. Evelyn gave out tips on how to walk and smile and be suggestive without being vulgar or slutty.

Then the fates decided to dump on us.

Although we had all the permits in place and the liquor license on its way (I chewed my fingernails to the bone over this and it arrived by courier only hours before opening night), a man from the city building department came in one day demanding to see our rest room plans. "We already have two public restrooms," I protested, "one male and one female."

"Now son, that jest ain't enough," he drawled, a dead cigar stub rolling in his lips.

Walking me to the men's room, he looked inside and said, "Y'all got to have at least eight more toilets in here."

I was appalled. Where were we going to put eight more toilets?

Looking around some more, he opened the door at the end of the bathroom that was the clean-up closet room for the maintenance crew. It was filled with mops, vacuums and other paraphernalia.

"Well looky here!" he boomed, "this here is *plenty* of room for at least five more toilets, and y'all can move those other ones closer to each other and get three more in!"

I called the builder in, and after talking to the man from the city department, he grudgingly agreed that with a lot of work and some tearing up of the floor, he could get five toilets in the janitor room and line three more in the main room—with very little space to move around if you counted the privacy stalls that legally had to also be put up. "The law says y'all don't have to put doors on all the stalls," the city man smirked, no doubt thinking this would turn the rich fag on and the public bathroom would become my hangout.

I told him I would take his advice under consideration and let him know. "Son, it ain't my *advice*, it's what has to be done or you don't open this club." And he left.

The next day I received a stop work order on The Palace from City Hall, pending proof that we would submit legal plans to bring our public toilets up to code. I had an entire crew charging by the hour standing around doing nothing, and a deadline of less than three months away. With the permits all in place and the liquor license assured, I felt that someone or something else was behind this ridiculous demand for more male toilets.

Nothing had been said about the women's loo, which only had four toilets, and classically, seeing the lines always outside women's restrooms at public places, it seemed the percentages should be reversed if anything.

20

Thank You, Governor Bill Clinton!

$\mathcal{I}$ decided to play politics first, and drafted a formal letter on EVDAN Corp. stationery to the Honorable Tom Ellsworth, Mayor of Hot Springs, in which I invited him to officiate at the opening of The Palace Dinner Theatre and present the Descendant of Desoto and Arkansas Traveler Awards to country music superstar Conway Twitty. Conway had been named for Twitty, Texas and Conway, Arkansas, and I had been told to try to book him as an opening act to ensure a huge crowd—but I hadn't even talked to an agent about it yet.

The two awards I mentioned were official State and City awards, and I felt sure Ellsworth could hardly refuse to present them unless he was sick in the hospital or out of town. I also thanked him on behalf of Mrs. Evelyn F. Williams for helping us expedite our permits and all his other assistance on behalf of the tourist trade organizations, the show people in town and the many people needing jobs that were in short supply. I poured it on thick.

Then I rang Mort Cox and told him what had happened, and after a moment he admitted that it sounded like someone did not want us to open on time—but he'd gone as far as his influence could take him, and the only person who could lift the stop work ban and override the City Building Commissioner was the State Building Commissioner at Little

Rock and The Governor, Bill Clinton.

I had already written a formal letter to Governor Clinton, inviting him and his wife Hilary to the opening. Evelyn had created quite a sensation a few weeks before, appearing on the Little Rock Television Easter Seals Telethon, by phoning not only every businessman in Hot Springs for a donation, and a Rabbi, but the Governor's office as well—which I'd heard Bill had gotten a kick out of. I got her listed to appear on the telethon along with other local notables and she acted as if she were starring in a major motion picture. The camera was on her more than anyone else manning the phones. It was during that time, carried away by the marathon appearance success, that she demanded that she be given an official tour of the Maybelline Plant outside Little Rock. Thinking this was a great idea and also more good publicity, I wrote the Plant with her request. A week later I received a terse and short reply from an underling at the Plant, declining any official visit by Mrs. Williams who was only a minor stockholder in Shearing Plough and had nothing to do with any promotion of Maybelline Cosmetics. Furthermore they "suggested" that she stop using the title "The Maybelline Heiress" so no unfortunate action could be taken by Maybelline Cosmetics.

Furious at this (I of course did not show it to Evelyn, knowing she would be hurt), and since I was largely responsible for The Maybelline Heiress legend, I went to our attorney Eudox Patterson and showed him the letter. He chuckled and said it was ridiculous. She had only been offering them free publicity as well and that the plant was not really a Maybelline headquarters at all, just a satellite plant and not as glamorous as she imagined. He also suggested that we drop the word "*The*" and refer to her only as "Maybelline Heiress, Evelyn F. Williams," which technically she was, no matter how little stock she held.

I ended up finally referring to her everywhere as "Miss Maybelline." When Evelyn asked if the company had replied, I said "Nothing yet, it basically is just a warehouse," and then The Palace plans and my toilet problems took over everything. Hurriedly sketching the required toilets on a sheet of draft paper, I made an appointment with the Building Commissioner in Little Rock, telling his secretary (who had seen Evelyn on the show) that it was a dire emergency and that hundreds of people's jobs were at stake! Either she believed me or my histrionics intrigued her but I got a half hour audience if could make it to Little Rock by 2:00 PM. Never had the Corvette streaked to Little Rock so fast!

He was a pleasant man and seemed very interested in what we were trying to do and impressed that I was getting Conway Twitty as opening act—Conway was a favorite of his—so I promised front row seats for him and his wife, along with the Governor, should he come. I was running out of seats. When I rolled out the draft paper and showed him what I had sketched and then the notice from the City and the remarks made by the inspector, his eyes narrowed and he mumbled "Someone up there is afraid of you for some reason—this is bullshit!"

After thinking for a few minutes, he grabbed up the sheet and said he would be right back. After cooling my heels for half an hour, answering his secretary's questions about who we were having play The Palace, and what was Mrs. Williams really like and was she as pretty in person as on TV, he came back in with the sheet rolled up and taped, and with a big smile on his face.

"I'll tell you what to do King. I have made a few notations on your drawing and signed it. I'll have my gal here type up a lift on that stop work order. You go ahead and have your crew put in those toilets. We can send some down from a community warehouse here that is refurbished from condemned buildings, and they won't cost you a cent. I know it will look like a damn army barrack's pisser, but later on you can take some out if you want—claiming they are a public nuisance. The thing is young man, you need to get your crew working and get open; you don't have much time and I and the missus want to see Conway Twitty."

Politics, I learned, is all about bend a little, give a little and get a little back.

Whoever got to the Mayor or people at City Hall to put the stop work order on me was interested in me losing time and not being ready. The Mayor or City Hall issued the citing and that was all they could do. The State observed the citing, and went ahead and authorized the plans for me to fulfil the request for more toilets and lifted the stop work order so I could do it fast. Everyone was happy except the party that wanted to stop me.

Knowing Evelyn would never see the men's room, I said we needed some plumbing upgraded in there and the team went back to work. Later I unrolled the draft and looked at his notes and suggestions that the builder ignored, and down at the bottom was the stamp of The State Seal—with the Governor's initials scrawled beneath it.

He had taken the plans to then Governor Bill Clinton!
I was impressed.

In the years that followed, I not only voted for Bill Clinton each time, but campaigned for him. Because of the experience I had just had, to me, I saw a man who not only addressed small things to help people, but kept his word.

I was surprised at all the hoopla that surrounded the Clinton-Lewinsky debacle. I'm not saying that what went down was right, but I think in his own mind, Bill actually meant it when he announced on national television he "did not have sex with that woman." Besides, all boys in the South were just horndogs at heart. And, unless a good girl "went all the way," fooling around was not really having sex. It seemed to me that at the time, the accepted norm was that "hand jobs" and "oral activities" was not "going all the way" or having sex.

The few times I saw Clinton in Arkansas, he radiated warmth and charm, even across the room. It appeared to me that everyone thought so!

One New Year's Eve, I was in New Orleans with my Distributors for my company in Germany, one of them being Susan Hartung, one of the most beautiful women in Europe. Peter, a tall and well-dressed businessman, whom reminded me of a Senator. Since our hosts heard me call him that several times during the evening, they assumed he was a Senator. They took us to Jennifer Flowers' elegant Bistro for drinks. As I approached Miss Flowers, I saw this pretty, sweet-faced blond who managed to be demure and sexy at the same time.

"Well hello, Senator," she said as our hosts led me up to her after whispering something in her ear. Taking her hands in mine, I looked down at this little flower-like face and murmured, "I rather thought you'd have your sights a bit higher than a Senator."

She paused a moment letting this sink in and then burst into laughter, taking my arm and leading me around her new place. Her husband at the time, whom I immediately clocked as a rat and a hustler, was all over me like a cheap suit when he found out I was in aesthetic medicine and related fields. He kept asking me if I could get him a good deal in LA for his wife's breasts; he wanted them lifted or something.

Surprised that he would be so intimate about his wife's body to a perfect stranger, I replied, "They look fabulous to me and I am sure to others as well," and walked away. Later I was happy to hear that she divorced this cad, but at the moment she looked up at me before she laughed at my "higher than a senator" remark. I knew that she knew President Clinton, and well, perhaps not to the degree that was rampant in the press for a while but she knew him, and she loved him—everyone did.

With the remodeling work well underway, waiters and waitresses were being trained, sound systems and lighting were being installed and the stage was being decorated with giant gold tubes of shining Mylar and flat black paint. Rick Warren was rehearsing his boys for the dance music, and in between act numbers, I had started hiring some talent and getting Conway Twitty—without exactly knowing how.

I owed everything that happened in the next few weeks to veteran booking agent Chip Pay down in Nashville, Tennessee. I never actually met Chip, but we talked for hours on the phone after I called him up on another club owner in town's recommendation. I don't know if Chip is still with us now, I heard from a friend that his son took over his agency, but back then he saved our life!

It seems to me thinking back, that he was fascinated by what I was trying to do in such a short time. He had heard something about a Maybelline Heiress in Hot Springs and I think he liked our work with the kids. I told him everything—The Silver Ghost character, *Hollywood on Wheels* and what we hoped for now.

He seemed to like the fact we were giving a lot of down and out and young people jobs as well. Chip had dealings in the past with the big club owners, booking talent for them and some of his dealings went a little sour. That in itself maybe spurred him on to help someone who literally placed themselves at his mercy and expertise.

In a way I subliminally made him feel like he was creating The Palace Dinner Theatre, although to him he was just doing his job. Over the years I've learned that when you want the best out of anyone ask and defer to their opinions—never ordering them around or imposing just your opinion on them. They are the expert in their field and should be treated as such. I told him what we had, our facility and problems and our budget. He came back with a list of stars he felt would fill the needs of Hot Springs and we both agreed that a mix of Country and Classic Pop stars would be best for everyone. The availability of known stars in our budget range included Barbara Mandrell, Watermelon Wine Man, Tom T. Hall, Johnny Rodriguez, ragtime pianist JoAnne Castle and Rosemary Clooney.

Both Evelyn and I loved Rosemary, my favorite song by her being Love from White Christmas when she flees the upstate Inn and Bing Crosby and appears in New York all in black at a nightclub. George Chakiris was one of the dancers in that scene and I had a brief encounter with him a few years back—which makes that scene even more personal to me. She had been in rehab up until recently when I contacted Chip and in those days rehab carried a certain stigma. Nowadays it is practically mandatory for a star to be in rehab—great publicity! But then it was sort of hushing hush, making them seem to be perhaps a little risky. Her fee was not as exorbitant as I expected and we were her first booking after she got out.

I had the great idea that she be the guest of Mrs. Williams and I, good for publicity and better than staying in a hotel. Describing Maybelline Manor to Chip made him think it was a wonderful idea also, but he had to pass it by her first. We settled on the list he proposed and the dates and finally I gulped and said "Chip I would like to get Conway Twitty for the opening night if possible!"

He was silent for a moment and then said "Weeeelll, Danie, I know Conway pretty well, but his schedule is tight, and it will run you around $10,000 just for a one night stand."

I told him about the awards to be given to him based on the cities that he was named for and the Mayor and probably the Governor showing up. This seemed to impress him a little more. He said he would get back to me as soon as possible, but not to count on it—perhaps he could get Loretta Lynn or Dolly Parton for an opening show.

Late the next day an ecstatic Chip called me and said Conway would do it! He and his band were on a bus tour anyway to some other venue and could leave a day early and swing by Hot Springs and open the theatre. Thanking him profusely, I said "YES" aloud in my office and then got on the phone to the press and radio stations to set up Conway Twitty spots. Nearly every club owner in town who was a friend of mine called the next week begging for comps and good seats. I grandly told them I would do what I could IF they put our posters up in their clubs announcing the grand opening and helped to direct people our way.

I also promised that after every closing show, we would recommend any of the late night and after hours clubs from our stage. I was of the opinion that all show people help each other instead of competing all the time, something I learned from the Carneys at the Showmen's Association.

Tom T. Hall had done a commercial or two for Chevrolet Cars and trucks, so I hooked up the local Chevrolet dealer to run ads about The Palace in with their regular local commercials simply by saying 'and come see Tom T. at The Palace opening soon!" (The owner and his wife being promised good seats.) Of course with some of the good seats came comps for the dinner and Evelyn finally said, "Good Heavens, Dan, you are giving away the whole place the first night!" I reminded her that the first night was the one that determined the success of the entire Race Meet and that the drinks they would buy would more than make up for the free food.

Chef Coleman supervised the construction of the kitchen, made over from our concession stand and walled off from the club. I had to buy the range he wanted, the freezers and refrigerators and a Hobart dishwasher. I acted like it was his own kitchen and begged him to shop for the equipment like it was his own money. He did and got many good used items at low prices, everything up to code.

He really enjoyed designing the menus with Evelyn, she knew food and she knew people and where to cut corners and still look and taste great. I was touched to see this huge, somber African American man and the tiny little white lady poring over recipes and menus, their heads together. All the acts had accepted our offers and dates, although Rosemary Clooney had not yet indicated whether she would be our guest or not, a glitch that annoyed Evelyn, who had been planning on it. Rick's orchestra musicians were well rehearsed and all had their black tie and tuxes ready.

Nessie Berry and her group of assistants had the stage curtains hung and the dressing rooms arranged. We were almost ready. There was gossip that The Vapors was not too happy about The Palace. The Vapors was the most famous and longest running club in Hot Springs. It was to Hot Springs like Ciro's or The Mocambo was to Hollywood back in the 1950s. I did not know the venerable and well respected owner of the club, but I knew his son and he did not like me from the beginning. He was a good looking kid, typical rich kid, but had a sour and disdainful expression on his face every time I came into view. He ran or owned a small but exclusive high end clothing store and one afternoon shortly after I decided to settle in Hot Springs, I drove up and parked outside the shop, attracted by the window display.

There, on a male mannequin, was the most stunning jacket I had ever seen. It was fashioned like the classic World War II flight jackets that ace pilots wore, made of soft, butterscotch French leather with a high collar of soft Lynx fur. Beneath it, on the display floor, were a pair of matching high-top Italian styled boots with Cuban heels. I had to have both!

As I entered the store, the only clerk there came out from behind the counter, a sour expression on his face. Looking me up and down, asked in a flat voice, "Can I help you?"

Taken aback for a moment by this wave of hostility and wondering if my fly was open, I said, "Yes, I'm interested in that jacket and those boots. I nearly said, I *love* that jacket and boots, but something told me that anything that was less than macho would have him telling me the place was closed.

"Well they're both very expensive," he replied, a condescending sneer in his voice. "The jacket alone is $400."

At that moment I didn't care if they didn't fit me at all; he was suggesting I couldn't afford it and I was determined to show I could. Peeling off a few hundreds from my dwindling court appearance money, I told him grandly (and butch voiced) to box them up; I was already late for an appointment.

He reluctantly boxed up the items, although he informed me that if I wore the shoes and they did not fit, they were not returnable.

"They'll fit," I said cheerily as I swept out the door. He stood there watching me with the same sour expression as I roared off.

The boots fortunately did fit perfectly and the jacket became a legend in town—people never remembering seeing it in his window, and thinking it came from Hollywood. I was wearing it when they took my picture for the newspaper the day of the tragedy.

This shop owner would stare at me with increasing hostility whenever I saw him at The Sawmill Depot or other popular places around town while the construction of The Palace was going on. I chalked this up to resentment for all the employees we took from The Vapors and the musicians. A long time afterward, I was asked to meet my attorney at lunch and when I arrived, he was sitting at the table with my attorney and some other men. Nothing was said during lunch and in fact I was so intent on my problems and talking to George about my case, that I did not recognize the young man at first. After lunch we all got up and shook hands. When I came to him, suddenly I knew who he was but offered my hand anyway. He reared back his and snorted, "I wouldn't shake hands with the likes of you if my life depended on it."

After an embarrassed silence from everyone, I walked out the door, cheeks flaming. I have seldom met anyone in my life I could not win over with a little effort—if it were worth it. I knew that this person was, for some reason, a mortal enemy and to this day I don't know what role he played in any of the problems I had in Hot Springs or if he did play a role, but if anyone could have, it would have been him.

The night before the opening of The Palace was like a dream sequence, the calm after the storm. Everything was ready, checked and double-checked. The lights on the front and all their colors made the old Roller Rink look like an exclusive spot where only the privileged would go, very noticeable from the main highway.

Evelyn's image, looming high above the entrance, looked almost alive, her brilliant smile huge and inviting as her upraised hand welcomed everyone to come on in and have fun! *Helloooo, suckers!* Sure, it was a little corny in that Mae West costume, but it was show business and Hollywood, and that was what we were bringing to the Spa City of Hot Springs.

The next morning Evelyn was all atwitter with rehearsing her speech of welcome ("Dan, what if I forget the Mayor's name?") and having Steve polish all her jewelry, still not deciding which to wear with what. She finally decided on her silver sequined blazer and a long black satin pencil skirt, set off by her black cowgirl hat trimmed in sequin loops that she had designed herself. "I don't want to look too frou-frou," she exclaimed, "this is a horse crowd and we have Conway coming." She really didn't know who Conway Twitty was, except that he was a big country western star. I played his "Only Make Believe" hit for her on the record player and her only remark was, "Sounds like Elvis Presley." Elvis had just passed away and the country was reeling in grief and shock.

There had been an Elvis impersonator in town months before named Bill Haney. Bill looked nothing like Elvis, as most of the impersonators didn't, but he sounded uncannily like him. The club where I caught his act was run down and full of boozy middle aged women and sleazy, broken men. His Elvis jumpsuit costume was made of the cheapest material with the jewels glue-gunned on and tacky chains draped everywhere. The bell bottoms on his pants were "floods," being about 2 inches too high above his rundown and scuffed boots. Feeling sorry for him, yet impressed with his incredible voice, I bought him a drink during the break and offered suggestions and help about his wig, makeup and costumes. He was surprisingly open to my comments as he eyeballed my clothes and jewelry. Later I offered to drop him off at his motel up the road and his eyes almost bulged out when he got a load of the long, sleek white Eldorado he was getting in to.

"Man, is this the ride," he gasped as he settled into the deep leather seats. "I'm gonna get me one of these someday when my act gets to Vegas."

Impressed by his upbeat attitude over an act that was so low class, I asked him who made his costumes and he confessed that he'd rented them in a costume shop, all two of them, and then stole them, sacrificing his deposit. "My girlfriend fitted them better to me and put on all the studs and everything."

After leaving him off at the motel, I intended to help him with a new costume or two, and maybe feature him at the rink, calling it Elvis Night. I never did. Later, after Elvis passed away, I called Chip Pay to inquire about a fill-in act for the Saturday matinee. Rick had a couple of singers with his orchestra that were good, but I thought a novelty act might add to the attraction. During the conversation Elvis's untimely demise came up and I suddenly remembered poor Bill Haney and asked Chip if he had ever heard of him.

"Heard of him?" Chip laughed, "Danie, I can't get *to* him—everyone wants Bill Haney now that Elvis is gone; he's doing Vegas right now." I told Chip my experience with Bill and how bad I felt for him and his cheap, rental costumes. Laughing again, Chip informed me that Bill now had costumes as good as Elvis ever had, in fact exact copies, and backup dancers as well.

I was happy for Bill, although it was at the expense of a great Star passing away too young. He had a dream, did not give up on it—and it came true.

The next morning I sat in the office tense as a prostitute in an Amish prayer meeting, waiting for the liquor license to arrive. Not a drop of booze could be served by any of the bartenders or cocktail waitresses without it and I knew full well that an inspector would be on hand just waiting to catch me out.

At about 3 o'clock the man responsible for helping me get this vital scrap of paper, which asked to remain nameless, came beaming in and slapped it on my desk! Jumping up, feeling suddenly like a trillion dollars, I grabbed the frame I had waiting, inserted the license and walked it up to the bar telling the bartender to nail it up where all and sundry could see it. We were officially a club.

I drove home elated, after being assured by Barbara Wallace, Connie the head cocktail waitress, the bartender and Chef Coleman that everything was going to be fabulous. The Conway Twitty Bus (like a home on wheels) was parked at the side of The Palace, engine running and electric cable running into a hook-up through a back door. I wondered if Mr. Twitty was inside or at the Arlington Hotel downtown in a suite. The two arch lights we bought were being tested by some boys hired to man them, a crew was sweeping up the parking lot and setting up the valet stand. Inside, Rick and a piano tuner were going over his grand piano and I was told that every seat was booked with people wanting to pay for standing room only and eat off paper plates.

At The Manor I was confronted by a hysterical Evelyn who suddenly hated all her wigs, cursing that she had not ordered a new one. Settling her down, I proceeded to do her makeup, and putting a wig on her, I told her to place her hat on her head at which point I lifted and curled the hair in an upsweep in back with curls rippling along the tilted side of the hat. She loved the effect and shooing me out of the room told me to go down and get dressed. Steve had already dressed and had taken my car down to The Palace to be there to assist in any last minute crisis that may occur.

"Don't call here unless someone is killed," I warned him. "Evelyn and I need to be alone and get ourselves set for her entrance."

I had arranged for Rick to have the orchestra strike up a rousing refrain, "There Will Be a Hot Time in the Old Town Tonight," as we walked in. After putting on my tux, I met a glimmering and strangely quiet Evelyn in the hallway. She looked up at me and smiled, her small hand brushing away some lint from my lapel. "You look like Clark Gable, so handsome!" she whispered. "My Maybelline Prince."

"And you, my dear, are the very essence of Carole Lombard."

"Oh Lombard, a milquetoast, never could see what Clark saw in her," she snorted, as if they were next door neighbors. "Give me Crawford any time—now there was a girl with some guts."

"OK, Joan baby, let's go. I think we have a Palace to open—your Palace!" And I escorted her into the chill March air toward the waiting car.

She stopped me with a hand on my arm. "Dan, it's your Palace too. You built it; you put your heart and soul in it."

With tears springing unexpectedly to my eyes, I whispered, "Thank you darling, I won't let you down."

"I *know* you won't," she replied firmly and with a graceful twist of her body. Almost like a girl, she sank into the deep seats of the car and we were off.

We drove in silence, tense with anticipation. Evelyn had not seen The Palace at night with all the lighting effects, the tables dressed and the candles everywhere under the glowing chandeliers. I knew that the staff in their flowing costumes and the boys in their fitted black pants and tight vests would delight her; not to mention Rick's tuxedo clad orchestra and the stupendous buffet piled with prime rib, lobster thermidor, *pomme soufflé*, and *coq au vin du Napoleon*, would take her back to the grand Chicago days when supper clubs were lavish and elegant.

When we were nearly there and she saw the lights and the line of cars waiting to drive up to the valet stand, she suddenly clutched my arm and exclaimed, "Dan, will it be all right? Can we do this?" Her expression was a cross between frightened and curious.

"We can do this, Evelyn; we *will* do this," I said loudly.

"All right then, let's go make a million dollars!"

We swept up to the entrance and immediately the car doors were opened with, "Welcome, Ms. Williams, Mr. King."

There was a line of people in the hallway, waiting to get in, but our boys cleared a path. "Make way for Mrs. Williams! Make way for Mr. King!"

Steve's head appeared above the crowd, looked at me and nodded as he disappeared. All at once the rousing sounds of "There Will be a Hot Time in The Old Town Tonight" blasted forth as we were escorted to our front row table, everyone clapping and trying to shake Evelyn's hand at once.

After she breathlessly sat down, Connie, beaming and gorgeous in her white Grecian frock, took charge, ordering drinks and telling me that Conway's manager wanted to see me right way backstage. Evelyn waved me off—"Go, Dan, go"—as people started coming to the table to speak to her.

The rest of the night was a blur of color, faces and sound—like in a dream where things can fade in and out and suddenly change. You are sometimes looking at the action from afar, then all at once become part *of* the action.

Conway's manager wanted me to meet Mr. Twitty and to let him know when he was supposed to be presented with the awards Chip Pay had talked about. I said it would be best after the intermission—sort of a send-off for the finale of Conway's show. He agreed. Conway was standing there, shorter and thinner than I had imagined, but then most stars are when you see them in person. In the lights coming from the main stage where Rick and his orchestra was warming up the dinner crowd, I could see his skin was pitted with cuneiform acne scars and I secretly wanted to recruit him into some new acne treatments and scar removal products I was working on.

Recently Tommy Parsons, a makeup expert from Nashville and the head of our makeup department, told me he had done Conway's make up in the past and had to literally pound heavy makeup and powder into those scars to smooth his face out for television. Nevertheless, he was a pleasant and laid back man who had star presence, and when he walked onstage to a big fanfare, the crowd went wild—especially after "Make Believe." Grown women were gazing up at him with adoring smiles and tears streaming down their faces—such is the effect of beloved country western stars on their fans.

After the intermission, Mrs. Williams was announced. Mumbling the lines I had written for her, she made her way up to the stage—and found she was too small for the mike stand.

"Could somebody help a little lady?" she called out. Everyone laughed and a stage hand ran over and adjusted the mike. In a surprisingly clear voice she thanked everyone for coming, mentioned that the Mayor would be giving Conway Twitty two awards (how she remembered them I will never know), and then said, "Welcome to my Palace—and oh—*Helllllllooooo, suckers!*" as she waved her arms in the air. Clasping her hands over her head like a prize-fighter, she walked off the stage to a thunderous applause—Texas Guinan reborn.

The Mayor gave Conway the awards with much pomp and dignity, the show went on and Evelyn wanted to look around. It has all melded into one scene in my mind now: Evelyn at the buffet tasting things with her fingers and exclaiming how good it all was to the beaming Chef; Evelyn standing and gazing up at the chandeliers and wondering where I had gotten such big and gorgeous ones (forgetting she had authorized the purchase weeks before).

In fact everywhere she looked, Evelyn raved as if this were the most magnificent place on earth and she had nothing to do with it at all!

Thank You, Governor Bill Clinton!   185

In between her ooohs and aahhhs and whirling about with her hands clasped like a little girl, everyone wanted a photo of her. At one point she hissed to me out of the side of her perma-smile, "If I'd known I've have to grin so much, Dan, I would have put a coat hanger in my mouth."

She had been in on almost everything, had come down several times during renovations and saw how many things were tacked together temporarily to get us open. Shabby couches re-upholstered to look new and acres of flat black paint to hide flaws and roller rink walls, with the idea we would cover them better later. She knew that underneath the lights, the music, the beautiful costumes and the formally dressed people, The Palace was slightly shabby and makeshift. But on this night it was magic and wonder and perfect—and hers.

It was the last night of her life.

21

Elegant Courage

*A*s the Conway Twitty show wound to a close, his manager sat with me for a moment at the back bar and told me I really had a good thing going. From a seasoned pro, I took this as a huge compliment. I asked him if he had any suggestions. He thought for a moment and said, "Well, you have all this flat black paint everywhere except above those gold pillar things at the back of the stage. Looking over to the audience, I saw exactly what he was talking about—right above the faux Mylar pillars was the old roller rink white wall and it seemed to glare at me like a boil on a nose!

"Oh, no," I cried, my hands to my head, "how could I not have seen that?"

Smiling, he assured me that no one would really notice it at first, but just paint blasting it would finish it off. He went on to say that there was an energy at The Palace he had not seen in a long time, since the Grand Old Opry before it became a huge tourist attraction.

"You have *people's* people working here, Danie, and they all respect and love you. At least that is what it seems to me."

He went on to tell me that I had a good mix of talent and stars lined up, although he cautioned that Tom T. Hall could be a handful at times. Then he reminded me that we had a little business to transact and asked to see me in the office.

There, he informed me that Chip Pay had promised pay-upon-demand after the performance.

"Oh, of course," I replied, moving over to Evelyn's little bar to grab a Drambuie. Gulping it down gave me a chance to think. What had Chip negotiated for me? He'd mentioned $10,000 once, and in the flurry of getting everything else sorted out, I hadn't bothered to ask him how much we would owe. He already had deposits on all the other acts, and probably thought I would be good for whatever was charged by Conway Twitty's people.

Casually I looked over my shoulder and asked, "How much do we owe you?"

Looking at me levelly, a smile on his face that did not quite reach his eyes, he replied, "Oh, about $12,000—Chip really talked hard to Conway to get him down that much, this being a special side trip and all."

Thinking that $10,000 was the *possible* high end, I inwardly cringed. How could I have Evelyn sign a check that night for $12,000 without a major scene?

"Well, I'll have to get Mrs. Williams in here to sign a check for over $5,000." I smiled and turned toward the door, hoping her ecstatic mood would soften the blow.

"Ahem," he coughed. "We were told it would be in cash, you know, that's how we could discount it."

That's how you would avoid the IRS, I thought, and told him I'd have to go to the safe in my office. I rushed into the box office and asked the girl on duty how much was in the cash register.

"We had to empty it out a couple of times, Mr. King, but I got about $15,000 or so in this here bag on the floor," she said, pointing to a canvas bag. "And of course this isn't counting the main bar cash or the tabs and credit cards still open."

Somewhat relieved, I quickly counted out $12,000 and, writing up a quick receipt, ran back into her office where he was pouring himself a Drambuie. Grandly peeling off $12,000 in various denominations, trying to use only the biggest ones, I remarked, "OK then, there—it's a little bit unusual, but hell, Conway was worth twice that," and gave him the receipt.

Suddenly his smile did reach his eyes and he left with: "I think you have what it takes to run a real successful club, boy; call us anytime when Conway is free."

By today's standards, the cost for a major Country Western star then was almost laughably cheap, but it did teach me that everything always has to be understood up front—not that I would have turned down

Conway Twitty even if I'd known in advance it would cost $12,000. I'd promised the town Conway Twitty, gotten the Mayor and the Governor involved, fast-talked people into free promotions just to see the great man, and packed The Palace while emptying the Vapors and every other club in town. My enemies and friends were mounting by the moment—which group would win?

Evelyn finally admitted that she was tired and had to go home, and I was exhausted—as the photos in the press the next few days showed. As we drove home, Evelyn still chatting excitedly about who was there and how wonderful it all was, I remembered that the Ides of March were upon us, and on the 7th I would turn 34. I felt like a hundred.

At the Manor I fell asleep immediately, only to wake slightly when I felt Steve drop his long body into bed beside me, reeking of alcohol, as I probably did. We'd had his teeth capped and he still absorbed an odd liquor breath, although he was not a heavy drinker.

The next morning I woke up with a start. Steve was still asleep, his long hair falling over his patrician face, and the clock on my stand said 10 am. I pulled on a robe and dashed up the stairs to the kitchen where I heard Evelyn banging around. She was by the stove putting a large frozen chicken into a kettle of water. She was wearing slacks and a pullover and for some odd reason had on her big sunglasses.

"There's coffee, Dan," she said in a flat voice, as if nothing in the world had been going on, never mind an opening of a business such as Hot Springs had not seen in decades. She'd sent the girl we had (hired to help clean our place) down to the club to help with clean-up while Steve and I were putting long hours in getting The Palace ready.

"I'm defrosting this bird; I'm just going to make some nice chicken soup that we can all have when you get back this afternoon. We have to get ready for the second night and we don't need another big buffet dinner. I'm almost bloated from last night."

What she was really saying is that she had a hangover, and we needed a little of her famous "Jewish Penicillin," as she called it, to regenerate. I really did feel like crap and very tired. I was hoping to relax the entire day, only going to the club around 5 P.M. or so, to oversee the next show.

She turned and looked levelly at me from behind the dark glasses and said, again in a no-nonsense tone, "Dan, last night was wonderful, but it was an opening. Now you really have to make this pay—and that will take a lot of work. You need to get down there now. According to the box office girl, you gave away a lot of free meals and seats and a lot of cash to that Cowboy singer."

Mortified that she knew about the cash, I stuttered, "Well, dear, we *had* to make a statement the first night out, or we'd never have a chance to get the crowds for the rest of the Race Meet, and the other clubs would be laughing their collective asses off."

"I'm aware of all that," she responded coolly, "but the fact remains you cannot stop now. This needs your personal touch—all the way through, understand?"

Vowing that I did indeed, I poured a cup of coffee and ran down to get dressed, yelling at Steve to get his butt in gear. When we appeared back upstairs, bristling with fake energy, Evelyn's cheery mood had returned, although she said she was very tired and wondered if it was really necessary that she appear the second night—after all, she could not, at her time of life, be expected to always be clubbing, even in her own place. She also wanted to go over everything in the guest rooms where Miss Clooney was going to stay.

"Why don't you boys just come back at 3 o'clock. We'll have a little chicken soup and grilled cheese sandwiches and then I'll decide if I feel like getting ready. You can do my makeup like you did last night, Dan," she remarked cheerily as we slipped out the door.

"She'll go," stated Steve in the car. "She'll start thinking about last night and a hundred things she wants done or changed and how everyone was so glad to see her—wild horses couldn't keep her away."

Evelyn was right to send me down to The Palace. It was a nightmare of fights over tips from last night, the head bartender telling me we were totally out of beer and red wine, Connie complaining that one of the girls was sick and she was exhausted already, facing another crowd short-handed. Barbara also had bad news about the credit card machine being stuck and Chef Coleman dolefully reminding me that he was running out of prime rib, which I had forgotten to re-order.

Only Rick, calling in to tell me that he would be late but on time for the opening music, was positive and excited, recapping all the compliments and happy customers of the previous night. He said a lot of people were coming back for dancing to the Big Band Era sounds he was so good at and could we have dancing with dining first and then a longer intermission?

Yelling *yes* to everything the poor kid was so enthusiastically asking, I slammed the phone down and started barking back at everyone. They all stopped their squabbling and stared at me.

"Look, people, we had the night of nights last night and you *all* made great tips; I saw how much you were scraping off the tables." I glanced pointedly at Connie, who blushed and cast her eyes down.

"If you continue to fight over this, I'll start the share-the-tips equally policy like other clubs have, or better yet, build the gratuity into the check—customers see that and often don't leave anything extra." They all said, "no-no-no" to that and shut up.

I told Barbara to get someone to try and fix the credit card machine, squirt a little WD40 on it if it was stuck. This actually worked. Taking Chef Coleman aside, I apologized for forgetting to order the ribs. He grunted and said he could probably call a friend who had a barbeque joint downtown to tide us over for two days. I promised to tip his friend a little extra for helping out.

I then got up on my soap box and gave what was to be one of my inspirational speeches that have become my hallmark in nearly every country for years since. I told them they were not just waiters and waitresses and bartenders but that "they were *show* business people, all working together to create and build the finest Dinner Theatre Arkansas had ever seen." I told them, "We want to be the place where the celebrities who are playing the other clubs come on their time off to relax and have a great time. When the next Race Meets, I want the top stars to call Chip Pay and *beg* him for a booking at The Palace. We all have special talents," I added, and looked at each one individually. "We all have dreams of being something more than we are, and I think all of you who have known me and worked with me before this Palace was created, know me as a man who understands dreams and makes them come true."

Several nodded their heads, looking at each other and remembering when no one would give them a job. "Now you've watched me continue on with *this* dream against almost impossible odds with all of our competition thinking we couldn't pull it off."

In unison, most said, "But we did!"

"Yes," I agreed. "You've seen me do what everyone always says you *can't* do: *beat City Hall.*"

They all laughed and clapped, "Yeah, man, you sure did!"

With each statement I was getting into a rhythm almost like an Evangelist at a tent revival, and they were all swaying to that rhythm. In a hushed voice I said, "Now, there is a little Lady in the big house out there on Brown Drive with a big heart, who has put a large part of her fortune into this. She believes in us, she believes in *you*. Right now she's at home trying to decide what she is going to wear so she can come down here tonight and shine for *you*—to keep *your* dreams alive and to keep this place going until it is the brightest star in the nightclub circuit from here to New York City—*are we going to let her down?*"

"*Noooo waaaaay!*" they yelled in unison, Doug Berry pumping his fist up and down.

"Well alrighty then, let's get to work; we have a show tonight!"

I knew they were tired, and promised them regular shifts and hours. I told the girls and the waiters to go home, get a couple of hours rest and come back around 5:30. Barbara, Rod and Chef Coleman said they would stay on, Barbara said she could catch a few winks in Mrs. Williams' La-Z-Boy chair in her office, and Rod had a sort of RV he was driving where he could take a shower and relax—he offered this to Barbara and the Chef as well.

During this display Steve had been going around checking everything back stage, in the now famous toilets (a subject of much laughter from the male clients the night before). He reported that there was a bra left in one of the dressing rooms, which I thought strange, and one of the ladies room toilets was overflowing. After issuing some final orders regarding these details, I told Steve we had better go on home and eat chicken soup. I didn't like the fact that Evelyn was out there all alone for any extended period of time. There had always been someone around Maybelline Manor, usually Steve, but if he and I were busy elsewhere, one of the female staff would be assigned to keep her company and help her out. Evelyn would scoff at this, especially with Sam Saleem out of the way.

"I'm a grown woman," she would object, as I picked up the phone to call someone. "I'm not a baby and at times I *like* to be alone without anyone bothering me."

It was true. She adored going through her rooms and closets, setting up the many wigs she had me comb out after she rolled them up, each curl in small papers around the roller. Most of them were synthetic, so she would sit them on the oven door with the heat on low to "bake" the curl back in. Eventually I bought her a hood hair dryer from a beauty supply house, which was a mistake because then I had to roll them up—she couldn't manage to work the dryer. "You do such a better job, Dan," she would wheedle.

Sitting in the car with Steve, I was suddenly overwhelmed with the project we had taken on.

"Steve, I don't know how I can do this all the time," I said anxiously. "It takes enormous energy and tons of courage on a daily basis. I've learned a lot and know how to put on a show, but this is serious business and the competition has been doing it for decades. What if it fails and I waste the money Evelyn has left?"

"You can do it," Steve said. "You have all the courage in the world. Elegant courage I might add." Giving me an appraising look he added, "Danie, look at what you've pulled off already against enormous obstacles. Now that everything's in place, sure, there needs to be some upgrading of The Palace, but that can be done after the Race Meet when things slow down. You still have the townspeople as customers, and Rick will bring in the Village people. You can create musicals and shows and pageants. Pageant people are always looking for a great place to hold them and there are tons of talented young people desperate to get into legitimate shows with low pay—just to be seen."

He also reminded me that I had already met a lot of local talent agencies, small time to be sure, but with a need to showcase their clients. With a twinkle in his kind blue eyes, he finished with, "Don't forget, you are Mr. Showbiz in this town and you can attract anyone with a look—you attracted *me*."

I think I loved Steve in that moment more than any time since I knew him; he really was a good man, and a rock. My fears and anxieties started lifting as I thought about all the possibilities he had mentioned, and the idea that our goal was to make enough money to go into the age management and beauty spa business with the doctor, who had come to the opening with his wife and was even more keen to pursue our project based upon what he saw. "If we build the spa on your property, I guess I'll have to come up with some more money for my share," he exclaimed with a grin, "and we'll have a place for the patients to go for dinner and a show during their stay."

As we turned onto that winding road that leads to Brown Drive, I heard sirens in the distance. "Look!" Steve pointed, "there's a huge column of smoke."

There was indeed a massive, almost mushroom column of smoke above the trees in the distance. It was reddish brown and ominous looking. I thought of those old atom bomb movies they showed sometimes on TV.

"Oh it's probably one of those big houses on the other side of Lake Hamilton," I replied. "Evelyn is probably scared out of her mind."

22

"Tyger! Tyger! burning bright"

Somewhere deep inside I think I knew that only Maybelline Manor was big enough to generate that much smoke. But there are times in your life when confronted by extreme tragedy, events that are so devastating that there is nothing you can do; you just shut down with denial, thinking nothing this bad could possibly happen to me—these things only happen in the news or in the paper, to someone else, and far away from here.

But as I turned into Brown Drive I went numb—the scene unfolding before my eyes was a terrible movie or nightmare I would wake up from at any moment. About a hundred people lined both sides of the drive, cars were parked on neighbors' lawns, and the neighbors themselves stood around, arms folded, all gazing at the black hole that was the middle of Maybelline Manor. Most of them, seeing the big white Cadillac slowly approaching the devastation, looked at me with sad eyes and then looked way.

I took in everything in what seemed like a second. The center of the house and the kitchen were burned through, smoke still pouring out. There were fire trucks on both sides, hoses snaking everywhere. I saw an ambulance parked close to the house—I stopped the car with a jerk and leaped out, screaming, "Where is Mrs. Williams? Is Mrs. Williams all right?"

I remember thinking that maybe she'd had a heart attack and was in the ambulance—she would be OK. *I have to call Bill, where is the doctor, get her out of here…*all ran through my mind as I ran towards the ambulance. Steve had jumped out of the car even before it stopped moving—I remember him running towards what was left of the front door, hair flying, and long legs pumping. Then suddenly, as if through a fog, he was standing beside the driveway in front of the house, looking at me from under his cowboy hat, and his long fingers pointed down, down to a small form under a white sheet on the driveway. *Why, he looks like the ghost of Christmas future*, I remember thinking.

I started towards him and the fire chief grabbed me. "No, Danie, no, son, just calm down, you don't want to go over there."

"*Let me the fuck go!*" I bellowed, sensing that he was a kindly man but not a man who could stop me.

As I approached the form, Steve looked at me with a painful question in his eyes, a question that maybe he feared I did not want answered. Someone, an ambulance driver or one of the police, picked up the edge of the sheet and turned it back—another question in someone's eyes.

I knew it was her immediately even though the body had been burned to a charcoal black, an unrecognizable mummy, so black it looked almost fake, like a movie prop in a horror film. I did not know the human body could be turned to charcoal like that. But I could still see that elegant sweep of jaw, that elegant profile, and even though the eyes seemed melded into the face, they were her eyes, forever closed now in what seemed a grisly sleep.

My entire world fell apart. I screamed so loudly it echoed down to the lake. Crushing my hands to my face, I cried out over and over again, "Nooo, Evelyn, nooo!"

Chubby Les Beale, the *Sentinel Record* photographer, appeared out of nowhere and took my picture. It appeared on the front page the next day. I vaguely remember Steve leading me away while I babbled heavens knows what.

Before we got to the car, the fire chief stopped me again, and taking my arm, said very softly, "She didn't die in the flames son, those came later. She died of smoke inhalation and never felt a thing."

The thought of Evelyn shrieking in agony as flames consumed her had not yet crept into my mind. But I thought of it then and turned to him, hugging him, tears choking me as I said, "Thank you, thank you."

During this exchange the police had been talking to Steve, who also had tears streaming down his face. They wanted to take a statement from me, but after seeing me break down in the fire chief's arms they decided to let me go somewhere to calm down and then come to the station when I could. Steve told them we'd been at The Palace all day, a fact that they could easily check out.

I had no idea I might be a suspect in a possible homicide. My life as I knew it was over, my best friend, my *family* was gone and I did not know where to go—or even have a place to go to.

Danny, my early Silver Ghost spy who had helped me on my radio show, lived not too far away from Maybelline Manor. His father was a minister and for some reason I felt I needed a minister. It's ironic how much many of us don't think about religion on a daily basis, reserving our faith for church on Sunday, or Easter and Christmas—yet in times of real crisis, we turn to God through one of his emissaries. Since I had nowhere else to turn at the moment, it seemed right.

Danny's parents were shocked to see a trembling and shaking wreck, held up by Steve, at their door, but they'd seen the smoke, and they knew—and very gently brought me into their home.

I croaked, "Do you have a drink?" then felt guilty for asking a preacher for liquor. He hesitated and told me he thought he had an old bottle of scotch somewhere and brought me a glass. I gulped the liquor down, and the slow burn sharpened my thinking. "What should I do next?" I asked.

"Call Joe Lewis out in Los Angeles," Steve suggested. So with fumbling hands, I rang Joe.

He was very quiet while I hysterically told him what had happened. Then telling me to calm down, that Evelyn was gone and there was nothing I could do about it, he said I should call first the insurance company and then Bill Williams in Palm Springs.

"I can't!" I wailed. "He'll blame me for keeping her in Hot Springs." Never mind that it was Evelyn who had invited *me* to change my life and move there, and resisted all urges from her son to move back to Newport Beach.

Joe admitted I was probably right, and said he'd inform Bill. Meanwhile I was to get a hotel and continue running The Palace until Bill got there; the attorneys would handle everything in accordance with Evelyn's Last Will and Testament, a copy of which Joe had on file.

"*You'll be all right*," he assured me. "Probate takes time, and you're the VP of EVDAN Corp., which runs The Palace. Plus you're an heir. You'll be all right."

For once Joe Lewis could not have been more wrong.

Evelyn's Last Will and Testament would be the subject of conjecture for years. Bill's version was that shortly before the fire Evelyn had called him and said she wanted to "change her will and get rid of Danie King." If this were true, why did she go through all the hassle and work of opening The Palace? Why make a public appearance with Danie King at her side on opening night?

Evelyn was a good actress, but not that good—and we were very close. I would have known immediately if she were harboring some sort of secret resentment toward me. She was neither afraid of nor intimidated by me. If anything, the reverse was true! Evelyn was a very stubborn woman used to always getting her way, as her son well knew. I could gently "persuade" her on certain issues—walking on egg shells to do so—but she was not stupid, and if she said "no" to anything, she meant NO.

The only reason Hobby Derrick and Delyle Compton had manipulated her during the marriage was that they kept her drugged. Also, her pride got in the way and she didn't want to admit she'd made a huge mistake in marrying the con man. Only when she feared for her life did she wake up and take action.

And I had been with her when she amended her Will. It happened in her little home study, or "office" as she called it, after she expressed anger about how Bill was hounding her and trying to "run her life."

"I want to change my will, Dan. You have to be in it somewhere, and I've been thinking about how best to leave you all this Hot Springs business as my legacy." I assured her I was the least important person for her to worry about—my shares in EVDAN and my position as General Manager of The Palace were more than enough compensation, in my estimation. I was still young and sure of myself and was convinced I would be successful on my own in anything I set my mind to. Also, I didn't want Bill Williams to have a single tiny reason to challenge any benefits Evelyn chose to leave me in a Will; I knew all about how vicious families can be when it comes to inheritance. When greedy, how even love can fly out the window.

Most people fondly imagine they'll somehow be present when their will is read in the lawyer's office, delighting when a beneficiary they like is made rich and reveling in the groans of disappointed relatives they don't like. I pointed this out to Evelyn and reminded her she wouldn't even be there—hopefully she'd be flying around heaven on silver wings.

She laughed. "I know that, Dan, but I want the money to go where it is best invested—to people who will help you keep my interests going here, in my name."

She wanted to be remembered.

Pen in hand, she went down the list, asking me what I thought of each family member. She was adamant right off that Bill already had enough money in his own right and had married a wealthy woman, Gloria Rosan, to boot.

"But Evelyn," I said, "you have to leave him *something*, or he could contest everything."

Tapping the pen against her forehead, she thought for a moment, then exclaimed brightly, "He loves my Eldorado! I'll leave him that!" and wrote it down next to his name.

Then she came to her granddaughters, Billee Rae and Sharrie.

"Oh, Sharrie is married to a successful man and will always be well-off," she exclaimed airily, "and Billee Rae is beautiful and was brought up as a rich girl. She'll attract and marry some millionaire, Bill will see to that." She made some more notations on the paper. I forgot how much, if anything, she decided to leave to the girls, but it was Preston to whom she wanted to leave the bulk of her Estate—including the house, most of The Palace property and the land it stood on.

As for me, I was to receive a small share of The Palace and maintain my position as General Manager. Beyond that, all I asked for was the right to occupy the premises known as Maybelline Manor on Brown Drive for the period of one year after her "demise." At the time the will was made, I figured a year would be ample time for me to buy a place of my own.

Bill Williams and a great many other people thought I was "in it for the money," manipulating a well-to-do older woman for personal gain. But I don't think this way—never have. My nonchalance about money is known even today, after I made several million dollars. I've been down and out a few times, but always knew it was only temporary and things would go back up again. I've never even formulated a product based upon what I thought it might make in dollars—my focus has always been on what things will *do*.

"You get along with Preston," Evelyn said. "Do you think you could work with him running The Palace?"

For a moment I wondered if he would even be interested moving to Hot Springs—then I remembered how much he had liked Angela Chiarelli, and said I thought I could work very well with this intelligent but shy kid. Evelyn seemed satisfied, and folding the notes up in an envelope, she told me to make an appointment with Eudox Patterson the next day to officially record the will.

Not long after that I called Joe Lewis in LA and read him the Will. He murmured in that quiet, hesitant way of his, "Danie, you could have gotten a lot more—you deserve it and she'll go along with it if I tell her to."

"I'm quite happy with my portion," I said. "Besides, I don't want a major legal battle with Bill Williams. Please don't interfere."

After thanking the minister and his wife for their kindness, I left for The Arlington Hotel, where Steve had booked me a suite. I collapsed into bed, still not believing the nightmare that had just unfolded. Sleep eluded me as scenes about Evelyn repeated over and over in my mind. I just could not get my brain around the fact that she was gone. A line from William Blake's "The Tyger" (from Songs of Experience) came to mind: *Tyger! Tyger! burning bright, In the forests of the night...What the anvil? What dread grasp, Dare its deadly terrors clasp?*

How dare my sweet Evelyn be gone.

The fire chief had said Evelyn did not suffer; if she'd been overtaken by the flames, her face and body would have been twisted in agony. Instead they'd found her on the floor next to the door, lying on her back with her features relaxed in the expression of someone who had just gone to sleep. I'd seen this with my own eyes. Still, what *had* she gone through at the end, lost and frightened in the smoke?

Her rooms were located halfway down a long hall to the right of the main entrance. Perhaps she'd seen or smelled smoke and run out to see what was wrong. According to the firemen the smoke would have been like thick fog; after a few deep breaths even a younger person would have collapsed. Or maybe Evelyn had already been down in the laundry room washing undergarments when she'd noticed smoke creeping down the staircase. She'd rushed upstairs and groped blindly toward the front door, confused, coughing....

And she *had* reached the door...only to have the so-called "security" doorknob come off in her hand. Perhaps this was a blessing. Later I was told later that opening the door would have welcomed in enough oxygen to arouse the flames and engulf Evelyn entirely in fire. She would have fallen in agony onto the front driveway, and either died there or survived only to be hideously scarred for life.

Still, I cursed myself for leaving that doorknob simply screwed in place instead of going against Evelyn's wishes and getting it fixed. But of course we never know when the smallest seeming thing might be of utmost importance, do we?

After I'd tossed and turned and cried miserably for two hours in my bed, Steve called my GP, Dr. Fodio, who came by and gave me a massive sedative by injection.

I spent the next morning making calls to The Palace and being confronted by tearful employees who insisted I carry on business as usual while awaiting the arrival of Evelyn's family from California. I also called my lawyer regarding the will and was told that it contained exactly what Evelyn had proposed. Furthermore it stipulated that I continue our work in her name, with full signatory powers on the EVDAN account. I told him we should probably set up a meeting with Bill Williams when he got to town so we could make plans for a funeral and a memorial service at The Palace. This was something I knew Evelyn would have liked very much.

None of it happened.

Later I heard that even while I was ensconced in my suite at the hotel, Bill Williams had swept into town with Gloria in tow, and was staying in the same place. I was still too shaken and rattled to talk sensibly to the man who was about to become my nemesis, so I wrote him a long and emotional letter on hotel stationery and had Steven slip it under his door.

In the letter I offered genuine condolences, told Bill a little about what I had seen and how happy his mother had been the night before, and offered to meet with him the next day to at least plan a memorial. I realized he would probably want to take her remains back to California and bury them with a beautiful headstone in a family plot. I also pledged to make sure her legacy, The Palace, grew into the profitable business we had hoped it to be.

It had not yet sunk in that this arrogant man still envisioned me as some sort of silly little hairdresser fag, sort of a pet of his mother, certainly not a man to be taken seriously in regard to any business his mother owned.

A little while later I received a call from Gloria who, in a gentle voice, told me Bill was mourning his mother's passing and didn't want to see me at all—ever. He would contact me through lawyers only, and in the meantime I should make no attempt to speak to him.

Feeling Gloria to be a kind woman, I cried, "Why?"

She said Bill did not approve of my "lifestyle," and when I tried to pin her down to specifics, she said, "Oh, well, your extravagances—he saw all that when we were here; the beautiful maid—I've had some maids of my own, Danie, and none of them were as beautiful and *personal* as she was."

I almost screamed, "Why can't he make up his goddamn mind? Either I'm gay or a womanizer!" Ironically, Evelyn had gone to a great deal of effort and expense to make sure her son and his family had a wonderful time during their visit—and now he was trying to lay it off on my "extravagant lifestyle." On top of everything else, I felt the man was jealous, pure and simple—yet my very gay-ness gave him an excuse not to confront me openly like a man.

Gloria asked if I would not go down to my office for a day so Bill could go there and look around. She also requested I make the keys to the Cadillac available since they were going to be in town for a few days and didn't see the sense in renting a car. This seemed like a lot of requests from a man who had just indicated he wanted nothing to do with me, but I still had the idea that after the shock was over Bill would see the value of the things his mother and I had accomplished, and want to work things out.

Instead, it took him exactly one day to swagger around town intimidating everyone with his Palm Springs Millionaire act combined with a Grieving Son routine.

I've also come to the conclusion that there was some hanky-panky going on that involved a certain type of Arkansas lawyer—the kind who hoped to cash-in by going along with the Millionaire instead of Danie King, a man they already knew they could not put one over on.

In his arrogance, Bill thought he was dealing with a bunch of hicks, but Evelyn had experienced the reality, and so had I.

On day two I went to the office and found everyone acting nervous and frightened. They told me that Bill had come in, demanding to see all the books and receipts and announcing that he was taking over on behalf of his mother, and that things were going to change. He'd also assured them that they would keep their jobs—particularly Barbara Wallace—but that depending on what was left in the EVDAN accounts at the bank, some of them might have to be let go.

Neither Connie nor Chef Coleman, who had been in the club and restaurant business a long time and seen every type of high roller there is, trusted him. Later, Bearbra Coleman told me that the moment Bill walked in he'd felt like packing up his knives and leaving—but he wanted to wait and see what I had to say. "I work for you and Ms. Williams, not that man," he said, followed by "God rest her sweet soul."

Barbara, on the other hand, was totally changed; she was almost pompous and arrogant toward me. "I'll see to it the place is run better when the new management takes over," she said.

When I pressed her for details on what she meant, she stomped out of the office. I realized I should have gone to my office the day before, along with my attorney, and confronted Bill. He wasn't even a major beneficiary in Evelyn's will, inheriting only a used car, while I was officially the VP of EVDAN Corp and the general manager of The Palace. A will can take months to probate, and even my small portion of the ownership of the property was not to be questioned during that time.

As long as there were assets and a going business, The Palace should have been left to run out its pre-paid talent contracts, advance bookings and the Race Meet, until such time as probate was settled. Then it would have been up to Preston Williams, the largest beneficiary, to decide what he wanted to do with his share—work The Palace with me, fire me and work it alone, or sell out. But Preston was not present, and Bill was "acting on behalf of and in the interest of his son's legacy"—not his mother's, but rather, his son's.

I knew Bill had been furious when he saw the Will. There were stories that he wanted to contest it—that his mother had called him up shortly before the opening of The Palace, claiming that she had caught me having an orgy with several men and wanted to change her Will and oust me now that she "knew what kind of person I was."

To the more intelligent people in town, and the amusement of some attorneys this did not make sense. First, there had been no orgy; even if anyone had been so inclined, nobody had time during the overtime rush to get The Palace ready. Secondly, I was a minor beneficiary whom Evelyn could simply fire if she was so eager to "get rid of me." No, Bill Williams was acting in the best interest of himself, trying to salvage what money he could from a hick town he didn't like and blamed for his mother's demise.

I forget how I was ultimately told the news, but via some official communication from an attorney I was relieved of my job as General Manager of The Palace. I was not to come in or near The Palace at any time, or attempt to influence its employees. I was to remove any or all personal effects from my former office under the watchful (and triumphantly spiteful) eyes of Barbara Wallace and a sheriff's deputy.

The reason I was given for this action was that there was a possible criminal investigation going on, and I was listed as someone who could possibly be involved. I could no longer represent the deceased's interests, nor was I to leave town until such investigation was completed.

Looking back, this ridiculous communication was a joke that I could have easily swept aside if I'd stood up for my rights. But I did not— and I paid for that dearly over the next few months. I was interviewed by the police, whom I'd known well on better terms, including a detective who, feeling that this might be the case of his career, tried to act like Columbo towards me in order to trip me up. At one point he leaned over his desk, narrowed his eyes and said, "Why did you have her stuffed with cotton?"

I was taken aback. I didn't know what to say. Was he imagining some kind of kinky, geriatric sexual fantasy or worse? Death by cotton batting? Then I calmly asked him if he had ever heard of prolapse of the uterus.

He turned red. "No."

I explained Evelyn's temporary solution to avoiding a surgery she feared. He cleared his throat and changed the subject.

Rumors boiled like lava all over town about who had killed Mrs. Williams. Oddly enough, the same rumors are still all over the Internet to this day, whipped on by delusional people who have nothing better to do than to speculate on something that never happened. Some would say she was killed by the so-called "Dixie Mafia," sent in by competitive club owners who were afraid The Palace would get all the Race Meet revenues. Others said it was friends of the evil Sam Saleem getting revenge. Sam was a crook to be sure, but a crook for profit, not revenge. Others even claimed it was Zeke, also seeking some sort of emotional revenge. But I knew him and knew this could not possibly be true.

The Palace stayed open through the performances of Jo Anne Castle, Tom T. Hall and Rosemary Clooney. By then I'd hired a lawyer, a young civil rights-style attorney named George Callahan. He and his fiancée, a gorgeous girl named LaDonna Dollar, became friends of mine and immediately made my miserable life easier. George laughed at the demands that I not enter The Palace at any time, and had this rescinded. He also thought Bill was a joke—but a joke who had a lot of people fooled, so he advised me not to pressure Bill on anything.

The EVDAN account was frozen, with funds going only to the bare bones maintenance of The Palace in order to keep it open and avoid possible suits from booked talent and Chip Pay. I could get my position back, George told me, but only after a costly legal battle. I couldn't do that. I was broke and had nowhere to live except for with friends, some of them humble country people who apologized for the meager accommodations they offered Steve and me, saying, "We know y'all are used to much better than this."

I will never forget these wonderful people.

George advised that I lay low and wait things out until probate was settled. "The Palace *is* going to close, Danie," he flatly stated. "Bill Williams is running around here grandstanding, but he knows nothing about running a club—I hear he was in the dry cleaning business before. Without you and Evelyn, The Palace is a dead duck."

I conceded that he was right and felt terrible for all the people who had pinned their faith and hopes on us. For some reason none of them ever blamed me for The Palace closing; they knew what was going on, and every time I did go in there they treated me like a big celebrity, offering drinks on the house and the best seat.

The first time I went in, Barbara and one of her "security guards" tried to stop me.

"You can't come in here," Barbara huffed, eyes pig-like.

"Barbara," I retorted, "let's get on the phone and call George Callahan and then the police; you're obviously mistaken."

The guard stared at me with crazy eyes for a moment and then walked away, shaking his head. Barbara huffed and puffed some more, her lips working furiously, then also stomped off.

I yelled after her, "You still owe me $500!"

"Just try and get it!" she hollered back. Several customers at tables overheard this exchange and laughed.

Before going into the club I always sent Steve in first to make sure Bill was not there. By some twist of fate he never was, having always left just before I arrived, or not come in at all that day. I did see Rosemary Clooney for a moment backstage (Barbara's guard still trailing me with crazy eyes) and told her about Mrs. Williams, and our plans to have her as our guest at Maybelline Manor.

"Oh dear," she said. "Honey, I'm so sorry about what happened, yes, I heard about that and would have loved to have stayed with you, but I had my husband and son with me and didn't want to impose."

I thanked her for a wonderful show, letting her know she was an all-time favorite of mine. I also said that I "knew" George, the dancer from *White Christmas*. Knowing exactly what I meant, she smiled and said, "Oh yes, George is a cutie—he knew a lot of people back then."

Not long after this, Bill left town and The Palace closed. According to Bill, "There just isn't any money." (Years later I heard The Palace had re-opened . . . under the name The Centerfold Club.)

I don't know how much money there was or was not. We were okay after The Palace opening. There were no loans outstanding and I probably could have gotten one if I needed it. I know that had I stayed on as General Manager, The Palace would have made it and Bill could have left town with the assurance that not only was his son's inheritance protected, it would grow into something even more substantial. Instead, it was disaster for all.

I got a loan based on Evelyn's bequest, still grinding through probate, and bought a custom-made Malcolm Bricklin automobile. The ill-fated DeLorean, which came out much later, was copied from Bricklin's marvelous space-age design, except not as well made. Looking back, buying the Bricklin was a stupid move, but only 3,000 of the cars were built, and my owning one made a statement that Danie King was still there and there to stay!

I had finally been allowed to get all my belongings and clothes—smoky-smelling but cleanable—from the Manor. As the chief fire inspector and I walked around the sad and dark place that had been my home, he pointed out all the flaws behind the rumors swirling around the cause of the fire.

Entering the butler's pantry where the "second fire" was allegedly started, he pointed to the ceiling. There I saw a small circle of blackened boards. A few crumbles of burnt wood had fallen onto the unharmed tile floor below.

"Fires usually burn up from their original site," the inspector said in a scoffing voice, "not down. The walls in this little pantry would have gone up in flames if there was a second fire set here."

In fact the entire lower part of the house, including the bar, had not been damaged at all except by smoke. After walking upstairs, we entered the gutted kitchen and living room. Everything there was unrecognizable—even Evelyn's velvet tuxedo couches had become strange, melted forms that looked like dead animals.

"This is where it all started" the inspector said, pointing to where the stove—now nothing but a black and rusted metal frame—stood. "We found a pot with some bones in it. It was probably left unattended and caught fire. The overhead vent was full of grease, hadn't been cleaned in years. The whole thing smoked until a door got opened somewhere and it all went up in flames."

I told him about seeing Evelyn putting a chicken in a pot of water to cook, and how she'd done things like that before and then forgot about it. On the other occasions a maid had discovered it in time.

"Son," he said quietly, "Her death is a complete accident."

Later Steve and I assessed what we had left. The maid's quarters, including its full kitchen, were untouched. The roof of most of the house had not burned through. In fact, only the kitchen, living room and part of the dining room were totally burned.

"Why, we could live here," I exclaimed, and decided to call George Callahan, who was handling my probate and fighting Bill William's feet-dragging regarding what my percentage of the property really was.

Excited, Steve and I packed up all my things and went back to Johnny Angel's where we were staying.

George tried, maintaining that a line could be attached to the electricity of the maid's quarters, as it had separate electric boxes anyway. But the City insisted that living there would be too dangerous, even though Evelyn's will stipulated that I could stay on the property for one year.

Desperate for funds, I sent Steve out to the Manor several times to search for cash that Evelyn might have stashed away. I felt this was owed to me, as my last three paychecks written on the EVDAN account had not been honored, the account being first frozen and then closed. Steve was lucky twice, and each time I cast my eyes up and said, "Thank you, Evelyn."

Finally things began to turn. Roger Lewin and I started up a modelling agency and photo studio and became well-known in town, teaching classes at Garland County Community College with a charming young lady named Rhonda. Soon every girl in town and every bride and groom wanted to be photographed by Lewin and King.

Aspiring male models, many of them closeted and afraid to be themselves, *became* themselves after being around me. They had watched me from the sidelines during my very public ups and downs, and when I did not disappear, never to be heard from again, they came out of the woods themselves. I would see them sitting in restaurants with a new boyfriend, defiant against any prejudice—just like King would do. While Harvey Milk was leading parades for equality and diversity in San Francisco, I was, without knowing it, a Social and Civil Rights activist in my own way, in Hot Springs.

Hot Springs was not an openly homophobic town. There were too many eclectic people there for that, not to mention the show business types and gay celebrities that came for the Race Meet. You could be gay, you could even be a drag queen—as long as you stayed in your place and out of other places. But my style was to be who I was and what I was, anytime, anywhere and anyplace. Of course this only works if you do things with class and consideration and don't put all your business in the streets. Taste still *is* taste.

I met a young photographer, Kevin Ellsworth, who was in town as a horse photographer for the Race Meet. Years later he would end up as one of the best fashion photographers I had ever met, eclipsing even Harry Langdon, whose celebrity photos were legend. Kevin was the total "ladies man." Think of Johnny Depp suddenly appearing in Hot Springs and running around with the town's most controversial person. He had the energy of the Energizer Bunny which was necessary because girls of all ages were standing in line. He possessed a haunting beauty and a casual, laid back attitude that let women know he *really* loved them, not just wanted to go to bed with them.

Years later, in Chicago, Kevin and I did a photo-shoot of a very young Cindy Crawford. She'd been "Miss Corn Queen" of DeKalb, Illinois or something like that before photographer Victor Skrebneski made her one of his famous "young, hot icons." She was 18 years old the day she came into the loft studio where Kevin was doing the shoot. It was a miserably hot and humid day and the air conditioning had broken down.

This tall and rather severe-faced young lady sat down in my make-up chair, not moving a muscle as I tried to interpret her face. I knew instinctively she was an up and coming model—she had a hard edge about her that screamed "total focus." I thought her face had a dramatic "fifties movie star" look. But she had a natural mole that she was very concerned about, and asked if she should have it removed.

I said "no," and pointed out that it could become her trademark, like Marilyn Monroe's beauty mark (I didn't add that Marilyn's was fake and moved around from picture to picture).

When I was done and she looked in the mirror she went ballistic. "That is *waaaay* too much makeup!" she wailed. "Skrebneski says I need hardly *any* makeup!"

Kevin and I both thought she was stunning, but his assistant and then-girlfriend, Tria, sided with Cindy—both girls practically in tears over my rendition. Eventually I gave up and removed half the makeup, giving her the more natural look she thought was "her."

Years later I would note with amusement that she ended up with pretty much the look I gave her—dramatic and riveting. And she kept the mole.

Steve finally left me—I was so tied up with Roger, the business and getting my life back on track that I wasn't spending much time with him.

Chicago soul food restaurant Queen Mary Anderson became my patroness, and soon I was once again "somebody" in town, hailed by one and all as a mover and shaker who drove a Rolls Royce instead of an Eldorado. Mary loved to hear my Evelyn stories, and had me repeat them to any guests who came to her house.

Like me, she wondered what Evelyn must have felt in her last moments. Was it true that everyone had a number, and hers had simply been up? Evelyn had feared becoming infirm and crippled with age. I made fun of these worries, telling her she would never age; she'd go in her sleep without any pain. I like to think that she did just that.

I also wonder if, in her final moments as the carbon monoxide eroded her blood stream, she had a "release of the spirit" experience. If she found herself floating high above Maybelline Manor, looking down at the crowd of stunned spectators, police cars, fire trucks and the ambulance…and the tiny figure of a young man bent over her burnt body, sobbing with his face in his hands. Was she serving as an angel for me now?

If so, did she shake her head and say, "Oh, Dan, you'll be okay; you can do anything" as she smiled, her face then turning to the light.

We were such good friends. We were good business partners. And we had so many years of great and fiesty fun.

Evelyn, the "tyger! tyger!, burning bright" as William Blake had written:

When the stars threw down their spears,
And watered heaven with their tears,
Did he smile his work to see?
Did he who made the Lamb make thee?

PART: 2

First Star to The Left

23

The Gay Rights Lecture

Mary Anderson was coming out of retirement due to some misconduct by people she'd left to run her Queen of the Sea restaurant in Chicago. She had purchased two condominiums by the lake in tony Hyde Park, and wanted Roger and me and a very eccentric woman who lived with us to move up with her and stay in one of the condos while I continued my skin revision research. She wanted to turn it into a real business for African-American skin type.

I think she was lonely in Hot Springs Village, being the only African-American woman there. The charm of fishing and making superb sea food gumbo had worn off.

The "eccentric woman," Eileen, was in her early forties. She was attracted to our photography and thought she could model. She did have a Garbo-like face and had come from a mainline, blueblood family in Pennsylvania; she also had mental issues and little money despite her expensive wardrobe. I liked Eileen however odd she could be and moved her in with us. I think in her way she was in love with both Roger and me, but she'd always refer to me as "a Renaissance man."

My inheritance had finally come through, after much wrangling at court appearances by my Hot Spring lawyer George Callahan and even a visit from Joe Lewis, who tried to convince His Honor that when Mrs. Williams referred to "The Palace Dinner Theatre and the property it sat on," she meant the *entire* property at Gulfa Gorge, including the location where we were going to build the Spa.

The judge did not see it that way—perhaps he was tired of the Danie

King Show. He ruled that the Williams family was offering to buy out only my share of The Palace and its dirt. He suggested I take the deal. I did. After paying off the Bricklin loan and George's well-earned fees, I was left with a grand total of $30,000 to my name. It is hoped that I also made young Preston a wealthy man.

There was nothing more to be done. We planned to leave Hot Springs in a caravan of three cars and go to Chicago, home of Tom Lyle Williams and birthplace of Evelyn. It seemed fitting.

Just before we left I received a call from a man in some position with the FBI. He was tall and quietly spoken, not the Men In Black with sunglasses and a frozen face as I expected.

He said, "I want you to do a lecture on homosexuality for some FBI staff, Arkansas State Troopers and the police force."

I was taken back—I'd heard that something called "gay rights" was emerging, and at this same time Harvey Milk was being murdered on the steps of the very building he occupied as Mayor for speaking out on the rights of gays and everyone else. Although my audience was to be more controlled, I was scared nonetheless.

I asked why he'd picked me, and he said the gay community in the USA had made political gains, and law enforcement agencies were interested in better understanding how gay people thought, who they were, and what walks of life they occupied.

Although he was very casual, I felt he was talking about animals in a zoo. They'd picked me because I was a good writer; my little "Inside Out" column really *was* being watched by Big Brother! He also said I was very visible as a person and could speak to a crowd.

All at once, I knew exactly what I was going to do and say—so I accepted and rushed home to tell everyone I was going to lecture to the FBI and State Troopers.

I knew they expected to get a "personal" story from me, sort of a public confession, an expose they could lick their chops over. Instead, when they filed into the room, some in full uniform—mostly men but a few women—they were confronted by a serious young man as conservative as a Republican lobbyist in a black suit.

Beside me was a whiteboard I'd insisted on having. After everyone settled down, I introduced myself and then thundered, "HOMOSEXUAL!"

Everyone jumped as I scrawled the word in capital letters across the top of the board.

Then I calmly said, "The dictionary definition is 'the same as.'"

The same as *what*? they were all wondering.

I proceeded to categorize the different homos they would encounter in their daily work. They leaned forward, fascinated.

As if I were one of them, I described the butch or masculine gay—someone they could see everywhere in every walk of life. I pointed out that this would be the least likely victim of crime, inasmuch as he or she blended into mainstream, often under the guise of marriage. Some of the officers glanced furtively at one another.

I went through other descriptions: effeminate gay men, butch gay women, drag queens and transsexuals. I did psychological profiles on all of these "types" and why I thought they were the way they were, and how best to treat them in any legal or law enforcement issue. I sounded like a training manual. They were hooked.

I cautioned them about older gay men—that contrary to popular belief, they don't always prey on young boys—in fact the situation was often the reverse. I described the young hustlers out in the street, the blackmail that goes on after they've hooked their older prey, and how to spot it. Everyone was entranced, many taking notes.

It was all very positive until the end when I started to talk about real relationships and love. The State Troopers down front started to squirm, and one of them yelled, "Hell, I sure as hell love my fellow troops here but I wouldn't want to sleep with any of 'em."

I looked over the crowd for a moment and then said, "Well, I can see why."

They broke into laughter.

That was the end of my speech and I thought I had escaped putting myself in the picture until one very dyke-looking female officer called out, "Isn't it a fact that y'all yourself a homosexual, King?"

The crowd grew silent, waiting.

I looked directly at her. "Well, no, darlin', I'm not a homosexual last time I looked." My voice getting louder, I said, "And I am neither Bi-sexual, Asexual nor Heterosexual."

Red-faced, she demanded, "Well, what the hell *are* you then?"

I'd been waiting for a chance to use this one liner for years.

"I'm just sexual," I said, and the room erupted into laughter and applause.

Afterward the FBI agent told me it was the most informative social presentation he had ever heard. They had all learned a lot about people, and it would help everyone make better decisions in gay arrest or protection cases. He asked if I would be interested in going on a lecture circuit to other cities, on Government salary of course.

Who knows what might have happened if I had said "yes"? Harvey Milk paid in blood for his public speeches, and here I was being offered by a representative of the United States Government to be paid in money for my identical views.

I chose a different course, but in later years I would become deeply involved with The Harvey Milk Foundation and Harvey's nephew Stuart, and end up in the world of politics and international campaigns for diversity.

But at the moment I had a partner, a disturbed woman, and a wealthy investor to consider—and besides, I knew nothing about being militantly gay. I didn't feel I had to fight for any rights or march in parades. I was not one of those men who put on a bra, hot pants and a huge wig while wearing a beard and moustache, then walks down the streets shouting and waving his arms.

Sure, I'd had a few homophobic encounters, like with Bill Williams and the boys in my first week in Hot Springs, but I usually faced such things head on—and everything usually went my way. Why should I identify with any group by going around lecturing about them? I was not a liaison-between-enemy-lines type. My casual counseling sessions with young closet gays and just being myself always, was enough for me. I'd never been truly bashed or made fun of to my face, or beat up— why should I fight for something I already had?

24

From Danie King to Danné Montague-King, a "Pioneer and Legend"

My career in aesthetics really began when I moved to Chicago under the sponsorship of Mary Anderson. When I first arrived with my little entourage, Mary was genuinely trying to promote my skin revision range for black skin.

She and her female cronies were delighted when I posed the following question at cocktail parties and dinners: "Put a fifty-year-old white lady and a fifty-year-old black lady side by side, and who looks older?"

"The white lady!" they would all yell—and then cackle with laughter.

I would sober up this levity-fest with the hard facts of why this was so. First, that African skin has a more rapid cell turnover than most Caucasian skin, which means that new, baby cells are on the rise to the surface for most of their lives, albeit slowing down rapidly in advanced age.

Secondly, the downside of this is the keloid scars common to black skin—any injury or breach in the tissue results in a rapid proliferation of new cells that over-blow the site of injury, forming irregular, bumpy, raised scar tissue.

And three, that African skin is stronger. Back when the planet was born, all mankind was endowed with specific characteristics to enable them to withstand the assaults of nature. The copious melanin in black skin acts like a reflective shield against the harsh and direct sun rays of the African continent. As a result black skin suffers less ageing from solar damage than lighter skins do, and the farther north we go, the less sun there is and the less need there is for copious melanogenisis (pigmentation).

There are several other superior aspects to African physiology, but all these "pluses" become "minuses" if the wrong chemistry is used in daily skin care products. This included *all* the so-called African-American skin care ranges, which were modeled after Caucasian products with only marketing to define their use. A famous Black skin care guru once told me that I was going to "too much trouble" in formulating according to racial characteristics. "All I have to do is to tell 'em what to use and they use it," he bragged. I left his office outraged, determined to go it alone as a white scientist.

Mary's description of her people's skin after I did treatments on them was, "They will recognize their skin." What she meant was that when African-American people saw skin akin to when they were young—skin that was in full health and operating with the right chemistry—they recognized their younger skins. This is when I realized I was not really "changing" anything, I was merely helping skin to be the way it was meant to be. I didn't buy into the "cleanse, hydrate, massage and lubricate" methods that were popular with the skin care gurus of the day. That, plus the occasional granular peel and exotic ingredients in crèmes like duck eggs or seaweed were all just show business to me. They had nothing to do with the real physiology of the skin or what was required to revise it back to health. To regenerate it.

Despite this, Mary Anderson began to get further and further away from my goal of establishing a skin-care range in Chicago. There were endless dinners and meetings with top business owners, local politicians and prominent people in the beauty industry. All of them were "curious" about Mary's little entourage of two handsome white men and an odd but upper-crust woman. Eileen soon became tired of Roger and me spinning our wheels as we dressed up and attended one social and business event after another. Her huge eyes filled with tears, Mary wished me all the best and flew back home to Perkiomenville, Pennsylvania.

I never saw her again, but have often thought of her and the "Renaissance man" she thought me to be—and have tried to be ever since.

Mary and I finally parted ways, and shortly afterward I met an exotic woman who was already in the skin care business, a former South American Beauty Queen named Alma Palma. She wanted me to create a skin care range for her, but didn't like the spelling of my name.

"Danie is toooo common," she sniffed. "We must think of something more elegant—for the label to look good."

I told her I had a nickname given to me by my mother—sort of a French-sounding "Danné."

"But that's it!" she exclaimed. "And it fits with your Grandfather's name, Montague."

So I became Danné Montague-King for the rest of my life.

I created a professional skin treatment range under Alma's name and appeared in her high-end skin care salon many times, feeling like a bull in a China shop with her all female clientele, fancy pink and white decor and facialists in uniforms. I was not used to all the protocol of "facials"—things that had been developed in Europe decades before and brought to the USA by doyennes of beauty such as Ilona of Hungary and Christine Valmy. My approach was more "medical and clinical"— and Alma and I had a head on collision, after which I left the premises.

This same thing would happen many times over the years with glamorous and beautiful women who were entranced by my vision and focus—and on some level, personal attractions. But there was always their ego involved, and their name. I needed to be on my own and march to my own music.

The next Grande Dame of this nature was Betty Odem, whose Hyde Park salon was the top place for women of color to go to for facials, wigs and makeup.

Betty was, and still is, a remarkable African-American woman who was always the epitome of glamour and beauty—a true template for her clientele, which was replete with celebrities, heads of State and politicians' wives. I spent one hilarious afternoon cutting up with Jacky Jackson, the Reverend Jesse Jackson's wife, and her little kids.

Betty was a disciple of the French skin care range, Renee Guinot at the time (privately I thought it was a good excuse for her to go to Paris all the time), but I was opposed to this because in my opinion, the range was not chemically suitable for Black skin care. Still, I had to work my treatments around this range and sell the French product along with everything else. Again I went loggerheads with a strong, definitive woman and left—albeit under friendly terms. Years later I featured Betty's brilliant career in one of my magazine articles.

Each time I learned something to add to my arsenal of how to present treatments and products to people, but my concept of how skin regenerates, as well as to how to alleviate the many anomalies people suffer from, remained the same. As a result, I got an early reputation in the industry as a creative and talented genius—but also as a madman and an arrogant maverick.

Decades later the media and in articles and on the cover of magazines I was referred to as "Pioneer and Legend."

The respect is welcomed. Still, though, I want to continue to help people even more.

25

Oprah and Me...

It was a huge, overweight and overbearing Polish lady named Dora who finally brought the Mary Anderson dream to a screeching halt. I met her in a posh restaurant cocktail lounge, and Roger and I soon found ourselves moving out of Hyde Park and into a nice condominium in the suburbs with a lovely landlady who had old money and old class.

There was an underlying racist aspect to this neighborhood, as there were in many Chicago neighborhoods in those days. Chicago was like that. When you went into the Greek neighborhood you were in Greece; Polish—Poland; Italian—Italy; and so on.

On the surface or in the downtown area, everyone got along fine. But in the "hoods" prejudice reined and everyone knew it.

After helping me move and letting me keep the grand piano she had given me, Mary never came into that neighborhood to visit us; we talked on the phone but never saw each other again.

Dora had a huge salon with many employees. She ensconced me in a "special area" and helped me purchase the raw materials and containers I needed to create my Danné Skin Revision Range. Roger got a job downtown at a photo studio, so money was coming in. Dora's aggressive promotional methods had me all over the place. Soon I was lecturing on skin revision at the Council of Hairdressers Union. Dora held buffets and barbeques at various wealthy clients' homes where I would also appear.

Once I stood on a stage in front of 500 beauticians with my beakers,

Bunsen burner and a Mix Master, showing how I made my water-in-to-oil transdermal crèmes from a soy wax base. No one had seen this before; it seemed like magic. Later this "kitchen chemistry" act was repeated on *AM Chicago* TV—resulting in hundreds of calls.

Chicago was on everyone's lips during the late 1970s. Mayor Jane Byrne put the city there with her tough glamour and relentless promotion of the Windy City. I ran into Jane once at a hair salon we both patronized, and I couldn't help comparing her to Susan Hayward in the movie *I Want to Live*, where Susan walks down the hall to the gas chamber but insists on wearing her stylish high heel pumps. Jane had that same big-eyed, serious yet all-feminine look, the same trim ankles and the same penchant for stylish pumps.

Oprah Winfrey came later and kept the image going, but at the time she was only a local talk show host. I remember seeing Oprah at a fashion show that I helped promote downtown. She was very quiet and humble that evening, sitting at a back table with her hairdresser. Months later all of Chicago was screaming for Oprah and award after award was given to her for "what she had done for Chicago."

I met a totally different Oprah at a Variety Club bash—no longer quiet, surrounded by an entourage of people, and totally in command. I had no idea what she *had* done for Chicago, except to become the most sought-after celebrity in town. I tried to speak to her about my Black skin research on the off chance she would be helpful. I'd prepared a short paper with some "before and afters" to hand her. A friend of mine who was a Variety Club member introduced us, and in the noise of a very large reception I tried to convey my message. She listened for a moment, took the envelope and handed it to an assistant. I told her I'd met her once before at a fashion show at The Gentry—a very upscale "diversity" bar. She looked at me sharply and said, "That was the first time I'd been there, and the last," and turned away.

Sometime later, she featured Janet Sargent, a then-popular New York skincare guru, on her show. Janet made a big statement about how there was no difference between Black and Caucasian skin when it came to products. Perplexed that this woman would be featured on television while I was dismissed with my sincere and what many considered to be ground-breaking research, I wrote an article for a publication that printed me from time to time, disagreeing with Ms. Sargent's theory. I was secretly hoping that if Oprah had read this article, she would call me.

Oprah allegedly did see the article, because a long time after that someone who worked with her told me she was "mad" at me because I was, in a sense, attacking her show. I really wasn't—only her guest's comments. But my effort backfired.

My education with the media was beginning.

Over the years as I watched this remarkable woman rise to purpose-filled fame, I often wished I had communicated with her better regarding the skin care needs for Black women. Always in the public eye, always "made up"—and her skin paying the price for so much time under hot cameras and often with nerves on edge—she would logically find my work and products truely helpful.

Then again, had that happened, I might never have left Chicago, the years of research in South Africa may have never happened, and my road would have gone in another direction. I've found that whenever there's something that can create a real change in the world, it hinges on the many, not just on one person. This is, no doubt, a concept that the soulful Oprah understands.

26

The Birth of Danné Skin Revision

In my personal life it was a little different. Dora was getting very demanding—everything had to be her way or the highway. I chose the highway because I could see that her expenditures on my behalf were causing problems with her hard-working husband—and I didn't want to be accused of exacerbating this. It would not be the last time a woman would spend everything she could get her hands on to impress me and tie me to her. I definitely needed my own place.

My first clinic was on the famous Oak Street in Chicago, owned by a very eccentric and eclectic hairdressing family. There I continued with my Black Skin research and in addition had a great many local celebrities and politicians come in.

The clinic was designed differently than the standard Facial Salon such as Iona of Hungary down the street, Elizabeth Arden's Red Door, or Christine Valmay. All of these Doyennes of beauty therapy were European facial stars who controlled the beauty therapy industry with their "secret crèmes and facial massages and machines." All of it was focused on women—very few men would enter these establishments, settling instead for a hot towel and a massage by their barbers.

I foresaw something different. I knew that 50% of my clientele would be male if the presentation was right, so I created a clinical atmosphere, like a doctor's office. I trained my staff to "prescribe" home maintenance products the way a doctor would prescribe drugs. This took the "selling of products" out of the equation. It also ensured that the clients *would* take their home prescriptions, for my highly active treatments were only as good as the progressive results that came from daily home-use products tailored to the treatment itself. If the client underwent one of my intense enzyme treatments that kick-started the enzyme and vascular systems of the skin and then went home and used some other commercial skin care, the chemistry would be aborted and negated, thus wasting the client's money and the therapist's time.

During my time at the clinic—incorrectly spelled "Appropo" instead of "Apropos" (the sign was painted too large to warrant the expense of painting it over)—I'd become involved in a medical procedure called "Exordermology," apparently discovered by a female Eastern European physician and then brought to the USA by another doctor.

A few years later I realized that it was just another twist on the dated phenol acid, croatin oil peel that any physician could mix up and apply. Basically these peels just burn the heck out of the epidermis and become a "controlled scar" if not applied properly, leaving a line of demarcation at the neck. A great many elderly ladies went around with the ghostly plastic look that this type of medical peels results in—or chronic erythema (redness) and sensitivity. I'd had one such client back in my Newport Beach days, an odd creature who was not giving into age gracefully. Her face was tight, wrinkle-free and always red.

When I put wigs or hairpieces on her and accidentally touched her face, she would flinch like a nervous horse, screaming, "Honey, I'm *sooo* sensitive."

A quack without a medical license had performed her procedure in a motel and she was thrilled to pieces over her result, calling him a "genius."

I called him lucky to escape prison.

The Exodermology process, however, was much more controlled and performed by a very nice doctor named Noberto Augustine who ran a successful family practice in Chicago. After talking to him and his business partner, a substantial Polish young man called Yatsik, I decided that pretreatment and post enzyme treatments would maximize the results of the Exodermology and minimize the negative aspects of the deep peeling procedure, such as the definite line of de-pigmentation along the jaw and neck.

It was theory only, but based upon my way of logically thinking of how cells and other physical responses work in tandem—and it seemed to work on the four or five clients on whom we performed the $3,000 treatment at the Oak Street Clinic. The client would receive three advance enzyme treatments, then be booked for the "big day." On the day of the Exodermology, they would be anesthetized with an IV into "twilight" anesthesia. The serums would be painted on the skin with a surgical swab and the entire face (excluding mouth and nostrils) taped up for three days.

We had booked rooms at the Ambassador West Hotel a few blocks away, along with a nurse to attend the patient's needs. It proved to be somewhat of a weight loss program, too, because for those three days patients could drink only smoothies that I designed according to their dietary requirements and blood chemistry.

How I became involved in blood chemistry and food I don't really remember, except for a recollection of a man selling a diagnostic machine comprised of a microscope and a blood sampling device. A physician would draw a small sample of blood and run the sample under the microscope, which would blow the image up on an early computer monitor. Suggested food groups and diet plans were designed along with whatever the blood cells showed.

It was an extremely expensive setup and of course I could not afford it, and Dr. Augustine was not interested. However, I used a lot of the information in the promotional material the salesman left me to create nutritional smoothies for our peel patients. Years later I was gratified that I wasn't being too crazy when the book *Four Diets for Four Blood Types* came out—a lot of the book made a lot of sense.

The four or five clients we had were all male. I visited them every day to check on their progress, and each and every one of them expressed a strong increase in libido—often flashing me from under the sheets or making "suggestions." I thought this was amusing, given the fact that one could not be more unattractive than with one's face taped up like The Invisible Man no matter what other charms one is trying to expose. I informed them gently that bedside manner stopped at the bedside.

Each of the procedures came out better than expected, and Dr. Augustine admitted that our twist on Exordermology enhanced the results 100%, not to mention the follow-up treatments for facial muscle building and the continued income from the home prescriptives each client became hooked on. This was an entire new approach to what is now known as "medical aesthetics," during a time when European facial divas ruled the industry.

Had more people believed back then in my vision of aesthetic medicine combining medical procedures with skin revision treatments, we could have perhaps franchised or patented a concept that would be worldwide and controlled by one parent company to this day. In retrospect I think it's better this way; the main thing being that people have been helped and lives changed on thousands of different levels because of the use of my original concepts. Huge companies that control everything often become the victims of their very size, and a lot of good things fall through the cracks. If this had happened, our fine little clinic in Lhasa, Tibet, or way out in small townships in South Africa or Russia, would not be able to operate with their own resources or ways of dealing with patients.

During this period, Dr. Augustine went back to the Philippines on business, and returned to inform me that he had spoken to Imelda Marcos about me and she was excited about installing a few of my aesthetics clinics in her luxury hotels. This was the high rolling era for President Marcos and his family. The excesses and luxuries they lived by, not to mention the antics of their trendy young son Boom Boom, were huge fodder for the worldwide media.

Imelda's friends in Hollywood and with an American heiress were documented weekly, along with her famous shoe collection. Even the most well-heeled Fashionista of that period could not fathom having the time in any one year to wear all those shoes.

I'd been asked to judge a Filipino beauty contest and appeared on Filipino television, which might have been a reason Imelda was so adamant to do a deal. But I kept stalling on taking a trip to Manila. I trusted Noberto Augustine, but a gut feeling told me a partnership with the Marcos family would not succeed.

A few months later the crash on the Marcos family came down, investigations were rampant, files and bank accounts seized, people put in the glare of a spotlight just by association. I escaped all this by listening to my gut feeling and remembering that Grande Dames usually like things done their way—especially when they have an entire country, police and military behind them. To me, aesthetic/medical treatments were serious business and not some "fun and glamorous" part of the cosmetic world. If I had been a medical doctor in those days I might have very well pioneered the approach of being strictly physicians, and had my concepts licensed out to medical clinics, but I did not have those credentials.

In the late 1970s and early '80s, what I was doing was unheard of. I had to operate under the category of "cosmetic" with its more flexible regulations. Privately this always bothered me and still does.

Meanwhile, in Chicago, I stopped seeing eye to eye with the people who had invested in the Appropo Clinic. The husband of the woman who ran the hair salon below Appropo had an ego issue. He always alluded to "connections" (I assumed Mafia) in Chicago, and tried to appear Mr. Independent and Mr. Cool. For a long time I bought into his macho act, but after a while I grew weary of it and although I respected his wife, I thought he was a nutcase. I had to write him off. After a dramatic falling out I went on my own, taking nothing with me, and began the process of obtaining investment for my very own clinic.

Yatsik helped me a great deal in those times. He resembled a big kid with a pedantic view of life—but once he believed in something he focused and followed through until he obtained results. His brother, a doctor of some kind, bought my Brickland, which was starting to show wear and tear, and kept me in the good graces of Dr. Augustine so I could make a little money from referring patients for Exodermology.

Neither Yatsik or Dr. Augustine were interested in doing any further business with my previous "partners," who were surprised to hear this. They expected that the business I had built up would continue on as usual—they even hired a young male therapist who changed his name to Danné! Although they planned to carry on the business as if I did not exist, Appropo soon closed. Years later I heard that drugs and a stint in prison were what had happened to Mr. Cool.

I was renting a large and well-decorated condo near the north side of Chicago at an up and coming address on Sheridan Road. I watched a young Sean Penn almost every day for a couple of weeks during the shooting of his first movie. I held skin revision seminars, managed to create some home prescriptive products in my kitchen lab, and converted one of the two bedrooms into a treatment room—all not legally approved, as the address was not zoned commercial.

Sandra Dellinger came to my rescue.

27

Honcho Sandra Dellinger to the Rescue

Sandra, a former client from the Oak Street Clinic, was a honcho in charge of promotion for GMC trucks in a day when corporate women looked as butch as possible to fit in "with the boys." Of course they all thought they were doing this because of women's lib, which had been the rage a decade before, but Sandra stayed just as she was—Dolly Parton. Sandra was from the South, petite, curvy, dramatic and full of gusto—with a mind like a computer. She also was the type of person who, if she did not like something about herself, didn't cry about it—she changed it.

And she did. In a flock of women with cropped or short bobbed hair, mannish blazers and sensible shoes, Sandra glowed with big, red blond hair in curls, eyelashes, full makeup, long manicured nails and fitted outfits that showed she was all-girl in the right places. At every GMC Corporate function I ever saw her attend, she had all the men wrapped around her little finger. She was herself, but could be a hundred other people also—we got along immediately. Over the many years of our friendship, Sandra and I shared several dramatic episodes. Passing her off as Dolly Parton at a well-known Hollywood Costume Ball called the GGRC was one of them.

Part of the Ball was a walk on the stage to present your character. As I checked her Dolly Wig and costume backstage before she went on, I realized something was missing. I ran to the restroom, grabbed a ton of toilet tissue and shoved it into the bottom of her bra, increasing her cup size by 100% and boosting her cleavage. "*Now* you're Dolly!" I shouted as I shoved her onto the stage.

Later there were photos taken in the professional photo stand that always shows up at these events. The women who ran the stand took me aside after shooting Sandra about 50 times and whispered, "We won't say anything about her being here, but she is adorable—we know when to respect privacy—can you get us an autograph?"

Sandra was highly amused at this but refused to fake a Dolly autograph, having met the real Dolly a few times, so we snuck out of the Ball early before the ladies "blew the whistle."

One night Sandra called me up and in her gentle Southern accent asked about the Exodermology and how long it would take. I informed her that I was no longer at the Oak Street Clinic, but was consulting out of my condo, and the procedure was being done at the doctor's offices.

"Well, ah don't mind that Danyay (she called me Danyay for years); ah would just as soon as stay with y'all anyway."

With a silent "yippee" I put the phone down, called Yatsik with the good news and prepared for a first class Exodermology week, complete with a quiet room, nourishing liquid meals and limousine transportation from my condo to the doctor's office and back. Yatsik arranged for an inexpensive limo service from the South Side—he seemed to have tentacles everywhere. Sandra's appointment was for the late afternoon and she was coming by taxi from O'Hare airport only an hour beforehand.

At the time I was in a relationship with a tall, classically handsome young man named Kenny, who had a strong Irish-Swedish background and the kind of face that sold cigarettes on billboards back then, very much like the original Marlboro man whom I knew personally in Newport Beach—a fireman in real life. I was not "in love" with Kenny and I think he knew this, but he was kind, fun, and did love me. I suppose at some level my ego rationalized my lack of deep love and the subtle guilt by telling myself in a flippant way, "He looks good on my arm."

Not wishing to be around the serious business of in-house patients, Kenny decided to go bar hopping that night. Meanwhile I raided the bar at home, nervously waiting for Sandra, throwing down one vodka and tonic after another. About half a bottle later she arrived, and in an expansive mood I commanded Yatsik to "call the limousine, please."

The limo arrived, driven by an eager little gentleman whose eyes popped when he saw the glamorous redhead in a mink coat, accompanied by a slightly staggering man in a three piece suit, get into his stretch vehicle. I had about $350 dollars in cash put aside for the driver and incidentals. Clutching my bottle of vodka under my coat, I settled back after barking out the address to the clinic.

The driver's round eyes kept surveying us in the back seat. For some reason Sandra said nothing about my inebriation or the fact I took a few shots out of the bottle along the way. This was the early 1980s, and the upwardly mobile yuppie image and its conspicuous lifestyle was the trend. We arrived at the clinic to a smiling Doctor Augustine and staff, and I insisted on accompanying Sandra to the treatment room. I was also wearing a fur coat from my Hot Springs days; it kept flapping and pushing waiting room plastic chairs over in my drunken wake.

Later Neburto told me that the waiting room looked like a hurricane had gone through. Furthermore he informed me—with humor—that I demanded his nurse prep Sandra's skin with my Deep Pore Cleanser, which I had whipped out of my coat pocket, and then pushed her away, saying, "Never mind, I'll do this myself."

Then I fell over Sandra and almost passed out.

I don't remember much after that, except being in the limousine heading home with Sandra lying down on the back seat in her mink coat and slip. Dr. Augustine had told me that after they taped her up, they did not want to pull her tight sweater-dress on over her head, and it would not go up over her hips.

We arrived at the condominium just as Kenny was leaving. Later, this is what he told me he saw: "I was standing at the open limo door, waving my arms. He looked in to see a woman in a slip and a mink coat moaning on the floor of the limo, an empty vodka bottle rolling beside her. Thinking I'd gotten her drunk, he pulled her out just as Yatsik came down the steps. Together they hauled her upstairs. I was following, and watched them try to go through the front door at the same time. They got stuck. Thinking they looked like a Three Stooges movie, I started to laugh insanely.

"Kenny turned and shot me a dirty look as they trundled poor Sandra up to the condo and into her bed. Kenny left in a huff and I started to sober up. I also realized that the driver was standing at the door with his hand out, expecting to get paid."

"Of course, my good man," I said grandly. "Let me see, how much?" as I searched through my pockets and could not find a dime.

He announced the charge was $250 plus whatever I wanted to give him personally—and my search became desperate. What had happened to my money? All at once, my eyes narrowing in suspicion, I turned on the driver—he had been with us all the way to the office and back; he'd seen me flash the wad of bills in front of Sandra. I was yelling at him, screaming that I was going to call the police, when out of the bedroom down the hall I heard a faint cry: "Ook in my errrr cot."

It was Sandra. I rushed to the room and said "Are you okay, honey?"

"Rook in my eerrr coat," she croaked again.

Her fur coat! Of course! I suddenly remembered putting the roll of bills in the deep pocket of her fur coat. Sheepishly I gave the driver the entire amount with many apologies, and with a dark look and shake of the head that said, "Rich white people is just too crazy," he left.

Kenny phoned from a bar and asked how Sandra was. I could hear the people in the background and suddenly I wanted another cocktail and to have fun. After all, Yatsik was at the condo to watch her.

"Hold on, Kenny, I'll be right there. I'll give her a Valium and she'll just sleep." (Forgetting we'd already given her a Valium when she was put to bed.)

Suddenly a big, beefy hand reached past me, grabbed the phone and put it gently on the cradle. It was Yatsik, who had never challenged me at all before.

With dead serious eyes he said, "Go to bed, Danné, now. I'll sit up with the patient."

I did.

No one was a better and more contrite nurse than I over the next few days. Sandra was treated like a queen. When the tapes came off, her entire epidermis was one big oozing red mass. An orange-brown powder called Thymol Iodide was put over the entire face every half hour for the next three to four days until a thick, brown crust formed. "Cookie Monster" is the description that comes to mind.

Keeping up the patient's morale at this time is vital—also because that' when they can come off the liquid diet and some tend to overeat, having nothing else to do all day long.

On about the 12th day Crisco (or any vegetable based crème) is liberally applied to the entire face, followed by warm soaks with a wet face cloth. The Eschar crust starts to drop away and in a day or two, *voila!*—smooth and firm, albeit red, skin.

That is when my post treatments started, along with a contraindication crème and anti-inflammatory serums. The redness usually disappears by the 15th day, although in some cases areas of the skin may continue to come off like old wall paper. Under *no* circumstances should this sheeting be cut off, even with a sharp, sterile scissors—it has to epilate naturally. Sandra was one of those "sheeting" people. One third of her cheek was hanging like a flap of material after the rest of her skin looked porcelain smooth and pink.

This was a problem. There was a massive GMC Exhibition at McCormick place that weekend, and as an executive, she had to make an appearance. I softened the tissue as much as I could and made her up with a Marilyn Monroe look.

Wearing a smart, tailor fitted pale green jacket and skirt and spiked Italian heels, she strutted in like she owned the place and cheerfully intermingled with all the stunned-looking men who crowded the exhibition center.

The women had expressions on their faces that were hard to describe: a mixture of awe and resentment. "How dare she show up that way? What has she done?"

This was the person who found me an investor for my own skin care business: a young man named Daryl Shepherd, who also worked for General Motors.

Daryl had around $30,000, and was a capable administrator. He'd experienced my treatments and was convinced that men taking care of their skin was a potential market, particularly in the gay community where there was disposable income, a penchant towards looking youthful for as long as possible, and no children who required college funds or all the other expenses of heterosexual families.

I had already built up a male clientele ranging from bank presidents to warehouse workers, and many acne patients who found no relief elsewhere; so Daryl and I shook hands and found a wonderful two-story historical landmark building right across from Loyola University on Pearson, two blocks from Michigan Avenue—the Great White Way of Chicago.

The building had upgraded wood floors, high ceilings with skylights over each of the treatment rooms, and the latest in track lighting; the reception room boasted a marble fireplace and plush carpeting. There was even a shower for body treatments and space in the back for a small lab. A staircase and ladder led to a deck on the roof, perfect for sunbathing and relaxation.

It was called Hartwell House and had a British flair about it, combined with American High tech appointments. Despite the fact that we were running through Daryl's investment quickly, I felt confident and ready to take on the world. Thinking back, the daily act of going up the stairs every morning and opening the antique finished door reminds me of our clinic at 1 Harley Street in London that came years later, and exists to this day.

28

The Lion with a Golden Chain

When I'm asked about my life, I always say, "Which one?"

I spent my first 30 years creating myself around a concept of science that ultimately would change the way the world looks at aesthetics—and all the years afterward making it come true. Along the way thousands of people have been helped, lives changed, self-worth issues resolved and life-long careers created.

I've heard myself described in many ways. Australian Television presenter Renee Brack once described me as a "Lion with a golden chain around his neck, larger than life but with marvelous restraint—he lets you know just how far you can jerk the chain."

I've been called a madman by the press for my outspoken views about Alpha Hydyroxy Acids and the dangers thereof. In China I've been described as a "Teacher and Guru," and in Tibet a 30-foot-high photo of me in a white suit, looking rather like an American televangelist, is plastered across the side of a building.

I hear "genius," "visionary" and "legend" a lot (makes me feel old at times), and often the joke "Is there a portrait of you in the attic at your house?" when people view my visage, which does not look like the 70 year-old man I will be by the time you read this.

What do I personally think about this?

Nothing at all. It always seems like people are talking about someone else. I know I have to *appear* to be all these things from time to time— and as age creeps up, doing so gets harder and harder. But it's my obligation to all the thousands of therapists, practitioners and doctors out there to stay with the ball I started rolling for as long as I can, without dropping it. To myself I'm just an eccentric, homey and ordinary man.

I could retire in comfort—the years of work have seen to that—but as I look back over the achievements of several decades I realize it's only the tip of an iceberg; there is much more to do.

In truth, the success of the DMK brand did not all come from my convoluted brain. It was also formed by hundreds of therapists and physicians out there in the field, experimenting along with me and giving me feedback. Many of them are responsible for treatments we offer in thousands of clinics globally to this day.

Likewise, fellow scientists working outside the skin revision industry contributed to my concepts. Several were brilliant lab "nerds" who had no gift of communication outside their work, yet their observations enriched my epiphanies and ideas—becoming pieces of the many puzzles I could not get right on my own.

I have (and I said this long before Oprah did) ridden on the shoulders of giants, and I thank them all wholeheartedly.

After my personal battle with *acne vulgaris* as a teen, I never stopped experimenting with ways to treat the skin—based upon how the body actually works and what it needs to function in a healthy manner. What keeps skin firm and tight and naturally bouncing and moist as in the young? What attacks the chemistry of the skin, making it try to defend itself—which results in wrinkles, pigment disorders, and so on? What *is* the chemistry of the skin and what does it recognize or reject as any kind of maintenance? Gardens can be brought to life year after year— why not us?

Thinking like this all the time creates situations where you're always looking for something—again, pieces of a puzzle. For example, back in the 1960s everyone was selling collagen crèmes basically made from either chicken or beef by-products. I couldn't see how that would be beneficial in enhancing our own collagen—which, along with elastin, is produced by the fibroblast cells. It would be like a man with his arm cut off going into a morgue and trying to grind up another arm to rub on his stump to grow a new arm.

In the skin, like does not create like.

One day I was perusing my old worn copy of *Gray's Anatomy* and I came across "The Cytoplasm and Synthesis of Collagen in Human Skin." What caught my eye was a little paragraph about how ascorbic acid was the precursor of collagen via the fibroblast cell, which I thought of as a "collagen factory." At the same time, the eccentric Linus Pauling was touting the benefits of vitamin C for everything that ails the human race. After bugging a lot of people, I finally found myself on the phone with the great man and told him of my theory regarding human skin produce collagen via ascorbic acids.

"I think you're onto something, son," he rasped—and then went on to describe the various *types* of ascorbic acids, delivery systems and so on. We talked for over two hours and promised to meet in the future. We never did.

The one vitamin C he insisted was best for cells when topically applied was ascorbyl palmitate, the ester of ascorbic acid. Fortunately for me it was cheap—available by the gallon from a friend who owned The Home Orange Juice Company in Chicago. It was not liked by the cosmetic industry even as a PH adjuster or preservative because it had a habit of turning crèmes sort of yellowish after a few days. I did not care. I wanted what worked best.

Since I was making all my own products for my clinic in those days, I could educate my clients on the nature of more naturally-formulated products that might change colors from time to time. Herbs especially are not homogenous in color. One cup of tea will be darker or lighter than the cup before it.

I didn't make a big deal about vitamin C as a major component of my concept, rarely mentioned it in advertising, only to clients during their consults as education on how their skins worked. I never thought to create an entire range around vitamin C—but later several companies did, including one operated by a self-styled female guru who claimed to have discovered a *special* vitamin C ester.

It was plain old ascorbyl palmitate, the ester we had been using for years.

Later, of course, I devised better combinations of Cs that were more durable without being *too* stable (stable ingredients are often weaker than the unstable, raw material) and came up with several different delivery systems into the skin.

It was back in the 1970s that my research into the world of enzymes took full flight. In beauty therapy, enzymes like papaya and betaine powders were popular as mild decongestant media—munching up a few dead surface skin cells with their large, crude, macrophage mouths. I was more interested in how to kick-start and energize the enzymes already *in* our skin.

We are the body enzyme; no molecular or cellular action takes place in our bodies without the assistance or interference of an enzyme. Like organic computers (complete with tiny crystal chips), enzymes carry messages across cell membranes to other cells, telling them what needs to be done—now.

Enzymes can hydrolyze impurities, effluvia and all the other toxins that create imbalance in the system and show up as terrible skin problems. My experimental masques to create this natural phenomenon were started in Newport Beach California; I used them on surfer kids, friends and relatives, aging movie stars such as Dolores Del Rio, Jane Russell, June Allyson and Mamie Van Doren—the 1950s blonde bombshell whose breasts are still of legend.

Still, my most frequent guinea pig was Maybelline Heiress Evelyn F. Williams.

29

My Name on the Door

This was the first time I felt confident enough to put my name on the door of a business I owned.

My first establishment in Newport Beach years before had had various names, ending up with The House of U. My brief sojourn in the Chicago suburbs became a misspelled circus that nonetheless gave me a foothold in Chicago Society.

Daryl had no ego that demanded a proprietary interest beyond profit, and in fact he pointed out that it was time for me to create my brand.

A great many sports stars, all African-American, came to me for treatment in those days. Mark Aquirre and Walter Payton were the most outstanding. They were so tall that their feet and legs hung off the treatment trolley and we had to add chairs with pillows to accommodate these giants. Roland Burris, now a U.S. State Senator, came, as well as his lovely wife. But, my real research in Black skin was conducted on the poor people who began hearing about the treatments and came up from the South Side, wondering if "they could get an appointment."

The first time this happened was when a middle aged woman whom life had not been kind to walked in. My head therapist, Jeannie, a beautiful African American, sniffed when this woman entered and acted in a cool and haughty manner towards her.

I insisted that Jeannie take her into the consult room with a chart and get her ready.

I sat with the woman and asked her why she wished treatment. She replied that she wanted to change her life for the better and felt that if she looked good, she would feel good and have more energy to go out and seek a better job and lifestyle. She said too many of her friends had turned to alcohol and drugs to dull the despair of poverty and life's darker side, and she did not want that.

I diagnosed her and told her what we could do and how long it would take—at which point she shyly asked me how much it would cost altogether, including home prescriptives. Taken aback (most people paid by the treatment), I added it all up. She looked at the figure and said, "I'll be back when I have that much."

After she left, Jeannie sniffed again and said, "You'll never see her again; why waste your time, Danné?"

Three months later the woman returned and had her appointment, and after it was over she opened her bag and proudly pulled out a big roll of cash, mostly dollar bills.

I gave the embarrassed Jeanie a significant look.

The lady became a regular after that. Each time she came in she dressed a little better, had a new hairstyle and makeup—and yes, she did land a good job as a paralegal at an established law office that was looking for a mature woman of color.

As word got around, I started analyzing the differences in African and Caucasian skins even more deeply, having a lot of different subjects to work on. It became quite clear that one treatment, one skin range, could not suit all. It was not a question of race, it was a question of what defense mechanisms were we born with. Doing nothing or using the wrong chemistry to take care of the skin can turn defense mechanisms into skin problems, premature ageing and all the other anomalies that we don't like when we look in the mirror.

I also noticed that older people's skin around the areola of their breasts and on their buttocks are always 10-20 years younger than facial, neck, arm, décolleté and leg skin. The conclusion is that these two areas require little defense from outside environmental attack, being covered with clothing most of the time. The other areas are always trying to defend themselves from attack and the residual effects are dead skin cell buildup, trans epidermal water loss, weakened tissue—ripe for the Demodex mite (rosacea) acne—and all the other "baddies" that attack the beauty of our human race.

Armed with simple concept and truth, I strove to come up with chemistry and treatment protocol that would match the chemistry and histology of the human body. Many times I failed. Also, there was a lot of skepticism from the beauty therapy industry because this flamboyant, outspoken *kid* was doing everything in direct opposition to what was considered proper therapy.

Years later I would become good friends with Joel Gerson, who wrote the *Beauty Therapy* textbooks that were commonly used then and still are in beauty therapy schools everywhere. He told me that he wished we could have met when we were young; schools would have had an entire new approach to aesthetics. Another classic in beauty therapy, CIDESCO, the time honored epitome of Beauty Therapy Standards, approached me in similar way after I started to get a name in Europe. Baljeet Surey, CIDESCO Secretary at the time and owner of the Ray Cochran School in London, asked me if I would contribute to modernizing and upgrading the CIDESCO syllabus. This was a leap of faith on her part, but I had to decline inasmuch as it would have been a full time job to get it right, and I had promises to keep and miles to go.

My African skin research and clinical work brought me to the attention of a local beauty school in Chicago which maintained a large Black attendance. I found myself teaching classes in aesthetics before there was any licensing or courses offered as there are today. I would travel the El Train out to the snowbound Chicago south side suburbs to teach these young people—standing out in packed classrooms of dark-skinned people like a pale totem pole with a mouth. I found that humor always broke the ice, for in the beginning many people were resentful that a white man would come to teach them about *their* skin. What did he know?

That was when I learned to be funny, outrageous and a little bit crazy when speaking to a new audience. It worked and I have never looked back. I figured that *real* science speaks for itself. Paint pictures in people's minds with common analogies of life, and they start to think. When you get students to really think they often end up answering their own questions and then feeling empowered, as if they've discovered something on their own. Self-worth rises to the top.

For a company of Pakistani men, I created a retail Black Skin home regimen kit for men and women called E'ON 5. I then spent a year travelling the country appearing on TV and making appearances in stores.

The most outstanding moment came in Detroit, Michigan, where the head buyer for JCPenney's Cosmetics in New York had scheduled me to be on a late morning news talk show starring a lovely woman named Narissa Williams. Since a news/talk show could not back any commercial product, Narissa warned me in the green room before I went on that I could not mention E'ON 5 or any product by name; I was there to talk about African-American skin and how to treat it.

I assured Ms. Williams that there would be no commercial mention at all—only science.

And I kept my word. I used the analogy of the ageing differences of white and black skins, the superiority of black skin cells and how the right chemistry could seem to work miracles. At the conclusion of my dissertation Narissa said, "Well, Danné, that all sounds exciting. But how does a person find out what to use to correct their skin problems?"

Grabbing the moment, I replied, "I'll be at JCPenney's at the Northland Mall this afternoon at 3 o'clock and will be happy to diagnose anyone and answer their questions."

After the show she turned to me and with a wry smile said, "You tricked me—you were not supposed to be commercial."

"I can't help it if you got all excited—you *asked* me," I retorted with a laugh.

I knew she would personally be fascinated by aspects of her own skin, being a media person, so in a way I did trick her—I was learning how to be interviewed by interviewing the host.

That afternoon I arrived at the Northland Mall and there were around 300 people lined up in front of the E'ON 5 counter display, waiting to be looked at and talked to. I was soon "lecturing" to groups of men and women 6-feet-deep; many of them had brought their teenagers with acne and razor bumps.

Did I feel strange, like I stood out as the only white person in that huge crowd? Yes, in a way I did—but somehow I felt that I had to be there—was *supposed* to be there, and race had little to do with it.

One tall, sour-faced woman in an expensive belted trench coat approached me, yelling, "What do *you*, a white man, know about *our* skin?"

Taken by surprise, I tried to stutter out an answer. But several matronly women—women with families to raise and used to hard times with little money for designer trench coats—turned to her and yelled, "Shut your *damn* mouth, b——, and let the man talk; he knows what he knows."

Overruled, she slunk away, darting looks at me that would kill.

But triumphs like this turned out to be few and far between. I had trained several local Chicago girls to represent E'ON5 in stores and perform demonstrations. All of them were enthusiastic to be part of America's "first" black skin care kit, whose poster featured a beautiful male and female couple saying, "Finally, something for us." But the men who owned the company seemed to care only how much they could make with minimum investment in people. Several of the girls who went to stores far out of town and worked for two to three days on their feet were told to keep track of all expenses such as food, lodging etc. When they came back the expenses were deducted from their commissions. Not an incentive to be part of any "first" team. It became worse and worse.

My part of the bargain began to disappear as well, so I walked after informing store buyers that I was no longer involved and had no idea where the products would be made or under what conditions. I did make a subtle allusion to "some shabby little lab that these men owned that made cheap shampoos somewhere in Chicago," so I was not terribly shocked when one of the men called me a few months later, screaming, "The stores, they have dropped us!"

Too bad.

The original kits were made by one of my lab contacts in California, who was already fed up with people whose main motivation was greed. I decided it was time to pull up roots and move to Los Angeles, back home where I had more contacts and support, and where I could be with the person who was to be my other half and ultimately make me a wealthy man.

I had already added to my treatment range new ways to remove dead cells from the skin without burning the hell out of the epidermis like the standard medical TCA and Phenol peels did. A plastic surgeon in Chicago helped me by providing patients as test subjects. When I explained what I wanted to do he said, "Hmmmm, I always *thought* there should be a better way."

Dr. Kaplan was the first medical person to give me an open door. It was this experience that made me *think* more medically than standard beauty therapists did. It also gave me a bedside manner that made everybody I met call me "Dr. King," as if I were some kind of surgeon and not just a minor Ph.D. in Botany.

For decades I became used to being "Dr. King," then I grew weary of having to diagnose people at cocktail parties or being asked by airline attendants to help with heart attack cases in flight.

"*I am not that kind of doctor!*" I would yell—to deaf ears; I still had to help. Fortunately nobody died.

In more recent years I have insisted on being just "Danné"—sort of like Cher.

It was in California that I started up what became my series of companies, the first being the kitchen lab in my apartment. My partner, Randy, and I would hand-fill and label my products after they were ready, and I would sell them and my treatments at local aesthetic clinics up and down the state. I will never forget when I developed my first Enzyme Peel, which I called 3743 treatment (after my birthday). My client was the wife of Warner Brothers' Jack Warner. A tall, statuesque beauty of 55 and a European, she did not think my style was strange at all. "Even my country, darlink—you vould be *beeg* star."

The procedure, which took six weeks for the old skin to desquamate without the trauma and down-time associated with medical peels, seemed a miracle to her—a highly social woman who *had* no down time. Soon, others from the film industry were coming in, and suddenly I found myself with my own television show entitled *Skin Deep*.

Looking back now, that was probably the first "reality" talk show of its kind. I would interview plastic surgeons, facialists, fitness trainers like Suzy Prudence, body sculptresses, makeup artists and broken-down actresses wanting to make a comeback. My "pay" was eight minutes on each episode to talk about my treatments or show them. Often when I did show them, as in the case of my new breast lift, channel surfers who ordinarily did not watch Channel 18 would stop and look at the show after seeing a pair of green breasts slowly elevating before their eyes.

I was invited to appear on the Geraldo Rivera show in New York, Geraldo being the most famous American television journalist at the time. That appearance made my little show even more popular, but unfortunately our producer, a British gentlemen, disappeared with a young woman one day, along with all the money scheduled for the show. Talks of lawsuits flew about from sponsors, but everyone knew the disaster was not my fault, so *Skin Deep* simply went off the air—and with it my television career.

Now Europe beckoned me, and a change in tide came that kept me from doing business in my own country again—outside of a few scattered accounts that are still with us today.

30

Britain, Australia and Biofreeze™

I was asked to lecture on African skin at an exhibition at Earl's Court in London. The organizer, a beautiful American-born black lady named Phyllis Cardwell, had managed to get a huge crowd to the open lecture platform.

I became a dyed-in-the-wool Anglophile the moment I arrived in the UK—all my private school years in England and the specialty courses in botany later, *and* my Dad's Welsh background came to the front. There I stood, so veddy proper in my Saville Row suit and ball tipped shoes in front of a fascinated Black audience, talking about "what you put in your skin."

Suddenly a loud and dramatic voice trumpeted out, "Young man, it is a rule of beauty therapy that nothing can actually penetrate the skin—you cleanse, tone and hydrate—that is all."

I looked to the back of the room where the voice came from, and there stood a tall woman with a Wagnerian bosom and theatrical light blonde hair. She was dressed in pink angora from head to toe and was wearing expensive burgundy boots with stiletto heels. Her face was commanding, her large blue eyes blazing with confrontation and ab-solute certainty.

"Madam," I responded, "with all due respect, if what you say is true, then how does the little schoolboy who goes into the woods in short pants and brushes up against a stinging nettle bush come out with red welts all over his legs? Where does that come from if nothing can penetrate the skin?"

She seemed to freeze, frowned, put her head down for a second and stared at me again before wheeling about and grandly stomping off.

I could swear I saw a twinkle in her eyes.

A few moments later a mousy little girl, carefully made up and wearing a crisply starched beauty therapy dress, approached me with a note. It read "Please come round to my stand, I want to talk to you." It was signed *Lillian Maund.*

Lillian turned out to be one of the most famous, controversial and formidable characters in the history of beauty therapy. She was a self-made success from middle class beginnings who transformed into a regal duchess with all the protocol of royalty and English aristocracy. She was also one of the greatest actresses who ever lived, and had she not gone into beauty therapy would have been successful on the English stage. With her husband Charles, a handsome Peter O'Toole type who worked with a British law enforcement detective division, she created a dynasty called International Aestheticians that was, in fact, her way of getting back at CIDESCO and other beauty associations that she felt were not progressive. Lillian was ahead of her time, innovative and intimidating. Most people were afraid of her—she could be your best friend one moment and tear your head off the next.

I saw through her almost immediately, but I loved her style, including her grand "finishing school" setup at Bache Hall, her huge old manor house in Chester England; and all her theatrics.

When I appeared at her stand she was sitting behind a desk in the middle of *three* large stands, with flawlessly draped treatment tables for demos, posters tastefully presenting her college. At every corner of her stand a young therapist dressed and made up like the one who passed me the note stood at rigid attention waiting to answer any questions people at the exhibition asked. Mrs. Maund's ears and eyes were trained on them all, and woe to the girl who stuttered or faltered with answers or who said the wrong thing. Lillian was very keen on discipline, protocol and image.

"You are one of the few who has ever challenged me in public," she laughed as I sat down. "And you are perfectly right about the little boy in the woods—clever answer."

Shortly thereafter, Phyllis organized a lecture for me at Dartmouth House in London where President Reagan received his honorary Knighthood. She invited "Doctors only," including some of the more prominent plastic surgeons in the city. Decades later, when Her Majesty's personal therapist started doing DMK treatments on the Monarch, I actually fantasized about getting an honorary title in that very room. (Sir Danné Montague-King has a nice ring to it!)

As I waited in the pub next to reception for the guests to arrive, Ms. Cardwell anxiously informed me that a lot of beauty therapists had heard about the outspoken American scientist and were trying to attend. Should she turn them away? The attitude of the medical profession regarding beauty therapy in those days was less than gracious.

I said, "If these ladies took the trouble to come and pay their twenty-five pounds sterling, let them in, I'll handle the doctors."

I had Phyllis herd the gentlemen into the pub and stood them all to a gin and tonic (a sure way into any decent British gentleman's good graces). Then I informed them that a group of lovely ladies had arrived—and what sort of men were we that we could not survive the company of lovely females for a couple of hours?

Amongst a muttering of "quite, quite," we all went to the hall.

During those two hours, the therapists took more notes and asked better questions than the doctors did. Afterward they begged me to start up some kind of advanced course in London. But I did not have a clue about classic beauty therapy courses, English style, and had to make vague promises that I worried about keeping.

Lillian Maund came to my rescue shortly thereafter: She installed advanced skin revision courses in her huge Manor House/college/cum-finishing school up in Chester.

Soon I was travelling back and forth to the UK nearly every month and caught the attention of *Les Nouvelles Esthetiques*, British Edition editor, Peggy Slight. The trade magazine of The UK. Peggy asked me to put forward an article from the American point of view. I did one on collagen therapy and electromagnetic waves. It received such a response that soon I was a regular with pages entitled "State Side."

Exhibition and publishing magnate Mark Maloney purchased *LNE* from its French home base owned by Pierantoni (who was taken aback by my first French lecture at Versailles where the stage was stormed by beauty therapists screaming questions as if I were Elton John). Mark retired the elderly Peggy but I pointed out that it would be the "thing to do" to give her, a revered British veteran, a spot in the new magazine format. He did, and Peggy's Corner was a regular up until the day she passed away in her little cottage in Nottingham.

After that it seemed that every magazine wanted copy from me. *Skonnet OG Helse* in Norway, *Professional Beauty* (formerly *LNE*) in every country where it was published, and a few USA publications began running my dissertations. Australia's leading magazine, under the direction of editor Mary Kay and her posh American sidekick, Linda Murdaugh, were so supportive that at times it was embarrassing—it looked like *The Danné Magazine*. The first exhibition at which they invited me to lecture (before I had any representation in Australia) was beyond belief. I was taken into a large hall packed to the rafters. There were even fathers standing in the back with their therapist wives and their kids on their shoulders. I don't know what I said or did, but afterward they burst into an ocean of applause and once again I was swamped with questions, as I had been in France.

It was, in fact, a French therapist who had moved to Sydney who almost attacked the slightly gobsmacked Linda Murdaugh, screaming, "Vy don't you Peeeple geet more edoocaters like theees man over here for us instead of all theees fake speakers who only sell products?"

Mary Kay put on many pioneer projects with me after that. A spectacular event at The Skeleton Museum stands out—complete with strolling string quartets in tuxedos and lamb cutlets for starters instead of cheese and fruit balls. The guest list included an eminent endocrinologist and a very boring man who went on and on and on about hair removal.

I was last on the menu, and when I looked out over that half-asleep and squirming crowd, my first words were, "Anyone gotta go to the loo?"

With a burst of laughter laced with sighs of relief, they all did, and came back fully awake.

It was at that moment that I "grabbed" Debbie Dickson, a young beauty therapist who later on became one of the most respected educators in Australia. She and Daniel Dickson, her husband, are now our DMK educators and distributors. Daniel's "go for it and never look back" people skills and Debbie's relentless pursuit of practices in science have provided a successful template for our team members all over the planet.

Funny thing about the Dickson's: they were only dating at that time—she a one-girl-show beauty therapist working at a fitness center and he a popular sports physiotherapist.

He approached me after many relentless business plan letters of how DMK should run in Oz, and browbeat us, along with his formidable corporate-type sister, into his becoming the DMK agent for Australia. He was 23 years old!

When he and Debbie came out to Beverly Hills for their agent's training, I had no idea they were broke. But it turned out that after a day's work when we dropped them off at their up-market hotel… they immediately sneaked out the back and went to their rooms in a cheap, rent-by-the-hour motel—the kind with beds that vibrate for a coin. Then, after the training ended, they told us they were going to take a drive up the magnificent California Highway 101 in a trendy new rental car. Again, after we dropped them off they cancelled the snazzy auto and went to a rent-a-wreck agency to limp up the coast in an aged beater.

Now, of course, the Dickson's—happily married and with two fine sons—are the personification of success in this industry. With interests in several companies outside DMK Distribution, their reach has spread to Asia and other global outlets, but they have not lost their original passion and vision. They know it is the journey and not the success at the end that is the real reward in life.

Mary Kay also sponsored the first paramedical conference held anywhere—combining dermatologists, plastic surgeons, Australian Beauty Therapists Association icons, educators, and little me. I posed this idea over a rather boozy dinner at a grand hotel in Melbourne, and to my surprise Mary Kay and Linda pulled it off.

At that time such a concept was not only unheard of, but was taking a real chance. Nowadays dermatologists are all on the skin care bandwagon and what was once considered "beneath them" has become "Aesthetic Medicine."

Build a field.

Finally it was being said that I was the most published aesthetic journalist in the world. But that meant nothing to me compared to what occurred at a gala held on a boat on the Thames, London, sponsored by Mark Maloney. A gorgeous creature from Iceland, who should have been on the fashion runways, approached me and announced she was a therapist. "I never buy anything or try any new machine until I read what Danné says about it," she exclaimed with tears in her eyes. This was followed by a hug that knocked the breath out of me. It meant much more than any accolade or "title" ever could. It also installed a fiduciary obligation in my heart to never, ever sell out for just money and to always try to present the truth with facts to back it up—a responsibility that motivates me to this day.

It was the articles that put our concepts into every country. For many years we never advertised for distributors, and I never mentioned DMK treatments or products in any article. I feared that I would lose any respect or credibility I had in the scientific circles if I used journalistic privilege to flog my company. But therein lay a problem. When a reader would write me, saying "I have acne, what do you suggest I use?" I gritted my teeth and wondered how to say, "Well, we just happen to have a treatment for that." I encouraged my distributors to take out ads in all the publications, hoping that the reader would draw a parallel between the Danné Montague-King who wrote an article on roasacea and a DMK Ad in the same magazine.

BIOFREEZE ™ changed all that.

Most of you have either heard of or been issued a product called BIOFREEZE ™ by a health practitioner. It's a topical "cold method" pain product based upon cryotherapy.

It started out as a humble pain gel, based on the science of cryotherapy (cold method) that I hand -made for my ailing grandmother who was suffering from arthritic agonies.

The rise of BIOFREEZE ™—from handing out samples to friends and relatives, to being used by millions around the world, (and is a book on its own)—for now, suffice it to say that after the checks for royalties on the use of my formula and yearly profit distribution became embarrassingly large (I did not own the product outright, or make it—I just created it), I sold my interests to my partners at Performance Health USA for what I thought was a substantial amount (they always wanted to have the formula) and put most of the money into DMK and skin research. In this fashion I did not have to "sell" DMK products or treatments to just anybody to make a living, I could *choose* who represented us—and always seemed to end up with the very best people, and the most committed.

I think this is why, in comparison to other companies, DMK practitioners seem to be a bit fanatic, almost evangelical at times.

This takes forward-thinking people who truly care about healing others whose self-worth issues are compounded by skin anomalies that affect their personal lives and professional potential. The mantra "Save a skin, save a life" is much more than an advertising gimmick to us.

I thought my BIOFREEZE ™ days were long gone, but recently a remarkable man from Texas, John McCready (formerly Canadian), who owns a successful veterinarian products company, approached me with the idea of creating a pain gel for horses and other animals.

Being armed with some newer ideas about penetration (especially into horsehide which is much denser than human skin), I came up with a new version of cryotherapy which he entitled DEEP FREEZE ™.

Australian horses at the Dickson ranch, occupied by Daniel's parents (where the sweet scent of homemade banana bread and other goodies are always on the air), were the first to experience DEEP FREEZE—and the results were amazing. American farriers began secretly using DEEP FREEZE on their own bodies against aches and pains, and began clamoring for a human version.

Unfortunately one of the "wetting agents" I developed to ensure penetration into horsehide, smells like garlic on human skin. So a return to the drawing board and some double blind tests from the prominent chiropractor Dr. Jeff Talbot eventually launched DEEP FREEZE Human Pain Gel and Cool Down Shampoo, Turbo Freeze and other sports, pain and athlete's foot remedies.

Worlds within worlds—it seems that once one gets going, the domino effect never stops. I'm convinced that this only happens when one really cares about the needs of one's fellow man and not how much money can be made off a "trend" or buzzword.

31

"Brad Pitt's Skin Doctor" and Other Adventures

Over the years, my journey of education has also been an amazing magic carpet ride into places I never dreamed I would go. Of course there were "stuff ups" along the way (like creating mass hyperpigmentation on almost the entire Indian population of Durban, South Africa with a new, and quite effective—for Caucasians—peel. This treatment was also effective on Black skins, so I was amazed at this catastrophe).

Of course we sorted it out with a lot of gratis hyperpigmentation treatments, but the disaster took a while to live down. Then I repeated the same mistake in London where we took a huge apartment at Grosvenor House on Park Lane in which we did treatments on the press—all the major editors from the glossies and newspapers. Somehow, the dark-complexioned wife of an important foreign diplomat got snuck in, and I, showing off, instructed my London therapist of to really go aggressive with the treatment. The next day I left for Tel Aviv, Israel.

The patient tracked me down by telephone, screaming that I had ruined her life, and she was going to shoot me and then herself.

I tried diplomatically to calm her down, assuring her that the "brown areas" she described were normal and to trust the London therapist for a few more days.

Fortunately, what could have been an international situation at the highest level—with the Fleet Street tabloids having a field day as they ruined my life—turned out the way I assured her it would. Weeks later she sent me a lovely thank you letter.

But I learned from the experience. I learned about Indian and other deep-toned skins that were not African Black, and also that I must not be so cocksure when showing off to the press.

A lot of the media cannot be controlled when it comes to celebrities. The second-worst snafu that I endured was the great Brad Pitt fiasco.

In London, at the opening of our new Harley Street Clinic under the direction of Suzanne Williams of DMK UK (and a member of The Royal Academy of Medicine), I was interviewed by a fresh-faced female newspaper reporter who asked me about my work on Brad Pitt. I informed her that I had never met Mr. Pitt, although I admired his work. There was a story going around that one of our Los Angeles therapists had freshened his skin with one of our resurfacing procedures, in preparation for his role in *Seven Years In Tibet*—where he played a flawless-skinned young Nazi mountain climber whose life was changed in Tibet. (I thought of Brad as I walked up all those hundreds of stairs at the Polenta Palace in Lhasa in 114 degrees heat in the shade.)

At the time he was dating Gwyneth Paltrow, and I knew that her mother, Blythe Danner, was a client of our therapist, so I had no reason to doubt this rumor. But I hate to use celebrities to flog our work ("*I'm the star of this show*," I would laughingly tell people) and I told this reporter as much.

To my shock, on the plane going back home, I opened a newspaper to a half-page article complete with photos of myself and Brad, entitled "Brad Pitt's Skin Doctor." The article suggested that Brad would be less than handsome if it were not for me. It hinted that I worked only on the rich and famous, and went on to list my beach home and hilltop estate as proof of my money-grubbing wealth and celebrity success.

Needless to say, there was a lot of saber-rattling from the Pitt camp— from his publicist to a nasty-sounding man who appeared to be some sort of manager. I repeated the facts several times, but as the communiqués became more threatening, I finally got my back up and reminded this person that I could (obviously) get publicity, and since Brad had two new movies coming out—why, let's just keep this going! All kinds of tabloids that would love to run the story of the harassing movie star and the poor, innocent skin revisionist.

I never heard another word after that and could only hope that Brad Pitt, one of my favorite actors, was so insulated with many layers of people that he had never even heard of the altercation.

A South African woman named Rosalie saw my press photo in the British *Les Nouvelles Esthetiques* magazine and claimed I had compelling eyes that drew her in. (Years later a German therapist also said I had "magic augens," and the nickname stuck).

Rosalie came to the USA with her husband. An energetic woman who seemed able to take on any project with great flair, she needed only a few days training to become our first distributor in South Africa. She was fascinated with my work involving Black skins—even though apartheid was still firmly in place and there was little economy for that community, most of whom were employed as domestics or other vocations of servitude.

When I arrived in Johannesburg for the first time I was confronted by long row of people, Rosalie and her staff, holding a fifty-foot long banner that read, *Welcome to South Africa Danné Montague-King.*

I was impressed. I was further impressed with the huge ranch Rosalie and her husband lived on outside of Johannesburg. They had an enormous amount of house staff, all living in a compound on the ranch. There was Haley, the house boy, who saw to all my domestic necessities (although I refused to be bathed by him). There was one girl to do the laundry, one to press the clothes, a gardener; a pool man and an assortment of people taking care of the livestock and general cleanup. They were all paid what would be minimum wage in one of our poorer States, and a portion of that pay was given to "The Fathah" (Father)—Nelson Mandela.

One day I asked Haley how many Krugerrand he made per week. I forget his answer but I do remember him telling me that one third of it went to "The Fathah." When I asked him why, he replied with a huge, toothy grin "Because he promised us that one day we'll be free and have Madam's ranch."

Later I discovered that there were agents amongst these people collecting money from uneducated people of their own race by using Mandela's name whilst he was in prison. The exploitation of Africans by Africans did not start with slavery here in the USA, it started decades ago, right in Africa—and in some areas of the great continent it still goes on.

Rosalie was a good businesswoman and somewhat of a visionary. She had two daughters. One was tall, blonde and built like a ramp model, and married to an equally beautiful tall, blond man who was the quintessential entrepreneur—into anything and everything. He had the grand home, the flashy cars and other toys. South Africa was and still is a place where a person with energy and a smart mind, willing to take risks, can make a fortune almost overnight (and lose it).

His wife was the head of distribution for Dermalogica Cosmetics in South Africa—a popular skin range that started out as "professional only" under the direction of Jane Martin-Wurwand of Britain.

Jane was an aesthetician who came to the USA back in the late 1960s and opened a beauty school called The Dermal Institute. It was highly successful because of all the British and European protocol that American cosmetology courses did not even begin to approach. Also, in those days, London ruled the fashion world, so Americans thought that anything English was "proper," "elegant" and "the best."

Years later, after moving back to the UK, Jane returned to the USA and established the product range called Dermalogica, claiming it had nothing to do with her school for professional therapists. We of course all knew better, and in South Africa the rivalry between DANNÉ Concepts and Dermalogica raged like a wildfire. The blaze was actually fanned by Rosalie's other daughter, Tracy, who took over our distribution from her mother along with an energetic and handsome young businessman named Mark Chopin.

Tracy and her sister, Lee, were as different as night and day. Lee was glamorous, outgoing and fashionable, while Tracy was heavy set, quiet and shy at first. But Tracy noticed everything I did and soaked it all up like a sponge. She became the first of my subsequent "research therapists," and her endless exploration of knowledge and willingness to experiment led to some of our most remarkable treatments. In those days in South Africa there was no equivalent of the FDA peering over our shoulders. I could formulate as I saw fit (although always erring on the side of safety), and Tracy had an endless supply of human guinea pigs, not rabbits, to work on.

I will say that while Evelyn F. Williams gave me my career and Lillian Maund of England promoted it to Europe, it was Tracy Nathan of

South Africa who gave it the serious bells and whistles that we still have many of today.

She challenged me over and over again. "Dannnnneeee, we *must* go deeper into the tissue—ah tell you—*shame*—Dermalogica is saying that their peels are beeter—and you're mah beest." (In an English accent this would be "Dermalogica is saying their peels are better, and you, Danné, are my best guy. "Shame" is a common South African colloquialism that can mean many things, from "Oh, my" to "That's too bad").

When I look at some of the early "before" and "after" photos we took back in those research days, I'm humbled by the work we did and the risks we took. I'm not just talking about scientific risks; we worked with people living in below-poverty situations in townships that were segregated from the rest of the city, and those who lived behind high walls with gates armed guards 24/7. Robbery and even rape was not uncommon, a situation that unfortunately was all too rampant. Powerful Zulu King Buthelezi was in charge of all these people as "Minister of Housing," and as he told me personally at a private meeting at Parliament House in Cape Town a few years later, "This is a token job and title. Where am I going to find housing for all these people who have no schooling or skills?"

Privately, after I received a commendation from this highly intelligent and religious man for my work there, I thought he should have been President of South Africa.

Tracy and Mark showed me the magic of that great country in ways I never dreamed existed. We would stay at compounds deep in the many wild life reserves for several days, roughing it in huts (albeit huts with air conditioning powered by little solar panels).

On my first visit to the Kruger National Forest we decided to take a "night ride" in an open Range Rover driven by a pink-cheeked blond ranger from Devon, England. The rangers all wore khaki short-sleeved uniforms and "veldtschoen" (field shoes) with high ankles to protect from snake bite.

This particular chap looked *too* pretty and young to drive anyone into the pitch black African night, but there was an elephant herd at the nearby elephant pan (a place of water where they all bathed and drank), and the roar of lions. We were all keen to take it on.

As we motored slowly past the elephant herd, it seemed almost magical, like the movie *Out Of Africa*. There were bulls circling the perimeter and cows with their calves, squirting them with water the way humans take showers.

As we trundled down the road in the dusk, something alerted the herd and they started thundering down the road after us.

"Stay calm, they're not after us," admonished the Devon boy, who nevertheless put his carbine rifle across his knees under the steering wheel. I was too enchanted to be scared—the elephants overtook us as if we were not there, parting to avoid crashing into us, like Moses at the Red Sea. There was a soft gray mist of dust from their stampeding feet that gave everything an unreal, ghostly appearance, like we were flying with them.

Occasionally a mammoth head would pass me by and an eye full of almost human intelligence would roll towards me and vanish into the mist. "Hello there, sorry, but we have someplace else to go to."

After the main herd passed, a huge bull brought up the rear, no doubt looking for any strays or babies that hadn't kept up. As he approached the Range Rover from the back, his ears went back and then straight out as he lifted his trunk and let out a bellowing blast.

"Stay calm," the ranger hissed, his voice shaking. "Don't make a move, whatever you do, until he passes by—those ear movements don't look good."

Tracy, Mark and I sat as still as statues while the elephant approached the vehicle and slowly wafted his trunk over the Rover and then us. I could hear sort of a "sniffing" sound as the trunk, both hole like nostrils, swept over my body and head with the gentlest of touches.

My instinct was that I was being sniffed for fear, so I commanded myself to go dumb and "someplace else" in my mind while he Hoovered away for what seemed an endless time.

Mark was also stoic and passed the fear test, but when the elephant came to Tracy and started stroking her hair, she slapped the trunk and screamed, "Don't *touch* me you——so and so——!"

Surprised, the Bull jerked his trunk back up, looked at her for a second, ears flapping, and then rushed to the side of the road, pulled up a small tree by the roots and slammed it down on the road close to where she was sitting.

Then he ran down the road to his herd.

Tracy's signature mantra from then on—whenever she was angry or fed up with a therapist or something that went wrong at work—would raise her hand and arm like an elephant trunk and give out a blast.

A few yards down the road we found out what spooked the herd. The headlights of the Range Rover picked out movement in the grass along the side. Suddenly the cutest little Lion cubs bumbled out on the side of the road, as babies do, three of them.

"Ohhh how cute! Stop, let's help them," both Tracy and I demanded.

At this point the boyish ranger became manlier "No, don't touch them! The mother is about and any messing with her cubs could kill some of us and certainly hurt who would be left."

Nothing is more dangerous in South Africa than a lioness with cubs, and the show that followed was grisly proof of it.

With the elephant herd gone, the night became very quiet. Even birdsong had stopped, along with the far-off whiffles and sounds of other bush predators.

"Over there," exclaimed the ranger in a loud whisper as he pointed to a field at the opposite side of the road from the cubs.

Slinking through the grass towards the cubs was a jackal—his narrow and viscous head thrust forward like a snake's as his body slunk silently over the turf.

"Why don't you shoot it?" I begged the ranger—"Save those kittens."

He turned and looked at me, his periwinkle-blue English schoolboy eyes showing me he wanted to do just that but, as he pointed out, it was too dark to take a risk—not knowing what else was out there.

What was out there was a lot of other rangers in Range Rovers. In Africa, news gets around almost as if by jungle drums. The spooked elephants had alerted other camps, and their Rovers had driven up to points around the entire perimeter of the field where the jackal was stalking.

In the distance several sets of headlights switched on, illuminating the field in a soft, pale glow. As if waiting for this "spotlight cue," two lionesses sprang out from different sides of the field bush, rushed towards the now-squealing jackal and literally tore it apart in front of our eyes.

I had never seen an animal torn in half in what seemed like a second. The lioness with her jaws deep in his throat shook the jackal's lifeless head back and forth in rage—like my Jack Russell Terrier, Fiona, at home shook a rat she had just killed. Blood and entrails flew everywhere as the two ladies disposed of the predator that had stalked their children. I felt a human to animal bond and wanted to call out, "Come over here, girls, we got the kids safe!"

But Devon-boy had other ideas and got us out of there just as the two sets of glowing eyes turned on us and the lions started prancing across the field towards our vehicle. I looked back and could dimly see some sort of reunion as the moms found the babies, and also heard little squeals, like someone being spanked.

Thinking that nothing more could possibly happen to top all that drama, we motored back to the compound. As we approached the gate, something long, fat and black dropped from an overhead tree limb onto the hood of the Rover and slithered to the ground.

"What was that?" I asked.

"Oh, just a Black Mamba—usually we don't see them too much around here."

"Are they dangerous?" I queried with a shaking voice.

"Probably one of the most venomous—but no worries, mate—they seldom come inside the compound."

Knowing that my hut was full of spots where anything could slither in, I left the lights on all night and sat up reading until dawn.

Based upon those experiences in what was known as "roughing it camps" for the natural and macho types, Tracy decided our *next* visit to the wild would be 5-Star.

One thing that takes getting used to in South Africa is the fact you are not in some sort of protected "zoo" or preserve such as we have in the northern continent. The African veldt belongs to the animals. Rangers are there to help them, not herd them, and people are allowed to visit at their own risk.

The 5-Star camp truly *was* a resort, the grass-roofed huts luxury apartments inside, with every amenity.

There was something very Disney-esque about this place—it took being driven miles and miles across the Transvaal to get there.

I sat in the back of the resort's jeep and Tracy sat in front with the driver. She seemed to be talking his ear off in semi-Afrikaner, because he kept turning around a grinning at me with nearly all gold teeth.

When we got to the camp we were informed that Nelson Mandela and his entourage were in residence, and to avoid hanging about their huts.

Richard, the driver, acted like I was Mandela—he would not let me lift a bag or do anything. After checking in, he schlepped all my gear down to my huge "hut," constantly looking at me and grinning. I wondered what on earth Tracy had told him to cause so much joy and mirth. Once in the hut he told me in broken English that he was mine to command and that anything I needed day or night, just call him. Bowing and scraping, almost as if I were The Sultan of Brunei (whom I did not bow to in his Palace years later), he literally backed out of the door.

In the morning I asked Tracy what she had said to him.

Laughing, she replied, "Oh I just told him you were the Savior of all Black Skin and are here, at the same time as Mandela, to work out a plan to help all African people with their skin problems. I also told him you were a good friend of the Zulu King Buthelezi."

"Tracy," I yelled, "he'll never leave me alone!"

He did more than that. I'd purchased a pair of glasses with very expensive, gold Cartier frames. I'd left them on my pillow when I left that morning, preferring to wear my contacts so I could also wear sunglasses outside that day. That night I searched for them and they were gone. I called Tracy and she brought Richard down and we turned the hut upside down—no glasses. Richard had insisted he clean my hut himself instead of the maids, so Tracy and I both knew what had happened.

He had that guilty attitude one cannot hide from people who see things clearly, but I couldn't accuse him without putting up a big fuss and Richard being sacked. There would be fifty men lined up to replace him.

"Danné," said Tracy gently, laying her hand on my arm, "he took them as a souvenir of you, not to sell—you are like a god to him."

After I acknowledged she might be right and I could get another pair, we started making up stories about what Richard would do with my glasses. The best one was: a crude idol carved to look like me is somewhere in the bush, the glasses hung around its neck. The villagers nearby come and pay tribute at a Skin Festival once a year. And do the dance of skin.

Later, a real dance of skin *was* created by a young Zulu group, boys and girls who danced it around me at a DMK festival outside Johannesburg.

The next day I awoke early. No one else was up yet, so I wandered over to the forbidden zone near Mandela's camp. Suddenly the stillness was broken by the *whap, whap* of helicopter blades as a copter landed on a pad close to Mandela's multi-hut compound. I'd seen the activist briefly at an outdoor dinner held the night before, but the gamey-tasting Impala haunch had made me ill so I'd gone to bed without meeting the man-of-the-hour.

Now, as I approached his hut—the main balcony being higher than my head—I heard voices speaking English with European accents.

Some very well-dressed men, who looked like bankers or Wall Street moguls walked out onto the huge balcony. I overheard huge sums of money being mentioned, but could not quite make out the details. Then I heard a soft reply in a South African accent—I knew it was Nelson Mandela because of the respect in the other men's' voices.

Creeping closer and feeling like a CIA spy, I inadvertently kicked over a large stone, which tumbled down an embankment and started a noisy cascade of other rocks.

All conversation on the balcony came to a stop. After a few moments of silence, I heard the hurried shuffling of feet and a door slam. Nothing more was heard.

I've often wondered what those millions of Rands signified and who the suits who arrived in a helicopter were.

Over the next few years my magic carpet took me into, not just over, Victoria Falls in a tiny Micro Light aircraft (basically a bicycle with wings and a small engine); down into the catacomb-like rooms under Catherine The Great's Hermitage palace in St Petersburg, Russia, where I was shown the hidden great art of the world stolen by the Nazis during the Second World War. I was told that President Clinton was the only other American at the time who had been taken to view these treasures.

I've eaten lunch in a restaurant shaped like a giant Troll in Norway, dining with the King and Queen of Sweden, a most gracious couple. It was a private lunch for the Royal Family with security all over the place and the restaurant closed to the public, but somehow my people at DMK Norge got me in.

In China a women's magazine publisher, our first distributor there, built us a $25 million dollar training center designed by the best architect in Beijing. It looked like a flying saucer ready to take off, with every high-tech innovation possible.

In Germany, my head educator, *Susan of Germany* as we call her, went along with my plan to launch DMK Deutschland by inviting therapists, plastic surgeons and other doctors *and* the general public to my opening lecture. This had never been done before, but I pointed out that all of these people would be interacting with DMK treatments anyway, so why not show them the concept all at once and together?

She and her then-husband Peter had come to the USA for training. I had not yet been to Germany, and despite my years of facing the media and the public, I was very nervous to go. I was well aware that Germans in general react to things with a collective mentality and assume that they have the best labs and best science possible. For an American to come in with smooth and casual salesmanship, touting miracles, was a certain recipe for failure (which is why most American skin care companies don't do well in Germany).

Sure enough, the beautiful Susan (think Grace Kelly combined with Brooke Shields when they were young) did exactly as I suggested. I approached the podium at a 5-Star hotel confronted by a sea of dour, suspicious faces, especially the doctors'.

I froze. All my natural humor and dramatic delivery fled. I literally *barked* my lecture out at ear-splitting decibel levels. Eventually *some* of my humor broke through and my arm shot out in a "Sieg Heil" salute as my other hand tried desperately to clutch it back down. I think I even clicked my heels a couple of times. The naughty boy demon I'd had inside me all my life was taking over.

But no one was laughing.

Suddenly I realized no one was laughing because they were all taking me seriously.

After my final remarks barked to a standstill, the entire room burst into thunderous applause and the doctors rushed up, led by a prominent surgeon, Dr. Jurgen Esche, who grabbed my hands and pumped them up and down. "*Ja, sur gut!*" Esche hollered. "But you are so logical, Dr. King."

Escorted to the dining room by a beaming Susan and Peter, I was shaking like a leaf. "Conquering Germany" kept coming to my mind, and indeed we did so in subsequent years, marching across that fair and tidy country with pomp and circumstance and first class all the way.

There was the Schloss DMK Tour where every venue in every city was held in a castle. Germans love formality and we were skincare royalty. When the huge new music theatre below Neuschwanstein, King Ludwig's most famous castle, opened up with a musical commemorating this gifted and haunted king's life, they organized a coach with horses to deliver me and the Hartungs to the entrance. I was dressed like a modern day Ludwig, with my mad, blazing "blue augen" contact lenses in and a similar hairstyle.

The crowd gasped and whispered as Susan and I descended the coach steps like the king himself and Empress Sissy, his cousin (Susan looked remarkably like the Empress). I was called "King Ludwig *mit* his magic *augen*" for years by our German clients, and I was gifted and spoiled by many magical moments in that country that only movies are made of—it *was* a movie in fact—and could never be repeated again.

One of the most memorable situations was being taken to the Two Brothers Restaurant in the Alsace region of France not far from the German border. My grandfather's people were from this area and everywhere I looked I kept seeing my own eyes looking back at me.

The restaurant was in an old country house, with a reservation wait of sometimes two years, but somehow Peter got us booked for dinner and a stay at the Petit Chateau hotel on the grounds.

The dinner was beyond description, everything "built" at the table by the waiter and the sommelier. I forget how many exquisite courses were served, how many award winning wines, but one of the two brothers, an older man (now deceased) approached the table—attracted by Susan's beauty and my behavior. He was effusive in his welcome and we laughed and talked for 15 minutes, ignoring envious stares from the other patrons who had waited a long time to eat at the famed establishment.

We were informed that all the produce was grown by the family on the surrounding farmlands and that each dish was tested over and over again before serving. I suddenly knew who this congenial man reminded me of, and burst out, "But Monsieur, you look like Maurice Chevalier."

Glowing red and beaming from ear to ear, he bowed. "Oh, but you are too kind." Chevalier, the waiter told me, was a hero to him and he had met him in his youth.

The next morning I awoke in my suite under the eaves of the *maison*, birds warbling in the spring air, soft wind blowing the voile curtains which beckoned me outdoors like a pair of white hands. Shambling down the narrow staircase, I heard no one at all and wondered where I could get a cup of coffee. As I approached the bar area, the younger brother (my eyes again) suddenly appeared and wanted to know if Monsieur would like breakfast on the river?

Stunned by this proposition, I asked, "But how—?"

"*Regardez,*" he beamed, gesturing to the outside terrace with the river beyond.

Floating there, tied to the small dock, was a skiff. Placed in the middle was a full sized table with white table cloth, napery, crystal, china and silverware. On the sides of the skiff were wicker baskets full of soft boiled eggs, hams, sausages, warm breads, cheeses and condiments.

I stuttered, "B-b-but I have to wait for the Germans," just as Peter bellowed, "*Guten morgen, Danné!*" and, followed by Susan, stood with me and stared at the skiff in disbelief.

I began to feel that this might not be part of the regular hotel service after an elderly boatman appeared, complete with a flat brimmed hat and a red scarf around his neck, holding a long boat pole.

After being seated and gently floating away from the dock, we looked back and the entire family had come out on the terrace to wave us off. Even the mother appeared, actually wearing a long, black bombazine skirt, white blouse and her grey hair in a chignon, all very much like a Hollywood movie.

They waved and cried "*Bonjour, bonjour,*" as we entered the center of the river.

Bobbing gently into the sunrise, we dined while passing quaint farmhouses where farmers' wives were actually shaking rugs out of upstairs windows and also cried out "*Bonjour!*"

I had never experienced anything so romantic in my life, and yet like King Ludwig, I was alone—except of course for Peter and Susan, who were in the early days of their marriage. Their marriage ended a few years later and talk about irony and life being a circle; Susan is now married to my old Hot Springs Arkansas photographer buddy, Kevin Ellsworth, happily ensconced in Germany!

Their final gift was taking me to The Vienna Opera Ball, a yearly occasion attended by European royalty, complete with all the family jewelry on display and carefully designed gowns. The waiting list is years long and to be invited you have to be old money, old title, or sponsored.

Before the Ball I took eight weeks of waltz lessons, Vienna style, so I would not make a fool of myself spinning the elegant Susan with her Versace gown and towering coiffure around the floor in front of the *hoi polloi* of Europe. Paris Hilton was invited in later years and the US press made a big deal of it. I was amused at my having been there before Paris, and not a word said about it in the press.

I became fascinated with King Ludwig Von Bayerling of Bavaria, researching his life in the many books written about him. As I wandered the magnificent rooms of his many residences I could feel the genius of this tormented man's imagination.

I knew he'd influenced Walt Disney; it is obvious that Neuschwanstein, Ludwig's most famous castle, was a template for the Disney logo castle.

Ludwig created many fantastic special effects, including being the first European monarch to use electric lights powered by hidden batteries to illuminate not only the outside of his residences but also an underground grotto with its opera stage and swan boat that would glide over the underground pond to receive the artists and ballet stars he would invite.

His last effort, Herrenchiemsee, built on an island, boasted a hall of mirrors that made the one created by Louis the Fourteenth, whom Ludwig much admired, look small and worn out by comparison.

On one tour we took through Ludwig's summer party palace, Linderhof, the young Bavarian Guard kept pointing to every spectacular room, describing its use and ending with, "…and King Ludwig was always alone."

Finally we came to the famous private dining room where the table would disappear into the floor at Ludwig's command, descending into a kitchen where the next course would be loaded onto it and raised back up.

After going over all the details of this eccentric feature, the kid once again proclaimed, "…and he was always alone."

"Rubbish!" I barked, tired of this nonsense. "He had this designed so the servants couldn't see what he was doing with his young ballet star guests, or what other romantic interests he had going—he was gay as pink ink."

The startled English tourists standing around me grew quiet and muttered, "makes sense, quite right."

Red-faced, the guide tried to quiet me down, but the audience was interested and during the rest of the tour I regaled them with details I had ferreted out from my research. Obviously the Bavarian Tourist Board felt that "outing" their king would not be accepted by the world. But a few years later, after the musical created about Ludwig "hinted" at his true private life, secret diaries were found written in his own hand that detailed not only his interest in young men but his commands to search throughout Europe to find likely candidates.

Many times, anatomical and physical preferences were included. Ludwig was not a pervert or "chicken hawk." But he was not alone—he was *lonely*, and being a deeply religious and sensitive man in a time when homosexuality was hush-hush, King Ludwig hated being gay. Because of this he became a recluse, and although loved by his people he became more and more distant from his duties as a King, immersing himself in his castles. In Munich the Parliament, rife with men hungry for power, wanted Ludwig out of the way and attempted to have him declared insane, which resulted in the false nickname "Ludwig the Mad King."

It was while being held prisoner in "medical confinement" that he, along with his physician, drowned in the lake outside the castle. This created a mystery that has baffled historians for decades. It was said he committed suicide while trying to escape, but the details are too odd to support that conclusion.

I believe he was assassinated.

I often wish there could be a time machine in which I could go back and visit Ludwig. I feel that I could have saved him—convinced him that he was not only "OK" as he was, but that the beauty and miracles he gave to the world were critical. His patronage of composer Richard Wagner, the fairytale castles he built that generate millions of dollars in tourist income for Bavaria—these things prove that a mind rich in imagination can live on forever.

32

Irish Eyes Do Smile

The Emerald Isle is probably the most magical place on earth, and for me it became a place of heart, home and hearth on many levels.

I had already been doing business in Northern Ireland under the distribution of Roberta Mechan, an extraordinary woman of Joan Collins style-beauty. She ran a beauty school and a skin clinic in Belfast during a time when tanks roared down the street and men with carbines flitted in and out of alleyways.

Roberta was married to a fine older Irish businessman who looked and talked exactly like actor Barry Fitzgerald playing the Irish priest in the old 1940s *Boys Town* movies. He and Roberta lived in a stone and wattle, windswept house in the hills above Belfast with their dog "Wee Minnie." When I was a guest it was not unusual for us to be stopped by patrols on the way into town with "bomb warnings."

One afternoon at her clinic I had about five patients, including a venerable Vicor, the Reverend White, under enzyme masques. Suddenly a warden appeared at the door and shouted, "Everybody out; a bomb may go off any moment!"

Nonplussed, Roberta's capable staff moved all the clients onto blankets in the back yard of the pub next door, and we finished the treatments as if it were business as usual.

And it was. Looking back, I don't remember ever really being afraid—thrilled, secretly, that I was in the midst of a lifestyle one usually sees only on the news. I do remember thinking how odd it was that people would go about their daily lives with danger lurking at every corner—

yet laughing and loving and having huge splendid families—without any show of fear or depression. No one is more Irish than the Northern Irish—yet they were totally subject to Britain.

By contrast, the Southern Irish around Dublin are actually more British-acting, as far as I could see.

Roberta had lived an exotic life; she had lived in Africa and married an African chief in a time of tribal war. She'd borne him two sons, only to be trapped in the palace with the boys during a prolonged conflict—her husband caught up in the fighting. The Red Cross finally found them—thin and near starvation—and she was airlifted to the UK and then to Ireland, where she brought the boys up as a single Mum, proudly flaunting a mixed union in the face of everyone.

The boys became popular businessmen in the community, and one night after a few whiskeys Roberta confided to me that the Chief had suddenly appeared one day out of nowhere "only wishing to see the boys." As a proud woman who had been deserted, she asked him to leave, and he vanished like the ghost he had been for all those years.

I loved Northern Ireland, and years later I was invited for a weekend at a lakeside cottage in Donegal by my friend Sean Rafferty, a famous radio personality who had interviewed me on his show many times, once with British Actress Fiona Shaw (*Two Men and A Baby* amongst her many movies).

At the last moment Sean informed me to come by train to Donegal and book a suite at a local manor house because his cottage had become fully booked by unexpected guests from London.

It was autumn, and when the train arrived dusk had fallen over the sleepy station, so dark I could barely make out the cab that was waiting for me.

After what seemed hours of driving down narrow, twisting lanes with thorny hedgerows towering over us, we finally pulled into a long lane that wound up a hill with Wuthering Heights glowering at the top, yellow lights pouring from its tall Georgian windows. The cabbie deposited my luggage at the broad steps and the massive oak door creaked open and an older woman stood there in a pose straight out of a movie. "To be sure, it's Danné King, is it?" she exclaimed, patting her grey chignon and looking me up and down merry blue and rather piercing blue eyes glowing through rimless glasses.

She wore a white blouse with puffed sleeves, buttoned up to her chubby chin and fastened with a cameo broach. A long navy serge skirt completed the ensemble, and I felt as if I had been sent back in time to the turn of the century. With motherly briskness she showed me to my enormous second floor room with its four poster canopied bed and tall gothic windows with swaged curtains.

A peat fire glowed in the small hearth, and I was instructed to "Sort myself out and come down to the lounge for a drink" and wait for Mr. Rafferty to collect me for dinner.

Changing into what I considered "Formal Irish Country Proper"—a pair of Calvin Klein vintage jeans, a blue chambray shirt with an ascot, Dingo cowboy boots and a tweed jacket with patches on the elbows—I descended the stairs to the lounge where a huge fire was crackling and a few other guests sat with pints in their hands reading newspapers or chatting.

They all looked like they'd been born in the vast house; one old gent was a dead ringer for The Earl in the 1930s Freddy Bartholomew movie *Little Lord Fauntleroy*.

Feeling like everyone was secretly wondering who the Yank was despite my very good Mayfair British accent (which seems to come over me whenever I set foot in that part of the world), I nervously gulped down a whiskey and waited for Sean.

Sean sent a driver instead—one of his young guests. The young man looked like Sinead O'Conner (a highly-intelligent girl I met on a flight from Dublin to London one evening) would have, if she'd been male. He had a shaved head, and was tall and lanky with huge, beautiful cat-like-green eyes—that kept boring into me as if he were trying to figure out what I was doing there.

I didn't get much out of him as we bumbled along the dark lanes in Sean's Mercedes, outside of the fact he was some sort of artist (or maybe a photographer). I assumed he was Sean's special guest for the weekend—but this was never obvious.

Sean's cottage was like a movie set and one of the coziest, most charming places I have ever been in.

After passing through a red gate, the drive ended at a thatched-roof cottage directly on the windswept lake. Lights blazed from the many hobbit-like windows. I was ushered into the tiny lounge with its huge crackling fireplace and the most unusual group of people I had ever met.

They were all talking at once, it seemed, and without stopping trained their eyes on me. Completing this somewhat eerie scene was an older women sitting in a rocking chair whose eyes shone brilliantly with mirth and sophistication.

Her mouth appeared to have been slashed from one side to the other, thick scars curving far up into her cheeks, sort of like The Joker in the *Batman* movie. Trying not to stare while my professional mind went instantly to thinking of reparative surgery, I introduced myself. Sean immediately became effusive, hugging me and proclaiming my small fame as a scientist and accomplishments to all and sundry.

Properly tagged, the rest of the group felt comfortable to me as one of the weekend gang, and made themselves known by name.

There was a handsome dark-haired young man who reminded me of Clark Kent from *Superman*, wearing a hound's-tooth blazer *and* an ascot (which made me feel I had made one right wardrobe choice) and a rather plushly-built but pretty young woman who emitted the sort of almost angelic kindness only upper-class, old money people have.

Clark Kent immediately admired my cowboy boots and announced he was going to Texas in a fortnight and asked me to recommend a good brand. He also fingered my jacket and murmured "Hmmmm, a jolly good tweed you've got there."

I was privately amused at this as I had bought the jacket years before at JCPenney.

After a bit of chitchat about celebrities Sean had interviewed, we repaired to the tiny but beautifully-appointed dining room for a wonderfully prepared meal of roast lamb. New potatoes, spring peas and fruit compote served with a really fine port and Stilton cheese cut from a massive wheel the English couple had brought over as a house gift completed the elegant but homey meal.

For some reason the conversation turned to castles. I had recently stayed at the incredible Dromolin Castle in Limerick, and was going on and on about its classic amenities, when Clark Kent casually mentioned he had a castle somewhere in Ireland.

"Oh, really?" I asked. "I hear there are several old castles for sale nowadays."

"Oh, this one has been in the family for 600 years," he replied.

I gulped. "Does it take much staff to keep it up?"

"Oh, not really, only around fifty people most of the year."

The young English Lady turned to me and asked what kind of house I had in California.

Blushing, I told her it was a fake English Tudor but had a wonderful view, gardens and pool. There was no snobbishness here. They all genuinely wanted to know how I lived.

It turned out that Clark Kent was an Irish Lord and the woman a Lady and Peer of the Realm with a manor house outside London slightly smaller than Sandringham, her Majesty's northern England estate I was to visit years later.

The rest of the evening was filled with jokes and laughter, and we all seemed to be like old friends as we piled into a Range Rover they had arrived in to escort me back to the manor house.

After a brief tour of the premises by the bowing and scraping lady of the manor we all promised to meet for breakfast the next day. The next day was massive hangovers all round, melted Stilton cheese on toast under Sean's gas burner, and leftover wine.

Then we all walked on the beach in a high wind and mist, coats and scarves fluttering. We visited the lady with the scars at an Old Abbey she was renovating into a home (she told me the scars were the result of a dental surgery that went wrong) and then the aristocracy and the boy with the Sinead O'Connor eyes drove off to the city. Sean told me he would drive me back to Belfast later in the afternoon.

That was the last time I saw Sean or the magical cottage. He moved to London and went to work for the BBC. But during our rainy drive he confided many things to me, and underneath that clever, jovial and razor sharp sophistication I sensed a lonely man. A prophet in his own land who was afraid to speak.

I always hoped London gave him the life he richly deserved.

Roberta did well with my concepts, but she was unable to service the entire country beyond her own clinic and school. Not knowing what else to do—and becoming really fond of her, I felt I was treading water. Suddenly, Katherine Hurley of Dublin appeared at my table while I was having a coffee break in between lecture at a professional beauty exhibition in London.

Katherine Hurley was an explosion of golden curls, huge restless blue eyes, and the energy of a Jack Russell Terrier. She could also be the quintessential Lady if she had to. Her mother was dramatically a Grand Dame and her father a true aristocratic gent of the sort you don't see much anymore. An era was passing that I was lucky enough to see the tail end of it.

Now I *am* that era.

Katherine took over the DMK distribution of Southern Ireland with grim yet optimistic determination. This was during one of the worst times for the Irish economy. Yet she presented me as if I were the Elvis Presley of Skin, and financed huge hotel venues, inviting the public as well as members of the profession—something that had not been done before.

Looking back, I see that she had absolute faith in me and fearlessly pulled every string she had to get my concepts publicized, almost as I were a faith healer. I think this willingness people had to go outside their boxes for me was not due to any charms I have. I feel it was because of what I stood for in skin revision, how my concepts were so different than anything being taught in the beauty business (Katherine was also a Sotheby's of Paris Distributor)—yet it all seemed logical. In addition, all my worldwide distributors came to *me* after reading the articles I'd had published in trade magazines.

Because I never mentioned my concepts *or* products in my articles, only the science behind whatever subject I was writing about. I think for this reason alone people trust me.

And then there were the "cures" and amazing results. Often on my visits to Ireland I would be brought the worst skin disorder cases imaginable.

Katherine would book public appearances for me around the counties, tearing madly along narrow county roads at night with me hanging on for dear life, expecting that at any moment a sheep or cow would amble out of one of the many hedgerows and overturn us.

The venues ranged from grange halls to hotel conference rooms. Once, an old cathedral—that had a power outage due to an electrical fault—my old slide carousel ground to a stop (this was before the days of Power Points and laptops) and so I completed my lecture to the light of alter candles.

Before one of these "whistle stop tours" as they became known, I had appeared on one of Ireland's most popular TV shows hosted by Pat Kenny—sort of the Jay Leno of the country. The night before show the *Irish Times* ran an article about a teenage boy who had killed himself over having acne.

Acne cases are dear to my heart due to my own horrific experiences with the disorder as a teen, so I surprised Mr. Kenny by using this news story as my lead-in. I had already instructed our Dublin therapist to change our on-camera treatment demo to an acne treatment.

Mr. Kenny did not look too pleased by these sudden changes on live

TV but went with the theme, not skipping a beat. *Irish Times was* his local paper, after all.

This show ended up having far reaching impact on our "Whistle Stop" tour the very next day. When we arrived at our destination in county Limerick, the hall was packed with spotty-cheeked teenagers, old ladies with flaming roseacia cheeks; little kids sat on the shoulders of their dads in the back where there was standing room only.

I recall feeling a little but like a televangelist or faith healer, even to the white spring suit I was wearing. For two hours I attempted to teach, in layman's terms, how skin really worked and what did *not* work.

Never underestimate the intelligence of the humble public who faces conditions that they cannot afford to control on a daily basis. Not only did these people understand me as they brought some really tragic and often undiagnosed skin problems to me, their honest Irish faces shining with new hope, but I knew they would act upon what I told them to do.

Many times I felt like a blind man fumbling in the dark. I was not an MD; there were no drugs I could prescribe. But the body, which includes the skin, has its own incredible healing powers if given the correct environment and proper tools to help it along.

These we had, and between that, some common sense and the fact that our Limerick therapist was a skilled registered nurse, a great many of the sad cases were later reported to have gone into controllable remission or been totally healed. To say that I was often scared and wondering why I was there in the first place would be an understatement.

People, especially good Catholic women, would take me aside and confess the most innocent and bizarre "sins" (usually involving their husbands' sexual habits) and wonder if these sins had brought on their skin disorders. I would turn priest and Father Confessor and assure them that this was not the case. The whole time I felt unreal, as if in a movie, and Maureen O'Hara would come sweeping out any moment and waltz me down the lane.

To top this first tour off, Katherine and I decided to take a break and have "elevenses" (small brunch) at the nearby Dromolin Castle.

Dromolin really is a fairy tale castle, complete with massive grounds, turrets, and a lake with swans gliding around. It's one of those small, Irish castles that are both grand but not so huge as to be daunting and cold.

The main rooms had roaring fireplaces, large floral arrangements and shining antique furniture. One almost expected a lord to come ambling out, pipe clenched in teeth, saying "Top of the morning to you."

We were informed by a haughty butler-type chap that breakfast was long over and there would be nothing until luncheon. Disappointed, Katherine apologized to me and said we could probably grab at holdover snack at a pub.

As we turned to go, a pretty little girl with black hair and blue eyes and wearing a maid's uniform walked by us pushing a Hoover. Her name actually *was* Bridget the maid. She stopped, peered into my eyes and exclaimed, "Oooh it's that man from TV! From the Pat Kenny Show."

All at once we were set down in a cozy window nook, and a huge silver trolley appeared with smoking bacon and eggs, toast, coffee, juices and marvelous pastries. The staff buzzed around us, asking questions about their skins.

Life again imitating the movies.

33

Aerie Hall

To put a timeline on my journey would be impossible. Certainly styles and trends change every few years, but only superficially. How many outfits do we all have in our closets that we bought years ago and never threw away, because they *might* come back into fashion again? How many men throw away their shoes every two or even three years?

After a few years of going back and forth to the UK and South Africa, the rest of Europe seemed to open its arms to me all at once. Most of was due to Lillian Maund, my published articles, and word of mouth.

Lillian wanted me to purchase an "estate" or manor house similar to her 300 year-old manor house, Bache Hall, in Chester, England. This slightly spooky edifice had at least twenty-five bedrooms, long corridors and a history of "spirits" that the girls who attended her beauty therapy/cum finishing school said they saw many times: a pale young girl in a shawl, gliding down the grand staircase.

I never saw this apparition myself, but there was a definite "feel" at Bache Hall that the living occupants were not the only denizens of the huge pile of brick and stone. One was always conscious of being "watched" by windows to rooms not occupied, especially the lone window high up under the eaves of the front entrance.

One weekend night, I had gone to bed in the main dormitory wing. The students had all gone home. My little room was in the middle of very long hallway with tile floors that would echo any footsteps. All the doors to the other rooms had been closed and locked by the inhabitants while they were away.

I had just laid my head upon the pillow when my door reverberated with a loud *boom, boom, boom*!

Looking up, I expected to see it bulge inward like in the movie *The Haunting*, yet I was somehow not afraid. I immediately jumped up and threw the door open. No one was there, the hall totally empty and very cold. Shivering, I dived back under the covers, wondering who could possibly pound on my door in the middle of the night, then abruptly disappear down a very long hall with no footsteps heard at all.

Who…or what?

Teaching courses at Bache Hall taught me the tools of educational protocol and restraint. My accent became so British that at times, when I listened to some of my BBC interviews, it was like hearing someone else speak.

Mrs. Maund could be the kindest, most understanding person in the world, capable of great generosity—or, she could flip-flop and be the most stingy of dragons, often waxing hot and cold within moments. It was a constant egg-walking exercise with her, a minefield of what to say and how to say it to keep the benevolent Countess on hand and the dragon at bay.

Today's psychologist might say "Definitely Bipolar II," but back then, this chemical imbalance was relatively unknown, or at least not talked about. Many times I felt she was perfectly aware of her talent for high drama and got a kick out of it.

No one dared defy her—not even the girls from very wealthy families who could have told her off after some of her histrionics (a word she hated me to use) and marched out of the academy.

She had a way of challenging people to go beyond themselves—to dare to dream and then try to make it come true. She put me on the spot many times in front of the public, both in the UK and when we did business in the USA. She would stand me up in front of well-known people in the industry—medical doctors and experts—and then tout me as "the absolute authority on the subject" and leave me standing there trying to muster up to the accolades while she sat back, eyes wickedly glinting and her painted on lips curling at the corners.

"Larger than life" applied to Lillian Maund with her impressive figure, like that of an ancient sailing ship, towering pale gold coiffure and wardrobe straight out of the TV series *Dynasty*.

She would "enter" a room in a cloud of expensive perfume, long legs flashing beneath chiffon skirts, and everyone would automatically stiffen to attention, even if seated.

Charles Maund, her husband and some sort of British detective, was tall, affable and handsome in sort of a Rex Harrison way. He got along with Lillian very well although he would shut up whenever she exclaimed, "Oh, Charles, naff off!" I often saw him smiling somewhat wickedly during one of her high drama moments—I think they truly enjoyed one another and the grand role they played in the industry.

Lillian started up an organization called International Aestheticians which, at its inception, was a contender to CIDESCO, the two-hundred year-old training syllabus revered by therapists the world over as *the* standard of what aesthetic training should be. Lillian thought CIDESCO was antiquated and impractical for the existing job market and economics, and at times I agreed with this as far as certain CIDESCO chapters were concerned (mainly in the USA, which has tragically low education standards).

AIE (International Aestheticians) had a real foundation to it when it started, and I was happy to be a small part of it. Lillian had great vision but was crippled by poor follow-up and world financing. She would go into countries, taking me with her, especially into Asia, where everyone would be awed and dazzled by us; and then we would leave. Whoever was left behind would end up doing things the way they saw fit, and Lillian's carefully-planned courses and protocol would fall apart.

There was wonderful madness going on with her all the time. I learned a great deal and many of those lessons are with me today. In many ways, Lillian Maund took over where Evelyn Williams left off. I can honestly say that I was finished by her finishing school, and the experience led to the hilltop estate in which I live today—my castle.

Certainly Lillian had as many enemies as friends and paid dearly for some of her more innovative ideas; but for people like her there is little room for middle ground. She would often remind me: "People take kindness for weakness, so be kind only where it counts." Of course this lesson never really sank in and I've long been a sucker for nut cases, con artists and the downright insane, escaping only after I finally grew bored with the stress of unproductive drama.

Lillian decided to create a student exchange program. She would send six English therapists to train in the USA for three months to round out their abilities and get ready for the aesthetic marketplace as a career.

Convinced that every proper British Girl needed the All-American "go for it" presentation and self-confidence that I could teach, she also felt that our undereducated and bad-mannered American therapists would benefit by three months at Bache Hall.

In many ways she was right.

Back then I didn't have the money for a "Bache Hall" to house the students, so a friend and I desperately looked for real estate that could somehow be construed as "a manor house," even a fake one. After a few false starts and a terrible fiasco involving greedy landlords who tried to get in on the project, I finally drove up a hauntingly beautiful drive with oak trees bending their giant boughs over the road, allowing ribbons of sunlight to stream down. The drive wound up and up and finally, on a hilltop overlooking a 390 degree view of the San Gabriel Valley and Hacienda Heights canyons, I saw HOME.

The house was a faux English Tudor that wrapped around the front drive like arms embracing you. Tall pines soughed constantly around the property, with feathery canyons and banks of wildflowers everywhere. It had a huge pool in the middle of very English grass, bound by brickwork and rose gardens. The house sort of wandered about inside, with few square lines so it all felt open and breezy yet intimate and cozy at the same time.

I knew it was mine, and even with no money and a lot of finagling with the help of a real estate sharpie, I took possession and tried hard to create a Bache Hall out of it, naming it "Aerie Hall" (aerie meaning a high place for birds, which did and still do abound) and proceeded to establish an American Training School for upper-class British Girls.

The first wave of these young ladies included Mrs. Maund herself.

As I approached the baggage section of LAX of British Airways, I could saw her standing there, majestically ordering the girls about, garbed in a flowing afternoon coat, coiffed to perfection and flawlessly made up. She did not look like someone who had just flown for ten hours across the Atlantic Ocean and the USA.

The six girls were also heavily made up, hair scraped back into ballet dancer chignons and all in matching track suits. The other passengers assumed they were indeed a dance troupe ("We are Lillian Maund Beauty Therapy students," they would chirp back, almost in unison).

They unfurled an American flag and we had to do "Arriving in America" photo ops for Lillian's newsletters and my magazine articles.

I was nervous about what Lillian would think of my faux British Aerie Hall as compared to her massive and real Bache Hall manor house, but as we came up the drive she was enchanted.

So were the girls with their little cozy beds, two to a room, upstairs; the pool, of course; and Mrs. Leffy Watson, an older, still beautiful Newport Beach socialite who, with her Ava Gardner looks and tall figure, had half the men on the west coast champing at the bit.

Age and bad luck had taken its toll on Leffy, but she was a wonderful cook and a clever seamstress. It was she who had helped me get Aerie Hall together with custom made Austrian draperies constructed of sheets stuffed with tissue, and a fabulous, inexpensive menu. In return I gave her what money I could, and room and board. She had nowhere else to go.

I think she liked the proper-sounding English girls who called her "Mrs. Watson" and dipped their heads in respect. She found out later that these sweet and proper girls were not so proper after hours, and local young men started sniffing about—many situations of sneaking downstairs in the dark and cars silently rolling down the hill with headlights off.

I feared pregnancies and parental repercussions from the UK—one young lady's father being a prominent London Attorney—and this led to many late night counselling sessions with the girls to enforce the fact that they were in a foreign country and none of these boys would come forward on their behalf if precautions were not taken. I knew that the Puritan tactics most adults used would not work; I had to show them I was "cool" and understanding, but worried about *them*.

We had many adventures that nearly stopped traffic. The casual time uniform, insisted upon by Lillian, was navy blue sweat suits, silver Mary Jane shoes and chignons held back with silver scrunchies. The daily school uniform was Lillian Maund's specially-designed crisp, starched white uniforms bristling with achievement medals, the upside-down British ribbon watch, and not a wrinkle *dared* to be in sight.

Of course the young ladies had a few personal evening garments and heels stashed away—but only allowed on formal occasions (and late at night when Leffy Watson was sleeping).

The first traffic-stopping event occurred when my 30 bazillion dollar Cadillac burnt to the ground after we had just pulled off the freeway to visit Beverly Hills and Hollywood. "Bazillion dollar car" was the nickname of this majestic vehicle because it was as close to a Rolls Royce as I could get in those days. And it was constantly in the shop for repairs. It was a 1984 black Eldorado Biarritz that I bought cheap from Dr. Julio Guarnaschelli of Florence, Italy, a physicist who had opened my eyes to the miracles of electromagnetic therapy, combined with my enzyme treatments—the forerunner to our Dermafield that's used in clinics worldwide to this day.

Julio, an expansive and dramatic man, made extra money on the side whilst pursuing investors to back his machines by buying and reselling older luxury automobiles. The Eldorado was custom made for the original owner, who might well have been a Las Vegas pimp. It had rolled and pleated black leather upholstery, every high tech device popular at that time, a leather coupe top and a massive chrome grill that gave it the "Rolls" look. I thought about trying to find the "Winged Victory" hood ornament, but decided that it would be too tacky.

The car ran on diesel fuel, available in California but not at all gas stations. I had to plan weekly where I would be in order to fill it up.

I arranged to pick the girls up in the early morning, and on a bright and sunny day, the long Eldorado filled with pretty, laughing English girls, we set off for Hollywood.

The car started making funny chugging noises as we approached the Santa Monica off ramp. Worried, I told the girls we had to get off the freeway immediately. I had just had the engine and all the vitals checked and nothing major seemed wrong, but the sounds were getting louder and louder. As we descended the off ramp, there was a loud "clunk" and the engine started losing power. I literally *prayed* us around the curve, and suddenly everything went off.

Being a heavy car, without the power on the steering wheel was frozen and I used all my strength to keep the vehicle on the curve to the bottom of the off ramp. Suddenly one of the girls screamed, "I smell smoke!" And indeed, smoke started curling up from underneath the dashboard, along with a strange, electrical smell like wires burning. Jamming on the brakes just as the monster vehicle nosed into the intersection at the bottom of the ramp, I jerked the park lever back and yelled: "Out of the car, everybody!"

We dived out and I herded the worried young ladies to the side of the road just as the engine burst into flame—like in the movies. It is very odd watching your one and only luxury car burn down in front of your eyes. The hood buckled, flames licked over the front, and the tires began to burn, deflating and dropping the car front onto the pavement.

The girls were crying as I desperately tried to call 911 on the huge cell phone I had back then. Sirens sounded in the distance and eventually the police arrived, silently looked at the scene and doused the flames with chemical foam.

Somehow I arranged to rent a van through Enterprise Rental Cars, a company that comes out to you instead of you going to an agency, and the sniffling girls got in, prepared to go back to Aerie Hall. "We're so sorry about your car, Dr. King," they moaned.

Thinking of stiff upper lips and what Lillian would do in this circumstance, I said, "Nonsense, we're booked to tour Hollywood and Hollywood we will see."

And we did—actually having a marvelous time while I secretly wondered what I would do without a car.

The man who towed the car happened to be a Cadillac collector, and he called to ask me how much I would want for it. Amazed that it was worth anything at all, I accepted his offer of $700 only to find out later that the engine was miraculously not ruined, nor was the main body of the car. He eventually restored the car to almost new and sent me a photo.

It didn't matter. In a month I had a new Lincoln Town Car, and have never bought a used car again.

34

Queens and Other Ladies

*M*oving to Los Angeles and then onto the world stage was not an overnight journey, but looking back, everything seemed to happen at almost the same time.

Since I didn't have the finances to buck both the American marketing machine where a new product is released every five minutes with an even newer miracle ingredient *and* the plethora of self-styled gurus that abounded in the skin care game, I went where my published articles opened doors: always overseas. Germany, England, South Africa, Taiwan, Hong Kong and Korea were the countries where I seemed to spend most of my time.

The British Invasion at Aerie Hall dwindled as I spent more and more time out of the country. I simply didn't have the time or deep enough interest to run a school at the same level as Bache Hall.

Lillian took me to Taiwan with her girls for a conference and I ended up living in a Chinese home for a month with a well-meaning but irascible woman named Suming Wang. Ms. Wang never became a full-fledged distributor of mine despite her efforts, and seemed more fascinated by showing me her many business interests in Taiwan (none having to do with beauty therapy) and the lifestyle there rather than actually setting up distribution. I did learn a lot about domestic Chinese culture by wandering around the seaside with her, stopping by a fishing boat and buying crabs and fish and then carrying the fresh catch to a little woman with an outdoor wok who cooked the seafood along with fresh vegetables.

We often visited the famous Grass Mountain district of Taipei City, where natural hot springs abounded; the water was even piped up into the mansions of the wealthy for private use. We would rent rooms with hot spring tubs in them and sit in the sulfur-smelling water for an hour; afterward an attendant doused us with buckets of cold water and we enjoyed a "three style fish" dinner al fresco with a lot of Chinese families. No one seemed to notice the rather flamboyant American man with the butch-looking little Chinese lady. (Suming was very masculine and after a few shots of whiskey, had a mouth like a sailor, but denied being a lesbian.) Every morning we would go to the marketplace with her "Ahma" (the lady who took care of her house and offices) and shop through an amazing array of fish, vegetables, fruits and herbs, many of which I had never heard of before.

I recall an eel the size of an elephant's trunk, which Suming had sliced and served that night with a ginger sauce that was out of this world. I ate a great many things that ordinarily would gag me to even contemplate. Several herbs such as *Mao Huang* led to the creation of products I would develop in the future. This was my early experience in choosing ingredients I had seen with my own eyes and obtained from the actual source as opposed to buying pre-made extracts, which is common in the cosmetics industry. I would see a plant or herb; learn what I could about it locally, then file it away in my mind in case someday it fit with the pieces of another puzzle and became a tool for a skin treatment.

At the same time, Hong Kong was opening its doors to other Asian countries, mostly through the Chen Family. I forgot exactly how I met Dorin Chen and her brother William, who was one of the most striking Chinese men I had ever seen: tall and stately like a matinee idol. He owned a popular bar in Singapore and had his fingers in other business interests, including partners in Thailand.

The details of how I got to Singapore have also vanished from memory—all I seem to remember is a very modern and aggressive Dorin asking me if I would do a seminar there at some point. She had a friend named Jesse Lau So Har who was in the beauty business in Brunei, home of the Sultan of Brunei, then the richest man in the world.

In those days Dorin acted and looked more like a Chinese-American than Suming Wang of Taiwan or Alice Lau of Hong Kong, but then Singapore was and still is a melting pot of many nationalities, very upscale and well-run by its government.

I had never seen a city-cum-country as clean as Singapore. Nicknamed the Fine City, back then it was still extremely pro-British with its famous Raffles Hotel, manicured streets, impossibly well-run airport and gracious homes and apartment buildings. There was of course a modicum of poor people, but they were hidden well.

The government had strict rules about everything. One was heavily fined if one threw any trash on the street or was seen spitting by a law enforcement agent. But so much morality can become boring, so they "allowed" a bit of corruption on one famous street called Boogy Street. From the late 1800s until the turn of the century, Singapore was a port city that offered every entertainment possible to the sailors who came in. Boogy Street was the most notorious with its houses of delight and diverse fleshly offerings. Even as late as the 1970s both ends of the street would be periodically closed off to flow-through traffic, and as the purple dusk settled over the city little doors would open up all along the streets and beautiful female impersonators would emerge gracefully to stroll up and down in exquisite gowns—to unknowing eye, the most beautiful of young women.

Of course this passed as a tourist attraction, with tips and applause handed out to members of the parade, but private clients were subtly engaged to follow "the girls" back to their apartments or rooms. The impersonator parade was eventually banished, until only one bar on the street featured a drag show. It starred an Indian queen who became famous as a comic—using the audience as material for his jokes.

The new and stricter laws stated that anyone appearing in drag, even in a show, had to wear a black, male body stocking under their costume. It was disconcerting to see beautiful young queens with full fashion makeup, elaborate wigs and sparkling strapless evening gowns over clumsy black t-shirt topped leotards.

My first class in Singapore, arranged by Dorin Chen, was packed with therapists and a few doctors.

Midway into my lecture the door burst open and an attractive Chinese woman in a smart business suit bustled in, softly apologizing for being late, sat down, whipped out a pen and immediately started writing down every word I said.

Her name was Jesse Lau So Har. Jesse was very Western in her thinking, and seemed to understand the conceptual side of my methodology almost at once. Like most advanced thinking therapists of that time, she was starved for real education and real results as opposed to the pampering facials and product hype that were normally offered. Jesse Lau ended up being my distributor in Singapore, and Dorin, who lived in Singapore, ended up opening a DMK distribution in Thailand—with the help of her brother, William, and his contacts. At the same time one of Dorin's best friends, Violet Lee of the huge Lee Pineapple fortune, was elevated from being a well-heeled client who had special treatment whenever I came into Singapore to Distributor of DMK Indonesia—where she was well-connected to the President and First Lady.

Jesse Lau had an up-market clinic in Brunei that she went back and forth to, and she arranged for me to do a special lecture at The Sultan's Palace by special invitation of His Majesty. Everyone seemed to be interconnected during this time—all three ladies friendly to each other's faces but resentful of each other's territories and relationship with me behind their backs. Jessie's relationship with Brunei's royals trumped Dorin and Violet.

The invitation to Brunei listed His Royal Highness's names—about 30 of them, it seemed—and was very formal. I was very nervous about what to wear and how to act. Although I was familiar with British royal protocol, I knew nothing about a Muslim monarch. I was calmed by Jesse, who told me I would be meeting the queens and the rest of the family, not the sultan—this was to be an "all women" affair, followed by a high tea. I was instructed to carry several papers and the invitations with me when entering Customs after I flew into the tiny kingdom—and to bring a large bag of extra products, as Jesse had booked me to perform my Pro Alpha Six Layer Peel, the first professional AHA treatment ever presented in Asia, on about 20 women.

I had borrowed a large, old fake Louis Vuitton bag from a friend to pack the extra products. Jesse said if there was any additional excise tax on the good she would be waiting in Customs with a checkbook.

As I flew from Singapore to Brunei in first class on the Royal Brunei Airlines, I could not help but notice the stark black and white signs all over the plane that grimly stated, *Possession of drugs is punishable by death.*

This same sign was repeated all over the airport, and as I approached Customs, confidently waving my papers, a guard looked confused and summoned another guard. I was marched off to a side room and told to wait.

An hour went by as I cooled my heels in a small room with nothing to do but look up at the portraits of His Majesty and his two wives on the walls. I was beginning to feel afraid and wonder what was going on…which soon led to anger. I was, after all, an American citizen there by invitation of the man up on the wall.

The door finally opened and an older guard walked in, my papers in his hand. I jumped up and yelled, "Your *boss* here invited me—what the hell is going on?" as I gestured wildly at the portrait.

He actually bowed low and murmured, "Yes, Doctor King, we know, we are so sorry for inconvenience. Airport rules changed two week ago. There is no need for visa paper or special invitation now; your papers confused our employees."

Somewhat mollified, I swept out to passport control, and the guard waved me through.

My luggage was stacked up before the final security point—they were going through everyone else's bags, it seemed. But the guard waved the customs official away, actually lifting up some of the bags himself and saying, "It's okay; no need to detain Dr. King any further."

I saw Jesse outside the exit door, checkbook in hand and a worried smile on her face.

"Nothing to pay, Jess," I said, "just get me to the hotel."

On the way I could see that Brunei was very lovely and exotic city that seemed to be just barely beating back the jungle. There were hundreds of monkeys in the trees jabbering as we passed Colonial-style apartment buildings interrupted by lavish mansions and the odd little house with a tin roof.

The Hotel was part of an American chain and the only 5-Star in town at that time. As I checked in, Stevie Wonder was leaving the lobby with his crew walking back and forth loudly complaining: "No booze allowed. No nuttin'—let's do this gig and get outta here!"

The Sultan was a man who could (and did) hire Michael Jackson or Stevie Wonder for a private party the same way we would hire a local garage band. But he ruled his people through their religion and stuck firmly to the rules in all public places. For example, the hotel lobby was also replete with signs saying *Possession of any drug is punishable by death*.

Finally alone in my room, I started to unpack and get ready for the next three days. As I took the bottles and jars out of my fake Louis Vuitton bag, I noticed a zipper on the side I had overlooked. I unzipped it, felt a small lump inside—and pulled out a small plastic sack of very old and dried-up marijuana.

Frozen with panic, I wildly around the room to see if there were any hidden cameras. Positive that security guards were marching at that moment to arrest me, I dashed into the bathroom and dumped the contents of the bag down the toilet, thinking at the same time that the band members downstairs would have given me a lifetime pass to Stevie Wonder's concerts if they knew what I had in my hand.

The toilet didn't flush everything away, and in desperation I scooped up what was left of the herb and gobbled it down with copious amounts of water, thinking that even the plumbing might be monitored. I could see the headlines: "American Scientist Executed for Drug Possession."

Jesse rang the room just about then and asked if she could talk to me for as few moments about my fees in US cash to perform the Pro Alpha Six Layer peel. She claimed that all the booked clients were quite excited by the treatment; certain other medical peels were getting a bad reputation in Singapore due to the amount of chronic erythema and hyperpigmentation that they left behind. My approach and previous results assured her that my treatment was specifically tailored for Asian Skin and the special chemistry thereof.

"They cannot pay $1,000 U.S. dollars, Danné," Jesse informed me concerning my normal price for face, neck and upper *decollate*.

"Oh well, why quibble?" I countered grandly, still rattled by my near-execution experience from an hour before. "After all, there are twenty of them. I'll come down to $600, but not a penny less—even with your five nurses attending it's still a lot of work."

"You don't understand, Danné—for only $1,000 they will not think it is expensive enough and won't work—can you charge at least $5,000?"

I stared at the phone in disbelief. She was talking about *$100,000* in U.S. money—my first introduction to people who have so much disposable income that unless something is outrageously priced it is assumed to be substandard.

Years later, after opening a clinic in Riyadh, Saudi Arabia, I became used to this conspicuous consumption. I once saw an Italian-designed *Palacio* by the Red Sea that a Sheik covered with a huge airplane hangar so the people in a nearby high-rise could not look down and see the members of his harem walking in the gardens. Huge openings in the roof slid up and down to let in the sun.

I personally visited palaces with ballrooms as big as football fields, and dressmaker's workshops packed with designer gowns, worn only once within a private family palace, out of the public eye. The gowns were encrusted with jewels, rivaling anything Valentino designed. In one room I watched dozens of Indian men, specialists in hand beading, painstakingly sewing jewels and beads in intricate patterns over the sheerest of silks.

One highborn princess sent her personal beauty therapist to me while I was speaking at a conference in Dubai, to offer me $50,000 for a personal consultation. Under advice from my distributor at IMDAD medical, I reluctantly declined. Apparently I could become "her favorite doctor" for a month or two—then be dumped for the next popular guru. In the meantime, the DMK brand would be compromised forever by the royals who ran the Kingdom.

My first visit to Brunei was staggering to me. I was determined to give the best lecture of my life, and the most detailed treatments on the 20 clients.

The lecture room was vast, modernly ornate and equipped with full multimedia gear. Again, this was before the days of PowerPoint presentations and laptops, so I used slides to illustrate my lecture. I'd grown used to the creaky old carousels that held the slides, and a flip chart where I outlined the functions of the skin with cartoon-like drawings that everyone understood.

But the Royal Brunei technology insisted in showing itself off. The slide screen was of Cinemascope size, with glittering curtains that swept open and closed between each slide. The screen itself also descended silently from a pocket in the ceiling between slides. I had to wait for the curtain to close, the screen retract, and then come down again and the curtain to re-open before I could carry onto the next slide. In addition to all this, there was translation to wait on.

I thought all this very funny, but hid my amusement, sensing that the royal family and their friends beaming up at me from the plush auditorium chairs were proud of these modern features.

After a very proper and long evening tea where I had to "diagnose" every woman's problems in front of all the other women and yet not make them seem too bad off (always find *one* feature you know someone has complimented her on), I had to attend a small dinner for the staff at Jesse and her husband's home.

Food seemed to be the only entertainment allowed in Brunei. There was plenty of it and all of was good. By the time I belched my way back to the hotel and fell into bed like a bloated whale, it was 6 AM and time to get up and perform magic on my $5,000 clients.

The day actually went smoothly. I managed to make each expectant Asian face looking up at me from the treatment table a special landscape. I really did get into each and every one on a personal basis, customizing my serums as I went along and addressing each woman's private concerns. Women have always been open to me—and some of the personal things that bother these women, including things that they didn't like about their husbands and relatives, would fill a hundred tabloids.

A few of the women were hiding ailments that needed medical attention, fearful of looking "used up and weak" by their husbands. I gave advice where I could and told them to attend to these things secretly while on shopping trips to Singapore, using our offices there as a contact and referral point. Jesse Lau hurriedly agreed to participate in this—and increased her business about 70 percent after I left. In Brunei women could not take the action I recommended, even to help themselves, unless a male figure other than their husband set it up and made it "a thing" to do.

Violet Lee also had dealings with the Royal Family. As my distributor in Indonesia, Violet spared no expense on the "Headquarter" clinic. Located in the entire top floor of one of Jakarta's highest building, the salon was ultra-modern with every innovation possible; it even had a huge infinity swimming pool on a deck that swept out over the city.

Amongst over-the-top fanfare common to Asia, there were masses of orchids everywhere and lines of shy and smiling young Asian girls in uniforms. I gave my opening lecture and then set about the long, exhausting business of diagnosing and giving treatments to the queue of VIPs Violet had invited.

Amongst them was the President of Indonesia's wife and her attendants. The First Lady looked and acted like a queen. Dressed in some kind of robe-like ensemble, she appeared to be both humble and imperious, and highly intelligent, understanding everything I explained to her as I looked at her lovely, elegantly-sculpted face and began the treatment.

Outside the room came hushed whispers from a crowd of employees and other clients who were supposed to be waiting their turn. Annoyed, I stuck my head out the door and gave them a fierce look and a loud "ahem." They scattered like leaves.

That evening there was a party in my honor on the pool deck. Beautiful fairy lights and candles blazed on tables covered with exotic native dishes, three bars were set up, and Cristal Champagne flowed. Violet had spared no expense, and watched me with glittering and excited eyes as I took it all in.

Suddenly music split the humid night air, and a troupe of female impersonators danced out to perform classic Indonesian dances. Some of the boys looked seductively up at me from under long, fluttering eyelashes.

I kept my face impassive, and the glances sputtered out. I was not hiding anything, but at certain levels of celebrity in Asia, one does not flaunt one's lifestyle or take advantage of what might be offered. I was Doctor Danné Montague-King, distinguished scientist there on serious business—not some Hollywood queen trolling for young guys like a lot of American tourists did. Plus, I had just treated local royalty—twice in two weeks. I have never believed in "just being yourself" in all circumstances, not in business anyway. One has to respect the situation one is in if one expects to succeed. "Have no agenda in places where you do not live" has always been my motto.

I broke this rule only twice—once in Thailand with a Royal Personage, and once in Russia. Both times I was not the aggressor, and the Russian situation actually saved a life from drugs and degradation, and restored a person who had drifted into madness back to the bosom of a family that had given up all hope.

The Royal was a one night in Bangkok that now seems like a dream sequence, so improbable was the situation. Following the grand opening of the DANNÉ Headquarters there, Violet had organized a six-city tour via van through Indonesia. The trip was sponsored by a large, multi-level company for which I had created a special sunblock and Vitamin C anti-ageing, skin brightening lotion.

Multi-level sales schemes at that time were fanatical and almost like a religion. Everyone wore matching polo shirts or blouses with the company logo emblazoned on the front and the back in vivid colors. This had nothing to do with my company—which was all about high-end professional treatments—but Violet felt that a massive tour featuring me and the Danné Team would bring a lot of publicity to our project.

But we were not prepared for the hundreds of identically-dressed people who turned out in every city we came to, jumping up and down endlessly shouting out motivational mantras—very much like the American multi-level sales schemes popular a decade earlier.

We started out in Bali, which did not live up to the exotic native paradise I had heard about. To be fair, the venue was held at a hotel on the side of the island crowded with 3-and 4-Star hotels bristling with Australian and German tourists whose main occupation seemed to be to get as drunk as possible and pick up young and attractive local girls and boys. The beach itself was a nightmare—far from the movie version of clean, white sand bordering an untouched blue ocean cooled by soft and balmy breezes. I asked for some beach time after the morning presentations and tried to lay in a hired chaise lounge and relax, only to be approached every five minutes by a hawker offering local hand-made souvenirs, massages, beads to put in my hair, and often, themselves. Some tired-looking women carrying back racks weighed down with tacky "native art" also had a child on each hip who would stare at me with huge, accusing eyes that asked why I wasn't buying Mommy's goods to keep them from starving. Only Egypt, outside the Pyramids with its constant "one dollah, one dollah," was worse.

Disgusted, I went to my room and sulked until Violet knocked on the door and asked if I was okay.

When I told her how terrible the afternoon had been she exclaimed, "But why didn't you *say* something, Danné? I belong to the Hilton Club on the other side of the Island."

After telling me to dress up, she had us driven to the stately Hilton and we headed for the beach area for drinks and dinner.

It was paradise. Gone were the hawkers, kept off the sweeping, pure sandy beaches by security patrols; the grounds and the pools were dramatically lit and had beautifully-appointed lounges and tables. Uniformed waiters silently took care of our every command—the air redolent with floral spice and the mouthwatering aromas of grilled seafood and meats.

As the moon rose over the glowing indigo sea, I forgot all about the afternoon nightmare and looked at Violet, lovely in her flowing white silk gown, diamonds and emeralds glittering on her slender fingers, and murmured: "I wonder how the poor people are doing?"

Later that evening we were invited to a special "voodoo show" somewhere in the center of the island.

The outdoor theatre was in what seemed like a tropical forest, dark and torch-lit. Laughing tourists were taking their seats as we arrived, and suddenly, with a lot of drum banging and eerie music, the "show" started.

Except it was not really a show.

It seemed to be pure New Orleans Santeria Voodoo—the figures on the stage dancing and whirling with the whites of their eyes showing through blackened faces. Whiskey was drunk and spat out—voices rose and fell, and there was no interaction with the audience as one would expect from a typical satirical tourist show. The suddenly-silent crowd might as well not have been there.

After the twirling around of a screaming rooster and the chopping off of its head, blood sprayed over the footlights and a hunched creature suddenly stared at us with baleful and challenging eyes. "This is *real*," I whispered to Violet. "Let's leave now."

You could feel a malevolent presence in the air—dark forces gathering, and the air became very close and still. We got up and walked around the crowd to the side of the building that housed the open theatre. No one looked at us; all eyes were glued to the stage. As we passed the side of the building a door suddenly opened, and framed in the back light of whatever room the door led to was the huge, tall muscular figure of a man nude except for some sort of leather loincloth. His hair hung in long dreadlocks decorated with feathers and beads, his goatee was long and pointed under full lips and extremely large tombstone teeth that gleamed in an evil smile in the darkness. He was holding some sort of long serrated blade in one hand while the other propped the door open, and his eyes shone with intelligence and a crazy light of devilish delight.

Violet gasped and froze in her tracks. I stepped in front of her and looked up at him; I knew somehow he was the head honcho of this voodoo pact—the Witch Doctor.

In a rumbling basso voice he said, "Good evening, Doctor, do you not enjoy or little show?"

Taken back by the familiar title—how did he know me?—I replied, "The lady is not feeling well, *doctor*; good night."

As I turned away, he smiled even broader and breathed "*Ahhhh…*" As if he knew that I knew what he was. It was a moment of Shaman to

Shaman recognition—and a very odd feeling. But I also believe it saved us some trouble, the least being some money.

Over the years, I or one of my therapists often personally encountered royalty.

Queen Norr in Jordan, lovely and accommodating from my therapist's report.

The Queen of Norway, apparently so down to earth that she could be seen pushing a cart at the supermarket. I was at the Royal Norwegian wedding in which the Prince married a commoner—and every monarch and members of the aristocracy in Europe, along with heads of state, was in town. It was dream-like to be part of this fairy tale affair, idly watching Prince Charles walk by along with dozens of other royals as if it were a neighborhood wedding, while thousands of cheering commoners waved national flags as part of the special effects.

Whenever anyone looked at me, or bowed slightly or smiled, I wondered if *they* wondered who the young-ish man in the white suit and yellow and black Versace tie was. Royals are brought up to be over-polite when confronted by someone who seems to be someone but they are not sure.

The Saudi Royals were somewhat different—although many are educated in the UK and have adopted a few of the British Monarchy protocols. I've actually enjoyed my many visits to the Kingdom despite the strict adherence there to religious rules regarding alcohol, theatre, clubs and the fact there can be no advertising where the human form is displayed. That alone was a bit depressing for a "before and after" business like mine.

The thing that stands out most to me about Saudi Arabia was the hours of good conversation I had over endless cups of coffee or tea with doctors in flowing white robes. I was aware of the religious aspects of Riyhad and the *Matowa*, the so-called religious police that monitored everyone and everything. There were strange and shocking stories of what the *Matowa* could legally do in regard to women who were judged unchaste in public. On the other hand, their power could work against them if, for example, they accosted a woman with a walking with a man they suspected was not his wife. If they ripped her veils off to proclaim her an adulteress (an offense punishable by death in a public place) and she was actually the wife of the gentleman, the husband could shoot the *Matowa* on the spot and not be arrested.

On the personal front, I could conduct none of my lectures or classes in a hotel conference room or other public hall unless it was for men only. My Saudi distributor, an elegant young Syrian named Tamer Wali, organized all the lectures in hospitals with a *Matowa* sitting at the door. Only in such a venue could the doctors who wanted to learn the DMK concepts, some of them females, be present together. Even then the men and women sat in different parts of the room.

My first class in Riyhad was about acne treatment. A local female with *acne vulgaris* was scheduled to be the model for the practical portion of the class. I had a very clever Filipino nurse helping me—and, masked and gloved, I awaited the subject. They brought her in trembling in her head-to-toe *abaya* and veils, only her eyes showing. She lay on the treatment trolley staring up at me with eyes filled with terror. When I asked that she remove her veils so we could see her skin, she shook her head violently—as if I, the evil infidel, was going to corrupt her.

I looked around the room at the Imdad Medical Group, my agents, who stood impassively, offering no assistance.

Finally I shouted, "This is ridiculous! How we can show a treatment over veils?" I ripped the veil from her face.

She was frozen in panic, as was the rest of the room with the exception of one young Egyptian plastic surgeon, Ihab, who had a smile on his face at my audacity—we later became good friends.

I told the Filipina nurse to cleanse the girl's skin and start the treatment.

With my hands behind my back, I gently counseled the woman on what she should do for her condition and what would happen in the treatment, and promised her lovely, blemish-free skin if she adhered to the program religiously.

She actually started to relax, giving me a few, tremulous smiles, and we got on with the program.

When the old *Matowa* finally *did* look in, his long white beard waving in the air conditioning, he saw the American scientist talking to the group of doctors while waving his arms with fervor, and a female nurse working on a woman behind his back. Later, I went out of my way to talk to this geezer personally, asking him about his righteous work and thanking him for helping to keep unwanted people from the classroom. Smiling with a few teeth missing, he actually puffed up his chest—being singled out for thanks by "the famous American" for doing a thankless job.

I was told by Tamer and his staff that we were often "lucky to leave our classes alive." There was a certain levity to this of course, but he was a Syrian and some of his main staff were Egyptian, all living under the sufferance and rulings of the Royal Saudi Kingdom—so some of these humorous remarks were made between clenched teeth. As an American, I could politically be "excused" for any small lapse of "religious decorum." The Saudis did not have to be so careful with their other Middle Eastern brothers.

I was not stupid. And I acted with dignity and full appreciation of religious regulations. I could, however, clearly see that a lot of ancient Bedouin practices and tribal laws, although not appearing anywhere in the Koran, had melded into the religious aspects—especially when pertaining to women's rights.

Some Saudi women were very comfortable with having to depend upon their husbands for everything, and staying within the confines of family and home. Others were not.

On one occasion after I had been given permission to address an entire audience of high-born royal women in the auditorium of a hospital theatre, they held a "cocktail reception" (Arab Champagne being juice and soda water). One of the lost outspoken women, a tall, slender beautiful creature wearing a bandage from a recent rhinoplasty surgery, asked me if I had cellulite treatments. I assured her that we indeed did treat all categories of cellulite.

"So what type do I have?" she asked, her eyes sparkling with challenge and amusement as she lifted the hem of her *abaya* and displayed a cellulite-free thigh.

Glancing at my male colleagues out in the hall, all of whom were looking elsewhere or at the ceiling, I said, "Ahem. Well, madam it appears that all you need are *preventative* treatments against future cellulite."

At first I thought she was toying with me, testing me to see how far I would go to break rules of propriety before she summoned the *Matowa* to frog-March me off to prison and, later, having my hand or some other body member publicly amputated. But we were in a hospital, not a public forum, and I had not touched any female at all. In addition, during the lecture she had asked the most frequent and intelligent questions. All at once I realized she was a sincere, highly intelligent woman and very high-born. She wanted to share knowledge and show off her status in order to do so.

So we jabbered away like old friends and soul mates for about a half hour while my colleagues stood silently in trepidation. She finally asked me to email her, then snapped her finger for a servant to give me her email and private phone number. Afterwards I was told how lucky I was to receive this, and how very highborn in the Royal Family she was.

I emailed her a few weeks later, bit got no reply. But months after that, a very attractive Arab women, smartly dressed and confident, walked onto our Beverly Hills clinic just to "stop by and say hello."

She acted like I should know her. Then when she saw the puzzled look on my face, she smiled and said, "Ahhh, the nose bandage. It's Princess..."

She claimed she'd never received my email, but informed me that she had run out of some of my products. The Saudi Headquarters was also waiting for new stock, so she'd sent her jet to LA and a courier to the clinic to get the products.

Four products.

I was flabbergasted but acted like this happened all the time. I sensed there was a spirit of rebellion going on with some of the Saudi women.

I had an appointment with a female Indian doctor at a private compound where Arab women go for aerobic classes, treatments and other hobby classes to spend their leisure time. It was thought that the DMK treatments would do well in this type of facility, but I had to personally endorse it. I came on a day when no women were on the premises, so I had *carte blanche* to see everything.

I noticed a colorful tent in the courtyard and was told that it held an exhibit of paintings done for an art show by local women. I asked to see it, and as I gazed at the paintings on display, some quite good, others amateurish, my mouth dropped open. In every painting the subject was females in some kind of bondage or trapped. I asked the little doctor, "Am I seeing something here?"

She quietly answered, "Yes."

35

$\mathscr{B}intang\ in\ \mathscr{C}hina-and$ $\mathscr{E}lsewhere$

The China portion of my career is still ongoing, and to tell you all about the 12 years I've spent going there would require another whole book. But I will tell you some. For sure, China is a vast, diverse and incredible country where I feel quite safe and totally at home.

I had no intention of going to mainland China in 2001, having spent years in Hong Kong, Korea, Singapore and Indonesia, and was "Bintang" in each (at least that was the word on all the signs that appeared before my name when I visited. It means "star").

It was at a CIDESCO conference in Hong Kong that I was approached through a translator by a quiet and attractive Mainland China lady and her outgoing and dramatic companion (whom I discovered later was the wife of a top Communist official. We had an awkward luncheon together. I was not too sure what the woman wanted.

She kept pointing at a stack of well-designed health and beauty magazines she had with her while her companion beamed and nodded. According to the translator, the woman wanted me to write articles for the magazine and was asking what I charged.

I had suffered phony journalist schemes before, where pay never came for articles I had worked hard on, so I waved my hand and said,

"Oh, about $600 U.S. per article," thinking I would never see the two ladies again.

A week later I received a bank draft in the mail for $600. I hurriedly wrote an article based on "The Truth about Asian Skins" and sent it to the email address.

Three weeks later I received an invitation to be the keynote speaker at a *Health and Beauty Magazine* conference, a first class Air China ticket, and all expenses to be paid upon my arrival in Beijing.

I decided that mainland China might exist after all.

I was met at the airport by an entourage of ladies and assistants bearing tons of elaborate floral arrangements, including my signature flower, Star Gazer Lilies.

How she found this fact out, I will never know.

Among the lineup was a young dermatologist, Dr. Andrew Ang, who spoke flawless English and had the same timber of humor as me; we became fast friends immediately.

A childlike lady named Liu Ling, both humble and opinioned at the same time, was to be my interpreter. She described herself as "plain," but her personae outshined her appearance. I felt there was much more to Liu Ling than just an interpreter.

Years later would prove me right: she was not only Dean of English at Beijing University, but respected in the USA by many of her students who had gone on in life, migrating to the States and had huge success. She would also be the one to bail out the DMK China Company when it went through various Chinese Opera changes and fiascos. I don't know whether it's just me, or the nature of the beauty business, that changes ordinary young businessmen into wannabe James Bonds or Mathew Bornes. Marriages were wrecked, embezzlement schemes came and went and sides were taken, each sending me copious emails pleading their causes with overly-flowery sentences always starting out, "Dear and compassionate Leader..."

At the time Ling was simply the woman who, insisted we rehearse my two-hour. I entered the massive suite trailed by the entire company, who stood silently starring at me.

When I asked why, Andrew informed me they wanted to know if I was pleased with the accommodations. Were they luxurious enough?

Assuring them they were, I asked if I could possibly get the hotel to change U.S. dollars into Chinese currency. The lady publisher immediately barked an order to one of her assistants, who produced a thick paper bag with a flourish and handed it to me.

"No need for U.S. dollar," she said, "plenty Chinese money here."

Taken aback, I reached inside and withdrew a thick wad of Chinese currency: about $3,000 worth.

Puzzled, I turned to the publisher, who informed me (via Ling) that this was advance article payment for incidental expenses during my visit.

They then insisted I go and view the auditorium at the convention center which was next to the hotel where I would give my presentation the next day. On the way I spotted a few health and beauty posters, but none of the beehive activity of booths being set up which is normal to Western exhibitions. *Maybe they do it all early in the morning,* I thought.

Ling went through my PowerPoints that evening, and I assured her I was used to translations and she would be just fine—emphasizing a few of the scientific terms I always used.

After Ling left, I was preparing to go to bed. Suddenly, there was a soft knock on my door. I opened it to a smiling Madam D., all alone and of course speaking not one word of English. Perplexed, I invited her in and she sat on the couch just smiling. Embarrassed, I talked as rapidly as I could and tried to use body language to convey what I was saying. I kept stammering how pleased I was with the room, how I would do a good job for her at the lecture in the morning, and anything else I could think of.

She just kept smiling and occasionally patting my hand. Did she think...? Was this a....? Some sort of East meets West middle-aged boy-girl deal? I'd been hit on by Asian women before, including one I would have sworn was a lesbian, but Madam D. seemed too shy and classy for this.

After many not-so-fake yawns, I finally made a couple of "I need sleep—long flight" gestures and with a final, delicate hand pat, she disappeared out the door, her Mona Lisa smile lingering like that of the Cheshire cat in *Alice in Wonderland*.

In subsequent years it became apparent that infact, there really was a romantic feeling in her. A crush, so to speak. But, she never approached me alone again. I never discussed my private life in China, but I think at some level she knew.

The next morning, wearing a white suit (which would become sort of a mascot for me), I entered a hall packed with over 500 people, male and female.

My PowerPoint was up on the screen, and Ling—plainly garbed in blues and browns—poised on the edge of her chair ready to bring my words to her people.

I was scheduled to speak for two hours with two breaks. I spoke three hours with no breaks at all, and after my final "*xie, xie*" (thank you), the entire audience rose as one and flooded the stage screaming, "picture, picture."

Cameras went off like flash bombs as the glazed-eyed crowd pressed closer and closer to me, some scrambling up the side of the stage and grabbing my pant leg.

I began to panic, feeling suffocated, and a small army of security appeared as a "flying wedge" to escort me through the wings and out of the building. I remember thinking this must be how Mick Jagger felt after a concert.

But before I left I glanced back into the auditorium and was halfway down, when there, standing just inside a door, was the publisher wearing a small Mona Lisa smile on her lips as if to say, "Aha, I was right! My people reacted to you as I thought they would."

I was told to relax in my suite, then change and come back to the area at nine for the banquet that followed the exhibition. As I walked toward the hotel I still saw no booths or other beauty companies represented, and a small doubt niggled in the back of my brain.

I was ushered into a massive banquet room in the conference center full of people packed like sardines and all speaking very loudly. I was placed at a table of important-looking but dour-faced businessmen with tiny bird-like wives who kept their eyes down, offering me a shy under-the-lashes smile occasionally.

After nursing a glass of white wine through several "toasts" with beer and whiskey glasses waving around, one of the gentlemen asked me in broken English, "How you like you banquet, Dr. King?"

"*My* banquet?" I asked. "But this is the *Health and Beauty Magazine* banquet."

Looking a bit puzzled, he replied, "Ahhh, but Madam D. organize for your honor."

Dumbfounded, I sat back as the show began. It featured an extremely talented group of young Mongolian folk dancers followed by an hour of speeches, some of which resulted in the entire room looking at me and applauding. I kept a fixed smile on my face as Ling vainly tried to translate this copious Chinese, excitedly stating that I was welcome to China and they were very honored by my esteemed presence.

After a dinner with far too many dishes for anyone to consume, we were all herded into yet another auditorium where Ling hissed into my ear that I had to make a speech at the end of the evening's performances.

Suddenly a white baby grand piano was wheeled out on the stage and Ling, with a big smile, said, "And there is your piano."

Somehow Madam D. had found out about my Liberace years ago and automatically assumed I would perform!

"No," I protested, "tell Madam that it would not be suitable for me to be presented as famous scientist only to become an entertainer." (Two years later I was snowballed into playing "Somewhere in Time" on the grand piano in front of 4,000 people—Madam D. getting her little concert at last.)

Nodding a sagely at this advice, Ling ran to deliver my message, which was received with equally sage nods. I did not realize it at the time, but this was my first excursion into how the Chinese think and communicate.

What followed was a spectacular series of performances emceed by male and female TV personalities as slick as any ive ever seen. There were young rock performers and dancers and soloists that would make *America's Got Talent* drool; boy bands rivaled any American group I'd ever seen or heard.

After the hoopla was over I was summoned backstage and told to wait for my cue. I located the male TV star and asked him what I was really supposed to do. Looking blankly at me, he said, "Don't know, I'm only hired."

My name was called with a drum roll. I approached the podium and looked out over what seemed to be a vast and silent crowd throbbing with expectation. Heaven only knew what Madam D. had said about me, so tossing aside any customary "I'm happy to be here," I said, "Ladies and Gentlemen of China, I stand before you not as a citizen of The Unites States of America, but as a citizen of the planet."

They went wild with applause.

Then, my mind racing ahead of my mouth, I went onto a monologue about things planetary and common to all people, and somehow tied it all up under health, beauty and scientific commitment to sharing discoveries and success.

Over the years that speech would be repeated by Ling and others many times over. It instantly took me out of the status of "Western man trying to do business in China" to "Guru."

After that I tried very hard to keep my promises there. *Education* became my mantra, and I really did end up exchanging ideas with government-funded laboratories and medical projects.

Their technology was suburb and their work ethic enormous, but I was the man with the ideas, a freethinker with imagination. This has since changed a lot, but back then it was media fodder and I was interviewed on every television station in Beijing. And, my classes were always packed.

The following day it was announced that Madam D., Teacher Ling, Dr. Ang and the colorful Mrs. Wu of Communist official wifedom, would all journey to a private and exclusive natural hot springs resort once inhabited by emperors and their courts. It was a beautiful place with graceful hot water lagoons winding in and out of traditional pagoda-style buildings where intense or gentle massages were performed by Geisha-like women whose hands were as strong as those of truck drivers.

Dr. Ang and I shared a monster suite where we talked like schoolboys all night after being soaked in the hot lagoons while baskets of herbs were poured over our heads. It was like steeping in a giant tea cup.

Ang had no idea what Madam D. wanted of me; he said only that she was an extremely wealthy and well-connected single mom. Years before she had hiked all over China with a backpack and then written a book about the women of China which became a bestseller. One more book and a partnership with a printer had given her the means to start her publishing empire. *Health and Beauty* was the top selling magazine of the day.

The next afternoon the ladies appeared at my suite, Madam D. acting as shy and coy as ever. Ling and Dr. Ang took turns translating while Madam D. told us about the dream she'd had where a scientist from the West would appear to her and together they would elevate the aesthetic arts in China to the highest level. She had read an article by me in an English publication, and wondered if I was that man. Hearing that I was a keynote speaker at CIDESCO in nearby Hong Kong, she'd booked a flight, along with Mrs. Wu, so she could sit in the audience and "look into my eyes"(I wore my fake blue contacts that day). Apparently my eyes said "I'm it!" because there I was, in a luxury room surrounded by Chinese strangers—yet I somehow felt at home.

After an hour or so of trading personal anecdotes, I finally came right out and asked Madam D., "Why the fake exhibition, the lecture, banquet and stage show?"

She replied that she just wanted me to see what she could do—and now she wanted to know what I wanted to do.

I was again speechless.

Evelyn F. Williams had been extremely generous with me, but the Maybelline years paled by comparison to what this woman was apparently offering. And she had political clout, to boot.

What I did not know was that this was but the tip of an iceberg.

I finally told her that the best I could come up with was that she become a DMK Distributor for all of China and Hong Kong. Taiwan was hinted at, too, but something told me that the political winds would be against this.

She seemed perplexed over what "distribution" entailed. I emphasized that we looked at education first and sales later, and this seemed to fit into her "dream." I also agreed to make as many trips to China as necessary to get it started.

A few days later Ling came to my suite and in hushed tones told me we were "invited to Madam D.'s private home that people seldom get to see—a real honor!"

Believing this, I dressed for the occasion. A private driver in a red BMW swept us to a towering series of high-tech condo complexes complete with guards, passwords and private elevators. Madame D. had a three-story penthouse with forty-foot-high ceilings in the common rooms. Guest room levels ended up in a charming loft at the top, where French-style windows overlooked the city from every angle. There was also a gym set and massage chair. The rest of this grand place was furnished rather sparsely, to my way of thinking.

In the center of it all was her fatherless son—a sad and lonely teenage boy who weighed nearly 350 pounds and looked like Jabba the Hutt. I hate elephants in rooms, and in this case it was literal—so, putting on my scientist mantle, I immediately approached Madame D. about his weight problem. I could not, after all, pretend he wasn't there and wasn't obese.

She sadly admitted his problem might be her fault. She was hardly ever home and worked hard all the time building her empire (that word again!), and the servant taking care of him spoiled him with sugar and fattening food. Madam D. herself hardly ever ate, claiming stomach problems; all I ever saw her do was pick at a few raw vegetables during even the elaborate dinners.

I asked her if I could spend some time with the kid and devise a program that would allow him to lose weight—and then maybe make it up to that gym on the top floor. Again she clutched my hand with tearful eyes and indicated that she'd hoped I would do this very thing, which is why I was invited up to her private home in the first place. It occurred to me that few of her friends and colleagues had ever seen her child, at least as he was now.

I spent the next few days with the boy, off and on. First I found out what he liked and wanted to be involved in: computers, of course. Then I offhandedly mentioned that at one time I had been overweight, and how it affected my self-esteem (in reality it had been a very short time and my self-esteem was fine, but he had to not feel all alone).

I asked him if he missed school and was tired of private tutoring. He said yes, but he was too fat to go to school and did not want to be made fun of by the other kids. I inquired if there were other fat boys in the classes and he responded, "Yes, but I'm the fattest of all."

I laughed. "We should put on a fat contest, then."

He chuckled and said he would win it.

I used the word "fat" in every sentence rather than avoiding it. "Fat" became the joke and the enemy and something we could get rid of if we wanted to.

I'd already found out he was not overweight between the ages of 7 to about 13, when his mother began her empire building in earnest. No word about a father was mentioned, and in China you don't ask.

"So you aren't a fat boy inside, right?" was my final question.

He put his head down and muttered, "No."

I explained to him about eating habits and food, including the fact that it would not do any good for me to design the diet for him that Madam D. wanted from me. He had to understand his own body chemistry intimately if he was to be empowered to allow his subconscious to take over his life—restoring the thin boy within.

"Fat is not really your enemy," I said. "Meats, cheeses and dairy have some fats to them—and of course, yum-yum bacon."

Leaping to my feet, I bellowed, *"SUGAR! SUGAR IS THE FIEND HERE, YOUR WORST NIGHTMARE!"* Then, lowering my voice, I said, "And just how much sugar do you eat?"

He admitted that the servant brought him a lot of sugary things, pastries and starches. He would gobble bags of chips while working late into the night on his computer.

I explained to this highly intelligent, English-speaking young man about the chemistry of sugar versus proteins, and thermogenesis in the body. I spoke of good fats being like a fireplace (brown adipose tissue) and bad fats being the wood to be burned (white adipose tissue).

I detailed various ways to create thermogenesis with foods, shivering, cold showers, coffee and as much cardio as he could manage until the weight dropped off. The goal: walk up those stairs to that little gym under the eaves.

I left a diet plan with Madam D., with the threat that if she did not see it carried out I would be very disappointed in her. Immediately her "loss of face" syndrome took hold.

In the business realm, Madam D. moved heaven and earth to impress me that her dream was valid and could be realized. At the first real beauty exhibition, held in another city, she "announced" me to the Chinese beauty therapy world and whatever competition was currently in China.

I was the keynote speaker, opening event speaker and winner of the Global Cultural Award gold plate and every other award they had going. Needless to say, I was embarrassed about jumping up and down to go on stage under the smirks of some of my old cronies from Hong Kong, especially my Dragon Lady's nemesis, Ching Ming Ming. A longtime adversary with her schools and products, Ching was surprised when, as an award giver, she had to hand the prize to me.

Her eyes widened with shock as she raised her head with the award in her hand, only to be confronted by me. Taking note of an addition to her body, and I murmured, "Nice boobs, Ching," as I took the award from her and bowed.

I could feel daggers in my back as I walked off the stage.

Madam D. was taking no chances that any other company might trump our presence on the exhibition floor. She took an entire room. The ceiling was decorated with panels of undulating green and white silk, my personal colors. Futuristic but comfortable divans and chairs were arranged like mini living room settings here and there, with mounds of lilies and orchids on pedestals in between.

A bank of computers against one wall showed my PPT programs and past international lectures, while my products were displayed in open-sided glass cases with uniformed DMK nurses at hand to tell visitors about us. There was a treatment clinic as well where VIP guests could get a free treatment.

Since I was featured in every magazine, I had to personally autograph copies for the attendees. The line stretched for blocks, and each autograph had to be accompanied by a photo op. I could not, in good conscience, just sign my name—who was I? Not Michael Jackson or Cher. I had to write something that would inspire the younger people. So I wrote "Knowledge IS power," over and over. That night my hand swelled up and I wished I had a coat hanger to put in my mouth to create a "perma smile."

The entire weekend was unreal. Out of nowhere, the man and wife who owned the fitness center I used in Beverly Hills appeared; they were attending a baby-adopting conference being held in the same hotel. Then I met the incredibly sexy and talented Australian Rock Star, Con Delo, who was playing at the local Hard Rock Café. I went to his show and almost made a fool of myself when he swaggered off the stage during the break, stalked up to my table—his Macedonian Greek eyes flashing, sat down and put his chin in his hand. He looked into my eyes and said "Who are *you*, a celebrity?"

Despite his Zeke-like chemistry, Con was a total ladies man with kids all over the place, and since that night we—including his lovely wife Nina and kids—have been the best of friends. (There are times in life where "might have been" is a better memory than "was"!)

Soon I was in Thailand to officiate over the opening of a very high-end DMK Spa. Attending the ceremony was a rather snotty and much face-lifted member of the powerless Royal Thai Family. She kept insisting that I be lower than her in any photo, *after* they brought her forth in a sedan chair. Knowing all about her shenanigans and boyfriends in the USA, I almost told her where to shove her height issue. Then I glanced at the pleading face of my client, the owner, and with a sigh, I sank to my knees alongside the Princess, who favored me with a smug smile.

So, while the paparazzi flashed away, I let my right hand steal softly up alongside her back, and pinched her sharply in her skinny derriere. She gave out a shriek while I looked innocently straight ahead, hands on my knees. As women rushed around the princess to help her up, she gave me a sharp and rather evil look. I shrugged shoulders and walked away.

I took many photos of this spa because it was simply beautiful, the epitome of what good taste and money can do with Asian Fusion themes. A wandering glass brick path wound through the entire place along curving walls done in tiles with muted DMK greens and whites. Waterfalls were tastefully displayed behind indoor gardens and pools. The treatment rooms were rounded as well, with every amenity possible, including closed circuit TVs, maid and food service, and fluffy towels and slippers with our logo on all.

It was fortunate that I took the photos because a day later I received word from Beijing that Madam D. had hired the best architect in Beijing and wanted samples of our standard training center for the DMK facility she was ready to build.

I panicked. This reeked of serious money, and I realized the Chinese went by Western standards with Capitol "W" and "S." We did not have any. All of our distributors chose their own look when it came to a training center. We enforced only our colors, products and marketing materials; the rest was up to them. Norway, for example, had huge, rustic rooms and hallways with exposed beams overlooking canals; South Africa was rather modern and spa-like with a grand arch over the entrance…but No. 1 Harley Street in London, albeit a *very* exclusive address, featured the small, genteel shabby-chic that the upper class British favor so well: the worn Aubusson carpet, the dusty crystal chandeliers and small winding staircases one has to climb if one does not take the rattling ancient lift. Anything newer or smarter would be suspect and not serious business.

Finland and Sweden were starkly modern, Ireland was England except bigger—a three-story Georgian House with painfully clean chandeliers. Our Beverly Hills clinic in the USA was totally medical-looking.

There *was* no "DMK look"—what could I tell Madame D.?

And then I remembered the photos I'd taken the Thai Spa Launch. I had a staff member download them onto a computer, and sent them off with a casual memo stating, "This is our normal standard look and décor; however, you have permission to elaborate if you like."

I should not have written that—I forgot about Chinese "face" and competitive spirit.

I saw the site and the demolition of the interior months before the grand opening of DMK China. It was huge and not in the very best part of town, so I had reservations on the final outcome but said nothing to the excited Madam D. when she presented her architect, a tall handsome Indian gentleman who seemed to know his business. Later on it turned out he really *was* one of the top architects in China.

The Grand Opening was planned in great detail even from our side of the pond. We flew in Daniel and Debbie Dickson, our young Australian distributors, and our most progressive team in sales. I also flew in an old journalism colleague, Marian Mathews from London. She was one of the most respected members of the British press and could be either an opinionated "dragon to be feared," or your best friend. We became best friends and I wanted good press from her, plus to have her as a showpiece for Madam D., who had named her magazine after one that Marian wrote for in the UK.

We all arrived and I was requested to once again wear only white suits. We had one day of rest at the hotel where I met Dr. Ang and his assistant "The Jack Russell," a young lady who could do everything and anything with unlimited energy. I gave many of the DMK staff nicknames that stuck and became their names for all time. Since Madam D's driver was always asleep when we walked up to the car, he became known as "Sleeping Driver." The young assistant became "Jack Russell" (despite the Chinese difficulty in pronouncing the English "R" and "L"), and one particularly bossy and obnoxious therapist with huge teeth and bulging eyes became "Horse Face."

Everyone used these names in serious conversation, even the conservative teacher Ling.

It was a very hot day at the grand opening, with temperatures soaring to over 110 degrees, and high humidity. As we drove up a large crowd swarmed the parking lot in front of the three-story building, and with many curious stares, exclaimed "The *Bintangs* are here!"

Daniel Dickson and my partner Randy Larsen looked smart in business suits; I was in the dreaded white-like evangelist suit, while Debbie Dickson, a cute and curvaceous natural blonde, wore a Marilyn Monroe-ish dress with cut-out sides.

Of all of us, she suffered the least in the heat. Several of the women stared at her, oooing and ahhhing, and one remarked loudly, "Ahhhh, you are the most beautiful woman in China." (We haven't let her live that down to this day.)

Marian Mathews appeared as a the classic British professional she was, assisted by a long line of uniformed girls blazing the DMK logo and kowtowing to each of us as we ascended the long staircase, rather like a linear version of the "wave" often seen at ballgames. We entered the DMK Training center.

And fainted.

I dimly remember Marian saying, "Good God, Danné, you've arrived."

We stood there in the reception room, mouths literally gaping. The entire three floors, including the basement, were round—all the walls of glass brick interior-lit with "DMK" etched deeply at regular intervals. A massive artificial oak tree that started at the basement level and was complete with fake roots. It winded up through the center of all three floors, it's branches coiling over the ceilings of the pie-shaped treatment rooms and then bursting out on the top floor, where the media lecture room and the corporate offices were housed. The lecture room came complete with surround-sound and theatre lighting. One could stage a full production or film a TV series in it!

The entrance opened onto a raised, glass-tiled floor where the reception counter and waiting area were—the only off-note, I thought. Dramatic to be sure, including the gold clothed pleated ceiling, but just a tad disco-ish if you blurred your eyes.

Well-decorated and modern consultation rooms were off to the sides. On the opposing wall of the round main hallway on the main floor, was curving glass, backlit display shelves bearing DMK products.

All the bedding, sheets, towels, head coverings and other appointments in each fully equipped treatment room were of top-quality material emblazoned with my logo. *I've trumped Pevonia* at last, I thought, reflecting on an annoying competitor whose ads always seemed to be about beautiful models in gorgeous robes and headbands.

But it was the basement that was the real triumph.

Taking my word that Chinese men would definitely go for skin revision treatment—if it were presented in other than a feminine manner, Madam D.'s architect had had a field day. The vast woodsy lower floor looked like a quiet forest with the huge fake tree trunk the center of attention (was there some male imagery going on here?). The massage rooms were wonders of wood, steel and glass, all in warm strong tones with deep cushions and beds dressed in green, gold and rust with a few subtle gray accents here and there.

A doctor's office was the reception area, staffed by a popular young physiotherapist and his nurse wife. There were steam rooms and saunas that did not look like steam rooms and saunas until you were in them and the mechanisms turned on. They looked like comfortable lounge rooms. There was a bar and restaurant and juice fountain with private rooms available for meetings in comfort, privacy and secrecy.

Heads of state could come and have serious skin revision, spa treatments or massage and still do business in the most discreet manner. And they did. I recall personally treating the next man down from the President and his wife. Looking at these impassive and powerful faces under my enzyme masques was a very other-worldly feeling: *Why am I here?* This feeling passed through my mind many times.

After the grand tour, and accompanied by the ever-present Chinese paparazzi (much more polite than the EU or USA variety, but also more persistent), we went back to the main entrance to the building where an even larger crowd had assembled. In China, and I guess everywhere else, wherever a small crowd is gathered, more and more curious people will join in regardless of what is going on—or maybe just to see what is going on.

By this time the VIP guests had also arrived: ministers of the state, local politicians, actors of note, and media. A huge stage had been erected in front of the steps and we were all told to stand on the stage at the back so as to be presented during the official opening ceremony.

Daniel, Debbie, and me being somewhat taller than most of the guests, stood at the back sweltering in the heat as Chinese officials droned on about Madam D. and her accomplishments and contributions to the arts. Mrs. Wu gave one of her regular, spirited poetry readings (she did this at every event and class for years)…and I fell off the platform.

I had taken one step back too far—as it shows in the video, which I still watch with amusement—and *wham*. The entire audience gasped but I popped right back up again, slightly bruised.

Then it was my turn to speak.

Ling and I had planned a short, but what we felt was inspiring, speech. I recall saying something like "This center represents education and dedication to the medical and aesthetic arts, and will work ceaselessly towards China being the brightest jewel in those fields in the crown of Asia."

Or something like that—arms raised, voice deepening and coming from somewhere else.

Much applause, and then out of nowhere a long line of models, all impossibly beautiful with impossibly small waists and long legs, walking slowly and snakelike onto the stage, holding a wide red ribbon. All were wearing the classical Chinese silk dress with the high neck and long slit up the side in red and gold embroidery. I was pulled back and placed in line again by somebody as the girls faced us and bowed deeply.

What on earth? I thought. I wished they'd tell us what was going on.

Large gold scissors were placed in our hands, and people in the audience mugged cutting motions with huge smiles.

So we all stepped up and cut our sections—the models undulated off the stage, fireworks cracked and flashed, and thousands of white doves were released into the air.

We were open for business.

DMK China is a work in progress even to this day—carried along by my guru status and unfailing belief in the DMK concept of Remove, Rebuild, Protect and Maintain. The country itself and Madam D. have afforded me some of the most exciting and exotic times of my life—including sailing on the very last ship to go up the Three Rivers Gorge to the very last city on the river. Along the way we saw ancient villages that would be flooded when the new hydro-dam project was finished, new homes and apartments being built for the people higher up on the hillsides.

I saw the "wind coffin" cemeteries where people were buried in coffins nailed to tree branches overhanging the river—that would soon be gone. And the centuries-old wooden road that was built literally jutting out from the center of the rock cliffs—the only transportation up and down the river for untold years accommodating foot traffic as well as carriages and animals. When I looked at how long this road was, I marveled at the ingenuity of the Chinese people and their determination to succeed despite any barriers put up to stop them.

It was this very quality that made me call them "The Water People." When I first used this description in a lecture, I was confronted with puzzled expressions. "Nothing can stop water when it gets going," I explained. "If it comes up against something like a dam, for instance—it somehow finds its way around it eventually."

They liked that analogy and applauded. This "Water People" tag has been quoted many times since.

All of this was magical and certainly out of the category of things a tourist would get to see—but beneath all the display and guru respect, the DMK China project was sliding downhill.

Personally I think that Madam D. had overextended herself financially to impress me and realize her dream through me, as if my very presence would somehow pull it all together and the DMK concept and education would become a "movement" and a standard of aesthetics in China.

She tried very hard to fulfill everything I said. If I mentioned schools, we would visit top schools. When I talked about medical aesthetics being the future, I was taken to the plastic surgery wing of a top medical hospital and introduced to the venerable Dr. Wang, who presented me with a set of his own specially-designed surgical instruments. He also showed me one of his recent face-lifts on a man still in the hospital, and I remarked, "Your technique for the male is very good."

"Ahhh," he replied with a toothy grin, "plenty chance to practice and work out mistakes."

I smiled politely.

Madam D. started not paying us the invoices for the shipment of products on time. There would be two or three outstanding bills, yet another new order would come in. Each time I arrived in Beijing I found that the previous manager had been fired along with half the staff. And with each firing, files with educational materials, videos and PPT would also walk out the door.

Madame D. kept on one girl, Big Linda we called her, who was sort of a protégé of mine. This young lady from a far-off country town understood my concepts and me from the very first day, yet spoke no English. Fortunately she kept copious notes on everything, (in Chinese) so the business was able to limp along, giving me the illusion that all was well.

Of course the over-the-top dinners, TV interviews and meetings with clients continued, but it soon became apparent that Madam D. was not hands-on with DMK and listened mostly to sycophants who told her what she wanted to hear, not what must be done.

And she was running out of money—25 million Chinese dollars later.

It was the humble Teacher Ling, my translator, who plugged the leaks in the dam with loans to Madam D. It was Dr. Ling, actually, Dean of English at Beijing University and member of a successful family. I knew none of this for a long time, nor that Ling had a similar dream as Madame's. But Ling's came from translating my lectures and watching peoples' reactions. She felt DMK China really was the future of aesthetics in that vast country, and did all she could to support me.

She is in charge today. I had to finally tell a tearful Madam D. that we had to dissolve her distribution contract.

Ling had already obtained a young executive gentleman and a female medical doctor who felt that they could restructure DMK properly. Not with all the bells and whistles Madam provided, but with solid business practices and a focus on education.

My business partner and advisors had become very skeptical about China, and with typical Western prejudice were no longer buying into my, "It will be our biggest and best distributor" prediction. I was forced to act, and finding out that quiet and humble Ling was now out-of-pocket because of DMK China, made it easier to release Madam D. Still, I loved her bells and whistles and scope of vision—in that way she was like Evelyn F. Williams. But unlike Evelyn she did not have that absolute confidence of female power and sexuality that says "Hey world, here I am! Let's do this! Let's make it happen."

I still think about Madam D. now and then, and miss her in many ways and, I hope that her now-thin son has found himself, and has a life of his own.

36

Tibet—and "the" Indigenous Wild-Growing Plant

A year later came the time for me to visit our clinic in Tibet. There I was taken to an incredibly advanced lab in the middle of Mongolia near a town that sounded like "Hahahoheteh" and where a sea of buckthorn plants, berries, roots and leaves grew wild on the Mongolian steppes. These plants were the most botanically powerful of their genus in the world.

I found the Mongolians to be a proud and vigorous people living in a clean and windswept land, rather like Texas. They are also proud of their young technology and entrepreneurship. They work hard and also party hard. They also still revere Genghis Kahn, despite the fact he murdered and raped and pillaged freely. I also discovered that the Mongolian women can out drink the men at social events and often fall red-faced on the floor at private barbecues—where mystery meat is rampant!

We were to fly to visit our clinic in Lhasa, Tibet—Randy, myself and teacher Ling. Madam D. had other appointments, but suddenly informed us that she wanted her son to see Tibet and to go with us. I had not seen her son for nearly a year, and words cannot express how I felt when I saw a tall, good-looking and *slim* young man walking towards me with the big smile on his face. He had done it: "Fat Boy" was gone, never to come back, and his shyness was also disappearing.

Telling him how proud I was of this he said, "YOU did it!" You were a huge part of my "new and improved" self.

"No, I only pushed the buttons to release the cage from the boy who was inside it," I told him. "But *you* did all the work." I was so proud of him.

We had heard about the "mountain sickness" that hits most people when they encounter the thin and rarified air of the Himalayas and Tibet. To counter it we took regular drugs, homeopathic drugs and oxygen packs. We thought we were prepared.

We were not.

Deplaning at the Lhasa airport was like climbing out of a cloud and going into pure and clean light. Everything seemed so clear and pristine, making the world below appear as if under slightly gray glass. The Himalayas, though miles away, appeared as if they could be touched just by reaching out. I kept mentioning to Randy that I felt no different; it was easy to breathe—sort of like being in a bubble waiting for the oxygen to run out.

Ling and the boy also were fine.

There was a train from Beijing to Tibet we could have taken—it slowly decompresses the oxygen the higher it gets towards Lhasa, so when passengers get off they are automatically acclimated to the thinner atmosphere. But we were in a hurry; I had people waiting to see me and hear me for the first time. *Bintang* again.

As we approached a surprisingly modern and well-appointed hotel, we were besieged by television cameras, so I had to stop and make statements, with Ling valiantly trying to translate. At that point *she* was then translated into the local Tibetan dialect. A simple sentence took five minutes to process…and I was suddenly aware I could not get a full-lungful of air.

Even so, there was so much excitement, I took it all in stride. One of the reporters asked me if I liked my Lhasa photo. I told him I did not know what that meant, so he tugged at my arm and motioned for me to walk a little ways down the street. He then indicated a building with a huge photo permanently placed on the side that depicted a smiling Tibetan woman in a uniform—and a dark-haired Westerner in a white suit.

It was me!

The DMK clinic was of course inside the building, but this huge photo gave me a sort of Richard Geer (who is a Buddhist but not allowed a passport to Tibet due to his close association with the Dalai Lama) status that followed me everywhere I went on the streets of Tibet—especially with the kids who wanted to tug at my shirt or write my name down on something.

Bintang.

"That photo is obscene," Randy said in a wry voice. "Next thing you know they'll be outlining your image in neon light tubes, wearing that damn white suite and place it on buildings all over China like The Kentucky Colonel." He shuddered at the thought.

"Well," I responded brightly, "if DMK fails, they can always use the image for DMK Fried Duck."

Ego aside, I must admit that even now, I feel secretly humble yet proud that there is a huge over-painted photo of me on a building in Tibet!

And then it happened. The mountain sickness hit us all full force that night, Ling suffered the least according to her, because she was up half the night playing nurse to Madam D.'s ill son. It occurred to me that both she and I had become surrogate parents to him—his own mother being distant for so long—and it had changed his attitude a great deal.

To feel better, Randy and I gulped medicine, snorted oxygen packs and then went to a nearby "spa" for the treatment and massage recommended by the hotel management. It was a dark place with darker hallways and figures lurking in shadows. Incense filled the air. We passed through one huge room with a lot of couches and a massive flat screen TV showing old American action films. Local men lounged casually, watching the film and drinking tea or local beer.

My therapist was a retired (or more likely defrocked) monk from the gigantic Polenta Palace on the mountainside that I was to visit in the next few days. In nearly pitch darkness he hand-examined me with the feathery touches, and informed me that I didn't drink enough hot water.

As it turns out his advice was sound for a person with chronic stomach problems, and I sensed this as I looked up at his seamed but kindly face glowing gold in light of yak-butter candles.

After we paid our fees and were walking out, I noticed a thin, effeminate young man lounging against a doorjamb. He had on a tight, cropped tank top, equally tight Capri-cut jeans and pink flip-flops. His eyes were rimmed with kohl and mascara, and he gave me simmering and knowing looks.

"Good grief," I said to Randy, "hustling—even in Tibet."

The lecture at the DMK Clinic was well attended and the audience highly intelligent and a lot more serious than most of our therapists in Beijing had been. Afterward the owner took me aside and told me that a group of local doctors and research scientists wanted to meet with me and discuss a special project. I told her I had the next morning free. Luckily the nausea and shortness of breath had faded away enough that a small hike up the hillside where the research center was located would not bother me—especially if I had to face the famous 200 steps of the Polenta Palace the following day.

The doctors and their team were young and very serious people, seeming to live only for their work. What I first mistook for chilly politeness was, in fact, fear that they would not be able to convey to me the project they had in mind, nor their passion about it. But I was already aware that Chinese stoicness covered many deeper emotions, and focused learning all I could about the precise records they kept on all their research. They showed me specimens under their microscopes with careful reverence.

It was quite special, all boiled down to one plant, an indigenous, wild-growing plant for which they were convinced had special properties. This they learned from folk medicine people in the higher villages near a mountainous area where the only real source of the miracle mineral *shilajit* was originally found.

I looked at the field specimens they had and admitted I had not seen anything exactly like it before. I remembered my recent experience in Inner Mongolia where I had found the most powerful source of seabuckthorn plants.

What these young scientists wanted was for someone with resources and connections, someone they felt they could trust to take their study and plant, examine it further so as to assess its properties, and, to see if it could be commercially used. What "find" that would be! It could literally change their lives for the better. Their hope was this would then elevate their incomes, their families' life-styles and their children's educations. (Advanced education outside the monastery had only recently come to Lhasa. These young doctors had all had to get their degrees in Beijing.)

I asked them if I could possibly see the plants growing in their natural soil. Getting excited, they exclaimed "Yes, yes," and we all piled into cabs and drove farther out of town to a hilly, wilderness area. There were copious amounts of the plant everywhere: tall spindly stalks with tiny pale flowers that gave off a strange, pungent smell when squeezed.

Picking a few and smelling them, I too, became excited, and silently vowed to help these people, most especially if there was anything at all to these plants being used for skin products. And of course Madam D. could use this as a great human interest story for DMK China, and with her political connections, pave the way to export the plant to the USA or Europe after harvesting.

My mind spun as I gathered specimens (hoping Customs would not root through my luggage and scream "drugs!"). Then, shaking the hands of the now-beaming young doctors, I set off to spend the afternoon with my Tibetan therapists in a private guided tour into the Himalayas.

The Himalayas really are the top of the world. At the time, villages there were constructed like they were hundreds of years ago: not a television antennae in sight.

We stopped some people who had Yaks with saddles and took photos of us sitting on them. We ate a packed lunch by a lake so smooth and so clear it was like an invisible cloud that had come to earth. A little boy who kept smiling at me and then disappearing into tall weeds presented me with a flower necklace he had made out of the very plant I was to research.

As he placed it over my head, Randy said, "Give him something, Danné."

I opened my wallet that still had some U.S. dollars in it and as I was about to take out a couple of one dollar bills, the boy, with a huge smile on his face, reached his slender fingers up and touched a twenty-dollar bill.

This kid is nobody's fool, I thought as I handed over the money. He bowed, giggled and ran off.

"He'll buy candy and rot his perfect teeth," I remarked to our guide.

"No," said the guide. "He will buy notebooks and pencils and other things for the new school that is opening in the village."

I wished I'd given him all my U.S. dollars.

On and on. One delightful experience after another

The next day was the tour of the fabled Polenta Palace, one of the most fascinating and mysterious edifices in the world, and far more impressive than any palace I'd ever seen in Europe, Russia or the UK. Thousands of years old, it was built over a subterranean lake which no one has seen, though you can hear by simply putting your ear against a stone bowl placed over a stone pipe that goes down through The Palace to the water below.

Appearing to be made of solid granite, the upper portions of the vast building are actually made of poinsettia twigs packed tightly together, formed into blocks and then faced with thin sheets of stone. This allows flexibility in the very high winds that from time to time tear through the Himalayas, proving that a willow in the wind is sometimes stronger than a house.

Yak hair curtains, hundreds of years old, hang everywhere—yak hair being impervious to practically everything, including insects and fire. I purchased an unbelievably expensive yak hair carpet and after all these years, find that it resists stains and bugs and even a dropped cigarette or two.

A lot of the rooms of The Palace were already familiar to me from seeing them in movies and, like Brad Pitt in *Seven Years in Tibet*, I climbed the two-hundred some-odd steps to The Palace in 108 degree heat. I almost passed out near the top.

Except for a few administration offices, the entire building was lit with yak butter. Village women bring tubs of it in every day. Most rooms, large and small, are filled with senior monks giving lessons to younger monks, using textbooks made of ancient manuscripts rolled in leather. The libraries that hold these manuscripts could be examined by anyone—I was amazed that I could just reach up and grab one without a guard appearing and demanding I put it back. As a scientist, I wondered about wear-and-tear on things so old being handled daily—but perhaps yak leather and other special treatments unknown to the Western world maintain them.

Or, perhaps they are not so old after all.

I was amazed at so much.

And I couldn't wait to begin testing on the indigenous wildgrowing plant the doctors had told me about. I was certainly interested in seeing if its properties could be used in my on going research and work in developing skin care products.

I did take the indigenous Tibetan plant home with me. Though carefully wrapped in plastic, I sweated all the way through Customs—imagining a security guard pulling me aside for smuggling cannabis into the USA.

I macerated half of the plants in cold water for two weeks, drawing off the extract for independent lab studies. The other half I dried and powdered, sending it off to a lab-rat friend in Texas, for much more in-depth testing to determine botanical vibration and frequency potential.

The reports came back with a load of information about a ton of amino acid content, as much as soy would have. There were also traces of phyto-estroegen content and similar prostaglandin aspects to Evening Primrose oil.

In my opinion, the cellulose of this plant would make an excellent part of a creme base—if formulated into a water-into-oil creme. I sent these findings and suggestions back to the Lhasa Biologists. But, I never heard anything back from them.

In the least, I kept my word and can only hope I opened a small door into something financially viable for those who hoped it might be.

37

Russian Rhapsody, Sort of

On her first visit to the USA, Dr. Ayshat Omorova was in culture shock. An elegant and dignified young lady, she stood in one of our local supermarkets staring at the dairy case and yogurt display with tears streaming down her face.

"What's wrong?" I inquired.

"So many brands," she whispered. "At home we stand in line waiting for one brand."

She told me that her mother, a gynecologist, treated most of her patients for food or household goods.

Before Ayshat left she wanted everything I had to give: old videotapes of hair transplant procedures, old manuals, books, notes, samples—anything to learn from or use. I was humbled at the comparison between our lives, and realized how priviledged I really was.

Russia was a place where marketing ploys as it related to skin care, was not tolerated. American buzzwords meant nothing to the "dermatologs" who came to my classes and furiously wrote down every word I uttered. They knew their physiology, anatomy and chemistry, and if things did not sound logical, they were not interested. After years of deprivation and make-do, they wanted *real* results and were willing to work hard to get them.

This kept me focused and on my toes. I could not let these special people, these serious learners, down. Energized by their focus and desire to be the best, it sharpened my own thinking beyond anything I ever had imagined before.

I fell in love with Russia and it fell in love with me.

Evelyn F. Williams would have loved the passion and culture of Russia. The teenagers would pack into the Bolshoi theatre and sit with intense attention through operas and ballets that most kids would snore through. Despite the poverty and the unbelievably dark underbelly of the Mafia-run city streets and clubs at night where horrors that defy the imagination lived, the youth still worshiped their culture.

My aristocratic demigod friend (himself a youthful victim of the streets who ran away from a highly placed diplomatic family at age 14) and I walked amongst the herds of tattered kids living in the squares and subways trying to sell anything, including themselves. No one harmed us, though I was hassled twice by local police trying to shake a rich foreigner down for a few dollars, only to be released when a superior officer arrived, attracted by my loud and arrogant voice, and saw in my eyes something he had not seen before: a person who knew who he was.

I was in Moscow on 9/11, taking a shower in my hotel suite, when my friend yelled, "Danné, Danné come look what's happening in your country!" I peeked out the door to observe the first plane going through the towers and said, "Oh, that's just an old Bruce Willis movie." My mind was unable to comprehend that such a thing could happen to us in real life.

When the second plane hit I sank to the floor in shock.

Later, when we went down to the streets to find a restaurant, ordinary Russian citizens, hearing my American English and outcries, came up and put their arms around me, murmuring, "So sorry, so sorry, Americanski, what happened to your country?"

I was surprised to be greeted with such empathic comments.

Our very best test trials in scar revision, acne and even children's scars from accidents were performed by our Russian and Ukraine doctors. Our trauma center in Donesk, Ukraine under the direction of Dr. Lunina and Dr. Andry Sotnik, have provided our international team with before-and-after results on extremely bad accident cases. They wanted my information and therefore I had a huge sense of obligation to always do my best for them.

One night, flying in late to Kiev, the driver took me to the wrong hotel. Normally I stayed at the legendary Premier Palace, but on that night I was dumped off by the no-English-speaking driver at a place that advertised a casino.

Being very tired, I thought I could bear one night and sort it all out in the morning with Mr. Aleve, my Distributor, and the doctors. My room was a disaster with a sagging bed and a small refrigerator that contained no water, only an old bag of dried cheese and garlic. Parched, I stumbled down to the bar to buy water and noticed it was packed with scantily dressed women of all ages, and a few middle-aged, tired-looking men.

As I asked the bartender for some bottled water, sidled one of the younger girls sidled up to me. Knowing what she wanted, I fished a $20 bill out of my wallet, waved it at her and said, "Previet (hello), could you tell me where the local gay bars are?"

I was too dog-tired to try to evade her propositions any other way. She gave me a big grin and said, "Sure, I have friend I can call," in very good English. Then she looked at me closely, squinted and exclaimed, "Aren't you that American doctor who was on TV?"

After I admitted I had been on TV, she hopped on the stool next to me, shoved her face into mine and wanted to know if I thought she needed Botox or fillers. I'd already gulped down a bottle of water, and, reluctant to go back to that grim room, I ordered a shot of Russian vodka and asked if she wanted one also.

We commenced discussing skin and what the DMK Kiev clinics could offer her. Some of the other ladies started joining us, asking questions about their skins—and soon I was in the middle of an impromptu lecture to a large, rapt group of women—al prostitutes!

38

Still Driven, after All These Years

The years since I turned 60 were repeats and revisits to all these countries. I was, and am, driven by the feeling that I cannot rest on my laurels and stay home surrounded by the American dream like so many of my contemporaries have after they sell out.

For a long time I imagined that fate allows only one Biofreeze per person. I counted that as the best business deal I had ever negotiated, a real life Horatio Algiers story of a kitchen chemist with an arthritic grandma parleying a cold gel into millions of dollars.

Then one day, while working with some young scientists in a government-funded nanotech lab outside Beijing, watching them render sheets of silicone impossibly thin like skin tissue, epiphany hit me again.

Silicone tape had been around for several years for scar reduction, but this skin-like version gave me an idea. After requesting that my colleagues get this type of silicone rendered into a fine powder, I took an eight-ounce jar of it back to the USA and called a friend of mine in the makeup industry, Tommy Parsons. For some time Tommy had been urging me to create a makeup line and hire him. When I asked him to take me to the best lab, he did not hesitate.

I was introduced to a pragmatic little woman of middle years who had done work for some of the top cosmetics companies in America.

When I told her I wanted the silicone powder made into a crème base she replied with a steady, flat look in her eyes: "Impossible, cannot be done."

"Why not?"

"Because all classic oil-based crèmes are cooked at 84 degrees Fahrenheit, not hot enough to render this pure silicone powder into a liquid or a blendable crème."

I insisted she raise the temperature of her cooker and go against "the way all cosmetics have been made." I pointed out that what she told me about how standard make up was always made was why her mother and her mother before her, along with all the other women in the world, were always in the ladies' room powdering their shiny faces or reapplying their makeup: because their own body temperature melted it in a hour or so.

Her eyes started to sparkle. She told me she had heard I was a very definite person about my ideas, and promised to try.

About a week later I was told that at a temperature of 230 degrees we had a crème. A weird crème, but a doable crème nonetheless.

Tommy Parsons soon developed all the international colors and components, and DMK Cosmetics was born.

It was very strange to be told by top professionals in the film industry that this foundation was the first of its kind.

After delivering a presentation to the members of the Cosmetics Union Local 706 in Hollywood to a group of hardcore veterans who have used everything over the years, someone said, "You're the new Max Factor."

Thrilled by this accolade, my head soared with all kinds of ideas. But in the end, the Foundations of Skin was where I decided to stop creating. I was a skin revisionist, after all, not Tom Lyle Williams with his eye shadows, pencils and lipsticks. I had created this makeup for doctors and therapists to apply on people suffering from acne, rosacea and other dermatitis, or post-plastic surgery. These were cases where oil-based foundations could attract bacteria or prevent the regular respiratory systems of the skin from functioning in a maximum healing mode.

My silicone base and a skin pore would be like placing a ping pong ball on an oil well. It would not clog or plug when the well decided to "blow." Once applied, it stayed on all day without powdering down to cut shine. Having been "cooked" at such high temperatures, it never moved nor melted, even during the most strenuous activity.

One makeup artist who was on a shoot to make up a popular action hero of African lineage forgot one of her kits in the trunk of her car. When she retrieved the kit she was dismayed to find that the hot desert sun had melted all the cosmetics in the case—except my foundation. Due to taking samples to top film professionals such as Emmy Award-winning makeup artist Brad Look, we had worked any bugs out of the foundation before final production. But this incident entered us into the movie and TV makeup artists' world, not just the paramedical world where I was comfortable.

Dancing with the Stars, a popular television series, was one of the first productions to use our foundation. This was due to my good friend David Levinsahn, one of the head cameramen, and his famous makeup artist wife Gloria. But when the dancers found out that the foundation did not sweat off after their first act, nor at any time during the entire show, the word got around. Soon movie after movie had our foundation on the set. It was popular with male action stars because unlike oil-based foundations, The Foundations of Skin defied the all-seeing eye of the new high definition cameras. This was a major concern of men like George Clooney and Will Smith, who understandably did not like looking "made up," particularly in action scenes.

Where this goes from here, I don't know. I did recently get a call from CHER's Personal assistant, a highly intelligent girl who reported that CHER, having been gifted with my foundation by a mutual friend, loved it but wanted to know if it could be made into a stick? Like the old fashioned pan stick by Max Factor?

Knowing this would be hard to do given the nature of our unique production, I hesitated, but one does not often get asked a favor by an icon whose fame is the same level as Elvis, Marilyn Monroe and Michael Jackson. Besides, she was one of my favorite actresses whose stunning performance in Tea With Mussolini alongside British legends such as Judy Dench, Joan Plowright and Maggie Smith made me so damn proud of her, I could not refuse!

I somehow pulled it off and shortly afterward the famed Australian makeup artist Rae Morris, one of the world's current top ten experts in the field and author of five remarkable make up books fell in love with my foundation and requested I "do her up" a special alabaster shade for rock icon PINK whom she travels with at time and actress Nicole Kidman. I was humbled and amused.

DMK Cosmetics, one diva at a time!

BIOFREEZE™ gave me my first big start, but re-engineering my old formula for horses, DEEP FREEZE, proved to be the ultimate "comeback kid."

Getting the pain relief factors in the formula through horse hide and hair involved effective but unpleasant wetting agents and new precursors. I also created a cool-down grooming shampoo for horses that seemed to almost put them to sleep.

I knew that animal owners would eventually try it on their own aches and pains, and when this indeed happened, the company I was formulating for asked me to create a human version that would include a cool-down shampoo for athletes coming off the field and a cool-down antifungal foot spray to avoid the locker room nightmare that all athletes fear.

The trials for the cool-down shampoo were hilarious. I did not factor into this product the effects the "cold" agents would have on peoples' "private parts." In the beginning there were a few howls of surprise from the showers at my own house. We had to plaster precautions on the labels.

The company wanted to place "by the creator of Biofreeze" on the products. Inasmuch as it was for horses in the beginning, I thought, "Why not? I'm the creator and can prove it."

However, when the DEEP FREEZE for people came out, there was a saber-rattling letter from the legal firm representing the now-multimillion dollar company BIOFREEZE™. It was very cleverly written. While admiring that I *was* the original creator of BIOFREEZE™, the company's clients would be confused and led to believe that DEEP FREEZE was somehow another product made by BIOFREEZE™—and because it was allegedly stronger they did not want to be liable for any complaints.

Reluctant to get into any legal hassles, and confident of my own branded name, Danné Montague-King, I asked the DEEP FREEZE people to remove the BIOFREEZE™ reference and put "created by Danné Montague-King" instead. I did not want to be liable for my old formula or product. When products get that big, one loses control of where they are being made and raw materials sources. I'm old-fashioned that way, which is probably why I'm not a gazillionaire today.

Bottom lines are great and there's nothing wrong with making money, but I like to stay hands-on and know where everything is and where it comes from.

A case in point is my DMK EFA supplements (essential fatty acids that keep the matrix of ageing skin puffed up and hair strong and glossy). I *know* what the seabuckthorn oil in the capsule can do; I've been to the source and the lab in Inner Mongolia. If I say it works, it *must* work. My name is on it.

My favorite success stories are found in the many cards, letters and Facebook messages from kids and adults around the world saying "Thank you for changing my life" even though I did not personally perform their treatments.

Sometimes I get thanks for *saving* a life.

I was asked to be a judge in the 2013 Miss Universe Contest in Melbourne, Australia. As I entered the lobby of the event hotel after a long flight from LA, I suddenly found myself in the arms of a very beautiful young lady who, with tears in her eyes, asked me if I was Danné Montague-King.

I gasped, "I think so, last time I looked," upon which she thanked me for saving her 17 year-old brother's life. He had terrible *acne vulgaris* and massive self-worth issues. A good-looking kid, he was socially inept and reclusive to the point of finding life not worth living. The family had him on suicide watch when his sister, Olivia Wells, auditioned and became a Miss Universe contestant.

DMK Australia was one of the sponsors of the pageant, and had been giving all the contestants free skin treatments in return for their filmed testimonials entitled "The DMK Diaries" on YouTube.

Finding that the treatments enhanced her already beautiful skin, Olivia took her troubled brother to our best Melbourne practitioner. In a few days he found his reddened and swollen skin clearing up for the first time, although he had been on many products and drugs prior to this.

His life took a huge turn for the better: no more "I'd be better off gone."

The last thing she said to me in the lobby was, "Thank you for saving his live and bringing him back to us."

That means everything to me—but was particularly poignant coming from a lovely young woman who is in medical school herself.

The following night, Olivia Wella became Miss Australia as her family and newly-reborn brother beamed on, smiling and smiling.

I'm often asked how I stay so young. My stock answer is, "Look like what you do or don't be doing it," but that's easier said than accomplished.

First of all, as Dr. Darren Weissman of the increasingly popular Life Line Method says, "The subconscious, not our conscious mind, rules and maintains everything."

This is true. I know for certain that somewhere inside me, Peter Pan does exist—and not in any Michael Jackson way. In fact I remember a Headmaster at one of the private schools my parents sent me to tearing at his hair after enduring a half hour of me asking direct and adult questions at age 12.

"You are an old man in a little boy's body!" he shrieked as he stormed out the door.

I was always *aware of myself*. I always knew who I was, or at least who I was going to be. It seemed there was always another person standing beside me looking on while the actual kid played and got into trouble by influencing the rest of the kids into participating in his games and schemes.

Dr. Weissman pinpointed the boy who has been subconsciously running my life as nine years old. It seems that at that age the child was merely misunderstood. In a way this makes sense. It was the 1950s with its false sense of morality, a gentler and simpler time than now to be sure, but with devastating boundaries that restricted a great many kids who had IQ' of over 160 and different sexual orientations that had to be hidden.

I never once felt guilty about anything I liked, enjoyed, imagined or dreamed of. Actually there were never any real dreams, only a lot of "someday when's."

When the "whens" did finally arrive I recognized them and never acted as surprised and grateful as other people thought I should be. To some, this bred resentment and the myth that I was arrogant and not appreciative. That puzzled me for decades; I was always appreciative of any hands-up along the road—just not surprised.

So the young man refuses to leave this aging body. That's reason number one for my not aging so much.

Number two on is "work and maintenance."

Although it does get harder with time, I'm often my own Guinea pig and have access to a great many powerful and exotic ingredients. One of the downsides of being in the skin revision field is that it's not financially viable to formulate with more than one or two potent ingredients at a time. Raw materials companies that make high quality ingredients also charge high quality prices, as they should. The production of certain enzymes and botanical marvels is often tedious, slow and costly. Most owners of these facilities think like I do—it either works or doesn't; if it doesn't, then don't bother making it.

Recently I had to opportunity to use a great many of my "big guns" in a product formulated as a fundraiser for the Harvey Milk Foundation, a worldwide equality movement dear to my heart. Called *Transgenesis*, this crème, placed in a package worthy of Gucci designers, produces results after ten days that literally looks like one had a total face and neck lift. This was fairly easy for me to develop as I was creating individual crèmes for my Beverly Hills clients, asking in return for a substantial donation for The Harvey Milk Foundation.

It was when those clients started asking for refills that my company took notice. Suddenly I was in the high-end luxury portion of the business, and top stores worldwide started carrying Transgenesis.

I can't help but think of the movie where the voice says, "Build a field and they will come."

When marketers put a product in a fancy package just to sell it at a high price it may sell for a while but never lasts; there is no real story behind it or a humanitarian reason for its existence. Recently, at a Harvey Milk and equality conference in Berlin, Germany, I was asked by CEOs of IBM, Google, Facebook and Coca-Cola how I managed to get our little company's name so talked about at the conference.

I replied, "Just put a story on your product before you offer it for sale—but make sure it's a real story."

I also give credit for at least 40 percent of my Peter Pan-dom to the Live Cell Therapy Injections I've been getting since 1983. These are performed by The International Clinics of Biological Regeneration founded decades ago by the late Sir Tomkins Smith, MD. Dr. Smith and his wife Judi founded the clinics for the sole purpose of offering ordinary people affordable treatment that was originally available only at exclusive clinics in Switzerland at a cost of thousands and thousands of dollars, much of if paying for peripheral services such as facials and high-end "spa rejuvenation for a week."

Simply put, live cell therapy uses cells from the fetus of an unborn lamb from the same herd carefully kept in Germany. The cells are flash-frozen and then resurrected in a solution for injection at time of treatment. The donor cell goes to the same organ in your body that it originally came from, "fooling" our ageing or diseased cells into becoming young and healthy again.

This is not one of those phony "one serum suits all" injections offered by medical con artists. Sir Tom was a highly respected scientist who held many patents for systems that improved life quality, including farm aids for better crops.

I know this therapy works. I have not only felt the differences year after year as they change my injections to assist my conditions as I age, but I've seen the lives of AIDS victims saved as well as friends who were supposed to be dead years ago and are still with us and disease free. One woman, a colleague, was given a month to live with her leukemia. Her physicians had run the course of what could be done. I told her about cell therapy and she said, "All I want is to stay alive long enough to see my daughter Mary K. married."

Mary K. has been married and divorced and Mom is still kicking, doing hair and DMK skin revision 20 years later.

Only 30 percent of the people who go to clinics around the world go for the rejuvenation benefits. The rest are terminal, and a huge percent of them go into what we have to call "a remission of some type." This is not to be confused with what I considered to be the rip-off of Stem Cell Therapy offered by South American countries where desperate AIDS and cancer victims are parted from their life savings with bogus injections often modelled after "The Doctor Feelgood" injections popular with celebrities back in the 1960s. Stem cells really are the future, but have to be surgically implanted as opposed to other cells—including our own fat cells, nature's best cosmetic fillers.

It's one of my pet peeves when charlatans take something that is scientifically viable and run amok with it. The current skin care craze involving products that have "stem cells in crèmes" is so ludicrous one wonders how the public can be so fooled. Yet because of the publicity generated by stem cell research during the Bush administration years, people leap at any product that uses those words.

At first the con artists just advertised "stem cell therapy anti-ageing crèmes. Then, after a little barking from the FDA, they switched to "plant stem cells."

How dead plant stems could possibly rejuvenate our own living stem cells and tighten our skins defies even the most hopeful and desperate imaginations. But the advertised "scientific research testimonials" manage enough pseudoscientific psychobabble to sound almost credible. Many times a Nobel Prize-winner from Norway seems to be involved. I guess they think the lovely, far off good people of Norway won't notice the scam as much as the more volatile Nobel winners from France or Italy, and being a wealthy country, Norway is not prone to litigation or rebuttal towards the mad marketing machines of the USA and UK where such schemes seem to flourish.

All of these things eventually run out of gas. Years ago I fought such rip-offs tooth and nail, usually in my published articles, which earned me many unsavory titles bestowed by the companies I was taking on.

I don't do this as much anymore because as Evelyn F. Williams told me, PT. Barnum really did say, to her personally, "There's a sucker born every minute."

He was right.

39

Becoming an Activist: The Czarina Elizabeth (Liz) Loren Maria Romanov

Around the time of my 60th birthday I was invited to attend a costume ball on a ship docked outside Venice, Italy. The theme of the party was "Hollywood's Golden Years," and we all had to come as a major star.

I'd recently started to attend events sponsored by the 50 year-old Imperial Court System, an organization started in San Francisco decades ago—before Harvey Milk—by Empress One Jose Sarria (whose life is currently being scripted from a play to be made into a major motion picture), a ninety-year-old gay rights veteran who changed many laws against gay people and helped raise millions of dollars for charitable organizations with his Royal Events.

Jose passed away recently, leaving San Diego City Commissioner Nicole Murray Ramirez as his heir. Some 3000 people, many in funeral drag, appeared in the cathedral for his State Funeral. The San Francisco

Police blocked all the streets leading out of the city towards the cemetery so that the long cavalcade of buses, limos and cars could attend the graveside services and say good-bye to this extraordinary man who was an Empress.

Primarily a popular cabaret performer doing comic opera for fans falling on the floor with laughter, Jose took the title "Empress One, The Widow Norton" after the death of controversial Emperor Norton, an eccentric San Francisco millionaire. Jose built this into an "Imperial Court System" with grand Coronations and Balls where everyone was a titled noble—the glitz and pageantry beyond belief to most people.

Years later, Nicole Murray Ramirez, also an activist, took up the royal mantle from Jose and turned the Court System into a more regimented political machine with a serious parliament and 66 chapters all over the USA, Canada and Mexico.

It was into this environment I wandered, having gone to a few Court events in Long Beach and Newport Beach in my youth.

I was curious to see how it had developed.

When I saw the Empresses, Princesses, Countesses and other nobles in their elaborate costumes, I kept thinking how fun it all looked, how theatrical. I remember thinking *I could do this—perhaps even better.*

My chance came at the Ship's Ball event. I decided to "do drag" for the first time—and not the comedy drag I did at the Roller Rink back in the '70s.

At a Palm Springs party I had met an incredible designer from the Ukraine, FEDOR. FEDOR had had cuneiform acne scars since teenage days, and was getting quite a lot of press at the time. Handsome apart from the scars, he offered to make me any garment I wanted in exchange for acne scar resurfacing at my Beverly Hills clinic.

After examining him I knew this would take six months and be costly, but so were his designs; he really was and is the next Valentino. So we struck a deal—and I decided to go to the Ball as a fellow Pisces, Elizabeth Taylor, in a FEDOR original.

Thus began the rounds of studios where friends made me prosthetic teeth modeled after Liz's. A specialty house, Classic Curves International, made the silicon and foam rubber body parts (they also do work for Drag Icon RuPaul and other Vegas performers) I had a custom wig designed, special jewelry modeled after Liz's, and Maurice Stein of Cinema Secrets helped me design the makeup.

Even I was stunned by the results—and after a few home rehearsals and one dinner party where close friends did not recognize me for over an hour, I swept down the grand staircase on the ship to the ballroom below, escorted by our suite butler in a tuxedo.

The decibels of sound the crowd made as I tremulously descended the staircase got immediately lower—and when I posed at the bottom for a moment, the room erupted into applause. *Evelyn would have loved this*, I remember thinking.

I reprised the same act later at a Royal Coronation—and immediately began getting royal titles in the Court System.

Many people did not know who I really was—and several assumed I was a transsexual. I was not a drag queen by lifestyle or a professional performer—I was something else that no one could define, and a mystery-legend began.

To me, I felt like a little kid getting away with something—like the characters I played as a child in the many home productions I roped my family into—the villain, the prince or sometimes the princess, to the chagrin of my mother as I tattered her old evening gowns and my dad's old tuxes and suits. My Liz was a totally theatrical performance in a crowd of Court Members who took it seriously—a Barry Humphries playing Dame Edna, except prettier.

I had no desire to be a woman—and unlike transvestites, did not get a thrill from wearing women's clothing (too uncomfortable after two hours). But I did enjoy the fashion, the theatre and the makeup portion—I had been doing this on real women for decades, and now, as a world class scientist, I could no longer pursue these hobbies as a profession.

In many ways it was an outlet for these things. I certainly had no sexual motive; the very thought of "coming onto" someone while being Liz was frightening. In fact, I was shocked how many men—from age 23 to 65—thought "Liz" was a "hot" item.

I suppose if I delved deep enough psychologically, I could find my dramatic mother in there somewhere; I seemed to take on her personae and class when doing "Liz." But it became work as I added live performances and speeches to the act. As Liz became more popular and eventually was crowned Czarina for Life by The Queen Mother of the ICS, Nicole Murray Ramirez, in San Diego, she became an obligation that ended up with me having to form my own 501(c)(3) nonprofit organization, *Emerald Kingdom*. This in turn became a vehicle to raise funds for the *Harvey Milk Foundation* and other charities focusing on the youth of today as our future of tomorrow.

A few years ago I was invited by Stuart Milk to walk the red carpet with him at *The Hollywood Hall of Fame Awards*. That year the awards were going to Barbra Streisand, Merle Haggard, Betty White, Serena Williams and a host of top American artists, scientists and authors. Since Stuart had only met me as "Liz," I asked him if "Liz" could walk the carpet on his arm. He informed me that I could appear any way I wanted—true diversity being the message.

At first I was all abuzz about what to wear on the same carpet as all these Hollywood greats. I arranged for a dresser to be on hand and a limo to take us to the venue. Randy Larsen, my partner, thought I had lost my mind "You're going in drag in front of Barbra Streisand?" he asked. "Where do you plan on going to the toilet?"

I calmly announced I would use the ladies room, as always—and then I sat down and thought it out.

Meeting all these celebrities at a private function could bring more awareness to our mission. Liz *would* attract a lot of attention, and not necessarily because she was a man in drag (Geena Davis pointed this out to me once at a Beverly Hills charity function where I *did* appear as Liz). But what kind of attention? Would the focus be on the *Harvey Milk Foundation* which I was representing?

In the end I went as myself, albeit dressed to the teeth—and the affair did turn out to be less Hollywood and more Kennedy Centre. Serious and dignified and none of the woman celebrities—outside of Serena Williams, who wore a sequined gown and matching sequin cast on her broken foot—looked especially glamorous.

Eventually the Czarina Liz Loren became more of a job than fun. Certainly there have been some fun times when people passing on the street stop and yell "Hey, Sophia!" and people who have known or worked with Sophia Loren come up and tell me how uncanny I appear.

Sophia Loren is the last of the truly great glamour stars and a reigning beauty worldwide. I admire her tenacity for life and for always appearing flawless—like a movie star should. I will never forget her walking tall and strong, carrying a portion of the Olympic flag, across the playing field at the Italian Olympics as Pavarotti sang *Nessum Dorma*.

The woman is ageless and indestructible, and if I can portray her in even the smallest way, I feel I've accomplished something.

Needless to say, it has been a "trip"!

Recently I was at a Jimmy James concert. Jimmy is one of the greatest live vocal impressionists on the planet and has many film star fans. Loni Anderson showed up along with her husband and agent at the Beverly Hills La Boheme Cabaret. I was at a head table Jimmy had organized. He is a big fan of my Foundations of Skin—the aforementioned medical silicone makeup base that covers everything, needs no maintenance once applied, yet looks like your own skin in broad daylight. It is popular with several famous singers. Divas who do one tour after another and enjoy the hassle free, younger look of this breakthrough makeup innovation.

So on this night Jimmy placed me and a group of my Beverly Hills supporters right by the stage.

Loni's agent, who had worked with Sophia Loren, insisted I pose with Loni and her husband. After one pose the entire Cabaret erupted as paparazzi appeared out of nowhere and people lined up to be photographed with the two sex symbols—Loni being the only real one!

In the end I think nearly everyone has a secret desire to be someone else, even for a little while. I just took it to another level to make a statement that should be seen and heard by all.

But look at the young people I'd always championed and encouraged. They're not all as fortunate as me. A lot of them *were* pushed aside by life because they were poor or misfits. Many got beaten up as they struggled for the right to belong to the human race. And some were literally crucified, like beautiful young Matthew Sheppard, a bright spirit loved by many and just being himself.

Then there were the countless teen suicides.

As I opened my eyes to the horrors still going on around me, I began to notice that a lot of young people in more liberal areas like Los Angeles were taking for granted the freedoms LGBT people now have. Many of these freedoms were the result of activists like Harvey Milk and Jose Sarria fighting discrimination openly. My life was privileged compared to theirs, and I regretted not taking that circuit lecture gig offered by the FBI man.

I always gave money to support groups, and devised ways to be a prophylactic against kids getting AIDS and being hooked on drugs. I found that when you get a group of professional actors, singers, playwrights, musicians and choreographers, and train young people who have dreams of being a star someday—but are poor and disenfranchised because they are different—stop dreaming and take drugs just to belong to a peer group or have indiscriminate sex to blend in and be accepted. But when you train them in the performing arts, you enhance their sense of self. Then, when you put them into shows and charity events where the donating public actually *sees* where their money is going, the kids shine—for a little while they are stars; each is "somebody."

It's a cycle of success: They take this confidence back to school, heads held high, and refuse anything but respect for who they are and what they are doing. Drugs and casual sex are not part of a healthy young performer who is going somewhere—these people have choices—at last.

After becoming involved with the *Harvey Milk Foundation* and possessing a "title" in the Imperial Court System, I started giving huge and elaborate Balls each year in Palm Springs, California—where a great many affluent gay people live or have homes.

Using the donated talents of friends and associates in the film, drama and dance fields, we would recruit poor and disenfranchised kids who held suppressed dreams of stardom but little hope of a spotlight ever shining on them. The Czarina's Ball became that light. In front of audiences of wealthy straight and gay people, many from old-money families in Beverly Hills, these kids did indeed shine. The transformation of their personalities was awe-inspiring to even the hardest hearts and the most skeptical.

I personally witnesses this, such as one of the young dancer girls who was hired by Disney, and others went onto Broadway—not because of the Balls and their considerable PR, but because the young people "felt like someone" at last and became more empowered to "go for it" with confidence.

Singing, dancing and campaigning in your late 60s while holding down a career is wearing. But Liz somehow became an iconic presence and a live message to young people all over the world that everyone has the right to be anyone they want to be, any time, any place "as long as it is done to entertain and illuminate—with grace and style." And so I was energized by this.

Over the years I'd grown tired of the media covering gay pride parades by filming the most clownish and tacky-looking guys, the ones with the beards, moustaches, huge bras and frightful wigs, with their music blaring. The "pride" I felt while riding atop vintage convertibles or floats in these parades was in giving the thousands of people lining the streets, smiling and waving, something pretty and classy. My Elizabeth Taylor was more cartoon drag than realistic—despite our common birthday and the fact that I related to her on some levels.

An actor and popular talk show host friend of mine, Ron Russell, pointed out that if I were to play an aging movie star character, I could pull off Sophia Loren much better. "No impersonator does Sophia," he explained. "They all do Judy, Liza, Cher and even Liz Taylor—but not La Loren."

He'd once been in a movie with Sophia Loren, and I'd briefly met her in London shortly before her 70th Birthday—so together he and I refined the look to a sometimes uncanny degree. I became a composite of both stars—Liz Loren.

To this day "Liz Loren" still campaigns and appears at events—but more often in upmarket straight venues, going after those corporate dollars, the checks often written by a stunned executive while his wife looks fondly at Liz's custom jewelry and designer gown.

Recently Liz was invited, complete with tiara, to speak at the Royal Purple Luncheon held by Crown Jewels, a west side women's-only club of Beverly Hills socialites—100 of the most powerful female movers and shakers in that city. My lecture was on age management, and was followed by a Paris-style fashion show by FEDOR which the girls are still talking about.

I was scared at the last moment as I stood behind the high, ornate doors of the venue. "What am I doing?" I hissed at my partner, Drue. "It's high noon in the daytime and these are prominent people—I am *not* Dame Edna."

"You *are* Danné Montague-King, now Czarina Elizabeth Loren Maria Romanov, and you can do this," he reassured me—as he pushed me and I sailed regally through the doors to an applauding crowd. I noticed, with a gulp, that there were two prominent plastic surgeons as guests.

As far as I know, this had never been done before, certainly not before the Crown Jewels group. I gave the classic lecture as I normally would, except in a softer voice, and of course I pitched the *Harvey Milk Foundation* with an invitation to my Ball (many showed up), and realized everyone was listening intently. There were no whispers behind hands, no smirks or eyes blazing with scornful amusement.

Later on I was introduced by some friends to Beverly Cohen, legendary builder of The Four Seasons Hotel in Beverly Hills. She looked up at me from her petite height and remarked, "You are perfectly lovely, my dear, and such an informative speech. I'm going to propose to the girls that you become a member of the Crown Jewels."

As I walked away I whispered to my friend, "Is she out of her mind? This is an all-WOMEN'S group!"

"She doesn't know, Danné," he whispered back gleefully.

Later I found out that about half the ladies did not know Liz was a man, despite the clear announcement of the twin personalities in the program. Many of them were of an age where their sight was impaired and they were sitting near the back of the room.

The statement was to be what you want to be anytime, anyplace, and get the message of diversity across with a good show. The event did raise awareness and support for the cause.

Probably the most scary Liz appearance was in response to a summons from Justin Knighten, of Lucas PR on the West Coast, to attend a daytime charity event known as "Maria's Buddies," for children who were physically and mentally challenged. This wonderful cause was created by Maria Shriver, and she specifically asked for Liz Loren even though she had met Danné Montague-King with Stuart Milk two years before at her *Hollywood Hall of Fame Awards* event.

Scared out of my mind, I called our Beverly Hills clinic director Rachel MacAurther, to ask her to help me dress and go with me as "a girl-friend." Rachel is so beautiful and sexy I felt she could deflect any suspicious looks from me. I also hedged my bets by asking Marci Weiner, the colorful and well-known Hollywood columnist, to join our group. Marci was the same age and wore similar makeup; we would look natural together.

Finally, needing an escort and driver, I asked a new friend, a former Washington, D.C. insider I had met at the Presidential Inauguration, Yale Scott. Yale is handsome, knew Maria from previous encounters while working for Laura Bush, and could also "work a room." I figured that surrounded by such glittering people, no one would notice that the tall glamorous Sophia Loren-looking lady in the Versace print frock and Giuzeppe Zinotti platform pumps, was actually an old man in drag!

Of course that meant ladies rooms, answering girl talk compliments on the outfit or where did I get that ring or who does my marvelous highlights—and all in the unforgiving glare of a California summer sun.

I know you are wondering; and I'm pleased to report, that it went off far better than I expected!

I'd been asked to donate some DMK products for the silent auctions, so my staff went all out to create nearly a booth for the company complete with banners and high-end decorations. One of Maria's volunteers, a gushing young girl, ran up to me and said, "Are you the cosmetic company lady?"

"Why, yes," I answered in my softer, higher Liz voice, "why do you ask, dear?"

"Well, Escada and Gucci sent gifts in just paper boxes, but *your* people sent everything wrapped so beautifully and your display is just gorgeous, people are already bidding."

A few women from Sacramento who were with Maria when she was the Governor's wife were there, and chatted with me like any group of older, upper-class women would.

A great many people recognized Marci and the hired press came to our table many times for photo ops and to trade business cards.

It was very fun—except the teetering to the ladies room on those platforms in the heat was a nightmare. I had to wait outside pretending to check my voice mail on my phone until I knew the bathroom was empty. If someone did come in while I was in the stall (tips of shoes pointing *outward*) I nervously waited until I thought they were gone. A few times I was fooled and swept out only to meet a women reapplying her makeup in the mirror.

Since my foundation was my new all-silicon based makeup, the only thing I had to touch up was lipstick and fluff the wig a bit. This must have been the thing to do because no one said a word, only gave me a cursory nod or stared at my shoes with the side glance women use when they're looking at what other women are wearing. It also occurred to me that drag queens usually all have a similar make-up and big-hair look, and would not be expected to be in the ladies room at 3 o'clock in the afternoon with political and social movers and shakers in the crowd at the Montage Beverly Hills.

Again, a little kid getting away with something!

Maria herself is a charming lady with the understated and earthy class all the Kennedy women seem to have. When we spoke she sounded like Tracy Lord, the character played by a young Katherine Hepburn in *The Philadelphia Story*. Maria invited us up to the VIP party in the penthouse after the event for some homemade ice cream that the Montage Bartenders had concocted. When we rode up in the lift, Maria's sunglasses fell off her head and broke at my feet. "Oh, damn, what a shame my dear," I said as I swept them off the floor and nearly fell over on top of her. Those damned heels.

"Oh, think nothing of it, Liz, these are just $19.95 ones I bought in the Cape."

I nearly laughed; anyone else would say $19.95 from Walmart. Hers were from The Cape.

Maria's sons and daughters were absolutely gorgeous, the girls a mirror image of their mother and the boys all wearing jeans with open-necked shirts and blazers with that casual style the well-bred seem to come by naturally. Even their haircuts had that Kennedy-sensual glamour. But what amazed me the most, was that they were all polite and courteous to what must have been a boring, much older crowd. The youngest son asked me if I wanted some ice cream and I accepted with a nod, fearing my voice at such close quarters. He brought it to me with a spoon and napkin, saying, "Is this okay, ma'am?"

Marci looked at me like she wanted to burst into gales of laughter, and as more and more "family type" people arrived I knew I had to either get out of there or face a blown cover and be forced to entertain in some way.

Maria's older daughter had been giving me some puzzled looks. "She wonders if you really are Sophia Loren," whispered Marci. I thought the girl had probably met the real Sophia.

Grabbing Yale and Rachel, we left, scattering tips everywhere to get the DMK display torn down and the car brought around.

A week later I received a charming letter from Maria thanking "Liz" for her support!

40

Aligning with the Harvey Milk Global Campaign

Human Rights, Social Rights, Civil Rights, LGBT Rights (Lesbian, Gay, Bisexual, Transgender): After all my travels over all these years, it seems only fitting that I would come to endorse and support the Harvey Milk Global Campaign. As I've said all my life, people should be free to be who they are, wherever they are.

The transgender community that is sometimes looked down upon by "masculine" gays and a few lesbians is actually one of the most powerful examples of people struggling for the right to be who and what they are.

My early work with transgender women back in the 1960s has helped me support the many powerful transgender women around the world today. Many of them are members of Parliament and other high political offices.

One of the best examples of how people can overcome extraordinary obstacles to be where they are is my friend Gina Duncan, a very successful businesswoman in Florida who was a well-known football star before her transition into herself. This quiet but professional lady is also running for office after being challenged by Stuart Milk. She spent a hard-earned fortune becoming what she felt she always was, and I asked her recently while we were having cocktails in Milan, Italy, how she felt *after* all the surgeries and everything was over and there was no turning back.

"As I walked down the hall to leave the hospital," she replied, "I felt in line with myself and the earth. I felt suddenly a real person."

Technically and emotionally, transgenders are not actually gay people. Their choice has little to do with their sex lives. But they must be included in our campaign for total human rights globally because they are an outstanding example of human courage and the need for rights for everyone to exist on this planet and live successful lives contributing to the human race.

My dear friend, actress Alejandra Boque of Mexico City, has a huge fan base with her wonderfully clever television show. She is another role model for the tragic transgender young people in Mexico and South American countries, some of whom are enslaved by prostitution—literally behind bars in brothels because they don't know where to turn when their families and friends turn on them.

I met Alejandra in Milan at the Cross Atlantic Conference where Stuart Milk, noting the positive affect Alejandra had had on her countrymen, invited her to be on an international panel.

I first met Stuart Milk while I was starting my "pay it forward" campaign. It was at an Imperial Court State Dinner in Lexington, Kentucky. I was a dignified and regal "Liz" on that occasion, and I approached him with the idea that with our mutual international connection we should somehow work together.

This humble and eloquent man took up the bloody banner his uncle dropped when he was assassinated. After the State Dinner we became fast friends, both of us travelling the world, for different reasons, Stuart not in the best of health and me aging. His agenda is the message of total diversity and equality and he preaches it in some of the most dangerous places on the planet, often facing down militia and hate mongers. He has the ear of presidents, royalty, politicians, heads of state, even the Vatican.

Stuart has my ear as well; he challenges people constantly to go beyond themselves, like I now know that FBI man was doing to me back in the 1970s.

In 2012 Stuart challenged me again by insisting that I extend a very long series of lectures I was doing in Spain, so as to speak on The World Health Panel in the City Hall of Milan at the first Cross Atlantic Global Conference. Here politicians, statesmen, top educators, activists for human rights and transgender women would be attending and some speaking.

Almost collapsing from fatigue, I arrived from Barcelona only to be whisked off by diplomatic limo to the American Embassy for a pre-conference reception, and greeted by a smiling U.S. Ambassador and his wife. Being told I had been cleared and listed by The State Department was heady stuff and for a moment made that old "running for office" feeling I had back in Hot Springs rear its head again, only to be put back to sleep by my age.

My speech on our mission on behalf of youth by giving them a hand up—not a handout—seemed to be well received, and I made many, many new connections due to this intrepid and challenging man who, like Evelyn F. Williams, has a way of making people go beyond themselves.

Stuart opened many doors for me that I did not imagine I would ever walk through. One evening he rang me up and asked me if I would like to attend the Presidential Inauguration with him. Taken aback and realizing the event was only days away with millions of people streaming into Washington, D.C., I was inclined to refuse. Getting a reasonably-priced hotel room and a flight to D.C. seemed like remote possibilities. But I accepted this huge honor and luckily was able to book all arrangements online in a half hour, including a private car to collect me at the airport—all at normal rates. It was like I was supposed to be there.

The private VIP coach that took us to the ceremonies on that very cold day was packed with "insiders" and actor/singer Ricky Martin and his significant other—who sat quietly behind me while Stuart and I loudly talked about the Harvey Milk Global campaigns coming up.

Ricky is taller and even more handsome than he appears on film or television, and extremely quiet and polite. He graciously posed for photos when we arrived and were taken by special guard through the throngs of people to VIP seats near the podium.

As I watched the stream of the most powerful people on the planet take their places—the Clintons receiving a standing ovation—I kept thinking, "Why am I here?" There seemed to be some sort of agenda that Stuart—a man who always challenged everyone to do what they could for the Cause—was priming me for.

His tall and good-looking young nephews, straight boys from New York, were almost like bodyguards to me. Flanked by the Jones Beach lifeguard muscles of these youths, I felt somehow special, yet frail.

President Obama's speech turned a corner that can never be turned back. In one fell swoop he went out on several political limbs and covered *all* bases with vigor and sincerity. I was seated in a crowd of left- and right-wing people, rednecks, sophisticated corporate types, middle Americans and coastal intelligentsia. Black, Hispanic, White and Asian were all represented. Yet for that one short moment, you could *feel* solidarity as Americans all.

For that moment in time, in history, we all believed what he was saying. In that time and space he became a leader to many.

The next evening we attended the Inaugural Balls, along with several thousand other people. The evening wear displayed ranged from the sublime to the ridiculous—I was constantly amazed by what some people assumed was "formal wear" for this most auspicious occasion. Many gowns would have looked better at a New Orleans brothel at the turn of the century!

The Black ladies of Washington D.C., however, strutted their stuff with style—especially the older ones. Every one of the black ladies had on a fur coat—and looked smug while they watched younger and less prepared women shivering in the long queues to get into the ballrooms wearing their skimpy shawls or boas.

I went to the Ball on a bus as the only white man aboard—and had more fun on that ride than at the Ball itself, which was too overcrowded and massive to really relate to anyone. Even the stars hired to perform seemed distant in the enormous crush.

What interested me most was how the powerful spotlight of Washington, D.C. dimmed the spotlight of Hollywood. In the VIP room where every celebrity seemed to know who Stuart was, as the power players made their entrances, I saw a very quiet Meryl Streep, Ben Affleck and others fade into "ordinary people."

The following day I was invited with the Milks to attend a Nancy Pelosi Reception in Capitol Hill. We decided to have lunch first in one of the many cafeterias on The Hill. Again, it was eerie to me to casually be in a line with a tray along with senators, congressmen and other movers and shakers we normally see only on CNN. It appeared that once you were "inside" and accepted, it's a family affair. You could walk around and talk to anyone—you belonged.

I saw how seductive politics could be.

At the Pelosi affair the room was packed with notables, yet Nancy announced "Stuart Milk is here" during an impassioned address that reiterated Obama's groundbreaking speech of the day before. Stuart and his towering nephews took this all in stride, Stuart looking as humble as he actually is. I don't think he's ever really come to terms with his fame and presence—or maybe he really has, and remains true to himself and his Cause, even so.

I met Caitlin O'Neil, who was closest to the Obama family, and we were joking and laughing like maniacs after being introduced. I found her to be one of the most perceptive yet laid-back women I had ever met—felt like I had known her for years.

There was a sense of urgent networking in the room with some of the attendees. Eyes sharply looking around at everyone to see "who was who" and how a confrontation would be beneficial to an agenda. But all in all it was more like a friendly cocktail party—with the exception of many, many young interns and fledgling politicians coming up to Stuart to heap praise on his stand and his work. I basked in the leftover light and passed out Emerald Kingdom cards.

Finally I found myself being introduced to Nancy Pelosi. As I looked into those burning eyes I took both of her frail hands in mine—suddenly aware that we were in the same boat, age-wise—and a lot still being expected of us. I complimented her on her stirring speech—and then for some reason I blurted, "If time were not against us, you'd be giving Hilary a run for her money."

Her eyes widened at this boldness, then she smiled. She knew exactly what I meant despite the somewhat blunt age reference. She shook my hands back and said, "Why, thank you."

Fortunately the queue behind me prevented any further conversation because, appalled at my pushiness, I could think of nothing more to say. But later, as I moved through the crowd I could see her glance over at me from time to time, a puzzled look on her face as if to say, "Who *is* that strange man with the long flowing hair and beard?"

The fact that I somehow *look* like I'm supposed to be somebody will, no doubt eventually get me into hot water!

My most recent tour with Stuart Milk again segued off a DMK launch, in this case for my fund-raising luxury crème Transgenesis, which is probably the best (and most expensive to make) formulation I have ever created. It debuted at Saelins, a tony high-end retail store in Hamburg, Germany, after which I accompanied Stuart to an incredible diversity conference entitled Stick and Stones in Berlin. This conference was the brainchild of Stuart B. Cameron, a handsome young Berliner whose organizational skills are unparalleled. Although there are a lot of well-run LGBT (Lesbian, Gay, Bisexual, Transgender) conferences around the world, Herr Cameron managed to mix Euro-rock with fashion, big business, show business and political savvy all at the same time!

"Hey everybody, let's have a lot of fun, whoever and whatever you are—but let's also change the world into a better place." This was Stuart Cameron as we walked on stage, each wearing the head of a unicorn, the mystical symbol that a different animal can be, and is, magical.

We arrived on a chilly day at the most bizarre hotel I had ever stayed in. It presided over a river front where segments of the old Berlin Wall, still standing, were covered with local art—some of it quite good! The hotel featured electric guitars and hookups in the room where you could record or do impromptu performances for guests. The décor was beyond eclectic, more like a pop night club than a residence—my room an overload of Pepto Bismal pink, including the robe and the slippers.

The conference area was packed with passionate German youths of all sexual persuasions, as well as politicians. The CEOs of IBM, Coca Cola and other top corporations had booths in place promising jobs to any and all who might be different or thought of as misfits.

Stuart was the keynote speaker, and faced an attentive and passionate crowd that went into an applause frenzy over his astounding message, which started with his Uncle Harvey's life and ended with a reference to me and my company's courage in daring to put the same message on a product that sold all over the world—along with a donation from each purchase.

I was in shock, sitting there in the back row—and then suddenly in a spotlight I did not expect! Later several corporate honchos came around and asked me how I dared to do this, and how was it done? (Normally they all just donate large amounts which no one really knows about.) I replied, "Make an excellent product that everyone will buy and use, and put your message on it—if you truly believe we are all brothers under the skin."

But it was later, when one of Stuart's friends from the government, then-Member of Parliament Machtild Rawert, took us on a private tour of the Reichstadt, that another unsung community of "misfits" came to my attention.

Miss Rawert was not what I expected of a female German Member of Parliament, many of them so mannish in look and demeanor. But she was a zaftig, bubbling lady with a dramatic trilling voice that echoed through the quiet, tomb-like halls of the vast seat of German government. She wore knee-high caramel leather boots, tight jeans and a jazzy sweater, and her child-like face beamed out from under an improbable red feather-cut gamine hairdo that had to stand out during parliamentary sessions. This was a woman of extreme intelligence who likes to be seen *and* heard—and is.

She was recently appointed Minister of Health, and uses her powers to equalize human rights on many levels—including being a quiet champion of inter-sex people.

I've known a few inter-sex people in my time—the cruel name being "morpaphrodites"—back into the 50s and 60s. There are more of these people around than one could imagine, and many of them have miserable lives.

In Germany it was common, when a child was born with double genitalia, for the doctors and parents to decide on the spot what the child's sex would be—giving them no choice whatsoever of who or what they wanted to be for the rest of their lives.

After a tour of the Reichstadt, Miss Rawert invited Stuart to speak at a local Catholic cathedral following a Mass for an inter-sex person who had just passed away. We arrived in a somewhat shabby neighborhood in Machtild's chauffeur-driven Government car, and were confronted by a large group of smiling, slightly odd-looking people on the steps of the fine old Byzantine-style church. When I say "odd" I mean this: despite the fact that most of them were either regular-looking women or a few "soft"-looking men who would pass unnoticed in daily life, you sensed in each case that there was someone else inside the visible form. This had nothing to do with a transsexual look—or a drag queen trying to "pass." There was little flash or glamor here. Trannies and drag queens have a choice; these people had none, and were doing the best they could with what the physicians left them.

It was heartbreaking.

The service was moving, as one by one people stood in the pulpit and honored the life that had passed as one of their own. Stuart more than rose to the occasion. Standing in the pulpit under a dramatic overhead pin spot, he took on a Pastor-like dignity I had not seen before. The speech he delivered was last minute and certainly not prepared, but his sonorous tones rumbled through the vast cathedral as if he were to the Priesthood born. He said exactly the right things, and you could feel the deep appreciation from the assemblage that this famous American activist had come to officiate at their almost secret Mass.

Afterward we had intended to take the Member of Parliament Rawer out to a posh restaurant, but the inter-sex group had prepared a humble dinner of *gemulse* (vegetable) soups, bread and sausages at the parsonage next store. We could hardly refuse.

It was at that little supper that many of the inter-sex people, hearing I was some kind of health specialist from glamorous Beverly Hills, California, approached me with their personal stories.

In my opinion they were *all* victims of terrible and tragic medical "experiments," and I got caught up in it.

Later, while standing out in front of the parsonage, I was confronted by one person who told me that her doctors had said she had to accept being a "funny lady" for the rest of her life, and had placed her on an appalling hormonal medication roller coaster.

Some of the inter-sex people looked like masculine lesbians, a few like mannish school teachers from another era, and a few were totally feminine women, the kind most men would give more than one look at. Nearly all of them felt like men inside, yet their testicles and other penis aspects had been removed, in most cases, during infancy. The rest of their lives had been lived in secrecy and shame, nature's boo-boos. By virtue of mutilated genitalia they had very little chance at the normal love lives that gays or even transsexuals could enjoy.

I found myself becoming a diagnostician, and my questions more and more detailed. They were candid and open about everything. Through it all I noticed that Mechtild Rawer was listening and watching me keenly out of the corner of her eyes, no doubt thinking, "What is this inquisitive American going to do about all this?"

I promised to carry the message back to the USA and my friend Sheena Metal, a talk show host on LA Talk Radio and an open Inter-sex person. I would have her deliver a message about how these people could be helped, although our medical organizations are much more understanding and open to suggestion than those in Germany.

The suggestion was posed by me and agreed upon by everyone present that all inter-sex children should keep the genitals they were born with, as long as there was no threat to general health, until the age of at least fourteen, at which time the individual could make a decision whether they wanted to be male or female for the rest of their life.

That night it seemed to me that once again I was at some kind of crossroads, mingling with a group of people little known to normal society. And Miss Rawert was adamant about offering official support.

It seemed ironic that weeks later, after she was voted in as Minister of Health, that Parliament passed a law stating that all inter-sex children had the right to remain as they were born until the age of accountability—14!

I don't know what influence Stuart and I had that night except to give this sad and remarkable group some hope and a hand up from across the sea, or what influence Madam Rawert had on the passing of this law—I just know that it happened. I was there, and I marveled even more at the differences in the human race that make us really all the same, and my conviction that rather than shut our eyes, recoil or smugly thank fate for our "normalcy" we should try to support our brothers and sisters everywhere regardless of what package they come in.

Going back in time, it became clear to me that Evelyn F. Williams, resting in her humble urn on the bluffs above Newport Beach, was a much larger-than-life person than I actually knew. She was the shining signpost on the road that said, "Go this way, Dan, not that way."

Certainly she was a very human being, subject to all the frailties and lusts of life, and she often paid a dear price for her dogged determination to live life to its fullest even if life itself became dreary and crippling.

I find that great and unusual people are often called self-centered and even selfish; they'll stop at nothing to gratify their whims. But these so-called "whims" are imagination made real, or as real as one can manage at the time. Evelyn had a vision and pursued it. She wanted love and went out and hailed it like one can with a taxi: miss one and another will be along shortly.

She was selfish when it came to self-preservation, knowing that she had to last a long time and wanting the front row seat to always have her name on it. Name me a star, leader or Statesman who doesn't. In the end, her generosity knew no bounds; she shared what she had as long as there was a song to sing.

It was Evelyn's faith in and expectations for me that kept me going for a very long time. How often in this tale have I written, "Evelyn would have liked this?"

I know she would have loved it all.

As was her personal and oft-repeated credo of "Miss Maybelline:" *If at the setting of the sun one thinks of the day that's done, and counting, thinks of the people whose hearts we have won, we can say our day was well spent.*— Evelyn F. Williams

About the Author

*D*anné Montague-King is a name synonymous with world-class skin revision and products available in over twenty countries. He is also the creator of several "firsts" that have helped humans and animals globally have a better quality of life. These include BIOFREEZE™, DMK Foundations of Skin, DMK Skin Revision, and DEEP FREEZE.

Danné has been a much-published journalist for the medical and aesthetic fields for over 40 years. He is the recipient of numerous awards, including the prestigious *Global Human Rights Ambassador Award* by the Harvey Milk Foundation.

Danné lives on a mountaintop estate in Southern California with his animals—both domestic and wild—his gardens, a guest wing where people from all over the world stay in homey comfort from time to time, and his longtime companion Drue Assiter.

Appendix: Photos

With Maria Shriver in Beverly Hills at a "Best Buddies" event.

My first "cover"!

The Czarina Liz Loren Romanov and Tsar Drue Konstantin Romanov at Night of 1000 Gowns, New York City. Liz's FEDOR Courtier gowns made the Sunday edition of *The New York Times*.

On Capitol Hill with The Milks' and Nancy Pelosi.

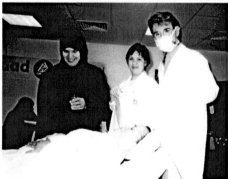

Removing the veils in Saudi Arabia.

Loni Anderson and Liz at a Jimmy James concert,
"Bosom Buddies."

Falling in love with Russia.

At the Presidential Inauguration 2013 with Ricky Martin—a very cool guy!

Waltzing with Susan of Germany at the Vienna Opera Ball.

My portrait in Tibet at "the top of the world."

Attaining "guru" status in China.

Hollywood On Wheels, the Star and the producer.

Lewin and King Modeling and Photo agency.

Evelyn F. Williams and me.

Other Books by Bettie Youngs Book Publishers

Hostage of Paradox: *A Qualmish Disclosure*

John Rixey Moore

Few people then or now know about the clandestine war that the CIA ran in Vietnam, using the Green Berets for secret operations throughout Southeast Asia. This was not the Vietnam War of the newsreels, the body counts, rice paddy footage, and men smoking cigarettes on the sandbag bunkers. This was a shadow directive of deep-penetration interdiction, reconnaissance, and assassination missions conducted by a selected few Special Forces units, deployed quietly from forward operations bases to prowl through agendas that, for security reasons, were seldom understood by the men themselves.

Hostage of Paradox is the first-hand account by one of these elite team leaders.

"Deserving of a place in the upper ranks of Vietnam War memoirs." —**Kirkus Review**

"Read this book, you'll be, as John Moore puts it, 'transfixed, like kittens in a box.'" —**David Willson, Book Review, The VVA Veteran**

ISBN: 978-1-936332-37-3 • ePub: 978-1-936332-33-5

The Maybelline Story
And the Spirited Family Dynasty Behind It

Sharrie Williams

A fascinating and inspiring story, a tale both epic and intimate, alive with the clash, the hustle, the music, and dance of American enterprise.

"A richly told story of a forty-year, white-hot love triangle that fans the flames of a major worldwide conglomerate." —**Neil Shulman, Associate Producer,** *Doc Hollywood*

"Salacious! Engrossing! There are certain stories so dramatic, so sordid, that they seem positively destined for film; this is one of them." —*New York Post*

ISBN: 978-0-9843081-1-8 • ePub: 978-1-936332-17-5

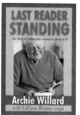

Last Reader Standing
... The Story of a Man Who Learned to Read at 54

Archie Willard
with Colleen Wiemerslage

The day Archie lost his thirty-one year job as a laborer at a meat packing company, he was forced to confront the secret he had held so closely for most of his life: at the age of fifty-four, he couldn't read. For all his adult life, he'd been able to skirt around the issue. But now, forced to find a new job to support his family, he could no longer hide from the truth.

Last Reader Standing is the story of Archie's amazing—and often painful—journey of becoming literate at middle age, struggling with the newfound knowledge of his dyslexia. From the little boy who was banished to the back of the classroom because the teachers labeled him "stupid," Archie emerged to becoming a national figure who continues to enlighten professionals into the world of the learning disabled. He joined Barbara Bush on stage for her Literacy Foundation's fundraisers where she proudly introduced him as "the man who took advantage of a second chance and improved his life."

This is a touching and poignant story that gives us an eye-opening view of the lack of literacy in our society, and how important it is for all of us to have opportunity to become all that we can be—to have hope and go after our dreams.

At the age of eighty-two, Archie continues to work with literacy issues in medicine and consumerism.

"Archie . . . you need to continue spreading the word." —**Barbara Bush, founder of the Literacy Foundation, and First Lady and wife of George H. W. Bush, the 41st President of the United States**

ISBN: 978-1-936332-48-9 • ePub: 978-1-936332-50-2

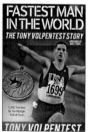

Fastest Man in the World
The Tony Volpentest Story

Tony Volpentest
Foreword by Ross Perot

Tony Volpentest, a four-time Paralympic gold medalist and five-time world champion sprinter, is a 2012 nominee for the Olympic Hall of Fame. This inspirational story details his being born without feet, to holding records as the fastest sprinter in the world.

"This inspiring story is about the thrill of victory to be sure—winning gold—but it is also a reminder about human potential: the willingness to push ourselves beyond the ledge of our own imagination. A powerfully inspirational story." —**Charlie Huebner, United States Olympic Committee**

ISBN: 978-1-940784-07-6 • ePub: 978-1-940784-08-3

Company of Stone

John Rixey Moore

With yet unhealed wounds from recent combat, John Moore undertook an unexpected walking tour in the rugged Scottish highlands. With the approach of a season of freezing rainstorms he took shelter in a remote monastery—a chance encounter that would change his future, his beliefs about blind chance, and the unexpected courses by which the best in human nature can smuggle its way into the life of a stranger. Afterwards, a chance conversation overheard in a village pub steered him to Canada, where he took a job as a rock drill operator in a large industrial gold mine. The dangers he encountered among the lost men in that dangerous other world, secretive men who sought permanent anonymity in the perils of work deep underground—a brutal kind of monasticism itself—challenged both his endurance and his sense of humanity.

With sensitivity and delightful good humor, Moore explores the surprising lessons learned in these strangely rich fraternities of forgotten men—a brotherhood housed in crumbling medieval masonry, and one shared in the unforgiving depths of the gold mine.

ISBN: 978-1-936332-44-1 • ePub: 978-1-936332-45-8

On Toby's Terms

Charmaine Hammond

On Toby's Terms is an endearing story of a beguiling creature who teaches his owners that, despite their trying to teach him how to be the dog they want, he is the one to lay out the terms of being the dog he needs to be. This insight would change their lives forever.

"This is a captivating, heartwarming story and we are very excited about bringing it to film." —**Steve Hudis, Producer**

ISBN: 978-0-9843081-4-9 • ePub: 978-1-936332-15-1

Blackbird Singing in the Dead of Night
What to Do When God Won't Answer

Updated Edition with Study Guide

Gregory L. Hunt

Pastor Greg Hunt had devoted nearly thirty years to congregational ministry, helping people experience God and find their way in life. Then came his own crisis of faith and calling. While turning to God for guidance, he finds nothing. Neither his education nor his religious involvements could prepare him for the disorienting impact of the experience. Alarmed, he tries an experiment. The result is startling—and changes his life entirely.

"Compelling. If you have ever longed to hear God whispering a love song into your life, read this book." —**Gary Chapman, *NY Times* bestselling author,** *The Love Languages of God*

ISBN: 978-0-9882848-9-0 • ePub: 978-1-936332-52-6

The Rebirth of Suzzan Blac

Suzzan Blac

A horrific upbringing and then abduction into the sex slave industry would all but kill Suzzan's spirit to live. But a happy marriage and two children brought love—and forty-two stunning paintings, art so raw that it initially frightened even the artist. "I hid the pieces for 15 years," says Suzzan, "but just as with the secrets in this book, I am slowing sneaking them out, one by one by one." Now a renowned artist, her work is exhibited world-wide. A story of inspiration, truth and victory.

"A solid memoir about a life reconstructed. Chilling, thrilling, and thought provoking." —**Pearry Teo, Producer,** *The Gene Generation*

ISBN: 978-1-936332-22-9 • ePub: 978-1-936332-23-6

Voodoo in My Blood
A Healer's Journey from Surgeon to Shaman

Carolle Jean-Murat, M.D.

Born and raised in Haiti to a family of healers, US trained physician Carolle Jean-Murat came to be regarded as a world-class surgeon. But her success harbored a secret: in the operating room, she could quickly intuit the root cause of her patient's illness, often times knowing she could help the patient without surgery. Carolle knew that to fellow surgeons, her intuition was best left unmentioned. But when the devastating earthquake hit Haiti and Carolle returned to help, she had to acknowledge the shaman she had become.

"This fascinating memoir sheds light on the importance of asking yourself, 'Have I created for myself the life I've meant to live?'" —**Christiane Northrup, M.D.,** **author of the New York Times bestsellers:** *Women's Bodies, Women's Wisdom*

ISBN: 978-1-936332-05-2 • ePub: 978-1-936332-04-5

Electric Living
The Science behind the Law of Attraction

Kolie Crutcher

An electrical engineer by training, Crutcher applies his in-depth knowledge of electrical engineering principles and practical engineering experience detailing the scientific explanation of why human beings become what they think. A practical, step-by-step guide to help you harness your thoughts and emotions so that the Law of Attraction will benefit you.

ISBN: 978-1-936332-58-8 • ePub: 978-1-936332-59-5

DON CARINA: *WWII Mafia Heroine*

Ron Russell

A father's death in Southern Italy in the 1930s—a place where women who can read are considered unfit for marriage—thrusts seventeen-year-old Carina into servitude as a "black widow," a legal head of the household who cares for her twelve siblings. A scandal forces her into a marriage to Russo, the "Prince of Naples." By cunning force, Carina seizes control of Russo's organization and disguising herself as a man, controls the most powerful of Mafia groups for nearly a decade.

"A woman as the head of the Mafia who shows her family her resourcefulness, strength and survival techniques. Unique, creative and powerful! This exciting book blends history, intrigue and power into one delicious epic adventure that you will not want to put down!" **—Linda Gray, Actress, *Dallas***

ISBN: 978-0-9843081-9-4 • ePub: 978-1-936332-49-6

Amazing Adventures of a Nobody

Leon Logothetis

From the Hit Television Series Aired in 100 Countries!

Tired of his disconnected life and uninspiring job, Leon Logothetis leaves it all behind—job, money, home, even his cell phone—and hits the road with nothing but the clothes on his back and five dollars in his pocket, relying on the kindness of strangers and the serendipity of the open road for his daily keep. Masterful storytelling!

"A gem of a book; endearing, engaging and inspiring." **—Catharine Hamm, Los Angeles Times Travel Editor**

ISBN: 978-0-9843081-3-2 • ePub: 978-1-936332-51-9

MR. JOE
Tales from a Haunted Life

Joseph Barnett and Jane Congdon

Do you believe in ghosts? Joseph Barnett didn't, until the winter he was fired from his career job and became a school custodian. Assigned the graveyard shift, Joe was confronted with a series of bizarre and terrifying occurrences.

"Thrilling, thoughtful, elegantly told. So much more than a ghost story." **—Cyrus Webb, CEO, Conversation Book Club**

ISBN: 978-1-936332-78-6 • ePub: 978-1-936332-79-3

Out of the Transylvania Night

Aura Imbarus
A Pulitzer-Prize entry

"I'd grown up in the land of Transylvania, homeland to Dracula, Vlad the Impaler, and worse, dictator Nicolae Ceausescu," writes the author. "Under his rule, like vampires, we came to life after sundown, hiding our heirloom jewels and documents deep in the earth." Fleeing to the US to rebuild her life, she discovers a startling truth about straddling two cultures and striking a balance between one's dreams and the sacrifices that allow a sense of "home."

"Aura's courage shows the degree to which we are all willing to live lives centered on freedom, hope, and an authentic sense of self. Truly a love story!" —**Nadia Comaneci, Olympic Champion**

ISBN: 978-0-9843081-2-5 • ePub: 978-1-936332-20-5

Living with Multiple Personalities
The Christine Ducommun Story

Christine Ducommun

Christine Ducommun was a happily married wife and mother of two, when—after moving back into her childhood home—she began to experience panic attacks and bizarre flashbacks. Eventually diagnosed with Dissociative Identity Disorder (DID), Christine's story details an extraordinary twelve-year ordeal unraveling the buried trauma of her forgotten past.

"Reminiscent of the Academy Award-winning *A Beautiful Mind,* this true story will have you on the edge of your seat. Spellbinding!" —**Josh Miller, Producer**

ISBN: 978-0-9843081-5-6 • ePub: 978-1-936332-06-9

The Tortoise Shell Code

V Frank Asaro

Off the coast of Southern California, the Sea Diva, a tuna boat, sinks. Members of the crew are missing and what happened remains a mystery. Anthony Darren, a renowned and wealthy lawyer at the top of his game, knows the boat's owner and soon becomes involved in the case. As the case goes to trial, a missing crew member is believed to be at fault, but new evidence comes to light and the finger of guilt points in a completely unanticipated direction. An action-packed thriller.

ISBN: 978-1-936332-60-1 • ePub: 978-1-936332-61-8

The Search for the Lost Army
The National Geographic and Harvard University Expedition

Gary S. Chafetz

In one of history's greatest ancient disasters, a Persian army of 50,000 soldiers was suffocated by a hurricane-force sandstorm in 525 BC in Egypt's Western Desert. No trace of this conquering army, hauling huge quantities of looted gold and silver, has ever surfaced.

Gary Chafetz, referred to as "one of the ten best journalists of the past twenty-five years," is a former Boston Globe correspondent and was twice nominated for a Pulitzer Prize by the Globe.

ISBN: 978-1-936332-98-4 • ePub: 978-1-936332-99-1

A World Torn Asunder
The Life and Triumph of Constantin C. Giurescu

Marina Giurescu, M.D.

Constantin C. Giurescu was Romania's leading historian and author. His granddaughter's fascinating story of this remarkable man and his family follows their struggles in war-torn Romania from 1900 to the fall of the Soviet Union. An "enlightened" society is dismantled with the 1946 Communist takeover of Romania, and Constantin is confined to the notorious Sighet penitentiary. Drawing on her grandfather's prison diary (which was put in a glass jar, buried in a yard, then smuggled out of the country by Dr. Paul E. Michelson—who does the FOREWORD for this book), private letters and her own research, Dr. Giurescu writes of the legacy from the turn of the century to the fall of Communism.

We see the rise of modern Romania, the misery of World War I, the blossoming of its culture between the wars, and then the sellout of Eastern Europe to Russia after World War II. In this sweeping account, we see not only its effects socially and culturally, but the triumph in its wake: a man and his people who reclaim better lives for themselves, and in the process, teach us a lesson in endurance, patience, and will—not only to survive, but to thrive.

"The inspirational story of a quiet man and his silent defiance in the face of tyranny."
—Dr. Connie Mariano, author of *The White House Doctor*

ISBN: 978-1-936332-76-2 • ePub: 978-1-936332-77-9

Diary of a Beverly Hills Matchmaker

Marla Martenson

Quick-witted Marla takes her readers for a hilarious romp through her days as an LA matchmaker where looks are everything and money talks. The Cupid of Beverly Hills has introduced countless couples who lived happily ever-after, but for every success story there are hysterically funny dating disasters with high-maintenance, out of touch clients. Marla writes with charm and self-effacement about the universal struggle to love and be loved.

ISBN 978-0-9843081-0-1 • ePub: 978-1-936332-03-8

The Morphine Dream

Don Brown with *Pulitzer nominated Gary S. Chafetz*

At 36, high-school dropout and a failed semi-professional ballplayer Donald Brown hit bottom when an industrial accident left him immobilized. But Brown had a dream while on a morphine drip after surgery: he imagined himself graduating from Harvard Law School (he was a classmate of Barack Obama) and walking across America. Brown realizes both seemingly unreachable goals, and achieves national recognition as a legal crusader for minority homeowners. An intriguing tale of his long walk—both physical and metaphorical. A story of perseverance and second chances. Sheer inspiration for those wishing to reboot their lives.

"An incredibly inspirational memoir." —**Alan M. Dershowitz, professor, Harvard Law School**

ISBN: 978-1-936332-25-0 • ePub: 978-1-936332-39-7

The Girl Who Gave Her Wish Away

Sharon Babineau
Foreword by Craig Kielburger

The Children's Wish Foundation approached lovely thirteen-year-old Maddison Babineau just after she received her cancer diagnosis. "You can have anything," they told her, "a Disney cruise? The chance to meet your favorite movie star? A five thousand dollar shopping spree?"

Maddie knew exactly what she wanted. She had recently been moved to tears after watching a television program about the plight of orphaned children. Maddie's wish? To ease the suffering of these children half-way across the world. Despite the ravishing cancer, she became an indefatigable fundraiser for "her children." In The Girl Who Gave Wish Away, her mother reveals Maddie's remarkable journey of providing hope and future to the village children who had filled her heart.
A special story, heartwarming and reassuring.

ISBN: 978-1-936332-96-0 • ePub: 978-1-936332-97-7

It Started with Dracula
The Count, My Mother, and Me

Jane Congdon

The terrifying legend of Count Dracula silently skulking through the Transylvania night may have terrified generations of filmgoers, but the tall, elegant vampire captivated and electrified a young Jane Congdon, igniting a dream to one day see his mysterious land of ancient castles and misty hollows. Four decades later she finally takes her long-awaited trip—never dreaming that it would unearth decades-buried memories, and trigger a life-changing inner journey. A memoir full of surprises, Jane's story is one of hope, love—and second chances.

ISBN: 978-1-936332-10-6 • ePub: 978-1-936332-11-3

The Aspiring Actor's Handbook

Molly Cheek and Debbie Zip

Concise and straightforward, The Aspiring Actor's Handbook is written for curious and aspiring actors to help them make informed decisions while pursuing this exciting career.

Veteran actresses Molly Cheek and Debbie Zipp have culled the wit and wisdom of a wide array of successful actors, from Beth Grant to Dee Wallace, and collected the kind of mentoring perspective so many in the business wish they'd had when they were just starting out. Get insider information and real-life experiences and personal stories that range from how to get your foot in the door to becoming a career actor. Get the inside scoop from successful veteran actors on how to work with agents and unions; manage finances; prepare for auditions; cope with rejection—and success—and much more.

ISBN: 978-1-940784-12-0 • ePub: 978-1-940784-02-1

The Predatory Lies of Anorexia
A Survivor's Story

Abby D. Kelly

"I want...I want you to think I am the smartest, the thinnest, the most beautiful..."

With these words, Abby Kelly encapsulates the overwhelming struggle of her 15-year bout with anorexia. Abby lays bare the reality of anorexia, beginning in her teenage years, when the predatory lies of the disease took root in her psyche as she felt pressured from family and peers for not being "enough." In her quest for a greater sense of personal power, she concludes "I'll be 'more', but it will be on my terms."

Her reasoning is a classic example as to why and how eating disorders dig in and persist as long as they do.

From this new self-awareness, Abby targets her body as the agent to show others that she is disciplined and focused. She sets out to restrict her food intake and adheres to an extreme schedule of exercise. While others close to Abby see a person who is dangerously thin, Abby, in fact, derives a sense of personal achievement from her weight loss.

Abby exposes the battles, defeats, and ultimate triumph—taking the reader on a poignant odyssey from onset to recovery, including how she set out to fool the many who tried to help her, from dietitians to therapists, from one inpatient treatment center after another, and reveals not only the victim's suffering, but that of those who love her.

This raw and passionate story eloquently describes how Abby finally freed herself from this life-threatening condition, and how others can find courage and hope for recovery, too.

"This beautifully written book paints an exacting picture of Anorexia, one that is sure to help legions of those suffering from this most serious and life-threatening condition."

—Amy Dardis, founder and editor of Haven Journal

ISBN: 978-1-940784-17-5 • ePub: 978-1-940784-18-2

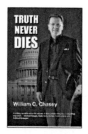

Truth Never Dies

William C. Chasey

A lobbyist for some 40 years, William C. Chasey represented some of the world's most prestigious business clients and twenty-three foreign governments before the US Congress. His integrity never questioned. All that changed when Chasey was hired to forge communications between Libya and the US Congress. A trip he took with a US Congressman for discussions with then Libyan leader Muammar Qadhafi forever changed Chasey's life. Upon his return, his bank accounts were frozen, clients and friends had been advised not to take his calls.

Things got worse: the CIA, FBI, IRS, and the Federal Judiciary attempted to coerce him into using his unique Libyan access to participate in a CIA-sponsored assassination plot of the two Libyans indicted for the bombing of Pan Am flight 103. Chasey's refusal to cooperate resulted in a six-year FBI investigation and sting operation, financial ruin, criminal charges, and incarceration in federal prison.

"A chilling narrative about the abuses of state power. Intriguing! Compelling. Important."
—**Michael Reagan, Radio Host, Author, Commentator and Political Strategist**

"An unprecedented first hand look into the chilling world of Libyan Leader Muammar Qadhafi by the man who risked it all to resolve the dispute between the United States and Libya over the Lockerbie bombing. This is sure to be an unforgettable motion picture."
—**Peter Tomaszewicz, Producer, Truth Never Dies**

ISBN: 978-1-936332-46-5 • ePub: 978-1-936332-47-2

News Girls Don't Cry

Melissa McCarty

Today the host of ORA TV's Newsbreaker, and now calling Larry King her boss, Melissa McCarty worked her way up through the trenches of live television news. But she was also running away from her past, one of growing up in the roughest of neighborhoods, watching so many she knew—including her brother—succumb to drugs, gangs, and violence. It was a past that forced her to be tough and streetwise, traits that in her career as a popular television newscaster, would end up working against her.

Every tragic story she covered was a grim reminder of where she'd been. But the practiced and restrained emotion given to the camera became her protective armor even in her private life where she was unable to let her guard down—a demeanor that damaged both her personal and professional relationships. In News Girls Don't Cry, McCarty confronts the memory-demons of her past, exploring how they hardened her—and how she turned it all around.

An inspiring story of overcoming adversity, welcoming second chances, and becoming happy and authentic.

"A battle between personal success and private anguish, a captivating brave tale of a woman's drive to succed and her tireless struggle to keep her family intact. The reader is pulled into Melissa's story... an honest account of the common battle of addiction." —**Susan Hendricks, CNN Headline News Anchor**

ISBN: 978-1-936332-69-4 • ePub: 978-1-936332-70-0

Cinderella and the Carpetbagger

Grace Robbins

Harold Robbins's steamy books were once more widely read than the Bible. His novels sold more than 750 million copies and created the sex-power-glamour genre of popular literature that would go on to influence authors from Jackie Collins and Jacqueline Susann to TV shows like Dallas and Dynasty. What readers don't know is that Robbins—whom the media had dubbed the "prince of sex and scandal"—actually "researched" the free-wheeling escapades depicted in his books himself . . . along with his drop-dead, gorgeous wife, Grace. Now, in this revealing tell-all, for the first time ever, Grace Robbins rips the covers off the real life of the international best-selling author.

The 1960s and '70s were decades like no others—radical, experimental, libertine. Grace Robbins chronicles the rollicking good times, peppering her memoir with anecdotes of her encounters with luminaries from the world of entertainment and the arts—not to mention most of Hollywood. The couple was at the center of a globetrotting jet set, with mansions in Beverly Hills, villas and yachts on the French Riviera and Acapulco. Their life rivaled—and often surpassed—that of the characters in his books. Champagne flowed, cocaine was abundant, and sex in the pre-AIDS era was embraced with abandon. Along the way, the couple agreed to a "modern marriage," that Harold insisted upon. With charm, introspection, and humor, Grace lays open her fascinating, provocative roller-coaster ride of a life—her own true Cinderella tale.

"This sweet little memoir's getting a movie deal." **—New York Post**

"I gulped down every juicy minute of this funny, outrageous memoir. You will not be able to put it down until the sun comes up." **—Rex Reed**

"Grace Robbins has written an explosive tell-all. Sexy fun." **—Jackie Collins**

"You have been warned. This book is VERY HOT!" **—Robin Leach, Lifestyles of the Rich & Famous**

ISBN: 978-0-9882848-2-1 • ePub: 978-0-9882848-4-5

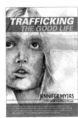

Trafficking the Good Life

Jennifer Myers

Jennifer Myers had worked hard toward a successful career as a dancer in Chicago. But just as her star was rising, she fell for the kingpin of a drug trafficking operation. Drawn to his life of excitement, she soon acquiesced to driving marijuana across the country, making easy money she stacked in shoeboxes and spent like an heiress. Only time in a federal prison made her face up to and understand her choices. It was there, at rock bottom, that she discovered that her real prison was the one she had unwittingly made inside herself and where she could start rebuilding a life of purpose and ethical pursuit.

"In her gripping memoir Jennifer Myers offers a startling account of how the pursuit of an elusive American Dream can lead us to the depths of the American criminal underbelly. Her book is as much about being human in a hyper-materialistic society as it is about drug culture. When the DEA finally knocks on Myers' door, she and the reader both see the moment for what it truly is—not so much an arrest as a rescue." **—Tony D'Souza, author of Whiteman and Mule**

ISBN: 978-1-936332-67-0 • ePub: 978-1-936332-68-7

Bettie Youngs Books

We specialize in MEMOIRS
...books that celebrate
fascinating people
and remarkable

If you are unable to order this book from your local bookseller, or online from Amazon or Barnes & Noble, or from Espresso, or, Read How You Want, you may order directly from the publisher at Sales@BettieYoungsBooks.com.

VISIT OUR WEBSITE AT:
www.BettieYoungsBooks.com

CPSIA information can be obtained at www.ICGtesting.com
Printed in the USA
BVOW03s1302110414

350178BV00001B/1/P